The Story of
THE MASTERS

By the Same Author:

Miracle at Merion

Making the Masters

Golf Courses of the U.S. Open

Golf's Dream 18s

Golfing With Dad

Golf Magazine's Golf Rules Explained

The Story of
THE MASTERS

Drama, Joy and Heartbreak at Golf's Most Iconic Tournament

DAVID BARRETT

TATRA PRESS

The Story of the Masters
Drama, Joy and Heartbreak at Golf's Most Iconic Tournament

Copyright © 2021 by David Barrett

Library of Congress Control Number: 2020945617

ISBN: 978-1732222724

First Edition: March, 2021

Tatra Press LLC

Distributed by Independent Publishers Group, Baker & Taylor and Ingram

Cover design by Mimi Bark

Interior designed by Isabella Piestrzynska, Umbrella Graphics

Media, special sales and permissions:
Chris Sulavik (Tatra Press) at tatrapress@gmail.com or 646-644-6236

Front cover image: Jack Nicklaus and his son Jackie at the 1986 Masters (Getty Images).

Printed and bound in the USA by Sheridan, Chelsea, Michigan

TATRA

Tatra Press
4 Park Trail
Croton-on-Hudson, NY 10520
www.tatrapress.com

For Mom and Dad,

Ludmila, Michael and Sophia

and the sportswriters of the *Augusta Chronicle* through the decades

Contents

Preface

The Conception

When amateur great Bobby Jones retired from competition, he didn't want to pull away from the game completely. After winning the Grand Slam of the U.S. and British Opens and Amateurs in 1930, Jones simply was tired of the tournament grind. His big idea now was to start a golf club.

As early as the mid-1920s, Jones had shared that vision with Clifford Roberts, a New York investment banker he met through a mutual friend. Upon Jones' retirement, Roberts set out to make the dream a reality and quickly found a piece of property in Augusta, Georgia, that seemed perfect.

Formerly a prominent tree nursery, the property known as Fruitlands had been the planned site of a resort hotel and golf course, a venture that fizzled out in 1926. The land was available for a good price during the Depression, and, when Jones first saw it, his immediate thought was "that this land had been lying here for years waiting for someone to lay a golf course upon it," as he later wrote in *Golf Is My Game.*

The location of what would become Augusta National Golf Club suited Jones in another way. Augusta was reasonably close to Jones' native Atlanta, where he now practiced law, but at a lower elevation with a milder climate in the winter months. That made it a winter destination for well-to-do Northerners (Roberts among them), who were just the kind of people that Jones and Roberts wanted to attract for their national membership.

That was all well and good, but there was a fundamental problem. During those hard economic times, it wasn't easy attracting members, even with the connections enjoyed by Jones and Roberts. The club faced serious financial difficulties and was delinquent in paying the costs of course construction. Without an influx of additional members, the outlook was grim.

Still, the club *had* managed to open, boasting an excellent course designed by Jones with architect Alister MacKenzie. The opening ceremony in January of 1933 attracted a number of USGA officials, who were fans and friends of Jones, the winner of four U.S. Opens and five U.S. Amateurs. They were very impressed with the golf course, so much so that they discussed it as a possible site for the 1934 U.S. Open.

Unfortunately, Augusta National was founded as a winter-to-early-spring club and wouldn't be open when the U.S. Open was held in June. Moving the Open to March was considered, but that was a problem because it was too early for sectional qualifying in the North. In April of 1933, USGA president Herbert Jaques wrote Roberts that "whereas we are favorably inclined toward this move in the near future, we do not think it is practical to attempt in 1934."

Roberts already had an idea of his own. What if Augusta National held a tournament itself? The publicity generated by the event would likely attract new members and help lift the club out of its financial troubles. A key to the event making a big national splash would be Jones entering as a competitor.

Jones had no plans, or particular desire, to ever compete again. But his greatest wish was to see Augusta National succeed, and he agreed that his playing in a tournament hosted by the club was the best way to make that happen.

Thus, the Masters was born—almost. It would take money to stage a tournament, and the club was short on cash. Roberts went to the City of Augusta asking for $10,000 to make the tournament a reality. Augusta's city council said yes, deciding that the tournament would attract out-of-town visitors from northern climes to fill resort hotels during tournament week, and that the publicity would serve as a promotion that would attract future winter-season visitors.

In August of 1933, the tournament was announced in a column by famous sportswriter Grantland Rice, who was an Augusta National member. Officially, it would be known until 1939 as the Augusta National Invitation Tournament, because Jones thought "Masters" was presumptuous. However, Roberts and other club officials had already pitched it as the Masters, and that's what it was called from the outset in the *Augusta Chronicle,* the wire services, and nearly every newspaper.

In December, Rice was interviewed by the local paper and predicted that the new tournament "will eventually equal the National Open [U.S. Open] in importance." He wasn't wrong.

1934–1942

The Early Years

The Masters didn't need any time to establish itself as one of the top tournaments in the game. The presence of Bobby Jones in the field of the inaugural Masters in 1934 garnered an elevated status. Jones had become an iconic figure by the time of his Grand Slam accomplishment and subsequent retirement at age 28 in 1930. Four years later, he was still young enough that his return to competition—even for a single event—drew more press coverage than any tournament outside the U.S. Open.

The results in 1934 and subsequent years made it clear that there was too much rust for Jones to play anywhere close to the way he did in his prime. As it turned out, the Masters didn't need that. In the tournament's second year, the press corps reported on Gene Sarazen's stunning double eagle on the 15th hole of the final round and subsequent playoff victory. Augusta National quickly became known as the stage for heroics by the game's best players.

Onetime boy wonder Horton Smith mounted a late charge of his own in 1936 to win his second Masters, Byron Nelson stormed through what would become known as Amen Corner in 1937 to establish himself as a coming star, and Ralph Guldahl shot a 33 on the back nine in 1939 to add Masters glory to his two U.S. Open titles. Masters champions Henry Picard (1938), Jimmy Demaret (1940), Craig Wood (1941), and Nelson again (1942) were all upper echelon players at the time of their victories.

Of course, starting a tournament during the Depression was no easy matter. Even with its prestige, the Masters faced its challenges, and, for the first few years, it wasn't even certain from year to year that it would be held. The financial support from the City of Augusta continued through 1936. Augustans then helped in a different way as businesses began to sell Masters tickets in the late 1930s, leading to increased attendance and revenue for an event that had initially been marketed more toward Northern visitors.

By the early 1940s, the club and tournament were on sound footing as the Masters had succeeded in its mission to attract enough members to ensure the club's viability and long-term prosperity. The tournament was less successful as a marketing tool for Augusta as a resort destination. The long-term trend of Northerners heading to the warmer winter temperatures of Florida was simply unstoppable, even for a city that now hosted golf's most iconic tournament.

1934

Anticipation for the first playing of the Masters centered around Bobby Jones' return to competition, which was seen as much more than a ceremonial appearance. Indeed, bookmakers had Jones and Paul Runyan as co-favorites at 6–to–1. In those days, bookies hung around the tournament, collecting bets and getting their odds reported in the newspapers.

The 25-year-old Runyan had won nine tournaments in 1933 and already three in 1934, including the Tournament of the Gardens Open in Charleston, South Carolina—a short-lived PGA stop held from 1933 to 1937—the week before the Masters with an eye-popping 273 total. The question for Jones, of course, was whether he was anything near the same player in the wake of a nearly four-year layoff from competition. Many thought he was.

"Championship golf…is not like boxing in respect to the angle that a long layoff is so costly in speed, stamina, and competitive edge," wrote Associated Press sports editor Alan Gould. "I'll be surprised if he doesn't finish among the first three at Augusta."

Jones fueled such predictions when he shot a 65 at Augusta National in early March. At just 32 years old, there was reason to believe the tournament host could contend. Jones returned to Augusta on March 14 to play practice rounds in the eight days leading up to the tournament, which was held on March 22–25. Clearly, he was serious in his preparation and did everything in his power to make a strong showing.

Unfortunately, Jones' putter didn't cooperate once the tournament started. He missed seven putts of five feet or less in a first-round 76 and a pair of 18-inchers in a 74 on Friday. So, despite ball-striking that should have put him in hailing distance of the lead, which was at 142, Jones was well back in the pack.

"I had no putting stroke at all," the tournament host admitted to writer Grantland Rice after the first round. "I honestly dreaded to look at a three- or four-foot putt, because I didn't feel that I could hole it."

Jones later said that he wasn't as tournament sharp as he had been in his competitive days, and was thrown off by distractions such as the whirring of a movie camera. But he did treat the galleries to some vintage ball-striking, hitting three par fives in two in the first round, including a second shot to four feet at the 11th (the hole that is now the second; the nines were reversed in 1934). Naturally, he missed the putt.

In the final two rounds, while paired with Walter Hagen, his friend and rival of the 1920s, Jones made six birdies on Saturday and five on Sunday. There were enough bogeys mixed in to leave him with a pair of even-par 72s, yet that was still good scoring in a week when the low round was 69. Jones moved up to a 13th-place finish.

Subpar scores were much harder to come by in those days than they are now. With the equipment of the 1930s, the course, even at 6,700 yards, played effectively longer back then. Also, while Augusta's greens were in better condition than most other courses of the era, they were not nearly as true as today's tour greens. Still, Jones did shoot that 65 in practice. For the tournament, however, the pin positions were placed in difficult locations, as noted by many players and the writer O.B. Keeler. Numerous mounds built into the greens produced significant challenges for both approach shots and putting. Another factor was the weather—it was downright cold. The high temperature was 52 degrees on Saturday and 47 on Sunday, causing spectators to don overcoats and players to battle chilly hands (as did the sportswriters, who were set up on the clubhouse veranda).

The leader throughout the event—but by a small margin or tied all the way—was a man who a few years earlier had been hailed as perhaps the next Bobby Jones. Horton Smith stormed out of Missouri at the age of 20 to win eight tournaments on the winter tour of 1928–29. By the end of 1930 he ran his total to 14 victories. Taking advantage of that success, he embarked on exhibition tours, primarily with Hagen. He was on the road constantly for 20 months, playing in some 130 exhibitions and 50 tournaments.

The rigorous schedule left Smith with a bad back. Then, in December 1931, he broke his wrist in a car accident, sidelining him for six months. Unsurprisingly, he won just one tournament in each of the three years from 1931 to 1933 and, in the latter year, it was only a team win with Runyan as his partner. While his star had dimmed considerably, Smith posted enough solid results in the winter of 1933–34 to be encouraged, even without a victory.

Steadiness was a virtue for Smith at this Masters, as he shared the lead with an opening 70, moved one ahead with a 72 in the second round, and held onto a one-stroke advantage with a 70 on Saturday. In second place through 54 holes was 1931 U.S. Open champion Billy Burke, with Craig Wood and Augusta National pro Ed Dudley two strokes back, and Runyan three behind.

Dudley, a semi-regular on tour and frequent contender in major championships in addition to being the pro at the host club, managed only a 74 in the final round and finished fifth. Runyan, perhaps the best putter in the game, was an early test case for a short-hitting player at Augusta National, where he found himself often laying up on par fives while others were going for the green in two. He dug himself a bit of a hole with a first-round 74 before shooting 71–70–71 for a share of third place at two-under 286. Also at that figure was Burke, who shot a final-round 73 with birdie putts that perched agonizingly on the lip of the cup on the last two holes. "The crowd each time yelled for him to wait for a breeze to blow the ball in," the *New York Times* reported. The breeze never blew, and Burke finished two strokes behind.

1934

1	Horton Smith	70–72–70–72—284
2	Craig Wood	71–74–69–71—285
T3	Billy Burke	72–71–70–73—286
T3	Paul Runyan	74–71–70–71—286
5	Ed Dudley	74–69–71–74—288
6	Willie MacFarlane	74–73–70–74—291
T7	Al Espinosa	75–70–75–72—292
T7	Jimmy Hines	70–74–74–74—292
T7	Harold McSpaden	77–74–72–69—292
T7	Macdonald Smith	74–70–74–74—292

In those days, leaders weren't grouped in the last starting times, and Wood was the first contender off the tee. He set the target for the others with a two-birdie, one-bogey 71 for a 285 total, pretty good under the frigid conditions.

"Craig Wood's score was posted. He could not lose a stroke anywhere," Keeler wrote. "And there were several thousand places, and then some, on that great course where the quartet of pursuers could lose a stroke, or more."

And this was no ordinary tournament. It was already a special event, heaping added pressure on the players, as Smith later observed. "Everyone was terribly keen to win," he said. "There was a tensity that I don't recall seeing at any previous championship."

Smith held up pretty well on the front nine, with a bogey on the third offset by a tap-in birdie on the par-five sixth. Holing a 15-foot par putt on the ninth hole, Smith knew, with Wood already finished, that he needed an even-par 36 on the back nine to win.

Things were looking up after a birdie on No. 10, but bogeys on Nos. 14 and 15, the latter on a miss from three-and-a-half feet, meant Smith needed a birdie down the stretch to win outright. The best birdie chance was the par-five 17th, where he took advantage by hitting a 75-yard third shot to 10 feet and holing the clutch putt. More drama unfolded on the closing hole, where Smith left his first putt three-and-a-half feet short, but he made that one for a 284 total to become the first Masters champion.

Thanks to the stature and presence of Jones, the Masters quickly ascended as one of the country's most prestigious tournaments. It received more press coverage than any event except the U.S. Open and was the first tournament other than the Open with a live radio broadcast. Perhaps the only downside was the chilly weather, which hardly advertised Augusta as a winter destination.

Great Shot

Craig Wood began the final round in third place, but was in terrible trouble on the first hole when he drove into trees on the right. His second shot hit a tree and ricocheted backwards (this is the hole that is now the 10th, but in 1934 it played 65 yards shorter at 430). Smith was now so deep in the trees, it appeared he would have to play backward into the adjacent ninth fairway. Instead, he found the smallest of openings and rifled an eight-iron shot through it. The ball hit close to the green, bounded on, and stopped an inch from the hole. "You can go out there and play shots from that spot until you are too old to any longer swing the club and never get one ball as close to the hole as Wood's ball," wrote Bob Harlow in

PGA Magazine. The unlikely par helped Wood shoot a 71, which didn't quite stand up as he finished one stroke behind Horton Smith.

....

1935

Gene Sarazen missed the first Masters, but not because he considered it unworthy. As it happened, he was already scheduled to head out on a worldwide exhibition tour arranged by Australian Joe Kirkwood—a fine tour player who doubled as a trick-shot artist—on the Tuesday of Masters week. In those days of low purses and a tournament schedule that didn't span the calendar year, players needed to supplement incomes. Most had jobs at clubs for part of the year, but the leading personalities—Walter Hagen, Sarazen and Kirkwood—instead made their extra dough in exhibitions. No longer affiliated with a club, Sarazen a few years earlier had bought a farm in Brookfield, Connecticut, and was given the nickname "the Squire."

The Sarazen-Kirkwood tour was a huge undertaking, lasting 10 months and covering five continents. Sarazen, who had won the U.S. Open and British Open in 1932 and the PGA Championship in 1933, entered only five tournaments in 1934 though in his prime at age 32. He was back on the tournament trail in 1935 and made a splash in practice rounds at Augusta, shooting a 65, a 72, and a pair of 67s for a 271 total for four rounds—extraordinary for that era, even with the course not set up at tournament difficulty.

Observers still felt that Jones was the man to beat, even though he was still retired and hadn't played a tournament since his lackluster Masters showing the year before. He entered tournament week as the betting favorite, with only Sarazen's sensational practice knocking Jones to the second rung at 8–to–1 with Gene at 6–to–1. But Jones would finish 25th, three-putting the first hole of the first round on the way to a 74 and finishing with a 78 on Sunday.

Sarazen opened nicely with a 68 on a good day for scoring—nice weather, for a change—and was a stroke behind Henry Picard's lead. Picard was riding a hot hand, having just won in Atlanta in a rain-delayed tournament that ended on Monday of Masters week. The 28-year-old had started playing the tour full time the year before, and showed enough promise to land a plum job representing Hershey Country Club. Unlike most clubs, Hershey didn't require Picard to spend much time there; the Pennsylvania resort was looking for someone who would play well enough on tour to boost its name recognition. The club chose wisely, as Picard posted three wins in early 1935, was leading the money list, and, in newspaper accounts, was being hailed as the Hershey Hurricane.

Picard followed his opening 67 with a 68 on Friday, spurred by four consecutive birdies starting on the 13th hole, opening up a four-stroke lead over Sarazen and Ray Mangrum, whose younger brother Lloyd would later make an impact at Augusta. Picard's scoring was spectacular, especially on the heels of a final-round 65 to win in Atlanta on Monday.

It came undone for Picard in the third round. He played the first part of his round during an hour-long wind and rainstorm, and was highly displeased playing without his heavy niblick (equivalent of a wedge), which had gone missing. Picard went four-over in the first five holes, recovered to play the next 10 in two-under, but threw those two strokes away by hitting into the water on the par-3 16th and making a double bogey (the 16th in those days was guarded by a creek on the right instead of by a pond on the left). He finished with a 76 and was two strokes off the lead. Picard might have been worn out from the hectic schedule of the two tour events leading into Augusta. The 72-hole North and South Open in North Carolina had been held on the previous Wednesday, Thursday, and Friday. The 54-hole Atlanta event started on Saturday with a scheduled 36-hole day on Sunday shortened to 18 by rain leading to a Monday finish. As a result of this crammed scheduling, only a handful of players entered both events before heading to the Masters, and Picard was one of them.

Sarazen, meanwhile, passed on both tournaments, instead devoting his time to familiarize himself with Augusta National. His second and third rounds of 71–73 weren't anything special, but he was still in the picture, three strokes out of the lead. The 54-hole pacesetter at 209 was Craig Wood, whose 68 in the tough conditions was the best round of Saturday by two shots.

Sunday was a bit nippy and windy, yet not so inclement to fully explain the leaders' struggles on the front nine. Wood had a three-over 39, needing a couple of par-saving putts even to pull that off. He was still one stroke ahead of Picard (38) and Sarazen (37), while Olin Dutra, who entered the final round one stroke behind, blew to a 42. Dutra, the 1934 U.S. Open champion, stormed home with a 32 on the back nine, ultimately finishing third at 284. Picard was fourth at 286 after a 75.

Wood had started his round earlier than the other leaders, and, with a spectacular finish, posted a number that made him appear a sure winner. The long-hitting 33-year-old took advantage of the par-five 13th and 15th with birdies, also birdied the 14th, and made up for a bogey on 16 by holing a 16-foot birdie putt on the 18th for a 34 on the back nine and a 73.

Sarazen was on the 14th hole when he was told that Wood had finished at six-under 282. At that point, Gene was three-under for the tournament, so he needed to somehow play the last five holes in three-under to earn a tie—on a cold day with the course not yielding low scores. To boot, he was standing in the trees after hooking his drive on the 14th when he found out what he needed to do.

"Well, Gene, that looks like it's all over," said his playing partner Walter Hagen, who entered the final round five strokes back and was on his way to a 79.

"Oh, I don't know. They might go in from anywhere!" replied Sarazen, as reported by O.B. Keeler, who was on the scene.

Sarazen hit a fine recovery shot and two-putted from 80 feet to walk away with a par on 14. His drive on the 15th left him 230 yards from the hole, over water—a creek in front of the green instead of the pond situated there today. Figuring he probably needed an eagle to have a chance, Sarazen went for it. Normally he would have hit a three-wood from that distance, but from a downhill lie he figured he would need a four-wood to hit the ball high enough to carry the water. He pulled out his Wilson Turf Rider club, which featured rails on the bottom to dig the ball out of tough lies. Closing the clubface slightly in order to gain a few extra yards, Sarazen watched the ball fly straight and true, barely clearing the hazard and rolling toward the flagstick—and dropping into the hole for a double eagle!

"I was afraid of the lie I had, afraid I couldn't hold the right line," Sarazen told Grant-land Rice after the round. "I was so tickled when it covered the flag that I couldn't think of anything else until I heard that roar from the crowd behind the green.... When that wild howl went up, I felt for just a second like crying."

1935		
1	Gene Sarazen	68–71–73–70—282*
2	Craig Wood	69–72–68–73—282
3	Olin Dutra	70–70–70–74—284
4	Henry Picard	67–68–76–75—286
5	Denny Shute	73–71–70–73—287
6	Lawson Little	74–72–70–72—288
7	Paul Runyan	70–72–75–72—289
8	Victor Ghezzi	73–71–73–73—290
T9	Bobby Cruickshank	76–70–73–72—291
T9	Jimmy Hines	70–70–77–74—291
T9	Byron Nelson	71–74–72–74—291
T9	Joe Turnesa	73–71–74–73—291
*Sarazen won playoff, 144–149		

That roar from the crowd could be heard outside the clubhouse, where the press gathered as reports from the course were relayed by radio. Soon the voice on the radio reported that Sarazen had made a two on the 15th. What?! That sounded like a mistake. Asked to repeat it, the man on the other end said, yes, it was a double eagle.

Sarazen had miraculously made up three shots on a single hole, but he still needed to play the last three holes in even par to force a playoff. He did it, but had to hole knee-knocking par putts of four feet on 17 and 18. "I honestly think those last three holes were the heaviest pressure I've ever known in golf," said the man who owned six major championships at that point.

There was no such thing as a sudden-death playoff in that era, and the Masters mimicked the U.S. Open by requiring the players to go 36 extra holes the next day instead of 18 as was the norm. After the thrilling ending of regulation play, the playoff was a rather dull affair. It was close for nine holes, as both shot even-par 36 on the front nine, but Sarazen quickly went ahead by four with a birdie on 10 followed by Wood bogeys on the next three holes.

After that 10th-hole birdie, the Squire put together a remarkable run of 24 straight pars, relentlessly hitting fairways and greens. On yet another cold day— with temperatures in the 40s when they teed off and never topping 55—it was a standard Wood couldn't match. Leading 71–75 after the first round, Sarazen went up by eight through seven holes of the second round and ended up winning by five, 144–149.

It was a bitter pill for Wood, who, after being congratulated in the clubhouse as a near certain winner after finishing his Sunday round, instead wound up in second place for the second straight year. "Last year I lost the championship because

Horton Smith holed two long putts," Wood said at the awards ceremony. "This year I lost it because Gene Sarazen holed a 220-yard putt. Next year I suppose they will be sinking even longer putts."

....

A Fortuitous Decision

The first Masters was played with the nines in reverse order than they are played today. However, that lasted only one year. The change to the now familiar configuration was actually a reversion to architect Alister MacKenzie's original routing. The reason stated by the club was to let the players get through their first nine before reaching the "intricate problems" (as the *Augusta Chronicle* put it) of the course's water holes, Nos. 11, 12, 13, 15, and 16. Those holes not only account for the severest penalties on the course, they also offer big rewards for outstanding play when players are bold enough to take on the risk. That's especially true on the par-5 13th and 15th holes, both guarded by water but reachable in two shots. Placing those holes on the back nine made the finishing stretch a great stage for drama. And, as it turned out, the setting for a shot that remains one of the greatest and most famous in golf: Gene Sarazen's Shot Heard Round the World for the double eagle on the 15th that got him into a playoff. Bobby Jones, who, as club founder, was undoubtedly involved in the decision on the nines, got to witness history. Having finished his round, Jones wandered down to see how his old friends Sarazen and Walter Hagen were doing, and arrived at the 15th just in time to see Sarazen hole his four-wood. "From duffer to star, we all dream of impossible shots that might come off," Jones said that evening. "This one was beyond the limit of all dreams, when you consider the surrounding circumstances."

....

1936

The big story of the 1936 Masters was the awful weather, with two scheduled tournament days completely washed out, requiring a 36-hole finish on Monday. In all, nine inches of rain fell between Wednesday and Monday. The first round was played in frigid, windy, off-and-on rainy conditions, sending scores soaring. A heavy rainstorm hit during the final round, leading the PGA representative to protest that the round should be canceled, but the players splashed their way around the waterlogged Augusta National and play was completed. It was less an alluring promotion for Augusta as a golf or winter destination, and more a cautionary tale. It could have been worse. The day of the final round, tornadoes ravaged the business district in Gainesville, Georgia, north of Atlanta, leaving more than 150 dead.

Bobby Jones was once again the talk of the practice rounds, this time posting scores of 64(!)–70–68–70 from Saturday through Tuesday. Could he play like that under the stress of competition this time? Once again, in a case of wishful thinking, many believed he could. Jones' odds dropped during the run-up, ending as the favorite at 6-to-1. Henry Picard, a two-time winner so far in 1936, was next at 8-to-1, while defending champion Gene Sarazen said on Monday that he "hasn't a chance" because he was off form.

Two inches of rain closed the course on Wednesday, and it remained closed the following day as well, with the first round postponed until Friday. It didn't rain on Friday, but strong, stinging winds buffeted the players on a day when the temperature hovered in the 40s. "Not in the memory of the oldest rocking chair observer was a round played under more discouraging conditions," wrote Joe Williams in the *New York World-Telegram*. "… It would have surprised no one if ice skaters had appeared on the water hazards, if ski runners had started down the rolling hills."

The varying direction and intensity of the icy winds wreaked havoc. So did the hole locations, many of them placed at the top of mounds due to the rain-soaked greens. When asked how he fared, Walter Hagen said, "Great. Broke 40 both ways." He shot a 77. Jones and Sarazen, playing together in the final twosome of the day, both had 78, Jones again bedeviled by awful putting. Eighteen players in the 53-man field shot in the 80s, including a stunning 88 by 1934 and 1935 runner-up Craig Wood, who lost a ball in the woods on the 10th hole and said, "It would have been better if I had lost myself."

In those conditions, Harry Cooper's round of 70 was extraordinary on a day when only five players shot better than 75. "It was the best round of golf I ever played in my life," said the 31-year-old, who had the best scoring average on tour over the past two years. Particularly noteworthy was a four-iron he rifled into the wind to six feet for a birdie on the 12th hole on a day when many tee shots ended up in Rae's Creek in front of the green.

The next day brought the only benign conditions of the tournament, and the scores reflected that. Wood bounced back from the embarrassment of his 88 with a 67, a 21-stroke difference that still stands as a tournament record for the greatest round-to-round improvement. Sarazen also shot a 67, with an eagle on the eighth hole, to play his way into contention.

Cooper, who led by two after the first round, extended his advantage to five strokes with a second-round 69 that included seven birdies and four bogeys. But he would have to wait an extra day, with a Sunday storm making play impossible and pushing the scheduled 36-hole windup to Monday.

Word from officials was that they would do whatever was necessary to complete play on Monday, even if the weather didn't cooperate. Said tournament host Jones, "In the event a couple holes are unplayable—say the 12th and 13th in the valley along the stream—we'll just omit them and go ahead and play the first and second over again. Or something like that."

The rain stayed away in the morning round, and Horton Smith made a move with a 68. The lanky Missourian had followed his 1934 Masters win with two more victories that year and three in 1935; so, while he wasn't quite burning up the tour as he had done in his early years, he was nevertheless still among a handful of top players in the game. Smith's four-under round followed 74–71 scoring over the first 36 holes, his 213 total moving him into second place within three of the lead held by Cooper after a 71 for 210. The only other player within five strokes was Paul Runyan at 215, with Sarazen heading a trio at 217.

Cooper began the final round an hour ahead of Smith, an advantage because he played more of his round before a driving wind and rainstorm hit Augusta. The course, already saturated from previous rains, couldn't take much more. Putts were leaving water trails across greens; iron shots from the fairway were producing splashes.

While the PGA wasn't running the Masters, PGA tournament manager Robert Harlow was on hand. As play continued, he filed a protest with the tournament committee. "There is no doubt the course was unplayable at one time this afternoon," he said Monday evening. "We proposed the final round be called off and played over tomorrow but enough of the leaders had finished or were sufficiently along on the last round to make it seem unwise for the committee to interfere."

In those days, if play couldn't be completed due to weather, the whole round was replayed. Suspending play and continuing the next day from where players left off wasn't considered. As the round was far enough along, the motivation was to continue playing—even under conditions where play would certainly be stopped today—rather than wipe out the portion of the round that had already been played.

"The players had decided to play through, rain or shine," said tournament chairman Clifford Roberts, whose committee quickly denied Harlow's protest. "Manifestly, it would have been unfair, much as we regretted conditions, to postpone play further, especially with the leaders fighting it out the way they were."

The pressure of leading from wire to wire might have been telling on Cooper. He went three-over on the front nine with four bogeys and a lone birdie. Somewhat steadying himself, he had eight pars on the back nine but made a bogey on 17 for an incoming 37 and a 76. Still, his 286 total seemed like it should have been good enough to win. In a scenario similar to 1935, the only players on the course would need unlikely heroics to catch or pass the leader in the clubhouse.

One of those players—again—was Sarazen. The defending champion ran across writer Grantland Rice on the 10th tee and *Atlanta Constitution* sports editor Ralph McGill in the 10th fairway, and told both of them he would shoot a 34 on the back nine, which seemed like a longshot the way the rain was coming down and the wind howling, not to mention his pessimism of the previous Monday. Sarazen did somehow put together a 34 on the back nine, with birdies on the 12th and 14th, for a 70 that matched the best score of the fourth round, but gave him a 287 total—one higher than Cooper.

The last challenger was Smith, who had five holes to play when Cooper finished and needed to play them two-under to win outright or one-under to tie. Smith promptly holed a 40-foot putt across the waterlogged 14th green for a birdie and followed with a seven-foot birdie putt on 15. Now he could win with three pars, but that was no lock on this day.

After a par on 16, Smith hit the green on the 17th, 40 feet away. Misjudging the pace of a green that wasn't quite as soggy as he had figured, he powered the putt 17 feet past. The man who had just been named the best putter in the game in a *Golfing* magazine poll of leading pros knocked that one in the hole for an adventurous two-putt to stay ahead going to the last hole. Smith faced another long putt on 18, this time coaxing it to within a foot of the hole to secure his second Masters victory in the three years of the event.

Rice, calling the conditions the worst he had ever seen, wrote that Smith's finish was "one of the miracles of sport— if you happened to be here and could see just what the job was."

1936

1	Horton Smith	74–71–68–72—285
2	Harry Cooper	70–69–71–76—286
3	Gene Sarazen	78–67–72–70—287
T4	Bobby Cruickshank	75–69–74–72—290
T4	Paul Runyan	76–69–70–75—290
T6	Ed Dudley	75–75–70–73—293
T6	Ky Laffoon	75–70–75–73—293
T6	Ray Mangrum	76–73–68–76—293
T9	John Dawson	77–70–70–77—294
T9	Henry Picard	75–72–74–73—294

It was hard luck for Cooper, who later in the year would also finish second in the U.S. Open and would end his career with 30 victories but no majors.

Jones, incidentally, shot 78–78–73–77 to finish 33rd. He would continue to play through 1948, never again considered a betting favorite but still drawing galleries and newspaper accounts of his rounds, which gradually became more and more ceremonial. The tie for 13th in the inaugural Masters would remain his best finish.

1937

Practice rounds in the early days of the Masters were spiced by competitive four-ball matches, particularly those arranged by Bobby Jones. There was a good one on Tuesday in 1937 with Jones and his usual partner, Augusta National pro Ed Dudley, squaring off against Sam Snead and Harry Cooper. Snead was a 24-year-old from the mountains of Virginia who had just ventured out onto the winter tour for the first time in 1936-37, winning twice. He earned one of two Masters spots based on the lowest scoring averages on the winter circuit by players who would not have otherwise qualified, and was playing in his first Masters. Cooper, the previous year's runner-up, also had two wins in early 1937.

They gave the gallery a good show, halving the match as both teams were nine-under with their best ball—Dudley the most impressive individual performer with a 66. Snead would have a disappointing Augusta debut, finishing 18th, while Jones would tie for 29th. Cooper and Dudley were the players to watch. Cooper, on his way to a seven-win year, was the betting favorite at 9–to–1. The local favorite Dudley drew the co-highest bid of $1,200 in the main Calcutta pool, matching two-time Masters winner Horton Smith.

The backing of Dudley wasn't misplaced. The Georgia native (born in Brunswick) was more than just the host pro: The 6-foot-4, 36-year-old owned 14 tour victories on the way to a career total of 15. In the first years of the Masters he had skipped the winter portion of the tour because it conflicted with the Augusta National season. However, in 1937 he made the West Coast trip and won the Sacramento Open in January. He finished fifth in the 1934 Masters and sixth in 1936, and would finish his career with 24 top-10 finishes in major championships—still the most of any player who never won a major.

The favorites were upstaged in the first round by a 25-year-old from Texas, now playing out of Reading (Pennsylvania) Country Club, who was just starting to make a name for himself. Byron Nelson had scored his first victory of note at the 1936 Metropolitan Open and was playing in his third Masters, having finished ninth and 13th the two previous years. This time, he jumped out of the gate with a tournament record 66, three strokes better than anyone else.

Described by the Associated Press as "a bashful youngster," Nelson was confident enough to tell Grantland Rice before the round that he was "hitting the ball well and going out for everything in sight."

Was he ever! With a following wind, Nelson drove the green on the par-four seventh, which then played at 340 yards and wasn't fronted by bunkers. It was just one feat in an extraordinary round of ball-striking where six of his seven birdies came on tap-ins and the other was from six feet. He was over the green in two on the par-five second and chipped within a foot, two-putted for birdie on the seventh and also on the par-five eighth, converted from six feet after his approach on the ninth, nearly holed a chip after just missing the par-five 13th in two, two-putted for birdie on the par-five 15th, and hit a mashie niblick approach to within one foot on the 17th. The only blemish was on the par-four third, where he missed the green and bogeyed.

Ralph Guldahl was second after a 69 that featured an eagle on 15. While Cooper and Dudley would lurk throughout, the tournament would mostly be a battle between Guldahl and Nelson. Guldahl, 25, was just two-and-a-half months older than Nelson and grew up in Dallas, not far from Nelson and future two-time Masters champion Ben Hogan in Fort Worth. All three tried their hand at pro golf at an early age, with Guldahl having the quickest success. He won a tour event, the 1931 Santa Monica Open, at age 19, and added another the next year.

Nevertheless, it was a rocky road for Guldahl. He didn't have the finances to play much more than the winter circuit in those years, and had a major disappointment in 1933 when he missed a four-foot putt on the 72nd hole to finish one stroke behind Johnny Goodman at the U.S. Open. Even with a win in another partial campaign in 1934, Guldahl became disenchanted with his play. With a wife and baby to support, he virtually quit the tour in 1935, playing only four events and turning down a Masters invitation. Now based in St. Louis, he inquired about a job as an automobile salesman, but decided to give the tour one more shot in the summer of 1936.

Guldahl's life turned around when he shot a final-round 64 to win the Western Open in Iowa and got a deal from a sporting goods manufacturer that enabled him to pay his bills and become a tour regular. He won twice more in 1936, including the Augusta Open in the fall—just about a mile away from Augusta National at the Forrest Hills course—and finished the year with the best scoring average and second in money to Smith.

Nelson maintained his three-stroke advantage with a 72 in the second round, making one birdie, one bogey, and 16 pars in a round when he didn't take advantage of the par fives or hit his approach shots as close to the hole as the first round. He vowed to be aggressive in the final two rounds. "I'm going for everything from here on, no matter where I finish," he told Rice. "The big poison in golf is trying to steer every shot when you have a lead."

Guldahl double bogeyed the first hole when his drive hit a tree, and also had three bogeys, but saved his round with five birdies for a 72 that kept him three back. He was tied for second with Dudley, who added a 71 to an opening 70.

The third round saw a reversal, as Nelson stumbled to a 75 and Guldahl surged to a three-stroke lead with a 68. Nelson's problems were mostly on the greens, as he had a ghastly total of 39 putts. The worst of it was a four-putt at the fifth hole, where he missed a second putt from four feet and then missed a two-footer.

Guldahl was even par on the front nine, then poured it on with a back-nine 32 that featured birdies on 13, 15, 16, and 17. He now had shot 32, 35, and 32 on the back nine. "I know this second nine is supposed to be the toughest, but it is the easiest for me," he said after the round. Considering what transpired the next day, those are words he perhaps should not have uttered.

Heading into Sunday, it was Guldahl at 209, followed by Dudley at 212 after another 71, with Nelson and Cooper (73–69–71) at 213. "Unless there is some bad cracking up or a miracle on the part of the opposition Ralph Guldahl will be hard to catch," wrote Rice.

It didn't take long to see that the catching, if done at all, wouldn't be by Cooper. His bad luck in majors continued when, first, his caddie didn't show up, leading to a scramble for a substitute. Second, he left his umbrella in the clubhouse. That was a mistake. After three days of perfect weather, the rain jinx had returned to Augusta. A morning downpour led to worries that the final round would be moved to Monday for the second straight year, but it cleared up to a mist and intermittent drizzle by the time the leaders teed off in the afternoon. Third, according to the *Atlanta Constitution*, Cooper was distracted by two loud-talking drunks at the first green and made a bogey.

Cooper shot a 39 on the front nine on the way to a 74 and finished fourth. Dudley also shot himself out of it early with a double bogey on the second hole, ultimately shooting a 74 for third place.

So, it came down to the two 25-year-old Texas natives trying to establish themselves in the top echelon of players. Both struggled on the front nine, shooting 38s, and then both birdied the 10th, leaving Guldahl comfortably in front. Or, so it seemed. But the crackup and miracle referred to by Rice occurred with stunning swiftness. Nelson made up six strokes on Guldahl in a span of just two holes, those being the water holes of 12 and 13.

Guldahl, playing about a half hour ahead of Nelson, went for the flag in a dangerous location on the 12th, his shot coming up just short, hitting the top of the bank and rolling back into the water, setting up a double bogey. On the par-five 13th, Guldahl went for it in two from a downhill lie, his shot again lacking distance

1937

1	Byron Nelson	66–72–75–70—283
2	Ralph Guldahl	69–72–68–76—285
3	Ed Dudley	70–71–71–74—286
4	Harry Cooper	73–69–71–74—287
5	Ky Laffoon	73–70–74–73—290
6	Jimmy Thomson	71–73–74–73—291
7	Al Watrous	74–72–71–75—292
T8	Tommy Armour	73–75–73–72—293
T8	Victor Ghezzi	72–72–72–77—293
T10	Leonard Dodson	71–75–71–77—294
T10	Jimmy Hines	77–72–68–77—294

and catching the creek in front of the green, leading to a bogey. "I can't swim. Never could," said Guldahl after the round, reflecting on his water balls.

Nelson hit his tee shot to 15 feet on the 12th and sank the putt. Considering that Guldahl had already stumbled on the 13th, that tied Byron for the lead, though in the pre-television, pre-leaderboard era nobody really knew that at the time. Nelson pounded his tee shot on the par-five 13th, was just off the green after a bold second shot, and chipped in from 40 feet for an eagle that propelled him to a two-stroke lead. Both protagonists played the remainder of the round in even par, Guldahl keeping himself alive with a birdie on 15 but driving into the trees for a costly bogey on 17. Nelson three-putted for a par on 15 and followed with routine pars on the last three holes to win by two.

Guldahl finished with a 76, while Nelson's 70—with a 32 on the back nine—was the only subpar round on Sunday. To hear Nelson tell it, he was more comfortable with the come-from-behind role in the final round than he would have been trying to lead all the way. "When I shook the lead during the third round, I felt I was going to win," he said. "I don't like the idea of staying out front."

Holding the lead at the Masters was starting to seem especially precarious, considering the pattern of heroics by players coming from behind. Gene Sarazen's double eagle in 1935, Smith's putting down the stretch on rain-soaked greens in 1936, and Nelson's birdie-eagle charge of 1937 were giving the fledgling tournament a reputation as a place where miracles happened.

Drivable No More

The original seventh hole played at 340 yards and was designed to be similar to the 18th at St. Andrews in Scotland, where players could hit their drives fairly close to the green (rarely all the way to it in those days) but were challenged by slopes on the green. Byron Nelson used a favoring wind and a good bit of roll to drive the green in the first round on his way to a victory. That feat was one factor in the hole being redesigned in 1938, as it showed it was too easy off the tee. At the same time, Bobby Jones noted, it was too difficult on the green, as the contouring was too severe. The green was moved back some 30 yards onto a little hill elevated above the fairway. There would be no more driving the green. Now the second shot required a precise wedge or short iron over fronting bunkers. Since 2002, the tee has been moved back twice, with the hole now measuring 450 yards.

1938

This was the only Masters scheduled to be conducted in three days with a 36-hole finale. That was the standard format for a tour event in that era, with the Masters pioneering the four-day tournament. In 1938, the PGA had to shoe-horn in several tournaments in a short time frame. The North and South Open in Pinehurst, North Carolina, finished on the Friday before Masters week, and the Greater Greensboro Open began the very next day, running Saturday to Monday. With that scheduled Monday finish in North Carolina, the start of the Masters was pushed back to Friday, with a 36-hole windup scheduled for Sunday.

As it happened, the weather hex struck again. Friday's scheduled first round was washed out by rain. They did play 36 holes on Sunday, but it was the second and third rounds, with the final 18 played on Monday.

Sam Snead won in Greensboro. He also had a date with Bobby Jones, Ed Dudley, and Henry Picard for a practice round in Augusta the next day. PGA tournament manager Fred Corcoran arranged for a flight to Augusta the following morning— Snead's first airplane ride. Just minutes after landing, Snead was already teeing it up at Augusta National. He and Picard beat Jones and Dudley in a four-ball match.

Snead arrived in Augusta with two 1938 wins to his credit on the way to an eight-win year. While not the bookmakers' favorite, he did earn the highest bid in the Calcutta auction at the Bon Air Hotel at $750. But the Masters would be his lowlight of the season. He started well enough with a 34 on the front nine of the first round, but skied to an astonishing 44 on the back nine for a 78. "It was the worst round of golf I ever played," he said. The second round was just as bad, another 78, on the way to a finish of tied for 31st in a field of 42 players.

His four-ball partner Picard also had a reversal in the first round, but in a very good way. Seeing Grantland Rice early on the back nine and standing at three-over, Picard said, "I can't play this course. I'm terrible." The Massachusetts native, who spent his formative professional years in Charleston, South Carolina, went four-under the rest of the way and finished with a 71.

That was three strokes higher than perennial contender Harry Cooper, who grabbed the first-round lead with a 68 that included a 33 on the back nine. Dudley appeared headed for a 67, but he triple bogeyed the 18th when he took three strokes to escape the trees after driving into them, and shared second place with Dick Metz at 70. Metz had a 32 on the front nine, but double bogeyed the 10th hole and had a 38 on the back.

Those hard-luck stories couldn't compare with Felix Serafin. The previous day, in one of the early groups off the tee, he played the first 11 holes in five-under. Then the rain came and didn't go away, resulting in the round being canceled. None of the play from Friday counted, as everyone started again from the first tee on Saturday. Serafin, to his credit, shot a respectable 72 and finished the tournament tied for sixth, but the 32-year-old Pennsylvanian, a three-time tour winner, could only wonder what might have been.

Before heading out for the second round, according to *Atlanta Journal* writer Morgan Blake, 18-hole pacesetter Cooper said, "You know for the first time in my life I was swinging my clubs just like I have been wanting to do all my life. Yes sir, I have finally caught on to how it's done. I am going to go out now and burn up this course."

He was just as wrong as Picard was about not being able to play the course, showing how unpredictable the game is—and how you should never say that you have it figured out. Cooper proceeded to post a dismal 40 on the front nine on the way to a second-round 77. That was the theme of the tournament, and especially the 36-hole day of Rounds 2 and 3, as nearly everyone was dogged by a bad round or a bad hole. Dudley appeared to take control with a 69 in the second round for a 139 total and a four-stroke lead. In the afternoon, he ballooned to a 77 with a crushing 41 on the back nine. Serafin went from a tie for second after 36 holes to a 78 in the third round. Defending champion Byron Nelson was tripped up by a single hole, making a six on the par-three 12th in the second round, the same hole where he started his charge with a birdie the year before. He followed a Sunday morning 74 with a 70 in the third round to pull within two of the lead, ultimately finishing fifth.

The star of the show on Sunday was 1935 champion Gene Sarazen with rounds of 70–68. He had opened with a 78, but by the end of 54 holes moved within one of first place. The 36-year-old said he would quit if he won the tournament, but instead shot a 79 in the final round to tie for 13th.

On this generally volatile day, it was steady play by Picard that enabled him to lead the race. A pair of even-par rounds of 72 gave him a 215 total that put him narrowly ahead, with four players one stroke back: Cooper, who recovered in the third round with a 71; Sarazen; Dudley; and Ralph Guldahl (73–70–73), who, after finishing as Masters runner-up in 1937, won the U.S. Open.

The last time Picard led the Masters was through two rounds in 1935, when he got off to an awful start in the third round on the way to a 76. Now more experienced, the 31-year-old was coming off a four-win season in 1937 and one victory so far in 1938 and showed no sign of faltering out of the gate this time. Instead, he drilled a 20-foot birdie putt on the first hole, chipped close to birdie both par fives on the front nine, and also birdied the fifth. With no blemishes, that gave him a 32 on the front nine and control of the tournament.

Picard couldn't completely shake Guldahl, however, as Ralph eagled the second hole and had a 34 on the front nine. Playing 45 minutes ahead of Picard, with Jones as his playing partner, Guldahl followed a bogey on 12 with birdies on 13 and 15. Picard, meanwhile, bogeyed the 10th with three putts from the edge and the 11th after a wayward drive. Guldahl's birdie on 15 put him three-under for the tournament; Picard was three-under after his back-to-back bogeys.

The difference down the stretch was the ability to handle Augusta National's devilish greens under pressure. Guldahl three-putted for bogeys on 16 and 18. Picard's ball-striking wasn't perfect down the stretch, but he parred his way to the clubhouse thanks to some deft chipping and several clutch four-foot putts, including one on 17 after an outstanding chip shot.

Picard finished with a 70 and a 285 total to finish two ahead of Guldahl and Cooper, who made a couple of late birdies for a 71. It was the second runner-up finish in the Masters for both.

"I had the touch of these tricky greens, and I figured I could win if the rest of my game held up," Picard said afterward, also crediting practice rounds with Jones giving him "winning ideas." The tournament host wasn't a factor in the battle for the title himself, but he was still influential.

1938			
1	Henry Picard	71–72–72–70—285
T2	Harry Cooper	68–77–71–71—287
T2	Ralph Guldahl	73–70–73–71—287
4	Paul Runyan	71–73–74–70—288
5	Byron Nelson	73–74–70–73—290
T6	Ed Dudley	70–69–77–75—291
T6	Felix Serafin	72–71–78–70—291
T8	Dick Metz	70–77–74–71—292
T8	Jimmy Thomson	74–70–76–72—292
T10	Victor Ghezzi	75–74–70–74—293
T10	Jimmy Hines	75–71–75–72—293
T10	Lawson Little	72–75–74–72—293

1939

By 1939, two expectations of the young tournament had already been firmly established in the consciousnesses of players and spectators alike—bad weather and heroic golf. This year featured plenty of both. Yet again, there was a day washed out by rain, which fell in torrents on Thursday forcing the postponement of the first round. And that might not have even been the worst of it.

The format was revised to three days of tournament play, with 36 holes on Sunday (the original 1938 plan). There was no precipitation on Friday, though a whipping wind challenged the players. Billy Burke and Sam Snead led the way with 69 and 70, respectively, each falling back after posting 32s on the front nine. Snead was now firmly entrenched as one of the game's top players—he was co-favorite with Ralph Guldahl and Henry Picard at 8–to–1—and he was finally figuring out Augusta National on his third try.

Gene Sarazen shot a 73, but said he was just glad to be three strokes ahead of legends Bobby Jones and Walter Hagen among the old-timers. "We all belong to the lost age—the forgotten men," said the 37-year-old 1935 champion. "But we did our share in our time. And we are still hanging around, hoping the four-foot putts will drop as they used to. If they do, we can still trim this young bunch."

The four-footers dropped for Sarazen on Saturday, and so did the 10-footers and putts from various other distances, as the man referred to as the Connecticut farmer shot a 66 that tied the competitive course record. No lesser authorities than leading golf writer William D. Richardson and legendary sportswriter Grantland Rice both called it one of the greatest rounds ever played—a bit of hyperbole, but perhaps justifiable considering the circumstances.

Sarazen played the latter part of his round through a wind and rainstorm that eventually brought hail reported as nearly the size of golf balls. There was thunder

1939

1	Ralph Guldahl	72–68–70–69	279
2	Sam Snead	70–70–72–68	280
T3	Billy Burke	69–72–71–70	282
T3	Lawson Little	72–72–68–70	282
5	Gene Sarazen	73–66–72–72	283
6	Craig Wood	72–73–71–68	284
7	Byron Nelson	71–69–72–75	287
8	Henry Picard	71–71–76–71	289
9	Ben Hogan	75–71–72–72	290
T10	Ed Dudley	75–75–69–72	291
T10	Toney Penna	72–75–72–72	291

and lightning, too, but in those days play continued through the flashes despite the danger. In 1936, for instance, the winner Horton Smith was accompanied by lightning flashes on his walk to the 18th green.

"I felt shaky and jittery over those last four holes as the hail came down and the flame of lightning went over my head," Sarazen said afterward.

But Sarazen somehow managed to play those holes 4–3–3–3, three under par. Sarazen called his second shot to the par-five 15th "as fine a golf shot as I've ever played." That's quite a statement, considering he holed a second shot for a double eagle on that very same hole when he won in 1935. This time he smoked a three-wood through the wind and rain over the fronting water hazard to within 12 feet before narrowly missing the eagle putt. The hail fell hard as Sarazen reached the 16th tee, and continued to the end of his round but didn't prevent him from making birdies on the last two holes.

Play was halted shortly after Sarazen finished, but fortunately the weather calmed down, the hail stopped, and play resumed after a clean-up job. Johnny Revolta, the tour's leading money winner in 1935, was pictured in the next day's *Augusta Chronicle* sweeping away hailstones from a green with a broom.

Guldahl also had an outstanding round, a 68 with birdies on all four par fives. He was at 140, one stroke behind Sarazen and tied with Nelson (69) and Snead (70), followed by Burke at 141 and Picard at 142. The final 36 holes promised to be a shootout among some of the game's elite.

The leading pack became even more bunched after Sunday morning's third round. Guldahl moved in front with a 70 that included 16 pars and two birdies for a 210 total. Sarazen had a 72 and was at 211, with Burke, Snead, Nelson, and Lawson Little at 212. Little moved into the picture with a 68, while Snead missed a chance for a low round as he offset six birdies with six bogeys in a 72.

While Guldahl had finished second in the last two Masters, he had gained confidence and boosted his stature in the game with back-to-back victories in the U.S. Open in 1937 and 1938. Speaking to reporters a few weeks before the Masters, Guldahl said, "I'm going to win the Masters this time. I've been runner-up twice—nosed out in the stretch. If there's any nosing to be done this time, I'll do it—maybe."

As the final round developed, Snead stamped himself as the man to beat. The earliest starter among the contenders, the 26-year-old Virginian who had won eight times in 1938 and twice so far this year, roared out of the gate with birdies on the first two holes. He birdied the seventh and eighth for a three-under 33 on the front nine, backtracked a bit with a bogey on 10 but birdied 15 and 17 for a 68 and a 280 total that bettered the previous 72-hole tournament record of Sarazen in 1935.

The 1939 version of Sarazen couldn't match Snead's pace, finishing with a 72 to place fifth. Nelson shot himself out of it with a 75 and Burke eliminated himself with a 37 on the front nine, rallying to shoot a 70 for a share of third.

When Snead completed his round, the announcement of his score was heard by Guldahl and Little, who were playing together and making the turn. With Guldahl posting a 36 on the front nine and Little a 34, they were tied with each other, and both knew they needed a 33 on the back nine to beat Snead or a 34 to tie. Little bogeyed 10 and 14 to drop out of contention, eventually posting a 70 to tie Burke for third.

It was down to Guldahl and Snead, who had partnered to win the Miami International Four-Ball four weeks earlier. The scenario was familiar. Snead was the clubhouse leader at the U.S. Open at Oakland Hills in 1937 when Guldahl topped him by playing the last 11 holes in one-under. This time Ralph needed to summon something even better. "I think I can do it," he said on the 10th tee.

He quickly backed up those words with a birdie on the newly lengthened par-four 10th after a four-iron to 10 feet. He narrowly missed a birdie putt on the 11th and hit his tee shot to five feet on the 12th—the hole that triggered his 1937 demise—but settled for a par. His tee shot on the 13th, the second part of the one-two punch that knocked him out two years earlier, was a short one as his foot slipped when he swung.

Other players had laid up short of the creek after drives longer than Guldahl's. In addition to the long carry, Guldahl found himself with a sidehill lie. But the two-time Open champion pulled out a three-wood and blistered a shot right at the flag that carried the creek and stopped six feet from the hole.

"It was an impossible shot…. You could hear the gallery gasp as big Ralph took out a wood," Grantland Rice wrote. "… Either Guldahl has the heart of two lions or no imagination—but the shot he played could have only been struck by a great golfer who had both amazing power and full control."

Guldahl followed the brilliant shot by holing the putt for an eagle. Suddenly, he was three-under for the back nine and could beat Snead by going even par the rest of the way. It was a development nearly as dramatic, and impressive, as Sarazen's 1935 double eagle.

Great as the eagle was, Guldahl, after the round, pointed to a birdie at 15 as the pivotal moment, because it provided a cushion. "I simply went for it," he said. "I hit as long a drive as I could, hitting a deliberate hook to gain length." That enabled him to clear the water on this longer par five with another three-wood second shot, this time catching the center of the green to set up a two-putt birdie.

That gave him an extra shot to play with, which he used up with bogey on the 17th. Still playing boldly, his approach went over the green there and he missed an eight-foot putt. Figuring that aggressive play had gotten him this far, Guldahl changed from a four-iron to a three-iron for his second shot on the 18th, hitting it to the back of the green 18 feet past the hole. A two-putt par gave him the needed 33, a 69, and a record total of nine-under 279.

The man who had arguably given away the Masters in 1937 and 1938 came through in the clutch in 1939. And once again a clubhouse leader was passed by a fast finisher on Augusta National's dramatic back nine.

A Local Boost

In the earliest years of the Masters, the crowd was largely drawn from visitors to Augusta, which was then still a winter destination for Northerners. Little effort was made to market the tournament to locals until 1939, when Augusta businessman Alvin A. McAuliffe formed the Business Men's Masters Tournament Association with the idea of selling Masters tickets at local businesses. It was a success, as the tournament drew its largest crowds (an estimated 8,000 on the final day), with another increase to come in 1940. Local ticket sales were important, because Augusta's days as a winter destination were on the wane, through no fault of the Masters. Additionally, the City of Augusta, which had provided financial assistance to the Masters from 1934 to 1936, had stopped that support. Indeed, throughout the 1930s, it wasn't absolutely certain that the Masters would continue each year, confirmation coming only with an official announcement, year by year.

1940

Ben Hogan and Jimmy Demaret could both make a case for being the hottest golfer heading into the Masters. No matter how you looked at it, both were red hot.

Hogan had won the last three tournaments with spectacular scoring—the cumulative 38-under par was a record. This represented a career breakthrough for the 27-year-old, as they were his first three individual victories on tour. Hogan had failed in his first attempt at the tour in 1932. The 135-pound battler from Fort Worth made another go of it in 1937, playing well enough to stay out there, and then won a team event with Vic Ghezzi in 1938.

He stamped himself as a player to watch in 1939, finishing second three times and impressing fellow pros with his dedication to practice. With three more runner-up finishes in his first six starts of 1940, the only doubt surrounding Hogan was his ability to seal the deal. He erased that uncertainty with three straight wins in North Carolina, beating Sam Snead by three strokes at the North and South Open in Pinehurst and following that with wins in Greensboro and Asheville with all eight rounds in the 60s.

Demaret came into the Masters with more victories on the year than Hogan, already having accumulated five, including his own run of three in a row in February. He then took some time off and wasn't in the field during Hogan's first two wins. He returned the week before the Masters, but withdrew from the Land of the Sky Open in Asheville after shooting a 74 in the second round.

Another Texan, hailing from Houston, Demaret was 29 years old, but this was the first year he would play more than 10 events on tour (he won once each in 1938 and 1939 in limited appearances). He was already making quite an impression, not just with his play but with his colorful wardrobe and his happy-go-lucky attitude, golf writer Charles Bartlett saying that he "regards every round as a lark."

This was quite a contrast to the grimly determined and focused Hogan, but the two would go on to become great friends and four-ball partners.

The two players with the hot hands were upstaged in the first round by a 25-year-old who, a month earlier, had won his first tournament, the Thomasville (Georgia) Open, one of the few events not captured by Demaret or Hogan. Lloyd Mangrum took advantage of good scoring conditions at Augusta on Thursday—greens softened by an early-morning rain that, for once, held up and did not interfere with play—to shoot a 64. While scores had come down in the 1930s after steel shafts supplanted hickories, this was still an extraordinary number. It was a record not only for the Masters, but also for any tour event.

Mangrum reportedly hit every green in regulation and all four par fives in two for two-putt birdies. He had one bogey, a three-putt on the 10th hole, and nine birdies in shooting 32–32. He played the last seven holes in five-under with birdies on 12, 13, 15, 17, and 18, saving his longest birdie putts for last as he sank a 20- and a 30-footer on the final two greens.

Demaret wasn't outshined by much, shooting a 67 for second place and setting a record of his own with a 30 on the back nine. After a three-putt bogey on the second and eight pars on the front nine, Jimmy blistered the back with birdies on 10, 11, 13, 15, 16, and 17. Four of those birdies came on putts of at least 25 feet, prompting Demaret to comment that he played about the same on the front and back nines, while playing partner Ed Dudley said, "I got dizzy watching that fellow play."

The low scoring grabbed the attention of the committee setting up the course, leading to a set of very difficult hole locations the next day, even more challenging since the greens were firmer. O.B. Keeler wrote that defending champion Ralph Guldahl (74–73) went on a mostly good-natured rant about the pin positions that couldn't be quoted in a family publication. Mangrum didn't explicitly complain, but noted after shooting a 75 that the difference between his first and second rounds was mostly on the greens.

Mangrum's 139 total was good for a share of the lead with Demaret, who shot a 72. They were two ahead of Byron Nelson (69–72). Hogan, unable to sustain his momentum from his winning streak, was eight strokes back after 73–74.

Ben made a bit of a move in the third round with a 69 that still left him seven behind. He would finish tied for 10th after a closing 74.

Demaret took the lead with a 70 on Saturday, notable because he did so during a bout of food poisoning leaving him with a terribly upset stomach and no appetite. In fact, he was so sick in the morning that the committee moved his tee time back so he would be able to play. Still, he was shaky during the round. "I only hope my legs can stand up and I can finish," he said on the 13th hole.

The key stretch came on holes 6 and 7. After managing pars on the first five holes, Demaret stuck his tee shot on the par-three sixth to within 10 inches for a birdie. On No. 7, he drove into the woods and watched his second shot hit a tree and bound into the adjacent 17th fairway. From there, he lofted an 85-yard shot over a guarding

1940

1	Jimmy Demaret	67–72–70–71—280
2	Lloyd Mangrum	64–75–71–74—284
3	Byron Nelson	69–72–74–70—285
T4	Harry Cooper	69–75–73–70—287
T4	Ed Dudley	73–72–71–71—287
T4	Willie Goggin	71–72–73–71—287
T7	Henry Picard	71–71–71–75—288
T7	Sam Snead	71–72–69–76—288
T7	Craig Wood	70–75–67–76—288
T10	Ben Hogan	73–74–69–74—290
T10	Toney Penna	73–73–72–72—290

bunker that incredibly stopped five inches from the hole for a par. "Too bad I couldn't see the break in the green from where I was," he cracked to Craig Wood, the two-time runner-up who accompanied him in the round.

Wood, incidentally, shot a 31 on the front nine to pull within two strokes, cooling off on the back nine for a 67 that still brought him into the picture, trailing by three. Demaret gamely hung on for a three-birdie, one-bogey round, three-putting for pars on 13 and 15 to miss a chance to extend his lead but getting up and down from a bunker to save par on 17. Mangrum had a similar round—he also didn't birdie 13 and 15 and had a late sand save on 18. But, with two bogeys instead of one for a 71, that left him one behind at 210. Wood and Snead (69) were next at 212.

The final round was a case of an exciting player winning with a dull, but relentlessly effective, round. Demaret, sporting a green felt hat cocked rakishly to one side and joking with the gallery the entire way, reeled off 17 pars and one birdie for a 71 to win by four strokes at 280. It was a windy day and tough for scoring, which played right into the hands of Demaret, a low-ball hitter who had already developed a reputation as the best wind player on tour.

On such a day, stray shots were inevitable, but Demaret recovered nicely whenever in trouble, overcoming poor drives on the second and third holes and getting up and down on Nos. 8 and 10 on the way to pars on the first 14 holes. His lone birdie came on the 15th, where he narrowly missed an eagle from 15 feet, and wrapped it up with pars on the last three.

Mangrum shot 37–37, but holed a 30-foot putt on the closing hole to claim solo second, afterward expressing surprise to a reporter that he was able to finish so high in such a class competition. Nelson was third with a 70, having shot himself out of it in the third round with a 74. Wood and Snead both struggled to 76s to tie for seventh. Their quests for a first Masters title would have to continue in future years.

Players and spectators had been anxiously watching the skies in the afternoon, but the seemingly inevitable rain held off until only three twosomes—of non-contenders—remained on the course. The impact was limited to the awards ceremony, a quick one held between rain showers.

1941

The last three tournaments before the Masters were won by Sam Snead, Byron Nelson, and Ben Hogan, who were establishing themselves as a great triumvirate of

American golf. But there was another player who bore attention—Craig Wood had two seconds, two thirds, and two fourths on the year.

Coming close was nothing new for Wood. Indeed, the 39-year-old had a record of agonizing near misses in big tournaments. Not only had he finished runner-up in all four major championships, he had lost in a playoff in each one—without managing to win any majors. Wood had, of course, lost the 1935 Masters in a playoff to Gene Sarazen after Sarazen's double eagle. He also lost a playoff to Denny Shute at the 1933 British Open, lost in extra holes to Paul Runyan in the match-play final of the 1934 PGA Championship, and lost a playoff to Byron Nelson at the 1939 U.S. Open. In the latter event, Wood shot a 68 in a scheduled 18-hole three-way playoff also involving Shute, but Nelson also posted a 68. Nelson holed a one-iron for an eagle on the fourth hole of the additional 18-hole playoff, further establishing Wood as a hard-luck victim of others' heroics.

Including his runner-up finish to Horton Smith in the 1934 Masters, Wood had five second places in majors. But it should be noted that he had 17 career victories heading into the 1941 Masters, so he was no stranger to the winner's circle.

Wood burst out of the gate at this Masters with a 66 in the first round to take a five-stroke lead, which still stands as the largest 18-hole lead in tournament history. He birdied five of the first eight holes, going four-under in that stretch, on the way to a front-nine 32. The gallery grew as the round continued—the club had just installed underground cables to enable a scoring system that included scoreboards around the course, so people were aware of Wood's assault on par.

The crowds observed Wood make his way around the back nine masterfully without a bogey, and picking up birdies on 13 and 15, chipping to four and seven feet after second shots that finished close to the green. The long-hitting Wood wasn't known for his putting prowess, but he was outstanding on this day. While his longest birdie putt was from 12 feet, he was nearly unerring from inside that distance, holing some key par putts as well as the birdies.

"Craig was incredible when he caught sight of that little tin cup," said playing partner Sarazen, who this time around watched Wood perform some magic in a round that was all the more impressive for being played in a wind that prevented anyone else from doing better than 71. Two of the four players at 71 were Nelson and Hogan, and there were 54 holes to go, so no one was conceding the tournament to Wood just yet.

Wood played the first nine holes of the second round in a drenching rain, ultimately shooting a very respectable 71 for a 137 total and a three-stroke margin over Nelson, who eagled the 15th on the way to a 69. Wood's lead would have dwindled further if not for his short game down the stretch. Even par for the day coming to the 15th, the Winged Foot Golf Club pro hit his second shot in the water on the par five but made an 18-foot putt for par. Wood birdied the 16th from eight feet, got up and down for a par on 17, and hit an excellent bunker shot from a half-buried lie to four feet to par 18.

Wood had four bogeys in the third round, yet was able to hold onto a three-stroke advantage thanks to five birdies for another 71. He hit approaches close to the hole

1941

1	Craig Wood	66–71–71–72—280
2	Byron Nelson	71–69–73–70—283
3	Sam Byrd	73–70–68–74—285
4	Ben Hogan	71–72–75–68—286
5	Ed Dudley	73–72–75–68—288
T6	Victor Ghezzi	77–71–71–70—289
T6	Sam Snead	73–75–72–69—289
8	Lawson Little	71–70–74–75—290
T9	Willie Goggin	71–72–72–76—291
T9	Lloyd Mangrum	71–72–72–76—291
T9	Harold McSpaden	76–67–80–68—291

for birdies on 16 and 17 before giving one back at the end with a three-putt bogey at 18. Ex-major league baseball player Sam Byrd was now in second place after a 68, with Nelson next but five strokes back following a 73.

The nice thing about an early lead is that it gives you a cushion, but the downside is that the pressure is squarely placed on your shoulders the whole way. For a player seeking his first major after missing so many opportunities, the pressure must be even greater. Wood sounded tired of hearing about his history in the big ones.

"They have turned on a lot of sob stuff for me," he said Sunday morning before heading out for the final round. "They think I never won anything.... I picked my spots to fall short I guess, and that's why they remembered it."

Of course, a first major wasn't going to come easily. Wood's mettle was severely tested on Masters Sunday, as he bogeyed the third and ninth holes to go out in 38 while Nelson, playing in the second twosome behind him, had a 33 on the front nine. After staying in front all week, Wood found himself tied for the lead and in a dogfight with one of the best players in the game.

The tide turned on the 12th and 13th holes. On the same bit of ground where Nelson had overtaken Ralph Guldahl in 1937, Byron let it slip away in 1941. The Texan hit his tee shot over the green and bogeyed the 12th, then hit his second shot in the creek to bogey 13. Meanwhile, Wood was conjuring up something akin to the heroics that had so often taken him down. Facing a difficult lie for his second shot on the 13th, Wood gambled by going for the green with a two-iron. His shot cleared the creek and finished on the edge of the green, from where he chipped to four feet and birdied.

After a hiccup on 14, where he three-putted for a bogey, Wood finished like a champion, hitting a three-wood to 12 feet for a two-putt birdie on the 15th and holing a 15-foot birdie putt on the 16th. Pars on the last two holes gave him a 72, a four-round total of 280, and a three-stroke victory over Nelson, who ended up with a 70. Hogan, incidentally, closed with a 68 but it only got him fourth place after a third-round 75. Snead had a final-round 69, finishing sixth after a 73–75 start knocked him out of title contention.

It was clear at the award ceremony just how much the title meant to Wood. "This is the happiest moment of my life," he told the crowd. It was his first major, but not his last. The blond bomber would add a second just two months later at the 1941 U.S. Open.

1942

In an attempt to court more agreeable weather, the tournament schedule was pushed back one week later, finishing April 13. It didn't completely work. The first round was hit with an afternoon rain that hampered late starters, though it didn't cause a stoppage in play. The rest of the week was neither horrible nor halcyon. The change to a second-Sunday-in-April finish wasn't yet permanent—until 1960, the Masters sometimes finished on the first Sunday.

The first-round co-leaders were a throwback to 1934, with that year's champion Horton Smith and contender Paul Runyan both shooting 67s. They also happened to be perhaps the two best putters in the game. But it was the ball-striking prowess of Byron Nelson and Ben Hogan that would be the hallmark of this Masters.

Nelson was one stroke back after a 68 on Thursday, and playing partner Jug McSpaden sounded a warning. "When he's hitting the ball like he is now, he's unbeatable," said McSpaden after watching Nelson play a bogey-free round while missing only one green.

The 1937 champion was even better from tee to green in Round 2, firing a 67 for a record-tying 135 total. "I don't mind saying that the round I played today was the best I've ever played," said the 30-year-old, noting the windy conditions and his many near misses on birdie putts. "I thought five putts would drop that barely missed the rim of the cup. To tell the truth I was hitting the ball so well I was afraid it could not last."

By his own count, Nelson had 34 putts and needed only 33 shots to get to the greens, hitting three of the par fives in two. Using today's standards, he had 33 putts not counting using a putter from the fringe on the first hole, which was the only green he missed.

Nelson went on to give the writers a provocative quote. "I know something about the course. I wish I could tell you what it is, but some of these guys might read it. I'm not joking, though. It's a peculiarity of the course I happened to see right at the start. I've never had a really bad round here." He promised to reveal his secret if he won.

That prompted Hogan to jokingly ask Nelson's wife, Louise, the next morning if Byron had talked in his sleep.

Hogan had won two of the last three tournaments and four already in the year. His disappointing rounds of 73–70 left him eight shots behind, the only encouraging sign being that there were just five players ahead of him. Sam Byrd, with a pair of 68s, was the only player closer than five shots behind Nelson through Friday, but in the third round Hogan would move into position as the main challenger. Ben put together a 67 on a day when the wind whipped up to as much as 35 mph and nobody else shot better than 71, moving into second place three strokes behind Nelson (72).

As the thinking man's golfer, Hogan gave himself the ultimate compliment after his round. "It was the best managing I ever did. I mean manipulating the ball, allowing for wind and roll," he said. He putted nicely, too, using only 28 putts, though not needing to hole anything longer than 10 feet to account for seven birdies.

Hogan's play "mesmerized an unbelieving but worshipful gallery," O.B. Keeler wrote in the *Atlanta Journal*.

Nelson, who had made only one bogey in the first 36 holes, had three on Saturday, including a three-putt on the 18th that trimmed his lead to three.

The bogey bug bit Byron on Sunday, and it almost cost him the tournament. One-under after three holes, he turned in the wrong direction on the fourth hole, where he missed a two-foot par putt. Nelson went on to bogey Nos. 6, 7, and 8, the latter after hooking his second shot into the trees on the par five and unable to reach the green from the underbrush.

Nelson recovered to hole a 25-foot birdie putt on the ninth hole for a 38 on the front nine. That moved him back into a one-stroke lead over Hogan, who matched par 36, and it soon became a two-stroke margin when Ben, playing about two holes ahead of Nelson, bogeyed the 11th. Each birdied one of the back-nine par fives—Hogan the 13th and Nelson the 15th—and as Hogan played the 18th hole he trailed by two.

A magnificent approach shot stopped three feet from the hole, and Hogan sank the putt for a clutch finishing birdie. Minutes later, Nelson fired his approach shot at the pin on the 17th, but found a fronting bunker. He missed a par putt from 12 feet, and suddenly found himself tied.

Nelson was in trouble with his tee shot on 18, which found the trees right of the fairway. He escaped brilliantly, hooking a five-iron through an opening and onto the green, just 15 feet from the hole. Two putts from there gave Nelson a 73 to Hogan's 70, and with matching totals of 280 they advanced to an 18-hole playoff on Monday.

The playoff would match two of the top three players in the game (the other was Sam Snead; see "A Barefoot Stroll", page 30), but there was more to it than that. Nelson and Hogan were both born in 1912 (Nelson age 30 and Hogan 29 at the time of the Masters) and moved to Fort Worth from smaller towns in Texas around the age of 10. Both got into the game as caddies at Glen Garden Country Club in Fort Worth. They first squared off on the golf course in a caddie championship at Glen Garden when both were 15, Nelson winning by one stroke on an extra nine after they tied in a scheduled nine-holer.

Nelson found faster success as a pro, winning his first tournament in 1935 and the Masters in 1937, while Hogan failed in an early attempt at the tour. Even when Hogan found his groove and led the tour in money winnings in 1940 and 1941—and so far in 1942—he was still coming up short in the big tournaments. While Hogan hadn't won a major, Nelson had captured the 1939 U.S. Open and 1940 PGA Championship in addition to his Masters title. What's more, Nelson had beaten Hogan in a playoff for the 1940 Texas Open in San Antonio.

The two were rivals who undoubtedly wanted badly to beat each other. But even with divergent personalities—Nelson the ever-polite gentleman, Hogan the bantamweight battler—they were friends who sometimes traveled together on tour. When Hogan heard that Nelson was sick to his stomach the morning of their playoff, which was scheduled for 2:30, he knocked on Byron's door at the Bon Air Hotel and generously offered a postponement.

Nelson didn't take him up on it, mostly because a nervous stomach before a big tournament day was almost a routine for him, and because he had often played well when it had struck him in the past. Not to mention that he would have seen a delay as improper and perhaps unfair to Hogan.

Byron started the playoff like a man who wasn't feeling well. His drive on the first hole sailed to the right and banged off a tree farther right, coming to rest nearly against a small tree's trunk. From there, he could only swing left-handed, not getting the ball quite back onto the fairway. He overshot the green with his third and made a double bogey. Both two-putted for birdies on the second, Nelson missed a short birdie putt on the third, and Nelson bogeyed the par-three fourth after a tee shot into the front bunker, giving Hogan a three-stroke advantage.

The turning of the tide came swiftly with a pair of two-stroke swings. Nelson birdied the par-three sixth after a tee shot to seven feet, while Hogan missed the green and couldn't sink a four-foot par putt.

Then came the shot of the week. Nelson lashed a four-wood second shot up the hill on the par-five eighth, the ball rolling to within six feet of the hole for an eagle putt that he made. Hogan was close to the green in two and chipped to four feet, but missed that one and settled for a par. Suddenly, he trailed by a stroke.

After the round, Hogan lamented those missed short putts on 6 and 8 as crucial, while Nelson pointed to a Hogan bogey at No. 10 as a key point. That gave Byron a two-stroke margin, and he felt he had it won from there. Of course, it helped that Nelson birdied the 11th with a long putt (matched by Hogan), birdied the 12th with a seven-iron to two feet, and birdied the 13th with a two-putt after reaching in two with an iron. Nelson had played an eight-hole stretch in a remarkable six-under. Hogan, despite being even par in that span (he birdied 13), watched a three-stroke lead turn into a three-stroke deficit.

Ben gamely battled back with birdies on 14 and 15, trimming the deficit to one as Nelson three-putted for a par on 15. But the par-three 16th was costly for Hogan, as his tee shot found a bunker and he missed from 15 feet, falling two back. Hogan remained two back going to the 18th, where the exciting shootout sputtered to an anticlimactic end as both hit their approaches into the left bunker, Hogan saving par and Nelson cautiously two-putting for a bogey and a one-stroke victory, 69-70.

Afterward, Nelson revealed his "secret" about Augusta National—play for the green on approach shots, not for the pin. "Once you start charging around here, you're going to start going over the greens, then you're going to start three-putting, then you get scared and start leaving yourself short," he said.

Oddly, Nelson didn't follow his own advice on Sunday when he shot at the flag on 17 and ended up with a costly bogey. But his overall green-hitting performance indicates that, for the most part, he pursued a "find the green in regulation" strategy. Of course, outstanding ball-striking also helped.

With the United States having entered World War II, the specter of war hung over the Masters. When Nelson holed the winning putt in the playoff, the cheers of the spectators were nearly drowned out by the roar of a bomber on a training run from nearby Camp Gordon. Military police from that Army training camp were

1942		
1	Byron Nelson	68–67–72–73—280*
2	Ben Hogan	73–70–67–70—280
3	Paul Runyan	67–73–72–71—283
4	Sam Byrd	68–68–75–74—285
5	Horton Smith	67–73–74–73—287
6	Jimmy Demaret	70–70–75–75—290
T7	E.J. Harrison	74–70–71–77—292
T7	Lawson Little	71–74–72–75—292
T7	Sam Snead	78–69–72–73—292
T10	Chick Harbert	73–73–72–75—293
T10	Gene Kunes	74–74–74–71—293

*Nelson won playoff, 69–70

brought in as marshals during the tournament, and many of the spectators were wearing Army khaki. Front-page headlines told of the fall of Bataan in the Philippines and a sports section story reported that, because of wartime manufacturing needs, the production of golf clubs would be halted on May 31. Golf ball production had already been banned on April 1.

The tour had gone on as usual at the start of the year, but the next tournament after the Masters would be the PGA Championship a month-and-a-half later. The U.S. Open wasn't played, no tournaments were held after August, and there was essentially no tour in 1943 with just four events played. The Masters wouldn't return until 1946, the year after the war ended.

A Barefoot Stroll

PGA tournament manager Fred Corcoran wasn't shy about promoting Sam Snead's hillbilly image. When Snead finished a Tuesday practice round, Corcoran suggested he go out and play a couple of holes barefoot, as he used to do in his formative years in the Virginia mountains, noting that he had done so at the 1941 Canadian Open and went on to win the tournament. Snead obliged and birdied the first hole with an approach to three feet, then parred the parallel ninth. "I feel better when I stand up to the ball in bare feet," he said. "Those thick soled shoes keep you too far off the ground."

The 1935 Masters champion, Gene Sarazen, representing the old guard, wasn't amused. As witnessed by Gayle Talbot of the Associated Press, Sarazen lit into Corcoran that evening at the Bon Air Hotel. "Is that your idea of publicity for the Masters, making a Huckleberry Finn out of Snead?" Sarazen said. "What we need these days are masters, not barefoot boys." Corcoran, who later would become Snead's agent, tried to explain it was all in fun. Maybe, but it didn't work out the way it had at the Canadian Open. Snead shot himself out of it with a 78 in the first round, eventually recovering to tie for seventh.

1946–1957

Snead, Hogan, and Post-War Growth

S am Snead and Ben Hogan were the key figures in the post-war years, combining for five wins and seven other top-three finishes in the first 12 years after the 1943–45 cancellation of the Masters during World War II. It took a while for Snead and Hogan to achieve their Masters glory. Snead's first Augusta victory came at age 36 in 1949, and he added titles in 1951 and 1954, joining Jimmy Demaret as a three-time champion and at the same time denying Hogan that accomplishment in a closely fought playoff. Hogan didn't win his first Masters until age 40 in 1951, with previous frustrations including a three-putt on the 72nd hole in 1946 to finish one stroke behind Herman Keiser. Hogan went on to set a 72-hole scoring record of 274 in 1953.

Demaret, with victories in 1947 and 1950 to go with his 1940 title, also made a mark. Cary Middlecoff, one of the top players in the game throughout the 1950s, took a back seat to Snead and Hogan in Augusta until 1955 when he scored a runaway victory. Also of note were two amateurs who came close to donning a green jacket only to fade down the stretch, Billy Joe Patton in 1954 and Ken Venturi in 1956.

The Masters excellence of Snead and Hogan continued to elevate the tournament's status, as a permanent press facility accommodated the growing press corps. Augustans continued to embrace the tournament, with local celebrations in the latter part of this period including a downtown parade and a coronation of "Miss Golf." The Masters developed a reputation for tournament innovations such as a telephone system for instantly reporting scoring from each hole.

1946

Byron Nelson and Ben Hogan. Or was it Ben Hogan and Byron Nelson? Those two were the clear favorites heading into the 1946 Masters, but it wasn't so clear which one was No. 1.

This was a highly anticipated Masters, and not just because folks were anxious to see a tournament at Augusta National after a three-year hiatus for World War II. It also had a lot to do with the way the rivals from Fort Worth were dominating the tour. Nelson and Hogan had met in a playoff the last time the Masters was played, four years before, and they had only stepped up their games since then.

Nelson, who was kept out of military service by a blood disorder, won 18 times in 1945, including 11 in a row, a record that still lives on and likely will forever. While the competition in 1945 was stronger than might be supposed, as a number of pros returned from service, it wasn't until the last two tournaments of Nelson's win streak that Hogan rejoined the tour. Little Ben, as he was known, quickly showed that he was up to the task of challenging the man who had recently earned the nickname "Mr. Golf." In the seven months from September 1945 through March 1946, Hogan won nine tournaments and Nelson six.

Bookmakers installed the duo as co-favorites with 3-to-1 odds. By the eve of the tournament, those odds had been adjusted to 2-to-1, perhaps because of what transpired in a Monday practice round. Nelson and Hogan teamed up to take on tournament host Bobby Jones and Augusta National professional Ed Dudley in a match followed by several hundred spectators, with Nelson shooting a 65 and Hogan a 66 (their best ball was 60).

A poll of the competitors rated Hogan as a slight favorite, but John R. Henry of the International News Service wrote that Nelson "seemed confident he will do the impossible, a third triumph in the Masters." He retained that confidence despite a slight ailment of the right wrist that caused him to cut short his Tuesday practice round and rest on Wednesday. "Nothing to it. Just like a crick in the neck," he said of the injury. "I'll be okay."

Several notables played the course during practice rounds even though they weren't competing in the tournament—the legendary Walter Hagen, 1913 U.S. Open champion Francis Ouimet, and six-time U.S. Women's Amateur champion Glenna Collett Vare. They drew considerable galleries, and their presence underscored the deepening significance of the event in the golf world.

"It's like the U.S. Open, only more so in a way," said Hagen. "There's no other competition like this one anywhere in the world. And I know from experience how easy it is to be trying too hard to win it."

The practice rounds were also noted for low scoring, swelling expectations that the tournament record of 279 would be broken. In addition to Nelson and Hogan, Sam Byrd shot a 65 and Jimmy Thomson a 66.

When the tournament rolled around on Thursday, however, the wind picked up and the pin positions were very difficult causing "considerable comment" among the players. The Masters committee apparently didn't want Augusta National to be a pushover.

The best scores were 69s by overlooked 31-year-olds Herman Keiser and Chick Harbert. Nelson, playing with Jones, shot a 72 admitting that he "went to sleep on three holes" leading to mid-round bogeys, while Hogan couldn't make a putt and had a 74. Sam Snead, winner of two events in March and third on the oddsmaker's board (starting at 4-to-1 and ending up 3-to-1), also shot 74. The 1940 champion Jimmy Demaret—picked by only himself in the pre-tournament player poll—had a 75.

Harbert, who had won three times on tour, played with a painful cyst behind his left knee, and arranged to have it removed Thursday evening in a minor operation. The cyst was gone Friday, but so was Harbert's game as he shot a 75 on the way to an eventual T7 finish. Keiser, meanwhile, shot an impressive 68 as he went without a bogey on a day when the pin positions were eased up only slightly. That left him with a hefty five-stroke advantage over Thomson. Hogan improved to a 70 and was seven back at 144, while Nelson had a 73 for 145. "It looks like I just can't play anymore," said Lord Byron, out of frustration, or perhaps sarcasm.

Keiser wasn't quite a nobody. He had won the 1942 Miami Four-Ball Invitational with partner Chandler Harper before embarking on a 31-month tour of duty in the Navy, where he was a storekeeper on the U.S.S. Cincinnati, bringing his clubs on the ship to play wherever they went ashore. While lacking an individual win, he had two runner-up finishes in 1946, losing a playoff to Hogan in Phoenix and finishing behind Snead in Greensboro. Still, it was anything but a sure thing that he would be able to withstand the pressure of leading the Masters.

Keiser hung in gamely during the third round. He made a great recovery from the trees on the 10th hole and saved his par five on the 13th with a 15-foot putt after finding the creek and playing out of the rocks. Jack Troy of the *Atlanta Constitution* wrote that "the gallery admired his fighting spirit and swung to his side," emitting a huge roar when he chipped in from 40 feet for an eagle on the 15th. That enabled Keiser to escape with a 71 and preserve a five-stroke lead, albeit now over the dangerous Hogan, who moved into a challenging position with a 69.

The final round was strictly a two-man battle between Keiser and Hogan, with Nelson and Snead ultimately finishing tied for seventh, eight strokes behind. While outwardly showing no emotion, Keiser was wildly up and down on the front nine with three birdies and four bogeys. He settled down with eight straight pars to start the back nine, one of them when a spectator's foot stopped his third shot from bounding well past the green on the 15th—in those days before gallery ropes, spectators were allowed behind the 15th green. They closely crowded all of the greens, and sometimes players even had to hit their approach shots over them.

Hogan heated up on the back nine with birdies on 12, 13, and 15, Keiser hearing the roars indicating that his lead was dwindling. Only a three-putt bogey at 14 blunted Hogan's charge, and Keiser had a one-stroke advantage as he played the 18th about a half hour ahead of Hogan. After a nice approach to 20 feet, Keiser faced a downhill birdie putt and knocked it five feet past—then missed from there. After only one three-putt in the first three rounds, Keiser had three on Sunday in shooting a 74 for a 282 total.

Hogan came to 18 needing a birdie to win or a par four to tie. "I hope he makes a three or a five," Keiser told a friend, not wanting to go into a playoff the next day.

It looked like a three was a good possibility when Hogan hit his approach to 12 feet. But he was putting down the same slippery slope Keiser had. After spending

1946		
1	Herman Keiser	69–68–71–74—282
2	Ben Hogan	74–70–69–70—283
3	Bob Hamilton	75–69–71–72—287
T4	Jimmy Demaret	75–70–71–73—289
T4	Jim Ferrier	74–72–68–75—289
T4	Ky Laffoon	74–73–70–72—289
T7	Chick Harbert	69–75–76–70—290
T7	Clayton Heafner	74–69–71–76—290
T7	Byron Nelson	72–73–71–74—290
T7	Sam Snead	74–75–70–71—290

a long time studying the green, Hogan's birdie putt missed and slid 30 inches past the hole. Stunningly, he missed the comebacker, and the title was Keiser's.

Years later, Hogan recalled that his first putt broke right as is went past the hole, "meaning it would have to break left coming back. But it didn't. It broke right again. I was told that the next day a half-dozen members tried to make the same putt and all of them missed on the right."

Hagen told writer O.B. Keeler that he and Jones agreed they would have been "a little more cowardly" on the birdie putts at 18 to make sure of a par four. Perhaps the dueling three-putts revealed the pressure of trying too hard to win that Hagen had referred to earlier in the week.

While the dark-horse Keiser would naturally be battling nerves down the stretch, Hogan wasn't immune. In fact, at age 33, he still hadn't won a major championship. Of course, the fact that he had no opportunities from 1943–45 (only two majors were played in that span, and Hogan couldn't compete in either because he was in the Army) didn't help. Still, his debacle on the 72nd hole was a bad sign— and an odd end to an otherwise compelling Masters.

Missing Putter

Lawson Little arrived at the 18th green of the second round without his putter, which had somehow disappeared on the 17th green or 18th tee. No one knew if it had been left on the ground or pilfered from his bag, but, either way, a spectator walked away with Little's blade. The 1940 U.S. Open champion hit his first stroke from the 18th green with a 2-iron, but got a ruling before his second putt that he could borrow a putter, which he did and made a four-footer for a par. While the incident didn't cost him a stroke, Little was distraught about losing a favorite club. "I've lost my bread and butter. I only hope that who found the club will be kind-hearted enough to send it back to me," he was quoted in the next morning's *Augusta Chronicle*. Apparently the "perpetrator" read the paper, because he brought the putter to Little the next day before the third round.

1947

This time around, Ben Hogan was considered a relatively clear favorite, though he ranked second to Jimmy Demaret on the tour's money list. Each had won twice individually in the first three months of the year, and they teamed to take the Miami Four-Ball Championship.

Hogan was determined to break through and win the Masters for the first time, heading to Augusta early to spend two weeks practicing while the rest of the tour played two events in North Carolina. Byron Nelson was also on the Augusta grounds more than a week early, but his situation was very different. He had quit the tour at age 34 the previous fall and bought a ranch in Roanoke, Texas, where he planned to raise cattle. Nelson hadn't played a tournament since the first week of October, nearly six months prior to the start of the Masters.

"I've been playing golf for 30 years, 14 of it on the tournament swing, month after month. Since I've been married, my wife never had a home until last year. Now we've both got one. I just got tired of it, that's all," he told William Tucker of United Press.

The Masters was one tournament that Nelson couldn't pass up. In fact, it was the only tournament he would enter all year. He hadn't shot better than 72 in 10 practice rounds, but was hoping he had shaken off the rust and that it would be more than a ceremonial appearance.

Once tournament week rolled around, the biggest draw during practice rounds was the great woman amateur (soon to be professional) Babe Zaharias, who had won the Titleholders event in Augusta a week earlier and was invited by Jones to stay over for Masters week and play the course Monday through Wednesday, where it was said that her group attracted more spectators than Jones' did. Another highlight was a shot-making exhibition and golf clinic on Wednesday afternoon that would become a fixture on the schedule for more than a decade, along with a long drive contest.

Also on Wednesday afternoon, Sam Snead and South Africa's Bobby Locke finally arrived in Augusta, making it to the course after 4 p.m. They were coming off an exhibition series in South Africa, where the homegrown sensation and runner-up to Snead in the 1946 British Open beat the great American in 12 of 16 matches. The timing and travel arrangements could have been better, though, at least so far as their Masters prospects were concerned. A 47-hour trip by air with various connections got them to New York on Tuesday, from where they took a train to Columbia, South Carolina, and finally a car to Augusta on Wednesday for some hurried practice before dusk.

Snead would hang within three strokes through two rounds before fading to a T22 finish, while Locke started slowly but finished strong with a 71–70 on the weekend to place T14—beating Snead again.

Early in the week, Nelson had said, "Who knows? I might get out there and start shooting some good golf.… It would be kind of nice to be in the spotlight again."

The Texas rancher got his wish in the first round, finding the spotlight with a 69 to share the lead with Demaret. The pair played together, Demaret saying afterward: "I saw a great round of golf. Byron could have been at least three strokes better with a few breaks on the putting greens." As for Demaret, he pleased the crowd

1947

1	Jimmy Demaret	69–71–70–71—281
T2	Byron Nelson	69–72–72–70—283
T2	Frank Stranahan	73–72–70–68—283
T4	Ben Hogan	75–68–71–70—284
T4	Harold McSpaden	74–69–70–71—284
T6	Jim Ferrier	70–71–73–72—286
T6	Henry Picard	73–70–72–71—286
T8	Chandler Harper	77–72–68–70—287
T8	Lloyd Mangrum	76–73–68–70—287
T8	Dick Metz	72–72–72–71—287
T8	Ed Oliver	70–72–71–74—287
T8	Toney Penna	71–70–75–71—287

by splashing out from the water hazard in front of the green to birdie the 15th (see: "A Big Splash", page 37).

Hogan struggled to a 75 in the first round, writing in his syndicated newspaper column, "I didn't play well at all. I hope you will excuse me if I don't say anything more about my round than just that."

Bantam Ben battled back with a 68 on Friday and added a couple more subpar rounds on the weekend to finish T4, just three strokes back, but he didn't elaborate on his good rounds in his column, either, instead focusing on what the other contenders told him about their play. He had plenty of opportunity to write about his friend and four-ball partner Demaret, who shot a second-round 71 to share the halfway lead with rookie pro Cary Middlecoff, and a third-round 70 to take a three-stroke lead over Nelson and Jug McSpaden.

Demaret's third round could have been titled "The Great Escape," as he surged ahead despite wild driving. "I was in the trees so much that several firms of tree surgeons wanted to sign me up," he said. But he was able to get out of trouble to a spot on or near the greens, and one-putted 10 times in shooting a 70.

Known for his colorful attire, Demaret dressed all in yellow on Sunday; "bright as an Easter egg in canary yellow," wrote Fred Byrod in the *Philadelphia Inquirer*. But he made sure that the round lacked a great deal of drama, shooting a rather workmanlike 71 as he stayed in front all day.

"I simply played steady golf. I figured a 70 or 71 would do the trick, so I played cautiously," said Demaret, who laid up on both par fives on the back nine—and birdied them both. A bogey on 16 and a second shot that bounded well over the green on 17 made for a few anxious moments, but he got up and down for a par on the latter hole and finished with a 281 total, good for a two-stroke victory over Nelson and rising amateur star Frank Stranahan.

Stranahan shot a 68 in the final round, but started too far back and would have needed a Demaret collapse to have a shot. Nelson didn't play poorly after the first round—and had an eagle in each of the first three rounds—but not quite well enough to win. Still, it was a remarkable showing after the layoff. "I talked with everyone Byron played with in the tournament and they said that if he had any luck at all with his putter he would have had a 65 every day," said Jones.

Demaret showed his fun-loving side in the runup to the tournament, grabbing the microphone to croon a few numbers with the band at the Bon Air Hotel on Tuesday night. But on the course, he was all business.

"The reason I won the Masters this year is I worked harder. I was more serious than ever in practice, I wanted to win this thing more than anything I know. I kept thinking about what Walter Hagen said. If you win once you are lucky, but if you win twice you are plain good," said the man who joined Horton Smith and Nelson as two-time Masters champions.

....

A Big Splash

Jimmy Demaret's second shot found the water hazard in front of the par-5 15th green on Thursday, but it served to showcase his flair for the dramatic. With his ball under water but very close to the bank, the colorful Texan took off one shoe and sock, rolled up his pants leg, and stepped into the water—then stepped out, took off the other shoe and sock, rolled up that pants leg, and stepped in again. Settling over the shot, he swung, sent a splash of water into the air, and watched the ball fly toward the hole and stop six feet away. Where it first looked like he would make a bogey, Demaret holed the putt and walked off with a birdie on the way to the first-round lead and eventual victory.

....

1948

The pre-tournament talk in 1948 centered on what might be termed the Stranahan Affair, which saw 1947 runner-up Frank Stranahan booted from the invitation list for reasons that were never precisely spelled out. The club would have liked to somehow keep the story under wraps, but the Augusta and Atlanta newspapers reported the Saturday before the tournament that Stranahan was probably out.

Both sides remained silent for the next few days—leaving it uncertain to the press and public whether the amateur standout would play or not—before Augusta National on Tuesday released a statement that Stranahan's invitation had been withdrawn because of "a disregard for regulations made for the protection of the golf course," noting that he had been guilty the previous year as well. It would come to light that the violations involved playing more than one ball in practice rounds, and that Stranahan was warned by Augusta National greenkeeper Marion Ira Luke not to do it again. The two men got into a heated argument, and it was likely the verbal altercation, more than a new violation, that precipitated the club's action.

This was a big deal. Stranahan, the son of the millionaire founder of the Champion Spark Plug company, was making an impression on the circuit playing as an amateur and had been runner-up in the 1947 British Open as well as the Masters. Unfortunately, some in the golfing world had the impression of him as a spoiled bad boy, which, fair or not, didn't help his cause in this incident. Frankie hung around hoping to get a hearing—he felt his side hadn't been heard, as the committee had based its ruling solely on Luke's report—but he was told that the case was closed. Ultimately, he bought a ticket and watched the tournament as a spectator (and was invited back to play in subsequent years).

1948

1	Claude Harmon	70–70–69–70—279	
2	Cary Middlecoff	74–71–69–70—284	
3	Chick Harbert	71–70–70–76—287	
T4	Jim Ferrier	71–71–75–71—288	
T4	Lloyd Mangrum	69–73–75–71—288	
T6	Ed Furgol	70–72–73–74—289	
T6	Ben Hogan	70–71–77–71—289	
T8	Byron Nelson	71–73–72–74—290	
T8	Harry Todd	72–67–80–71—290	
T10	Herman Keiser	70–72–76–73—291	
T10	Bobby Locke	71–71–74–75—291	
T10	Dick Metz	71–72–75–73—291	

There were no overwhelming favorites this year, as Ben Hogan had recently been bothered by a bad back. In a poll of pros at the Charlotte tournament, they picked Byron Nelson to win—even though he hadn't played a tournament since last year's Masters. Sam Snead was a relative longshot. As Grantland Rice noted: "The putter is one of the major clubs required to wrestle with par [at Augusta National], and Snead hasn't been speaking to his putter for more than two years." Indeed, the slumping Virginian would finish well back at T16, though he won the long-drive contest the Wednesday before the tournament.

Lloyd Mangrum grabbed the first-round lead with a 69, but in the second round was penalized a stroke on the eighth hole for causing his ball to move when he stepped on a nearby tree branch after a shot into the woods. The resulting double bogey contributed to a 73, which started a slide toward an eventual T4 finish. Unheralded Harry Todd led through 36 holes after a surprising 67 on Friday, but he followed that with an 80 the next day.

Claude Harmon was within a stroke of the lead after each of the first two rounds with 70–69. Undoubtedly a strong enough player to have played the tour, the 31-year-old Harmon had too good a life holding down two of the top club pro jobs in the country—Seminole Golf Club in Florida in the winter and Winged Foot Golf Club in New York for the rest of the year. The only year he entered more than eight tour events was 1945, when he played in 16 and had three third-place finishes. With tour purses being anything but a jackpot in those days, he was just as well off with his club gigs and could live the settled life of a family man—his four sons all went on to be club pros themselves.

Harmon took control of the tournament with a 32 on the back nine on Saturday, with birdies on 11, 12, 13, 15, and 17—offset by only a bogey on 14—for a round of 69. "I'm having a lot of fun out of the tournament," he told the press. "I haven't been playing in tournaments all winter like the rest of the fellows and I'm more relaxed." Only Chick Harbert, at 211, was closer than five strokes behind Harmon's 209. Hogan had been within two of the 36-hole lead, but shot himself out of it with a 77 in the third round.

Harmon had made a bit of news in 1947 when, in the third round, he aced the 12th hole while playing with Hogan. This time, a near ace on the sixth hole of the final round, his tee shot finishing 18 inches from the cup, fueled a surge that set up a cakewalk to the title. Harmon's birdie on No. 6 was followed by a birdie on the seventh from 10 feet and an eagle on the par-five eighth occasioned by a fairway wood second shot to four feet. Behind him, his closest competitor Harbert would make bogeys on Nos. 5, 6, and 8, and Harmon took an eight-stroke lead to the back nine.

A 37 on the final nine gave Harmon a 70 for a 279 total that matched the tournament record and a five-stroke victory over future Masters champion Middlecoff (70 with a 33 on the back nine), eight ahead of third-place Harbert (76). Walking off the 18th green, Harmon was greeted by two meaningful handshakes.

One was from 1941 champion Craig Wood, the head pro at Winged Foot when Harmon was hired as an assistant. Wood not only groomed Harmon to eventually take the head job there, he also provided swing instruction that Harmon credited as a key to his success.

The other handshake was from Bobby Jones, who had once shaken an 8-year-old Claude's hand. Harmon was born in Savannah, making him the first native Georgian to win the Masters. The Harmon family moved to Atlanta and Jones' neighborhood, leading to the handshake which came in the midst of Bobby's amateur exploits. The Harmons would move to Florida when Claude was still a boy, so he spent his formative competitive golfing years in the Orlando area but never forgot his Georgia roots.

1949

The 1949 Masters was notable for two absences from the field. Bobby Jones played what turned out to be the last round of golf of his life in June 1948 at East Lake, his home course in Atlanta. Suffering from spinal pain, he was diagnosed with syringomyelia and underwent an operation that fall. Unfortunately, his condition would continue to steadily deteriorate throughout the rest of his life until his death in 1971. Jones had played his last Masters in 1948; he was on hand as tournament host in 1949, mostly viewing the action through binoculars from the veranda of his cottage near the 10th tee.

Ben Hogan was absent from the grounds entirely. He suffered a fractured pelvis, broken collarbone, and broken ankle in a car crash on February 2 while driving back to Texas from the West Coast tournament trail. As if that weren't bad enough, he developed blood clots while still in the hospital, undergoing an operation to prevent the possibility of a large clot moving from a leg to his upper body, where it could be fatal. He was finally discharged from the hospital on March 31, seven days before the start of the Masters. Hogan was in the thoughts and hearts of the entire golfing world, including his fellow pros, who sent a framed photo of the Masters field and an engraved humidor from Augusta to Hogan's home in Fort Worth with their best wishes for a recovery.

With Hogan sidelined and Byron Nelson retired (though he would still tee it up at the Masters), the tour was down to Sam Snead as the lone representative of the triumvirate that ruled the game in the years just before, during, and after World War II. And the Snead of 1947 and 1948 was just a shell of what he had been in previous years. Still a wonderful ball-striker, Snead's putting turned bad enough to make observers cringe or turn away when he had the putter in his hands. He didn't win a single tournament in 1947 and just one in 1948 when he took a long break from the circuit and assumed a position at The Greenbrier in West Virginia.

He returned to the tour in the winter of 1948–49. By the time of the Masters, things had brightened considerably. Snead won a one-day event in Aiken, South Carolina, 15 miles from Augusta, in March and, more significantly, captured the Greater Greensboro Open in the tournament before the Masters.

Suddenly, he was one of the favorites in Augusta. On Monday, Randy Russell wrote in the *Augusta Chronicle* that, after wowing the fans with the accuracy of his shots in a practice round, Snead headed to the putting green for a practice session, where "he performed with a skill quite improper for a fellow who is not supposed to have any talent for putting."

Snead had switched to a new putter in Greensboro and received a couple of helpful tips from fellow pros. That was enough for Snead to break whatever mental block he had developed about his putting, and turn him into a new man on the greens.

Still seeking his first Masters victory in his 10th try—the runner-up finish in 1939 his only top five—Snead played with Lloyd Mangrum in the feature pairing of the first round. Mangrum, the tour's leading money winner, took the first-round lead for the second straight year, with a 69 in winds that were steady at 20 mph with gusts into the 30s. Snead pleased the crowd with an eagle on the second hole, but didn't make a single birdie as he managed a 73. After the controversy of a year earlier, Frank Stranahan was back in the field and back on the leaderboard with a 70 for solo second.

The wind blew again in the second round, this time negotiated most successfully by 1946 champion Herman Keiser with a 68 for a 143 total that earned a share of the lead with Mangrum (74). Stranahan struggled to a 77, starting a slide that resulted in a T19 finish. Snead shot a 75 for a 148 total that left him in a tie for 14th five strokes back, and it appeared the early-week optimism regarding him was misguided.

Snead didn't think he was out of it, though. He headed to the practice green after the second round to iron things out, and started holing putts from everywhere. "But will that stroke hold up on the course?" a friend asked. "You're damn right it will," Sam replied.

It did. Snead roared back with a 67 in the third round, with his new-found putting prowess at the forefront. He one-putted the first five greens, three of them for birdies, and added a birdie at the ninth for a 32 on the front nine. A bogey on 10 and birdies on 13 and 15 produced a 35 on the back nine to complete a round that saw Snead move within a stroke of the lead at 215. That lead was assumed by Johnny Palmer, as Keiser skied to a 78. Tied for second with Snead at 215 were Mangrum and Joe Kirkwood Jr., who played boxer Joe Palooka as an actor in a series of movies while playing himself as a professional golfer in real life.

Kirkwood exited the stage with a 75 in the final round, while Palmer hung around with a 72. Mangrum had a 70, but visited the pond on 16—the one that had been newly installed for the 1948 Masters by damming the stream that originally bordered the green—for the second straight day, this time making a bogey after a double bogey on Saturday. Those were three costly strokes, as he tied for second with Johnny Bulla, who closed with a 69, three strokes behind the winner's 282 total.

The weekend and tournament belonged to Snead, who shot another 67 on Sunday. It was a display of scoring unlike any seen at Augusta National before—the cumulative 134 for consecutive rounds was the best ever in the Masters to that point. His putting again was sound, as he took 30 putts with just 14 in a front-nine 33 that began with birdies on three of the first four holes.

1949		
1	Sam Snead	73–75–67–67—282
T2	Johnny Bulla	74–73–69–69—285
T2	Lloyd Mangrum	69–74–72–70—285
T4	Johnny Palmer	73–71–70–72—286
T4	Jim Turnesa	73–72–71–70—286
6	Lew Worsham	76–75–70–68—289
7	Joe Kirkwood Jr.	73–72–70–75—290
T8	Jimmy Demaret	76–72–73–71—292
T8	Clayton Heafner	71–74–72–75—292
T8	Byron Nelson	75–70–74–73—292

Snead gave his supporters cause for concern with bogeys on 10 and 11, reviving memories of past failures in big events—notably the U.S. Opens of 1939 and 1947—for which he was just as famous as for his many victories. There would be no collapse this time, though. Instead, it was a charge to the finish as he birdied four of the last seven holes. A birdie at the 12th got Snead back on track, and he hit the par-five 13th and 15th in two, narrowly missing eagle putts. He finished in style with a seven-iron from the rough on the 18th to 22 feet and a putt that, appropriately enough, found the hole for his eighth birdie of the day.

For his first Masters victory, Snead received the honor of being the first champion to be awarded a green jacket in the official prize ceremony. Augusta members had been wearing green jackets since 1937, so the idea—a brilliant one, considering how potent a symbol donning the jacket has become—was that winning the Masters made the player an honorary Augusta National member.

Upon returning to the clubhouse, Snead received a congratulatory phone call from none other than Hogan, who had listened to the radio broadcast in his home in Fort Worth.

1950

The big news in 1950 was that Ben Hogan was back, having made a spectacular return at the Los Angeles Open in January, where he reached a playoff before losing to Sam Snead. In three tournaments since then, Hogan hadn't finished better than 19th, so there were still lingering questions about his physical condition and form as he headed to Augusta for some early practice. Was he back to being the player he was before the accident? Nobody really knew yet. So, it was certainly promising when he shot a 66 in practice on the Thursday before the tournament, following that with 68, 72, and 67 in his next three sessions.

Snead, meanwhile, was playing the best golf of his life, posting five wins in nine tournaments, but there was a warning sign when he withdrew from the Azalea Open with a wonky back the week before the Masters.

Snead had a 71 and Hogan a 73 in a cold, windy first round, taking a back seat to a 35-year-old rookie pro. Skee Riegel didn't start playing golf until age 23, after playing football at Lafayette, but went on to win the 1947 U.S. Amateur and earn low amateur honors at the 1948 Masters before taking the professional plunge. In just his fifth event as a pro, Riegel shot a 69 to take the solo lead, one ahead of a group of five players including Jimmy Demaret and Australia native Jim Ferrier.

The 6-foot-4 Ferrier, coming in at a trim 195 pounds after losing 25 pounds over the previous year, jumped to a four-stroke lead with a 67 in the second round. Ferrier was a familiar figure near the top, having finished fourth-sixth-fourth in 1946–48, though in 1949 he followed a third-round 67 with a closing 79 and was T16. Playing the tour part-time starting in 1940, the Aussie had become an American citizen after being drafted into the Army during World War II. Playing the circuit full-time after the war, he had posted seven victories since 1947 (he would finish his career with 18).

Hogan had the only other sub-70 score on Friday, a 68, to move into second place at 141. He showed a fine putting touch with putts of at least eight feet for four straight birdies on Nos. 6 to 9, followed by a 10-foot par save on the 10th. Demaret was next at 142 with an eagle at the 13th saving a 72.

Ferrier still led by four through nine holes of the third round before a 38 on the second nine enabled Hogan to cut the margin to two. Ben had a chance to tie for the lead with a birdie on the 18th hole, but instead three-putted for a bogey. Many players, including Hogan, contended that the greens were too hard and too fast. "The second shot of mine was as fine a shot as I've ever made," he said of his approach to 18. "And then I come up there and find myself 25 feet away—and with the toughest downhill putt over a fast surface."

With a 54-hole total of 210, Ferrier would have to hold off a quartet of stars, with Hogan's 212 followed by Demaret and Byron Nelson at 214 and Snead at 215. Nobody else bettered 218, Riegel having gone 75–78 after his opener. Demaret eagled the 13th hole for the second straight day in a 72 marred by five three-putts. Nelson, still a player to be reckoned with in retirement, had a 33 on the back nine for a 69 and Snead climbed into contention with a 70.

Hogan was unable to mount a comeback victory—those heroics would have to wait until two months later at the U.S. Open. His legs perhaps not up to the grind, Ben shot a final-round 76 as the *Augusta Chronicle* said he was "spraying his tee shots all over the course." He tied for fourth with Nelson (74), while Snead had a 72 for third, as it became a battle between Ferrier and Demaret.

The Masters finished on Easter Sunday, as it had in 1947 when Demaret scored his second Augusta victory. Once again, newspaper accounts characterized him as looking like an Easter egg, this time wearing three shades of green. He started a charge to the finish with a birdie on the 13th, putting him at six-under for the week on that hole. He bogeyed 14, but birdied 15 and 16 for a 34 on the back nine and a 69. Having started his round earlier than the other leaders, Demaret posted a five-under 283 total when Ferrier had six holes to play.

Two-under for the round to that point, Ferrier was eight-under for the tournament, so he could win outright by playing the last six holes in two-over or better. He quickly threw away those two strokes to spare, driving into the creek on 13 and three-putting 14 from a long distance for a pair of bogeys. After only a par five at the birdie-able 15th, Ferrier's tee shot at the par-three 16th bounded over the green and he missed an eight-foot par putt. Now he needed two pars just to get into a playoff.

1950		
1	Jimmy Demaret	70–72–72–69—283
2	Jim Ferrier	70–67–73–75—285
3	Sam Snead	71–74–70–72—287
T4	Ben Hogan	73–68–71–76—288
T4	Byron Nelson	75–70–69–74—288
6	Lloyd Mangrum	76–74–73–68—291
T7	Clayton Heafner	74–77–69–72—292
T7	Cary Middlecoff	75–76–68–73—292
9	Lawson Little	70–73–75–75—293
T10	Fred Haas	74–76–73–71—294
T10	Gene Sarazen	80–70–72–72—294

Demaret was following the action, wearing headphones in the radio tower at the 18th green. He was giving his commentary to the broadcast, and also in asides to reporters at the scene. "If he ties me, I'll beat him tomorrow," said Jimmy after Ferrier's bogey on 16.

Ferrier bunkered his approach on 17 for another bogey, now needing a birdie on 18 just to force a tie. "He's mine, boys!" Demaret exclaimed, which became true enough minutes later when Ferrier three-putted 18 for yet another bogey and an ugly 41 on the back nine for a 75.

A little more than a month shy of his 40th birthday, Demaret had become the first three-time Masters winner, having outplayed Ferrier by seven strokes on the last six holes. "I'm going to adopt that 13th hole and take it home with me," he said.

1951

Jim Ferrier, who had let the title slip through his hands the previous year, came into this Masters on the heels of three straight victories followed by two runner-up finishes in his last five tour events. But while the Australian was the hottest player, he wasn't the most talked about. That was Ben Hogan.

Ben's victory in the U.S. Open had been the story of the year in sports in 1950. He was now playing a limited schedule due to circulatory problems in his legs and was entering only his second tournament of the year, having finished second in the 54-hole Seminole Pro-Am in Florida. The infrequency of his appearances, the indominable nature of his comeback, and his legendary focus and drive all fed what came to be termed the Hogan mystique. All eyes were on Hogan, and he was considered the favorite to win, even though he hadn't won a Masters in nine previous attempts.

Hogan, who confided to some other players that Augusta National didn't suit his game, arrived nine days before the tournament to begin extensive preparations and learn how best to handle the course. Playing it in different wind conditions and trying various shots—knockdowns, fades, draws, etc.—he devised a strategy. As the tournament approached, his game was in good shape and his mindset positive. Defending champion Jimmy Demaret, after playing with Hogan on Tuesday, predicted that Ben would win.

Sam Snead, who had won 11 times in 1950, had also been absent for most of the first part of the 1951 schedule. While finishing third at his first event, the Los Angeles Open, he discovered a fractured bone in his left hand, which sidelined him for two months. In the three events he entered, he finished 3–2–3, so he wasn't being written off at Augusta.

George Fazio, a role player in Hogan's 1950 U.S. Open victory, as he and Lloyd Mangrum fell in a playoff, took the first-round lead with a 68 but Snead and Hogan were very much alive with 69 and 70, respectively. Hogan eagled the second hole after a three-wood to 10 feet in an otherwise steady round with 15 pars, a birdie, a bogey, and the eagle. Mangrum, the year's second leading money winner, was tied with Snead at 69. Ferrier started with a 74 on the way to an ultimate seventh-place finish.

Skee Riegel, who faded after leading through 18 holes in 1950, this time went in front at the 36-hole mark thanks to a 68 for a 141 total, one ahead of Fazio and Hogan, whose round of 72 included 37 putts (counting using a putter from the fringe). Snead had a 74, hurt by a double bogey at 12, where his tee shot found the water, but was still in the hunt at 143.

Neither Snead nor Hogan was completely pleased with their third round, yet Snead ended up tied for first with Riegiel at 211 after a 68 and Hogan was one behind with a 70. Snead's score was aided by uncharacteristically fine chipping and putting, but he wasn't happy with his ball-striking and didn't feel completely healed. "I can't seem to get my hands together. My left hand is still weak," said the Virginian, noting that if he were playing from tee to green as he did in his 1949 victory he could have been eight or nine strokes better.

Hogan birdied all four par fives but no other holes and lamented his decision-making that led to his two bogeys—mis-clubbing on No. 6 and failing to account for a crosswind on No. 7. As someone who rightly prided himself on his course management, Hogan hated those kinds of mistakes more than anyone. A missed four-foot birdie putt on the 18th that would have tied him for the lead didn't help, either.

While entering the final round a stroke behind Snead and Riegel, *Golf World* noted that Hogan was the favorite in "Augusta wagering parlors." As it worked out, the bookies knew what they were doing.

Hogan went out last among the contenders in the final round and benefited as, one by one, the others faltered. First was Mangrum, who started two strokes back. He was even par through 11 holes, but hit his tee shot on the 12th over the green, where it partially embedded in the bank. Unable to take relief (or perhaps unaware that he could—the exact condition of his lie and the interpretation of the rules both uncertain looking back today), he punched the ball out with a putter but didn't reach the green and ended up with a double bogey. He ended up with a 73 and tied for third with 1947 U.S. Open champion Lew Worsham, who stayed on the fringe of contention all week without being a major factor.

Next was Riegel, who faltered with bogeys on Nos. 9 and 11 to go one-over on the round at about the time Hogan was on the first tee. Riegel recovered with birdies on 13 and 17 to finish at 282 and set the target for Snead and Hogan.

1951		
1	Ben Hogan	70–72–70–68—280
2	Skee Riegel	73–68–70–71—282
T3	Lloyd Mangrum	69–74–70–73—286
T3	Lew Worsham	71–71–72–72—286
5	Dave Douglas	74–69–72–73—288
6	Lawson Little	72–73–72–72—289
7	Jim Ferrier	74–70–74–72—290
T8	Johnny Bulla	71–72–73–75—291
T8	Byron Nelson	71–73–73–74—291
T8	Sam Snead	69–74–68–80—291

Snead, after a 37 on the front nine, needed a 34 on the second nine to match Riegel. He didn't come close, shooting himself out of it with a disastrous eight on the 11th hole. A new dam installed during the previous year had turned the creek to the left of the 11th green into a pond. Snead's approach found the water, and, after a drop, his next one did, too. It reminded observers of the eight Snead took on the 72nd hole to lose the 1939 U.S. Open. An unnerved Snead went on to take a bogey six on the 13th and a double bogey seven on the 15th for a 43 on the back nine and an unsightly round of 80.

Hogan, by contrast, played a bogey-free round. Not mistake-free, but a round in which his short game erased the few errors. A key was the par-three fourth, where his tee shot found the front bunker but he came out reasonably well and holed a 10-foot par putt. That preserved a strong start—he birdied the second after reaching the fringe of the green in two and birdied the third with a four-foot putt after his approach hit the flagstick. Some good fortune helped. Hogan's second shot on the par-five eighth struck a spectator and kept it from going further left, and his approach was halted on the back fringe by the feet of the assembled crowd. From there, he chipped in for a birdie.

Making the turn in 33, Hogan could see that Riegel's 282 total had just been posted, and he knew that an even-par back nine would give him his first Masters title. For a 38-year-old who had only known frustration in Augusta, with runner-up finishes in 1942 and 1946 and three fourth-places, he knew it was no sure thing. He played conservatively on the back nine, laying up with his second shot on both par fives. At the 13th, he pulled a four-wood out of the bag before switching to an iron— and ended up with a birdie after hitting his third shot to eight feet.

While that fits the enduring image of Hogan as a methodical grinder, his favored style of play was actually more aggressive than that. He said after the round that the safety-first play down the stretch wasn't the type of golf he enjoys playing. "There's no other way to do it, though. Why take chances and throw away the tournament?"

Hogan had eight pars and the birdie on 13 on the back nine for a 35 and a final-round 68 to finish two strokes ahead of Riegel, who professed himself quite happy with second place.

With a Masters title finally in hand on his 10th try, Hogan joined Gene Sarazen and Byron Nelson as the only winners of the Masters, U.S. Open, and PGA Championship—the three majors contested in the U.S.—at a time when few Americans ventured across the ocean to play in the British Open.

"I had begun to wonder if I could ever win the Masters," he confessed after the round. "The last round of it had become a complex with me."

1952

Sam Snead and Ben Hogan had been mostly absent from the tour in the first part of 1952, Snead playing in only two official events and Hogan none. Both entered two unofficial pro-ams, a 36-holer at Seminole in Florida and an 18-holer at Palmetto in Aiken, South Carolina, just down the road from Augusta. Snead won both, with Hogan finishing sixth and second.

Perhaps it was those pro-am results that led sports editor Randy Russell in the *Augusta Chronicle* to label Snead as the consensus favorite in the Masters. Also, Hogan had complained of a bad back during practice rounds, and there was the history of a defending champion never having won the Masters. Snead had performed impressively in the Jacksonville Open in March, where he tied Doug Ford for first place after regulation, but conceded the playoff without playing. Snead had received a favorable ruling in the third round, when it was determined that his ball lying outside the out-of-bounds stakes was actually in play. After the final round, saying that he didn't want anyone to think he was taking advantage of the ruling, Sam let Ford take the title.

Still, there were observers who doubted whether Snead could win in Hogan's presence. Snead's three post-war major championship victories, the 1949 Masters and 1949 and 1951 PGA Championships, had come when Hogan wasn't in the field. Hogan's six post-war major titles had all come with Snead on hand. It was believed by many that Hogan had Snead's number.

That may not have been the case, but it is true that Snead was irked by the acclaim accorded to his rival. It stuck in Snead's craw that Hogan was named Player of the Year in 1950 for winning just one official event while Snead had captured 11. In his 1997 book *The Game I Love*, Snead wrote that the slight so affected him that "I said, 'The hell with it,' and cut back on my playing significantly.... It hurts even now." Snead had spent the bulk of the winter of 1952 relaxing in Florida instead of heading out west to follow the tour.

Snead's first round got off to a bad start with a double bogey on the first hole when his punched five-iron from the trees hopped well over the green and behind another tree. It was the beginning of a crazy round. Snead birdied five of the next 11 holes, then hit his drive into the creek on 13, took two swings to escape, and made a bogey. He birdied the 14th, and missed a four-foot birdie putt on 16 that would have given him birdies on all four par threes. The wild ride ended with a bogey on 18, where, after a bad drive, he hit his approach onto the adjacent ninth green.

It added up to a 70, which was perfectly fine as it was only one stroke behind leaders Johnny Palmer and club pro Ray Gafford, both of whom would fade in the coming rounds. Hogan also had a 70, not sinking a putt longer than seven feet.

The game's leading protagonists, Snead and Hogan, were 1–2 after the second round, Snead shooting a 67 for 137 and Hogan a second consecutive 70. It was another entertaining round by Snead, which included a 40-foot birdie putt from the fringe on 1, hitting the flagstick with his approach on 5 to set up a birdie, and a smother-hooked second shot on 8 that hit a tree and kicked back into the fairway to preserve a par. Birdies on both back-nine par fives were pure spectacle. Snead hooked a tee shot so far around the corner of the dogleg on the 13th that Dow Finsterwald in the group ahead looked back in amazement when it nearly reached him as he walked the fairway. The massive drive set up a five-iron second shot and a two-putt birdie for Snead. On 15, his drive found a gravel-dirt maintenance road to the right of the fairway. Most thought he would lay up with a short iron, but Snead grabbed a long iron and took a mighty swing that dislodged a few rocks and sent the ball soaring over the water hazard and onto the green for another birdie.

Hogan's round was neither as wild nor as low, but he did make a 60-foot birdie putt on the fifth and a 20-footer to finish with a birdie on 18.

The third round was something else entirely. The temperature dipped to 45 degrees and a variable wind blew at up to 30 mph, causing scores to rise—especially Snead's. The 36-hole leader swelled to a 77, but still ended the day in a tie for the lead with Hogan (74) on a day when nobody bettered 71.

Snead was out of sorts from the start, as he was observed tossing grass in the air for more than a minute in the first fairway in a futile effort to gauge the constantly changing wind. His only birdie was on the second hole, and he proceeded to play Nos. 4 through 13 in six over with six bogeys, the last coming with a second shot into the creek on 13. "I've never hit so many good shots and scored so poorly," said a befuddled Snead.

Hogan nearly salvaged his round with birdies on 12, 13, and 15 after a poor start, but a three-putt bogey on 18 left him with a share of the lead instead of solo.

For the second consecutive year, the final round brought a stunning collapse that denied the tournament a down-the-stretch Hogan-Snead showdown. This time it was Hogan who faltered, posting an unsightly 79. The main culprit was his putter, a club Hogan used 40 times in the round. The stage was set on the first hole, where Ben knocked a 50-foot putt 15 feet past and missed the comebacker. It continued with misses from short range, with two more three-putts in the first six holes. A very good putter early in his career, Hogan at age 39 was coming down with a case of the yips, when he would sometimes have trouble bringing the putter back while standing over a short putt. It wasn't a pretty sight.

The next closest player to Hogan and Snead entering the final round was the formidable Cary Middlecoff, two strokes back, but the Tennessean stumbled to a 78. Conditions weren't as tough as they were Saturday, but there was enough wind to make it a stern test. The only round in the 60s was a 69 by Jack Burke Jr., a third-year pro who made noise early in the year by winning four straight tournaments. He had a roller-coaster Masters, with rounds of 76–67–78–69. Starting the final round seven

1952

1	Sam Snead	70–67–77–72—286
2	Jack Burke Jr.	76–67–78–69—290
T3	Al Besselink	70–76–71–74—291
T3	Tommy Bolt	71–71–75–74—291
T3	Jim Ferrier	72–70–77–72—291
6	Lloyd Mangrum	71–74–75–72—292
T7	Julius Boros	73–73–76–71—293
T7	Fred Hawkins	71–73–78–71—293
T7	Ben Hogan	70–70–74–79—293
T7	Lew Worsham	71–75–73–74—293

strokes out of the lead, Burke needed Snead and Hogan both to collapse to have a chance.

Tommy Bolt, five strokes off the lead through 54 holes, made some noise with eagles on Nos. 2 and 13, but bogeys on 15, 16, and 17 left him with a 74 and a 291 total, one stroke higher than Burke and ultimately tied for third with Al Besselink and Jim Ferrier.

It was Snead's tournament to win, if he could only avoid disaster. He did avert one on the par-three 12th. One-over for the round to that point after bogeys on 8 and 9, Snead debated with his caddie what club to hit. He wound up choosing the lesser one, and promptly dumped his shot short into Rae's Creek fronting the green. On his penalty drop, the ball ended up in a bare lie with "no more grass than there is hair on top of my head," he said after the round. He chunked his next shot, barely clearing the hazard and not reaching the green. Looking disgusted, he didn't take much time over his chip shot—and knocked it into the hole from 40 feet. A looming triple bogey became a relatively benign bogey and sent Snead down the stretch feeling confident.

It wasn't locked up yet, but a birdie on 13 got Snead headed in the right direction. He missed a five-foot birdie try on 15, and parred the rest until the 18th, which he birdied from seven feet after a huge drive that went left but finished harmlessly in the expanse of the club's practice range. An even-par 72 gave Snead his second Masters title with a 286 total that was four strokes better than runner-up Burke.

Doubling Up

The crowds were getting bigger at the Masters, and despite less than ideal weekend weather, the 1952 event drew more people than ever—an estimated 18,000 to 20,000 on Sunday. That was a boon for gate receipts, which in turn was good for the players. It was customary for the tournament to boost its announced purse based on the revenue from ticket sales. In 1950, the purse was increased by 20 percent and in 1951 by 50 percent. In 1952, the players hit the jackpot as the purse was boosted by 100 percent, so Snead won $4,000 for first place instead of $2,000.

1953

Ben Hogan had played only three official events in 1952. He bounced back from his final-round Masters blowup to win the Colonial in Fort Worth in May, but had another disappointment at the U.S. Open in June, where he led through 36 holes before closing with 74–74 to finish fourth. Now 40 years old, there were enough questions about his stamina and his putting to wonder whether his best days were behind him.

Hogan spent the winter practicing in Palm Springs, California, but not playing in any of the tournaments on the tour's western swing. He continued his routine of arriving to Augusta two weeks before the start of the Masters to prepare for his first full tournament in 10 months, having entered only the Seminole and Palmetto pro-ams in 1953. Despite the skepticism from the outside, those close to Hogan knew he was relaxed and confident heading into the Masters.

"I feel grand. I practiced every day of the winter," he told a writer before the tournament, commenting on Palm Springs that "the turf there is ideal for the development of your swing."

Hogan also found the turf at Augusta National to be to his liking that week, particularly compared to previous years. He would note after the tournament that, given the fine condition of the fairways, one could wholly focus on distance and execution on approach shots whereas "before, you had to worry about bad lies."

Conditions were good for scoring, as evidenced by Lloyd Mangrum's 63 in his Wednesday practice round—not officially a course record as it wasn't achieved in competition. Since Mangrum had won three tournaments already in 1953, and held the Augusta National course record of 64, he was clearly a player to watch. So, of course, was defending champion Sam Snead, who finished second to Chick Harbert in Wednesday's long drive contest.

It was Harbert who took the first-round lead with a 68, while Mangrum was far back with a 74. Hogan shot a 70 with bogeys on the last two holes, missing short putts. Snead also should have had a 70, but on the 18th hole, where he sank a 60-foot birdie putt, his fellow competitor Byron Nelson marked Snead for a four instead of a three. Nelson wrote a "70" as Snead's total score, but since the hole-by-hole scores added up to 71, that's what Snead was stuck with (he had signed his scorecard without checking it).

The scorecard mistake became less important the next day, as far as Snead's chances of winning the tournament were concerned, as Sam ballooned to a 75. He double bogeyed the fifth hole and tossed his ball into the pond in frustration on the 11th after a bogey there. Snead would go on to finish T15.

Hogan moved into the lead with a 69 marked by superb ball-striking while missing four putts inside five feet. He was in first place despite not making any putts longer than eight feet in the first two rounds. Hogan told one writer: "I'm playing well. I have no complaints at all," but, to another, fretted that he wasn't putting well enough to win. Mangrum had the day's best round, a 68, to move into T5 position at 142 along with Ed "Porky" Oliver (69–73).

Hogan was paired with Oliver on Saturday, and they put on a show the likes of which had never been seen in the Masters. Hogan shot a 66 and Oliver a 67, combining for a better ball score of 60. Oliver put the pressure on with birdies on Nos. 1, 2, and 4, but Hogan birdied the second and fourth himself, the latter with a tee shot inside two feet. Hogan's putter cooperated this day. Having already holed a 12-footer for

1953

1	Ben Hogan	70–69–66–69—274
2	Ed Oliver	69–73–67–70—279
3	Lloyd Mangrum	74–68–71–69—282
4	Bob Hamilton	71–69–70–73—283
T5	Tommy Bolt	71–75–68–71—285
T5	Chick Harbert	68–73–70–74—285
7	Ted Kroll	71–70–73–72—286
8	Jack Burke Jr.	78–69–69–71—287
9	Al Besselink	69–75–70–74—288
T10	Julius Boros	73–71–75–70—289
T10	Chandler Harper	74–72–69–74—289
T10	Fred Hawkins	75–70–74–70—289

birdie on the second, he followed a two-putt birdie on the eighth by sinking a 40-foot birdie putt on the ninth and a 25-footer for a birdie on the 10th.

After a hiccup on the 13th, where he three-putted for a par, Ben birdied the 14th from eight feet and nearly holed his second shot on 15, the ball rolling to the back of the green to set up a two-putt birdie that made him seven-under to that point. The course record of 64 was in sight, but Hogan's putter let him down in the closing stretch as he three-putted from 30 feet to bogey the 16th and missed an eight-foot birdie try on 18. Still, the 205 total for three rounds bettered Nelson's 54-hole mark by two strokes.

Oliver, who at 220 pounds made for an odd couple pairing with Bantam Ben, stayed in hailing distance with a 209 total for second place. Having slipped from his three-under start back to even par on the day with bogeys on Nos. 5, 10, and 11, Porky played the last six holes in five-under with an eagle on 13 and birdies on 15, 16, and 18.

Rain on Friday had dampened the greens, promoting under-par scoring, and Sunday started with heavy rain and wind in the morning. The early starters played through a downpour, including Bob Hamilton, who, at 210, was the only other player besides Oliver within five shots of Hogan through 54 holes. Hamilton would shoot a 73.

Oliver teed off at 1:00, paired with Mangrum (213 after a third-round 71), in a light drizzle. By the time Hogan started at 1:42, the sun was shining. Even the weather seemed to be favoring Ben as he set out on his bid for a second Masters title.

By then, it had become a tradition for Nelson—now a retired elder statesman though only months older than Hogan and Snead—to be paired with the 54-hole leader. So, the old Fort Worth friends/rivals set out together. On the first hole, Hogan faced a four-and-a-half-foot putt for par. He stood over it, backed off, stood over it, backed off, stood over it, and finally made a lunging stroke—and the ball found the hole. As Nelson later related it, Hogan said as they walked off the green, "Did you see that? Now how can I miss?"

Ben proceeded to birdie the second and fourth holes thanks to extraordinary shots—a four-wood hooked around trees to 20 feet for a two-putt birdie on No. 2 and a three-iron to a foot from the hole on No. 4. Hogan stalled with bogeys on the sixth (missed green) and eighth (three-putt), but he was still ahead by four at that point as Oliver had just bogeyed the 11th after a decent start.

Oliver would make a couple of birdies down the stretch for a 70 and a 279 total that matched the old record, but it wouldn't matter. Nor were there title implications in Mangrum tying the best score of the day with a 69 for a 282 total and third place. For it was Hogan who had the other 69 to win going away.

After pars on Nos. 9–12, Hogan fired a four-iron second shot at a pin tucked just over the creek on the 13th, finishing 20 feet away for a two-putt birdie. Afterward, a reporter asked why he took the risk there, particularly since he had mentioned that he played safe in the round. "If I couldn't have made that shot with an iron, I shouldn't be here," Hogan said. "But I did shoot away from the pin on 11, 12, 16, and 17 because I didn't want to take chances on them."

He also laid up on the par-five 15th, hitting his third shot to six feet and making a birdie. Hogan finished in style with a birdie from 10 feet on the 18th for a 33 on the back nine.

"It was the finest 72 holes I've played in one tournament," Hogan said. "I'm not talking about just hitting shots. You can hit your shots great and still shoot 80 because of poor judgment. The shots are 30 percent of the game. Judgment is 70 percent."

Hogan shattered the tournament scoring record with a 14-under 274 and tied the mark for victory margin at five shots. Gene Sarazen called Hogan's performance "the greatest four scoring rounds ever."

The winner looked at it as more than a four-day process, crediting his pre-tournament preparation. "Practice means as much as playing itself," said the man known as the hardest worker in golf—and one who now spent much more time practicing than playing in tournaments. "A tournament is anti-climax to preparation, the way I see it. Before the tournament in practice, I knew I was playing well, better than ever in my life."

The better-than-ever play continued. Hogan went on to win the U.S. Open at Oakmont and the British Open at Carnoustie in the only appearance he would ever make in that event, going a perfect three-for-three in 1953 majors (he no longer played in the PGA Championship, which required too many double rounds in its match-play format and, in any case, conflicted with the British Open that year).

. . . .

Presidential Postscript

Augusta National member Dwight Eisenhower had become president in January and would be a frequent visitor to the club during his eight years in office. He flew to Augusta the Monday morning after Hogan's victory, and Hogan met him on the first tee that afternoon and hit a few practice shots. The new champion stuck around to play a Tuesday round with Eisenhower, along with Nelson and Masters chairman Clifford Roberts.

. . . .

1954

Ben Hogan had played in only four official events in 1953, with a victory in the Pan American Open to go with his three major titles, making it a perfect year. With the

Masters again his first official tournament of the year in 1954, Hogan was naturally the center of attention, drawing huge galleries in practice rounds.

"Not since Bobby Jones in 1934 has a player been greeted with such enthusiasm," wrote Randy Russell in the *Augusta Chronicle*, going on to note that the once taciturn Hogan not only appeared relaxed and confident but also "as jovial as the next pro."

The driving contest was held on Wednesday, and it was won by a little-known amateur from the mountains of North Carolina. Billy Joe Patton unleashed a 338-yard blast on his first of three scheduled drives, didn't bother taking his last two, and emerged as the winner. Patton would be much more than a footnote in this Masters—he would become the story of the tournament.

The 31-year-old lumber salesman fired a 32 on the front nine of the first round and finished with a 70, a score good enough on that day to share the lead with Dutch Harrison. The temperature had climbed into the 90s, followed by a cloudburst late in the afternoon that gave the later starters a drenching (Harrison bogeyed 10 and 11 when the rain hit). Play was never officially suspended, but some players elected on their own to sit out the bad weather.

Probably a bigger factor in the high scoring than the weather were pin positions that were very difficult—perhaps a reaction to the low scoring of 1953.

The only other players to break par were Jack Burke Jr. and perennial contender Lloyd Mangrum with 71s. Hogan was at 72 with a round that included one birdie, one bogey, 16 pars, and a lot of missed putts. Not exciting, but good enough to stay very much in contention.

Scores were even higher in the second round due to another set of tough hole locations, a chilly wind, and overnight rains that made the course play long. There were no subpar rounds and just one 72, that from Australia's Peter Thomson, who had opened with a 76.

Patton's 74 gave him an even-par 144 total and the outright lead, one ahead of Hogan (second-round 73). Patton had barely made it into the Masters field, his invitation extended only as a result of being an alternate to the 1953 U.S. Walker Cup team. He had won the 1951 and 1952 Carolinas Open, but little else, and didn't play a lot of tournament golf. He would, however, go on to win three North and South Amateurs and play on five Walker Cup teams. He was using part of his vacation time to play in the Masters and had prepared in the cold Carolina mountains late winter and early spring by hitting balls on his lunch break. He was so little known that the *Augusta Chronicle* reporting on him this day called him "Billy Jo."

Patton was the type of pure amateur who played the game for fun, and boy was he having fun at the Masters. He endeared himself to the fans by chatting and laughing with them along the way and by his go-for-broke style of play.

"I'm going to play bold. That's the only way I know how," he told reporters after the round. Patton was essentially shooting for birdies on every hole—and it was somehow working on a course that was yielding few birdies.

Patton admitted that he had gotten some breaks. His third shot on the par-five eighth missed the gap in the trees he was aiming for, but made it through a bush and onto the green for a par. His second shot on the par-five 13th was hit into the azaleas left of the green, but somehow found a bare spot enabling a swing and a clear shot as he again escaped with a par.

He was a great story, but Patton wasn't expected to last. The headline in the *Chronicle* said that he was "tabbed for a blowup by experts."

Byron Nelson had played with Patton in the second round (after accompanying Hogan in the first) and while marveling at the amateur's power said, "I've never known anyone with that kind of power who could control the ball." With a strong grip that often led to a hook, the consensus view was that Patton wouldn't hold up under pressure.

Even Patton himself said, "I'm supposed to shoot 80 sometime in the tournament, you know, and I probably will."

Hogan, meanwhile, followed a steady first round with an up-and-down effort. After bogeys on Nos. 4 and 5, he got to two-under on the day with birdies on 7 (60-foot chip-in), 9 (25-foot putt), 11, and 12, then gave it back with bogeys on 13 (second shot in water, which he blamed on a wind gust), 17, and 18 (both three-putts).

While Hogan and Patton, who also bogeyed 17 and 18, were slipping at the end, two-time champion Sam Snead was shooting himself into contention with a 34 on the back nine. With rounds of 74 and 73, he was only three off the lead and in fifth place behind Patton, Hogan, and the 146 totals of Mangrum and Bob Rosburg.

It appeared that the expected Patton blowup was happening in the third round as the amateur bogeyed four straight holes starting at the third to go four-over. But he rallied in the middle of the round to get to one-over before bogeys on 16 and 18 left him with a 75. It wasn't an 80, but on a day with better scoring conditions it dropped Patton five strokes behind leader Hogan, who shot a 69.

Hogan missed five birdie putts inside 10 feet and had a three-putt bogey. He did make a 25-footer for one of his four birdies and hit two brilliant bunker shots within a foot of the hole, yielding a birdie at the second and a par at the 18th. When the dust settled after 54 holes, it was down to favorites Hogan and Snead leading the field, Hogan at 214 and Snead second at 217 after a 70 that included a three-putt on 18. Cary Middlecoff and Tommy Bolt joined Patton in a tie for third at 219, but it looked like a two-horse race.

Snead was the first of the leaders off the tee at 12:00 noon. When he bogeyed the fourth and fifth to go two-over for the round, most of the crowd abandoned him to watch Patton (12:30 start) or Hogan (1:00).

Patton gave the tournament a jolt when he flew a five-iron directly into the hole for an ace on the sixth. The report in *Golf World* called the gallery roar "more intense than any ovation ever accorded to a player in American golf." The commotion drew even more spectators to watch Patton, and his gallery continued to grow as he birdied the eighth and ninth holes for a 32 on the front nine (he had started with a bogey on No. 1 and a birdie on No. 2).

Hogan was in the third fairway when he heard the commotion from Patton's ace at the nearby sixth. Ben had bogeyed the first, but he got a stroke back with a birdie at the third. Still, Patton's birdies at 8 and 9 brought the North Carolinian within a stroke of the lead. When Hogan three-putted the seventh for a bogey, missing his second putt from 18 inches, he dropped to one-under for the tournament and into a tie with Patton.

Patton's play was a bit shaky early on the back nine. He saved par after going over the green on 11 and made a bogey after doing the same on 12. After a decent, but not great, drive on 13 he found himself in the go/no-go zone for his second shot. As the lumber salesman trying to pull off a huge Masters upset deliberated, his enthusiastic gallery got involved. "Go for it!" some shouted, while others counseled, "Play it safe, Billy!" Ultimately, Patton pulled out a four-wood and went for it. The shot had enough distance, but was off to the right, finishing pin high but in the creek.

Billy Joe took off his shoes and rolled up his pants, thinking he might try to play out of the water, but thought better of it. He took a penalty drop and quickly played his fourth stroke, still barefoot. He chunked the pitch shot, which barely cleared the creek but didn't reach the green. After a chip and two putts, he walked off with a double bogey.

As he walked to the 14th tee, Patton said to his fans, "Let's smile again." Looking back on it years later, he reflected, "I looked at the gallery and their faces were so somber. I probably said it as much for myself as I did for them. It was to lighten them up and get me moving."

It certainly got him moving. And his gallery got pumped up again when he hit an eight-iron within inches of the hole and made a birdie on the 14th.

Meanwhile, Hogan had come to the 11th hole thinking he needed to make something happen. Ignoring his usual rule of aiming to the right, he fired his approach shot at the flag—and pulled it just enough to land in the pond left of the green. The result was a double bogey.

Now Hogan was one-over for the tournament. But Patton had gone two-over with his double bogey on 13, getting back to one-over through 14. The forgotten Snead, playing up ahead in near isolation, had birdied the seventh and bogeyed the 12th. He drove into the trees on 13 but made a birdie after laying up. His second shot on 15 was long and well right, but his pitch shot from nearly 50 yards almost went in, setting up a birdie. That got him to one-over. As he was parring the last three holes, Patton and Hogan were falling back to him with their water troubles. Snead's one-over total became the target.

Patton hit a mediocre drive on the 15th, leaving him a long way from the green and with a bad lie besides. Nonetheless, he grabbed his two-wood and tried to muscle it over the water. Instead, he made poor contact and the ball ended up landing short of the pond and rolling into it. The bogey dropped him to two-over. His best birdie chance down the stretch was an 18-foot putt at the 18th. When that didn't drop, it left him with a 39 on the back nine for a 71, a two-over 290 total, and a what-might-have-been story.

Hogan's putting was a major problem on this day, and a three-putt bogey on 14 put him at two-over. He got the stroke back with a birdie on 15, going for the green in two for the first time all week and two-putting from 60 feet. He had a golden opportunity to pass Snead when he hit his approach to three feet on the 17th. But

Hogan jabbed at it and missed. A par there and another at 18 gave him a final-round 75. He had blown his chance to win in regulation, but at least he could look ahead to a playoff date with Snead the next day.

Patton had to settle for the low amateur medal, which he received in an awards ceremony after play was finished on Sunday. Billy Joe told the assembled crowd, "I don't feel bad about that six on 15 and I don't feel bad about that seven on 13, and I don't want my rooters to feel bad about them… I made up my mind I was going for the pin 72 times if I had the opportunity 72 times. I told myself I wasn't going to go around after the tournament thinking I could have saved a stroke if I played it bold. And the way I made those birdies is the same way I got that six and that seven."

It was an inspiring and heartfelt speech. Patton was no doubt right that if he hadn't played so aggressively, he wouldn't have had a chance to win in the first place. But there's one flaw in that argument—the two-wood over water on the 15th was a gamble that had almost no chance of succeeding. Years later, Patton admitted "that was the worst judgment I ever showed in a crucial situation in golf."

Bobby Jones wrapped up the Sunday ceremony by saying of Patton, "If anyone ever created a stir in golf, he did. He has no cause for regret, because he finished one stroke behind the two greatest golfers in the world."

Those two greatest golfers were about to meet in an epic playoff that would determine Masters bragging rights. Both owned two Augusta victories, so whoever won the playoff would join Jimmy Demaret as the only three-time Masters champions.

The playoff was a tense, tight battle. Not until the 16th hole was either player ahead by more than one stroke. Jones called it "an absolutely beautiful exhibition of precision golf." That was true enough on the full shots, though the putting left something to be desired, not surprising in this battle of 41-year-olds.

Both made routine pars on the first, birdied the second (Snead with a two-putt, Hogan with a pitch to tap-in range), and missed birdie putts of around six feet on the third. Snead fell one behind with a three-putt bogey on the fourth, before squaring it again with a birdie from six feet on the sixth. Sam was in trouble with his tee shot on the tree-lined seventh hole, then hit an exceptional recovery over and around trees to the fringe to set up a par. Both were just in front of the green in two on the eighth, and both ended up missing short birdie putts, before also trading pars on the ninth. They headed to the back nine each at one-under, having made the same score on seven of the front nine holes.

Snead provided the most dramatic moment so far when he chipped in for a birdie from 50 feet on the 10th to go ahead by one. It was back to level when Snead hit his tee shot into the back bunker on No. 12 and bogeyed.

To this point, Hogan had held the lead for two holes, Snead for two holes, and they were even with each other after eight of the 12 holes they had played. The head-to-head match would turn on the 13th. Hogan laid up after a drive down the right side, later explaining that he would have needed a wood to reach the green but couldn't have stopped the ball anywhere near the flag perched just over the water in front. Snead had busted a long drive down the left side and hit the green with an iron for his second shot, two-putting from 30 feet for a birdie.

1954

1	Sam Snead	74–73–70–72—289*
2	Ben Hogan	72–73–69–75—289
3	Billy Joe Patton	70–74–75–71—290
T4	E.J. Harrison	70–79–74–68—291
T4	Lloyd Mangrum	71–75–76–69—291
T6	Jerry Barber	74–76–71–71—292
T6	Jack Burke Jr.	71–77–73–71—292
T6	Bob Rosburg	73–73–76–70—292
T9	Al Besselink	74–74–74–72—294
T9	Cary Middlecoff	73–76–70–75—294

*Snead won playoff, 70–71

Snead missed a chance to go ahead by two when he couldn't convert a seven-foot birdie putt on 14. Both birdied the 15th, Hogan using a putter from the back fringe to get close and Snead making a five-footer for his second putt. Sam was now three-under and Ben two-under on a course that had played tough all week.

For such a hotly contested fight between two of golf's greats, the last three holes were a bit anticlimactic. Snead two-putted for a par from 20 feet on the 16th, while Hogan had a putting lapse that was a killer. Ben's 15-foot birdie putt pulled up a full three feet short—he said later that he was so concerned with the line, he forgot to hit the putt and, in fact, made contact with the ground behind the ball. A three-foot putt was the last thing Hogan wanted at this point, and he missed it to fall two behind.

Hogan went over the green on the 17th and saved par, but he still needed a two-stroke swing on 18. That became a possibility when Snead hit his approach into the left bunker, but Hogan missed a 20-foot birdie putt. Snead needed only to two-putt from six feet for the victory, and that's what he cautiously did for a bogey. The final tally: Snead 70, Hogan 71.

This would be the last playoff in any tournament between Snead and Hogan, and Snead was 2–0—a fact he wasn't shy about pointing out for the rest of his life. For Hogan, Masters playoffs continued to be his kryptonite. He was now 0–2 in extra holes at Augusta, having lost to Byron Nelson and Snead by a single stroke each time.

Hogan and Snead had now traded the last four Masters titles, and accounted for five of the last six. This playoff was the climax, as neither would win in Augusta again, though they would remain part of the story.

1955

Back in 1946, a dentist in Memphis, Dr. Herman Middlecoff, asked Bobby Jones to persuade his son Cary to remain an amateur. Cary had followed his father into dentistry, first as an Army dentist during World War II after finishing dental school and then in the family practice after the war.

Cary had met and played golf with Jones while stationed at Camp Gordon near Augusta in 1944–45. The young Middlecoff stunned the pros with a victory in the North and South Open in the fall of 1945 and played well in amateur events in 1946—so well, that he began to consider turning pro. Despite the talk from Jones,

Middlecoff came to believe that in order to realize his potential as a golfer he needed to compete on a weekly basis with the pros. If he didn't prove himself among the best in the game in two years, he told his dad, he would return to dentistry.

The golfer who would continue to be known as Dr. Cary Middlecoff never had to fill another tooth. He won a tournament in 1947, two in 1948, and six in 1949, including the U.S. Open.

While he continued as one of the top players in the game into the 1950s, Middlecoff's Masters record wasn't stellar. After finishing a distant second to Claude Harmon in 1948, Middlecoff hadn't placed better than seventh in Augusta. Nor had he won another major after the 1949 U.S. Open. Still, with two wins so far in 1955, he was considered one of the top candidates to supplant the Sam Snead-Ben Hogan duo and was reported to be "hitting the ball exceptionally well" in practice rounds.

Snead and Hogan naturally had to be considered the favorites, but both had questions about their physical condition and tournament readiness. Snead had played only six events in 1954. A neck injury bothered him at the U.S. Open, where he said before the event he might not be able to play, and the PGA Championship, where he needed treatment before teeing it up in the second stroke-play qualifying round. In December, he had to withdraw during the Miami Open due to a back injury. He didn't return to action until March of 1955 and had played only one 72-hole event before the Masters.

Hogan hadn't played a 72-hole event since the previous summer. While that was his annual situation since going to a four-event-a-year schedule, this time his preparation for Augusta was interrupted by a trip back home to Fort Worth to take care of some business. Also, he appeared to be bothered by a gimpy left knee and sat out the Wednesday practice round.

Everyone took a back seat in the first round to Jack Burke Jr., the 1952 runner-up, who stormed in with birdies on 13, 14, 15, and 17 for a 67. That was four strokes better than anyone else on a windy day coming from a direction in the players' faces on some tough holes, and with lush fairways making the course play long. Mike Souchak, a young player making some waves as the leading money winner so far in 1955, and 1952 U.S. Open champion Julius Boros were at 71 (they would ultimately tie for fourth with Bob Rosburg).

Snead would have threatened Burke if not for a disaster on the 13th, where his second shot plugged in a bunker and he took four strokes to escape the sand, making a triple bogey eight. Still, he managed a 72. Middlecoff also had a 72, while Hogan shot a 73, pronouncing himself satisfied with his ball-striking if not his putting.

Burke's lead vanished quickly as he stumbled to a 76 in the second round. His place at the top was taken by Middlecoff, who fashioned a four-stroke lead of his own thanks to a 65 that Jones called "the best round ever shot in a Masters."

The Tennessean set a record with a 31 on the front nine, where he birdied the first hole from 15 feet and the last four holes, all on putts of between five and eight feet. He would need only one long putt all day to post his low number, but that was a *really* long one. After hitting his second shot to the back edge of the green on the 13th, Middlecoff holed an eagle putt from 82 feet—a distance known precisely because it was later measured by tournament host Jones.

Middlecoff laid up after an errant drive on 15 but managed a birdie from eight feet. Now at eight under, he could par in and tie Lloyd Mangrum's course record 64, which hadn't been threatened since it was set in 1940. Alas, he left his approach a long way from the hole on the 17th and three-putted, missing the second one from six feet. Still, he was in control of the tournament.

Hogan had a fine round of his own, a 68, to move into second place at 141. Snead had to do a lot of scrambling, but came away with a 71 and shared third with Burke at 143.

In the middle of the third round, Middlecoff appeared to be backing up. He bogeyed No. 10 to go one-over for the round and hit his tee shot into the water on the 12th. But he saved a bogey on 12 after a penalty drop, pitching on and holing a 10-foot putt. His putter came to the rescue down the stretch, too. After a birdie on 15, Middlecoff holed a 10-footer for a par on 17 and a 25-footer from the fringe for a birdie on 18. Instead of seeing his lead trimmed to two strokes, Middlecoff ended the day with the same four-stroke lead he started with, as he and Hogan both shot 72.

The 72s were perfectly fine scores on a day when only three players broke par. Hogan, however, could have done better as he three-putted three of the par-threes, all from less than 20 feet. Reporters continued to note that he was limping on his left leg, and Hogan admitted that the hills of Augusta National were taking a toll.

Snead was in all sorts of trouble on the way to a 74, and Burke was the only other player within five strokes of Middlecoff's 209 total through 54 holes, as he shot a 71 for 214. Burke would shoot himself out of it with an 80 in the final round, including a nine on the 13th hole, completing a thoroughly erratic week.

Hogan teed off 30 minutes ahead of Middlecoff on Sunday, but couldn't put any pressure on the leader. In a five-hole stretch starting at the second, Hogan missed four birdie putts of between seven and 12 feet and three-putted the other for a bogey. Described by Charles Bartlett of the *Chicago Tribune* as a "wan, tired player," Hogan would finish with a 73, good enough for second place yet not enough to pose a threat.

Snead had one of the better rounds of the day, a 70, to finish third. The low score was turned in by a rookie pro named Arnold Palmer, who fired a 69 and finished T10 after a 76–76 start.

Middlecoff took care of business with a very good round of 70 for a record victory margin of seven strokes with a 279 total. It wasn't an easy day for the new champion, though. He admitted after the round that the longest hours he ever spent were from the time he woke up at 8 a.m. to his 1:42 p.m. tee time ("it seemed like a week," he said).

Always a fidgety sort, Middlecoff's jitters about trying to hold the lead might have been magnified by his memories of playing with Jim Ferrier in the final round of 1950 when Ferrier let his advantage slip away on the back nine. But Middlecoff used that experience as a lesson, remembering that while Ferrier had a couple of tough breaks, he also made a couple of bad decisions. "I kept thinking about that today, and played it safe," Cary said.

Being paired with Byron Nelson in the final round also helped. "Byron is one of my best friends, and he kept telling me just to keep playing golf when I showed signs of jitteriness." Nelson, often paired with the 54-hole leader, had now brought home six Masters winners in addition to the two titles he claimed himself.

1955		
1	Cary Middlecoff	72–65–72–70—279
2	Ben Hogan	73–68–72–73—286
3	Sam Snead	72–71–74–70—287
T4	Julius Boros	71–75–72–71—289
T4	Bob Rosburg	72–72–72–73—289
T4	Mike Souchak	71–74–72–72—289
7	Lloyd Mangrum	74–73–72–72—291
T8	Stan Leonard	77–73–68–74—292
T8	Harvie Ward	77–69–75–71—292
T10	Dick Mayer	78–72–72–71—293
T10	Byron Nelson	72–75–74–72—293
T10	Arnold Palmer	76–76–72–69—293

A front-nine 34 with birdies on the sixth and seventh essentially wrapped it up for Middlecoff. He got a bad break at the 10th when his approach shot came to rest in a heel print in a bunker, leading to a double bogey, but with nobody making a run at him there wasn't much to worry about. Cary finished in grand fashion with a six-iron approach to the 18th that spun around the hole, settling three feet away for a closing birdie.

Winning the Masters, Middlecoff told reporters, was "the biggest thrill I've ever gotten out of golf. I'd begun to wonder if I was ever going to win a big one again."

Looking Back

On the Wednesday before the tournament, the new Gene Sarazen Bridge was dedicated at the pond fronting the 15th green, commemorating Sarazen's double eagle on the way to victory in 1935. After the ceremony, 45 of the players in the Masters field hit shots from 232 yards out, which, as best could be determined, was the spot from where Sarazen launched his double eagle 20 years before. Only 10 managed to hit and hold the green with their effort. Not surprisingly, nobody managed to hole out, Fred Haas coming the closest at four feet, one inch.

1956

In a poll of tour players picking the favorite heading into the 1956 Masters, defending champion Cary Middlecoff led the way followed by three players in their 40s—Ben Hogan, Sam Snead, and Lloyd Mangrum. Another fortysomething, Jimmy Demaret, was reported to be playing well in practice rounds.

When the tournament got underway, though, a fresh and relatively unknown face shot up to the top of the leaderboard. Amateur Ken Venturi started with a bang as he birdied the first four holes, an unprecedented feat as far as anybody could figure. "I wonder who will be the low pro this year," quipped Demaret as he waited in the locker room before his tee time. Venturi, described in the *Augusta Chronicle* as "a 24-year-old San Francisco automobile salesman," went on to shoot a 66, two strokes better than the amateur record and one stroke ahead of Middlecoff.

Venturi's potential had been spotted early by Eddie Lowery, who owned a car dealership in San Francisco and knew something about great golfers—as a 10-year-old he had caddied for Francis Ouimet when he won the 1913 U.S. Open. In 1952, Lowery suggested to his friend, Byron Nelson, that he take a look at Venturi. Nelson liked what he saw, and not only became Venturi's teacher but took the young amateur along on an exhibition tour in 1953.

Venturi made the U.S. Walker Cup team later that year, earning an invitation to the 1954 Masters, where he finished T16. That was good enough to earn him a return invitation in 1955, but Venturi was serving in the Army and couldn't play. He got into the 1956 Masters via a special vote of Masters champions.

Able to pursue an amateur career as Lowery gave him a job as a salesman at his dealership, Venturi said he had no intention of being a pro. The month before the Masters, Venturi won the San Francisco City Amateur, which doesn't sound too impressive until you consider that in the final he beat reigning U.S. Amateur champion Harvie Ward.

Middlecoff put on an impressive display of his own with four birdies in a five-hole stretch starting at the 11th, while Hogan held up the honor of the old guard with a 69 made up of 15 fours and three threes.

Hogan had been concerned about his stamina, limiting his practice rounds to nine holes. Perhaps that had something to do with his shooting a 78 in the second round to drop from contention, though he blamed his putting. "I told you fellows years ago that I was a terrible putter," Ben told the writers. "I guess I had to show you today."

The wind was a factor, too, as it blew down part of the scoreboard next to the 18th green and blew scores upward, with only four players breaking par. One of those was Venturi, who had the low round for the second consecutive day, this time a 69. Venturi's 135 total tied the tournament 36-hole record of his mentor Nelson (1942) and Henry Picard (1935) and gave him a four-stroke lead over Middlecoff, who shot a 72 for 139. The amateur and the defender were running away from the field, as the next best total was 142.

The highlight for Venturi was a nifty chip-in from 110 feet for an eagle on the eighth hole, where he used a six-iron to run the ball up and over a greenside mound. He also chipped in from short range for a birdie on the third, but was only even par for the round through 12 holes before finishing with a flourish with birdies on 13, 15, and 18, the last one on a 23-foot putt.

Venturi exuded confidence in his post-round interview, saying, "I came here to win the tournament. It's bad for an amateur to come into any championship with the idea of just being low amateur." Asked he was if nervous, he responded, "Yeah, I couldn't sleep but ten and a half hours last night."

Middlecoff double bogeyed the first hole and had a 38 on the front nine, but rebounded with birdies on 13 and 15 for a 34 on the back to stay in hailing distance.

Among the par-breakers for the day was Jack Burke Jr. with a 71 for a 143 total. "The course played tougher than any day I've ever played it," said the man who led through 18 holes in 1955. "I sure feel good about my round and I sure wouldn't trade it."

If Burke thought Friday was tough, he would find Saturday to be even tougher. The wind gusted to as much as 45 mph and came from the opposite direction as the day before—into the player's faces on 13 and 15, rendering those par fives unreachable in two. What's more, the gusts were so variable that the wind could die down or pick up just as players were hitting a shot, wreaking havoc with the result.

In the locker room before starting his round, Middlecoff said if the wind kept up, the course would play harder than ever: "There's going to be a lot of 85s out there today," the defending champ predicted. "Don't talk like that!" retorted fellow competitor Walker Inman.

Nobody ended up shooting 85, but there were 10 scores in the 80s out of 68 players and none under par for the lofty average score of 78.564.

Middlecoff broke par on the front nine with a 35 and surged into the lead over Venturi, who scored 40. It was a reversal on the back nine as Middlecoff stumbled in with a 40 and Venturi recovered with a 35 to restore his four-stroke lead with both shooting 75.

Venturi insisted he didn't lose confidence after his 40 on the front nine. "The score said 40, but I wasn't playing 40 golf. I was hitting the ball real solid," he said, noting that he overshot several greens.

The California amateur slipped to five-over for the round with a bogey on the 11th before rallying with consecutive birdies on 13, 14, and 15, all of them from about six feet. He laid up and wedged close on both par fives and hit a spectacular seven-iron from the edge of the trees on 14 that caught the corner of the hole as it ran past. He bogeyed the 17th, then saved par from a bunker on 18.

The 18th was a big turnaround, as Middlecoff also found a greenside bunker and blasted out to six feet but took three putts from there for a double bogey.

That finish and a dislike of playing in the wind put Cary in a sour post-round mood. "You go crazy out there fighting the wind. If it's like this tomorrow, I don't even want to play. It's not golf."

Still, he was in decent position, the only player within seven shots of Venturi's 210 total. Doug Ford was third at 217 after a 75. Burke, playing with the leader, also had a 75 and was at 218, along with Mangrum, one of three players who managed to get around in 72.

No amateur had ever won the tournament founded by the world's greatest amateur, Bobby Jones. Venturi appeared to be in great position, but could he hold on under the pressure of the final round? He had a nice cushion, but his closest pursuer was one of the tour's elite, not the player you would choose to have on your tail.

Through the first eight holes, things were looking good for the amateur. Venturi stood on the ninth tee with a six-stroke lead over Middlecoff, who was two holes ahead, and Burke, in the immediately preceding twosome.

Middlecoff had mounted an early threat with birdies on the first two holes, then staggered badly midway through the front nine. After a bogey on the fourth, he four-putted from 40 feet to double bogey the fifth, missed a two-foot birdie attempt on the sixth, and made another double bogey on the seventh after dumping a pitch shot into a bunker.

Venturi was one-over through eight holes with a bogey on No. 7 and the rest pars. He missed a three-foot par putt on the ninth, an unfortunate sign of what was to come.

During an agonizing back nine, Venturi just couldn't seem to make a par. If he missed the green, he couldn't get up and down. If he hit the green, he would three-putt. There were no major disasters, just a slow-motion crash with bogeys on 10, 11, 12, 14, and 15.

At about the same time Venturi was messing up the par-five 15th, where he knocked his wedge over the green, Middlecoff was butchering the 17th, missing the green and taking three putts from nine feet for his third double bogey of the round, and his fifth of the tournament.

Venturi had friends keeping tabs on Middlecoff and reporting back to him on how Cary stood. He was relieved that he was now two strokes ahead—or so he thought.

Ken had forgotten about Burke, even though the 33-year-old Texas native was playing right in front of him. Jackie was quietly putting together a fine round, and with Venturi's collapse had made up most of his eight-stroke deficit, standing one stroke behind as he headed to the 17th. He was even par for the round, with birdies on Nos. 2 and 12 and bogeys on 11 and 14. That was good shooting on a day that was windy enough to make par a good score, though not as blustery as it had been Saturday.

Burke hit his eight-iron approach on the 17th to 15 feet from the hole. His putt crawled toward the cup—and fell in, he admitted, only because of a gust of wind. Burke's playing partner, Mike Souchak, picked the ball out of the hole and gave Jackie a bear hug. Souchak was on his way to a final-round 80 and, instead of dwelling on his own troubles, became Burke's most enthusiastic rooter. "C'mon man, they're still making bogeys out there. Play some golf, and you'll win this one!" he had exhorted Burke on the 17th tee.

Just as important as Burke's birdie on 17 was his par save on the closing hole, where he escaped a greenside bunker to four feet and made the putt. It was his sixth scrambling par of a round in which he needed only 28 putts, in contrast to Venturi's 38 putts and five three-putts. Burke's 71 matched the best round of the day (Snead had 71 for a T4 finish) and gave him a one-over 289 total.

The 17th was as pivotal to the third contender as it was to the first two. Venturi's downwind nine-iron landed on the front of the green but bounded all the way over the back and down a slope. After a pitch to 12 feet, he missed the putt and fell to two-over for the tournament, eight-over for the round.

It was only then that Venturi learned Burke had finished at one-over, so he needed a birdie on 18 to tie. The amateur's bid ended with a miss from 20 feet as a closing par gave him a sad 80.

Venturi had tears in his eyes as he walked off the green, and more tears at the award ceremony. Gaining his composure for the post-round interview session, he said, "I just wasn't getting the putts down I got on the first three days. The only tightness I felt was trying to get the ball too close. And I was playing Middlecoff, and that was wrong."

1956		
1	Jack Burke Jr.	72–71–75–71—289
2	Ken Venturi	66–69–75–80—290
3	Cary Middlecoff	67–72–75–77—291
T4	Lloyd Mangrum	72–74–72–74—292
T4	Sam Snead	73–76–72–71—292
T6	Jerry Barber	71–72–76–75—294
T6	Doug Ford	70–72–75–77—294
T8	Tommy Bolt	68–74–78–76—296
T8	Ben Hogan	69–78–74–75—296
T8	Shelly Mayfield	68–74–80–74—296

Burke, whose eight-stroke comeback still ranks as the biggest at the Masters, conceded he had no thoughts of winning when he teed off for the final round. He was just shooting for low pro money.

Once on the verge of stardom after winning four straight tournaments in 1952, Burke had gone winless since 1953, had never won a major, and was dispirited by his mediocre play so far in 1956 as he headed to Augusta.

"When you play as hard as I have and never won a major tournament, you begin to wonder," said Burke, who a year earlier shot an 80 in the final round of the Masters to fall from contention to a T14. This time he was the beneficiary of Venturi's 80.

"Ken and Cary were very nice to me, and I want to thank them," he said after a Masters that had been both won and lost.

Turning Sour

When he returned to San Francisco following his Masters collapse, Ken Venturi made news when he complained that he had been paired with Sam Snead in the final round instead of Byron Nelson as originally planned. Snead hardly said a word to him all day, and Venturi said he felt "lonesome." Another complaint was that his friend, fellow amateur Harvie Ward, who had gone out to watch the action after finishing his round, had been told by an official not to talk to him. Venturi also noted that winner Jack Burke Jr. had been paired with a friend, Mike Souchak. Venturi prefaced his remarks, which were reported by three wire services, by saying, "I don't want to be accused of sour grapes," but of course that's exactly what it sounded like.

On Saturday, Venturi telegrammed Masters chairman Clifford Roberts and Bobby Jones apologizing for his remarks and saying, "I wish to go on record as having no excuses for losing." It was true that tentative final-round pairings had been made showing Venturi and Nelson playing together. Since his retirement from regular tour competition in 1946, Nelson had often, but not always, been paired with the 54-hole leader in the Masters. In a statement, Roberts and Jones said that the preliminary pairing had been changed to avoid any possible charge of favoritism, since it had been widely reported that Nelson was Venturi's golf teacher and good friend.

1957

The 1957 Masters started the same way the previous year's ended, with Jack Burke Jr. shooting the low round on a difficult day with a 71. This time it gave him his second 18-hole lead in three years, though of course what he hoped for was ultimately a second victory in two years.

On a day when he otherwise putted conservatively, Burke sank a 30-foot eagle putt on the 13th that was moving so fast when it hit the hole "it would have gone in the lake," he said, meaning the creek next to the green. That was the blow that put him ahead of a group of five players, including 44-year-old Sam Snead, who had five birdies and five bogeys; 46-year-old Jimmy Demaret; Doug Ford, the tour's leading money winner; and Australia's Peter Thomson, winner of the last three British Opens.

Just after daybreak on Friday, tornadoes ripped through Columbia County, 19 miles from Augusta National, but Augusta only saw a morning rainstorm with winds less severe than the third round of 1956. It calmed down in the afternoon, and Snead was able to tour the course in 68 to take the lead in a bid for a fourth Masters title. He canceled a double bogey on the 12th with an eagle on the 15th and had four birdies. "I'm more relaxed than I've been in a long time," Snead said, noting that his putting stroke was much better.

Demaret was second at 142, two strokes behind, costing himself a share of the lead with three-putt bogeys at 16 and 18, followed by Burke at 143, Ed Furgol and amateur Harvie Ward at 144, and Ford and Thomson at 145.

The big news in the second round was who failed to make the cut. It was the first time the Masters instituted a 36-hole cut, and there were some high-profile victims. Eliminated were the two players named on the most ballots of 10 Masters champions when asked to pick the five players with the best chances of winning the tournament that year. Cary Middlecoff couldn't recover after an opening 79 and finished at 152, while Ben Hogan was at 151 after a 75 on Friday and missed the cut by one. Both had eight three-putts over the course of two rounds.

It led Hogan to suggest after the round that putting be eliminated as part of the game, with the (presumably) tongue-in-cheek suggestion of turning each green into a funnel that would take the ball into the hole. "I've always contended that golf is one game and putting is another," said the great ball-striker whose putting woes were becoming more and more pronounced with age.

Two years after winning the title, Middlecoff entered the week as the consensus favorite but during the practice rounds was quoted saying he was having putting troubles. He wasn't able to get over them. Other prominent players who didn't make it past 36 holes were Tommy Bolt, Gene Littler, Mike Souchak, Julius Boros, and Billy Joe Patton.

The absence of such accomplished players on the weekend drew criticism from players and the press, who argued that the cut not only dropped some top gallery draws from the field but also that players of the caliber of Middlecoff and Hogan would have been capable of coming back into contention if they had remained in the field.

The cut was started because the field had expanded, with 101 players in 1957, and also to accommodate television (the first broadcast had been in 1956). The committee led by chairman Clifford Roberts had made it an austere cut with just the low 40 and ties. As it turned out, the cut came exactly at 40—one more bogey by any of nine players at 150 and Hogan would have played the weekend. Roberts said field size and the number of players making the cut would be reevaluated for the following year, but the number making the cut wouldn't expand to 44 and ties until 1962.

Snead retained the lead after the third round, but his attitude was far less buoyant as putting woes set in and contributed to his 74. "Boy, I'm glad they didn't have any more holes out there today," Sam said. "If Hogan thinks he putted bad, he should have seen me today. Anybody got a set of 21-year-old nerves?"

Snead had five birdies, but seven bogeys kept him from pulling away as he finished the day at 214 chased by a bunched-up pack. Canada's Stan Leonard (68), rising star Arnold Palmer (69), and amateur Harvie Ward (71) were at 215, Ed Furgol at 216, Ford, Burke, and Demaret at 217, and five more players within five strokes of the lead.

After a three-year stint in the U.S. Coast Guard, Palmer turned pro late in 1954 at age 25 after winning the U.S. Amateur. He didn't command an army in Augusta yet, but was making a name for himself on tour, with one win in his rookie year of 1955, two in 1956, and two already in 1957—including the Azalea Open the week before the Masters.

For the second consecutive year, an amateur automobile salesman at Eddie Lowery's San Francisco dealership was a serious threat to win the tournament, and this time it was Ward. (Ken Venturi had turned pro at the beginning of the year and wasn't a threat through 54 holes, eventually finishing T13.)

Observers gave Ward a legitimate chance to come away with the title. So did he, thanks to inspiration from the showings of Venturi and Patton in recent years. "Until Ken and Billy Joe made their splashes, I always sort of felt that the amateurs came here just to fill out the field," said the winner of the 1955 and 1956 U.S. Amateurs.

Ward and Ford were the first twosome of contenders to hit the course on Sunday. While the amateur shot a respectable but unthreatening 73, Ford started hot and finished even hotter.

A year earlier, Ford was in third place through 54 holes, albeit seven strokes behind. Through nine holes of the final round, he was even with eventual champion Burke, only to blow up to a 42 on the back nine for a 77 and a T6 finish. He would better that back-nine score by 10 strokes this time around.

1957	
1 Doug Ford	72–73–72–66—283
2 Sam Snead	72–68–74–72—286
3 Jimmy Demaret	72–70–75–70—287
4 Harvie Ward	73–71–71–73—288
5 Peter Thomson	72–73–73–71—289
6 Ed Furgol	73–71–72–74—290
T7 Jack Burke Jr.	71–72–74–74—291
T7 Dow Finsterwald	74–74–73–70—291
T7 Arnold Palmer	73–73–69–76—291
10 Jay Hebert	74–72–76–70—292

His front nine was pretty good, too, with birdies on the first (four feet) and eighth (three feet) for a 34. Ford saved par on 10 and missed the green on 12 before chipping in from 30 feet for a birdie. He added a birdie on the 14th with a seven-iron to eight feet.

A pivotal moment came on the 15th, where Ford's caddie wanted him to lay up short of the water with his second shot and handed him a four-iron. Ford put the club back in the bag, grabbed a three-wood and told his caddie, "This is the ballgame."

After the round, he would say, "I never was a play safe golfer. I knew I could get there if I hit the ball good. I thought I should try." He made solid contact; still, the ball just barely cleared the water, landing just in front of the green before rolling on to within 35 feet, setting up a two-putt birdie.

Two more pars brought Ford to the 18th hole at five-under for the round, having moved into the lead. His seven-iron approach came up short, in the front left bunker and half-buried. Known as perhaps the fastest player in the game, he wasted no time walking into the bunker, setting his feet, and making the stroke. Knowing the ball would run out from the lie, he landed the shot well short of the pin and watched it roll into the hole for a birdie. Ford tossed his sand wedge in the air and whooped for joy as the crowd let out a roar. The spectacular finish gave the New York pro a 66 and a five-under 283 total.

Meanwhile, the other contenders were falling by the wayside. Leonard was well on his way to a 41 on the back nine for a 78 and Palmer was struggling to a 76. Demaret was shooting a 70, but, having started tied with Ford, that only lifted him to third place.

Snead was on the 13th hole when Ford finished, having just bogeyed Nos. 9, 10 and 11 to spoil a good start and slip to one-over on the round and one-under on the tournament. He added two more bogeys on 13 and 14 before finishing with birdies on 15, 16, and 18 that were meaningless in the title picture but earned him second place at 286.

"Back on eight, I thought the cake was mine and all I had to do was finish," said Snead of his two-under start through seven holes. "Boys, don't take up golf for a living."

Snead had six birdies on Sunday while shooting a 72, completing a roller-coaster week with 20 birdies and an eagle offset by 16 bogeys and a double bogey. Ford, by contrast, had 11 birdies and six bogeys.

Ford's position was so secure that he met the press wearing a green jacket for a winner's interview while other players were still on the course (his early start also meant that television coverage missed him completely).

The 34-year-old talked about growing up in Manhattan, where his father, a second-generation Italian immigrant who had changed the family name from Fortunato to Ford, was the pro at an indoor golf school. While golf was the family business, Doug also frequented the city's pool halls in his teen years. He would go on to do a lot of golf hustling in Westchester County after World War II before finally turning pro at age 27.

Ford won nine events in 1952–56, including the 1955 PGA Championship, and added another victory in early 1957. Still, six players were picked ahead of him in the pre-Masters poll of past champions. With his 66 that ranked as the best final round in the Masters to that point, he ensured that he would be joining those past winners each year for the champions dinner.

Festive Occasion

An estimated crowd of 25,000 lined Broad Street in downtown Augusta on Tuesday for the first Golf Parade as part of Masters Hospitality Week. Local businesses sponsored floats, high school and military bands marched and played, a squadron of Navy blimps flew overhead, Bobby Jones led the parade along with the Augusta mayor, and other Masters golfers were dispersed throughout in cars. On Wednesday night, the first Golf Ball continued the festivities, with "Miss Golf of 1957" chosen to "reign" over the Masters. The parade and ball continued annually through 1964.

1958–1966

Arnie and Jack

Arnold Palmer was the perfect superstar for the coming television age—and also for the Masters. He was truly dominant on tour in the years 1957–63, winning 39 tournaments in that span. And the way he did it attracted galleries and television viewers alike, striding the course with confidence, wearing his emotions on his handsome visage, and playing with a swashbuckling, "go for broke" style.

Augusta National was the perfect venue for Palmer, accumulating four Masters titles while earning a devoted gallery following that came to be called "Arnie's Army." His victories usually came in dramatic fashion, and even when he wasn't winning, the ultra-aggressive Palmer was creating drama by blowing chances to win. He and the Masters fed off each other in gaining popularity as he won in every even-numbered year from 1958 to 1964.

At the height of that popularity, Palmer was challenged by a young player who would carve out an even greater career and Masters record. Jack Nicklaus first dethroned the King at the 1962 U.S. Open, but it was in Augusta where the budding rivalry played out the most often and where Nicklaus shined. Like Palmer, Nicklaus would win the Masters more than any other major—six of his 18. While more conservative by nature than Arnie, Jack could hit the ball so far off the tee that he tamed Augusta National by making the par fives play like par fours. Add to that his deft putting touch, Nicklaus' prodigious talents propelled him to the Masters three times over his first five years as a pro (1963, '65, and '66), becoming the first player to successfully defend the title.

Palmer and Nicklaus combined to capture seven of the nine Masters in this period. The other member of golf's Big Three, South Africa's Gary Player, took one of the others, with the trio combing to win seven Masters in succession from 1960 to 1966.

By the end of this span, complaints were raised in some quarters that bombers like Nicklaus—and, to some extent, Palmer in his prime—held a disproportionate advantage at Augusta National. While it's true that Augusta's wide fairways and reachable par fives gave an edge to long hitters, the course's challenging greens and demanding approaches tested other parts of the game as well. Consistently producing the game's best players as winners is the hallmark of a great course, not something to be meddled with.

During this period, crowds continued to grow to such an extent that it became a problem. Estimated crowds already having reached 30,000 on the weekend by 1958, they swelled to 40,000 to 50,000 or more by the early 1960s. The accuracy of those figures is not known since the club never released attendance figures; in any case, the ballooning number of patrons led to the first restrictions on ticket sales starting in 1963 with the goal of keeping the crowds at a manageable size. Daily tickets were still sold at the gate but limited to an announced number of a few thousand depending on advance sales. Starting in 1966, there were no tickets sold at the gate on tournament days, as advance sales had reached what Masters officials considered capacity, based on available parking and their ability to ensure a comfortable experience for spectators.

1958

A pair of twentysomething golfers on the rise, Ken Venturi and Arnold Palmer, were labeled as the players to watch heading into the Masters.

Venturi, 26, had turned pro at the end of 1956 and won twice in his rookie season of 1957. He was on a roll through the first three months of 1958—in nine tournaments he had three wins, two seconds, and hadn't finished outside the top 10. He was the choice of the writers to win the tournament, impressing the golf scribes with his confident-but-not-arrogant approach.

The 28-year-old Palmer had compiled eight victories in little more than three years on the tour, including four in 1957. After a sluggish start to 1958, he came on strong in March with a victory in St. Petersburg, two seconds, and a third. "It is said of streak-playing Arnold Palmer that when he's hot, he's unbeatable," according to the *Augusta Chronicle* in an article that went on to note that he was improving his consistency.

The pair had something in common. Both had blown a chance to win the Masters in the final round, Venturi with his 80 in 1956 from the lead and Palmer with his 76 in 1957 from one behind through 54 holes. "I have a score to settle with that course," Venturi told the *Chronicle*.

Palmer was a late arrival to Augusta, having played at the Azalea Invitational and gotten into an 18-hole playoff there on the Monday of Masters week. In a strange affair, Palmer lost that playoff to Howie Johnson, 77–78, with Arnold calling a one-stroke penalty on himself on the 14th green when his ball moved at address.

Tired from his overtime work at the Azalea and now heading into his seventh straight week of competing, Palmer played poorly in a Tuesday practice round, where he and Dow Finsterwald took on Ben Hogan and Jack Burke Jr. In the locker room, Palmer overheard Hogan say to Burke, "How the hell did Palmer get an invitation to the Masters?" Arnie decided to work on his game on the practice range Wednesday while playing only nine holes.

On Thursday, Venturi showed that his man-to-beat status was deserved, as he took the lead with a 68. He did it with some great scrambling, missing eight greens but consistently chipping close and emerging with only one bogey. Venturi had plenty of company near the top, with 17 players breaking par. That included Palmer, who went out in 37 but came back with a 33 on the back nine for a 70.

After perfect weather on Thursday, it was cold and damp for the second round. It looked as if it would be a miserable day for Venturi, who struggled to a 40 on the front nine. However, he showed his moxie, and his talent, by coming home in 32 for a 72 that kept him in the lead at 140.

The lowlight of the front nine was a double bogey on the par-five eighth, where he got two bad breaks—a drive under the lip of a fairway bunker from where he could only pitch out and a fourth shot that hit the bottom of the flagstick and caromed 40 feet away. On the 10th tee, Venturi thought to himself, "I'm going to look awfully silly if I shoot 80 again."

The young pro promptly birdied 10 and added another birdie at 13. He stalled with a three-putt bogey on 14 and missed a birdie putt from four feet on 15. After that, Venturi stormed in with birdies on the last three holes from five, eight, and 20 feet. From the brink of disaster, he restored a one-stroke lead, with amateur Billy Joe Patton (a 69, low round of the day) and Billy Maxwell closest behind.

Palmer had a 73 and was tied for sixth at 143 with a couple of big names from the old guard—Sam Snead and Cary Middlecoff.

On Saturday, Palmer moved forward while Venturi went the other way. Arnold fired a 68 to tie for first place with Snead, who shot the same number. A key for Palmer was saving a bogey after hitting his tee shot into the water on the 12th, pitching to six feet after a penalty drop. One-under for the round to that point, he proceeded to hit both back-nine par fives with long-iron second shots for a pair of birdies. He finished in fine charging style, holing a 25-foot downhill putt on 18 that would have raced well past if it hadn't hit the back of the hole, popped up in the air, and dropped into the cup. "I looked at the board and decided to go for it instead of lagging it up," he said afterward in a declaration of a go-for-broke style that would become his trademark.

Snead was five-under through 14 holes and earned oohs and ahs from the crowd on 15 with a bold three-iron from the right rough that carried the water and settled on the fringe. He let a great round get away, though, as he took three to get down from there and bogeyed the 16th.

Venturi fell back with a 74 that included a double bogey on 11 and a three-putt bogey on 18, losing two strokes to Palmer on that green and finishing three back at 214, tied for seventh on a crowded leaderboard.

With a sense of drama, the committee paired Palmer and Venturi, the pre-tournament favorites, in the final round, sending them off first among all the contenders.

Despite the large cast of characters close to the lead, the duo remained the most compelling figures for almost the entirety of the round.

Neither reprised their Sunday collapses of 1956 and 1957 ("I'm more experienced now," Palmer said after the third round). Instead, it was Snead who fell apart with a double bogey on the first hole and ultimately a 41 on the back nine for a 79. "The harder I tried, the worse I pulled," Sam lamented. Middlecoff was another former champion who faltered. Starting one stroke out of the lead, he double bogeyed the third hole and shot a 75. Bo Wininger was tied for the lead at one point in the front nine before disappearing from view with a nine on the 11th hole.

Palmer looked a little shaky himself at the start, but he holed a 20-foot par putt at the first and parred the second after a drive into the woods. The scorecard showed that he never lost the lead all day, though he was often tied and there was always a pack a stroke or two behind. But in fact, for a couple of holes, the scoreboard showed him behind.

The confusion—and controversy—arose on the 12th hole, where Palmer's tee shot flew long and ended up semi-buried in its own pitch-mark on the bank just below the bunker. (He hit a four-iron because he didn't want to come up short in the water as he had done the day before.) He asked an official for relief but was told to play the ball from where it lay. Palmer gouged the ball out, only able to move it a couple of feet. From there, he hit a good chip but missed the short putt for an apparent double bogey that would drop him one stroke behind Venturi.

But Palmer returned to where his ball had been embedded, dropped a ball, and played from there, with the intention of getting a ruling from the committee on which ball would count. He got up and down for what he hoped would be a par.

After hitting his second shot on the 13th (more on that shot later), committee member Bill Kerr ducked under the ropes and had a two- or three-minute discussion with Palmer. Word spread through the grapevine in the gallery that in Kerr's opinion—though no final decision yet—Palmer had been entitled to relief and his score would be a par. On the 14th tee, Bobby Jones talked it over with both players. Finally, when Palmer and Venturi had reached the 15th tee, it was announced that Palmer's score on the 12th was a par, and the scoreboard changed to reflect that.

Meanwhile, Palmer had struck the shot of the tournament, a three-wood second shot on the 13th to 18 feet. When he made the putt for an eagle, the gallery let loose a tremendous roar. All of this with the rules situation hanging in the balance. Palmer said that the decision to go for the green in two had nothing to do with his score on the 12th, whatever it was to be. But as the tournament report in *Golf World* described it, Palmer hit the shot "with no particular show of bellicosity but perhaps with a visible pinch more of his always formidable determination."

Had the eagle given him a two-stroke lead over Venturi, who birdied 13, or merely drawn him even? That wouldn't be known for another 15 minutes or so.

The news that Palmer was in front didn't settle the tournament, as he proceeded to stumble his way to the house to leave the outcome in doubt. He had to lay up on 15 and settled for par, then bogeyed 16 from a bunker. Showing signs of nerves, Palmer got a big break on 17 when his drive hit a tree and caromed into the fairway,

1958

1	Arnold Palmer	70–73–68–73—284
T2	Doug Ford	74–71–70–70—285
T2	Fred Hawkins	71–75–68–71—285
T4	Stan Leonard	72–70–73–71—286
T4	Ken Venturi	68–72–74–72—286
T6	Cary Middlecoff	70–73–69–75—287
T6	Art Wall	71–72–70–74—287
8	Billy Joe Patton	72–69–73–74—288
T9	Claude Harmon	71–76–72–70—289
T9	Jay Hebert	72–73–73–71—289
T9	Billy Maxwell	71–70–72–76—289
T9	Al Mengert	73–71–69–76—289

but he bogeyed 18 when his approach went to the back fringe and he took three strokes with the putter to get down.

Venturi couldn't take advantage. With a fine round going at two-under for 13 holes, the Californian three-putted for bogeys on 14, 15, and 16 before a birdie on 18 gave him a 72 and left him two behind Palmer. "I putted myself right out of the title," said Venturi after eight three-putts in the last two rounds.

Palmer was in the clubhouse with a 73 and four-under 284 total that gave life to Doug Ford and Fred Hawkins, who were playing together 45 minutes behind the Palmer-Venturi twosome. Both came to the 18th at three-under and hit fine approach shots, Hawkins to 16 feet and Ford to 12. Palmer and his wife, Winnie, sat on a couch in Clifford Roberts' quarters and watched nervously on television as two players had a chance to force a playoff.

"Arnold was sure one of them would make the putt," Winnie said. "He was so fidgety, he couldn't keep still. He said he didn't want to watch—but he did."

On the flickering screen, Palmer saw Hawkins, who had birdied 15 and 17, miss his putt. With the tension increasing, Ford, one of the fastest players in the game, took more time than usual before failing to convert his putt. A relieved Palmer was the champion, while Ford had perhaps even more cause than Venturi to feel like he had let the title get away. Ford had 16 pars and a pair of birdies to match the day's best score of 70, but he missed a five-foot birdie putt on the 17th. Even worse, he three-putted from nine feet for a par on 13, missing from 16 inches on the second putt.

In reflecting on the tournament, Jones wouldn't focus on the unfortunate rules incident or the stumbles of various contenders. It was Palmer's second shot on 13 that he would remember the most, especially because it reminded him of the shot Gene Sarazen struck for his double eagle in 1935.

"Today Cliff [Roberts] and I were watching Palmer at 13 and the same exhilaration came over me as did when I watched Sarazen from that mound in 1935. I said to Cliff, 'He really hit that one.'"

Thanks to one bold shot and some good fortune down the stretch, a new Masters star had been born.

An Embedded Problem

An exciting final round was marred by the rules incident involving Arnold Palmer on the 12th hole. There seems little doubt that Palmer should have been given free relief for an embedded ball behind the green—*Golf World* and *Sports Illustrated* both reported that, because of soggy conditions on the course, a local rule was in effect allowing relief for an embedded ball through the green (i.e., anywhere except a hazard). Fellow competitor Ken Venturi agreed that relief should have been granted. But it wasn't, and when Palmer played two balls it created the unfortunate situation of not knowing his score while it took about a half hour for the committee to reach a decision.

If there is any lingering cloud over the incident, it is that Palmer waited to play a second ball until after completing the hole with his original ball and making a double bogey with it. Under today's Rules of Golf, it is required that the player declare his intention to play a second ball before making another stroke with the original. This ultimately created some long-after-the-fact controversy, but apparently it was not commented on at the time. In fact, the rule read somewhat differently in 1958 and it's difficult to say how a committee at the time should have ruled in this particular situation.

1959

So far, no defending champion or foreigner had managed to win the Masters. This time around, defender Arnold Palmer and Canada's Stan Leonard looked like good bets to accomplish one or the other of those "firsts," as they were 1–2 or 1–1 after each of the first three rounds.

Leonard was in front after the first round with a 69, spicing his round by splashing a shot out of the water hazard on the 12th hole to 30 feet and sinking the putt for a par. Palmer was tied for second at 71 along with Jack Burke Jr. and Chandler Harper.

Burke was the talk of the practice rounds with a 66 on Monday and a 64 on Tuesday—this on a course that for the first time was set up with green speeds and hole locations the same as they would be in the tournament. When Gary Player followed with a 64 on Wednesday, it was felt that tournament records were in danger.

Then on Thursday the winds came and only four players broke par. The challenge was not so much the strength of the wind as its sudden changes in direction and intensity. "You can't compensate for the wind if you don't know how it will be blowing when you swing," said Player, who wasn't displeased with a 73.

Friday was only slightly easier, and Palmer moved to the forefront with a 70 to take the lead at 141 despite a bogey on 18 for the second straight day. His game wasn't particularly sharp; still, he shot a 34 on the back nine despite hitting only three greens in regulation and had 28 putts for the round. Leonard slid to a 74 and was second at 143, with nobody else under par for 36 holes.

Burke must have regretted the unfortunate timing of his best play during Masters week. His practice-round form disappeared in a second-round 77, leaving him back in the pack. That was still better than Ken Venturi, the 1956 runner-up and 1958 challenger who was the pre-tournament favorite in a sportswriters' poll. He missed the cut with rounds of 75 and 76.

Through 54 holes, it was Leonard (69) and Palmer (71) tied for first at 212. Leonard was a 44-year-old from British Columbia who had played mostly in Canada until finally joining the PGA tour at age 40. The 5-foot-6 Leonard, a long hitter with big forearms that earned him the nickname "Popeye," had won the Canadian PGA Championship six times on the way to what would become a total of eight. His four years on the U.S. circuit had yielded two victories and a couple of strong showings in the Masters—he was one stroke back through 54 holes before a T11 in 1957 and finished T4 in 1958.

While Palmer's long game wasn't particularly sharp, his play around the greens continued to be superb as he had another scrambling round. He didn't birdie any of the par fives, but this time birdied 18 to earn his share of the lead. Arnie's driver had been erratic in the first round, his iron play shaky at times in Rounds 2 and 3. Still, he was in prime position to defend his title, saying, "I feel like if I can just get to playing a little better…"

The most serious threat to the leading duo was 1955 champion Cary Middlecoff, who shot a 68 on Saturday for a 213 total. For the second straight year, he was one stroke behind a pair of co-leaders heading into the last day.

Nobody was paying attention to Art Wall through 54 holes. The 35-year-old Pennsylvanian was leading the money list, but stood in a tie for 13th place six strokes behind at 218 after rounds of 73–74–71.

In the locker room before the final round, Wall told a friend, "I'm not going to try to set the world on fire. I just want to go out and shoot a good round." What he had in mind was a 70 that he figured might earn him third- or fourth-place money.

The low-key attitude was in keeping with Wall's soft-spoken nature. Known as one of the nicest guys on tour, and for his week-to-week consistency, he was one of the most overlooked of the top players. That was starting to change, as he won twice in 1958 and twice more in the first three months of 1959, including a win at the Azalea Open the week before the Masters. That event had a Monday finish, leaving only a couple days of preparation for Augusta.

Perhaps that had something to do with his indifferent start to the tournament, but things were looking up after he broke par in the third round. Wall surged out of the gate Sunday with birdies on the first two holes, then went into neutral and completed the front nine in 34 after a bogey at No. 7 and a birdie at 8. That pulled him within four of the leader, Palmer, who was a couple holes ahead of him and shot a 36 on the front nine. Middlecoff was two behind after a 37 and Leonard three back with a 39.

The defending champion was in the driver's seat. "I thought I had the tournament won when I went up to the 12th tee," said Palmer after the round. Then, suddenly, he didn't. His six-iron tee shot on the par three came up short in Rae's Creek. After a penalty drop, his pitch went just over the back of the green. Palmer chipped to three feet, and missed the putt, giving him a triple bogey. "I had considered using a five-iron, but was too sure of myself. I started hitting it good and figured I didn't need to worry."

Now Middlecoff was in the lead. Meanwhile, Wall was three-putting the 10th to fall three behind Cary and two behind Palmer. Not that he knew where he stood. "I had no idea what anyone else was doing out there. I didn't inquire," he said after the round.

Palmer rebounded with birdies at 13 and 15, so Wall didn't really appear to be much of a factor as he played the 13th, now four strokes out of the lead. Still just hoping to move up to a bigger paycheck, Wall hit the green in two, 80 feet from the hole, and left the first putt 15 feet short. His birdie putt hung on the edge of the cup—then toppled in while Wall was walking to the hole to tap it in.

1959		
1	Art Wall	73–74–71–66—284
2	Cary Middlecoff	74–71–68–72—285
3	Arnold Palmer	71–70–71–74—286
T4	Stan Leonard	69–74–69–75—287
T4	Dick Mayer	73–75–71–68—287
6	Charles Coe	74–74–67–73—288
7	Fred Hawkins	77–71–68–73—289
T8	Julius Boros	75–69–74–72—290
T8	Jay Hebert	72–73–72–73—290
T8	Gene Littler	72–75–72–71—290
T8	Billy Maxwell	73–71–72–74—290
T8	Billy Joe Patton	75–70–71–74—290
T8	Gary Player	73–75–71–71—290

Wall added a birdie at No. 14, holing a 20-footer. After a good drive on the 15th, he hit a two-iron for his second shot on the advice of his caddie and it was a beauty, finishing 15 feet from the hole. The eagle putt nearly fell; anyway, he had a third straight birdie.

After Wall parred the 16th, playing partner Julius Boros told him if he made another birdie he would have a chance. Up ahead, Palmer was stumbling at the finish for the second year in a row, missing a four-foot par putt at the 17th and a four-foot birdie putt at 18, where he was distracted by the whirring of a movie camera. With a 74, Arnie posted a two-under 286 total.

Wall was two-under for the tournament heading to the 17th, where he hit his second shot to 15 feet and made it for a birdie. Now a par on 18 would beat Palmer. But what about Middlecoff?

The Tennessean had bogeyed 11, birdied 13, and bogeyed 14. As Wall was teeing off on 18, Middlecoff rifled a three-wood second shot to within four feet of the hole on 15. He sank the eagle, moving to three-under and even with Wall.

Did Wall have yet another birdie in him? He did. Not known as one of the longer hitters on tour, he nonetheless crushed his drive on 18 and hit a nine-iron to 12 feet behind the hole located on the front portion of the green. Not certain whether the putt would break to the left or the right, he played it straight and watched it roll straight into the cup. It was his fifth birdie on the last six holes for a final-round 66.

Middlecoff parred 16 and 17, so he needed a birdie at 18 to force a playoff. His approach came up short of the green and his chip barely missed the hole, the resulting par giving him a 72 and second place alone.

In his press interview, Wall credited Doug Ford, a frequent roommate on tour, with helping him with the mental side of the game and course management. Wall's

66 matched the best final round in Masters history shot by Ford in his victory two years earlier. But Ford had only needed to pass five players to reach the winner's circle in 1957 and Burke had passed just three in his record eight-stroke comeback in 1956, while Wall passed 12 players in his six-stroke comeback. The quiet man had set the world on fire after all.

....

Who Needs Practice?

Ed "Porky" Oliver headed to the practice range on Friday to get ready for the second round, and wondered aloud where his caddie was. The caddie soon appeared, with the unwelcome news that Oliver was due on the first tee right away. Oliver had gotten mixed up on his tee time, and arrived at the course late. Now he borrowed a seven-iron from another player to hit one warmup shot, and rushed to the tee just in time. The lack of preparation didn't affect him, as he shot a 69, within one stroke of the day's best round. It was by far his best round of the week on the way to a T14 finish.

....

1960

The tournament would come down to Arnold Palmer vs. Ken Venturi, Chapter 2, with Dow Finsterwald also playing a prominent role, if ultimately an unfortunate one.

Palmer, who had turned 30 the previous fall, spent the first part of 1960 stating his case as the game's best player. He had already won four tournaments, including three in a row from late February to mid-March. Venturi was the oddsmakers' second Masters choice, having scored a victory and six top-five finishes in eight starts. One player who wouldn't have to be reckoned with was defending champion Art Wall, who was present but unable to play due to a kidney infection and a bad knee.

Palmer came to Augusta in the middle of the week before the Masters; however, he ran into a couple of bumps in his preparation. He seemed to be developing a phobia about the 12th hole, hitting his tee shot into Rae's Creek in his first four practice rounds—after blowing the tournament there in the final round of 1959. "I just can't seem to get it across there," he said on the Sunday before the Masters after his fourth straight drowned tee shot on 12. "If this keep up, I'm going to play it short of the creek and pitch it over."

Then there was a mild case of the flu, for which a local doctor prescribed a couple days of rest. Palmer didn't play a practice round Monday or Tuesday and, on Wednesday, played only a couple of holes plus the Par 3 Contest in the afternoon. This was the first year of the Par 3 event, which would become a Masters tradition on the nine-hole short course that had opened in 1958. The inaugural was won by 47-year-old Sam Snead with a four-under 23.

None of that held back Palmer in the first round as he shot a 67 in ideal weather to take the lead. His short game was outstanding; he holed a greenside bunker shot for an eagle on No. 8 (the previously bunkerless green area had been redesigned in 1956; it was restored to its previous state in 1979) and saved par after missing several greens. One of those was on the 12th hole, where he went over the green, being sure to take plenty of club. Ironically, considering the brouhaha in 1958, his tee shot embedded in its own pitch-mark, and this time he was granted relief right away. The only long putt Palmer made all day was an 18-footer for a birdie on the home hole.

Venturi appeared to be destined for the lead, and maybe a record round, as he shot a 31 on the front nine with a 35-yard eagle hole-out on the second hole and three birdies, including a 30-footer at the ninth. Stunningly, the 28-year-old with a history of Masters frustration skied to a 42 on the back nine for a 73.

He double bogeyed the 12th, where his tee shot went long and ended up sitting in a pitch-mark made by another ball (and thus not getting relief). Venturi also had three three-putt bogeys and sent his approach shots over the green on 17 and 18 for a pair of closing bogeys (he actually had a birdie in his 42). After the round, he was in surprisingly decent spirits, referring to his back nine as "a slick 42."

Four players were two strokes back at 69—Claude Harmon, Fred Hawkins, Jay Hebert, and Finsterwald. Make that three players: Finsterwald on Friday would retroactively be penalized two first-round strokes for taking a practice putt after finishing the fifth hole.

The infraction came to light when Finsterwald dropped a ball to take a practice putt after finishing the first hole of the second round, only to be stopped by fellow competitor Billy Casper, who said he didn't think that was allowed. It turned out Casper was right. Finsterwald told an official what he had done on the fifth hole of the first round. Having thus signed a wrong scorecard that didn't include a two-stroke penalty, Finsterwald was subject to disqualification, but the rules committee, as allowed under the rules, waived the DQ penalty due to unusual circumstances.

Finsterwald was a very good player who had already accumulated 10 tour victories by age 30 (he would finish his career with 12). He shot a 70 in the second round for a 141 total and was only one stroke out of first place—a lead that would have been his if not for the penalty. "It was stupid of me for not knowing the [local] rule when it was printed right on the back of the scorecard," he said. "Even if I had been disqualified, I couldn't have been bitter about it."

Thus, Palmer was able to stay in front with a 140 total after a 73 in a second round when he missed four putts in the three- to four-foot range and several others inside 10 feet.

Venturi put himself right back into contention with a 69 to stand just two back at 142. He bogeyed the first hole, later attributing the bogey to still being bothered by his 42 on the day before, but quickly turned things around and would have gained a share of the lead if birdie putts on the last two holes hadn't lipped out from eight and 12 feet.

"He had it close on every hole," said Jack Burke Jr., who played with Venturi. "He played like you just couldn't believe it."

Four players were one stroke behind at 141, including 47-year-old Ben Hogan after a 68, making him a factor for the first time in five years.

Palmer would cling to a one-stroke lead after a third-round 72, this time with five players one stroke behind him. One of those five was Hogan, who, after a 72 said, "I feel as spry as a young amateur out there." Alas, the next day, Hogan putted like a 47-year-old with a case of the yips, taking 38 putts on the way to a 76 in the final round.

For his part, Palmer struggled on the greens in the third round. "I've putted like Joe Schmoe two days in a row," he said. The 1958 champion threatened to pull away as he played the first seven holes in two-under. It started to go sour with a three-putt par at the eighth, got worse with a shot into the creek and a missed four-footer as he bogeyed 13 and bogeyed 17 for a 38 on the back nine.

Venturi was in the group tied for second at 213 after a 71—and would have been tied for first if he hadn't missed a two-foot par putt on 15. "I guess a lot of people thought that 42 on the back nine would finish me this year," he said. "But I was playing good enough that the 42 didn't disturb me. I am playing better golf now than I ever have in my life."

With Hogan, Casper, and Julius Boros—three of the players in the tie for second through 54 holes—all shooting 74 or worse on a windy, chilly Sunday, the final round became a fight between Finsterwald, Venturi, and Palmer in front of a huge crowd estimated at 35,000 or more.

This time Venturi and Palmer weren't matched head-to-head; it was Venturi with Finsterwald in a duel playing about four holes ahead of Palmer (paired with Casper). The earlier starters leap-frogged Palmer on the front nine, with Venturi getting birdies on Nos. 2, 3, and 6 for a 33 and Finsterwald pulling back within one with birdies on 8 and 9 for a 34.

Their scoring pace slowed on the back nine, but it was a tense battle as they traded birdies and bogeys, with either a tie or Venturi one ahead for the entire nine. Venturi saved a bogey on 11 with a one-putt after hitting his approach in the water and made a remarkable par save on the 16th, when he somehow stopped a short downhill bunker shot within inches of the hole. It came down to the 18th, where Finsterwald hit his approach into a bunker and Venturi countered with a marvelous second shot to six feet. Finsterwald blasted out to five feet and was given life when Venturi missed his birdie try. Finsterwald missed, too, allowing Venturi to take the clubhouse lead with a 70 for a five-under 283 total, one ahead of his playing partner for the day.

At that point, Palmer had completed 14 holes and stood at four-under for the tournament, so he needed to go one-under the rest of the way to force a playoff or two-under to win outright. Arnie had shot a 36 on the front with two birdies and two bogeys (and a missed two-and-a-half-foot birdie putt on No. 2) and overshot the green again on 12 before chipping to three feet and escaping with a par.

He had squandered a birdie chance on 13, when he reached a greenside bunker in two but missed an eight-foot putt. The 15th beckoned as another par-five birdie opportunity, but he hit his second shot well right of the green, rolled his third shot up the slope to 15 feet, and missed the putt. The task had just gotten a lot harder.

Palmer got a bad/good break on 16 when his 25-foot birdie putt hit the flagstick (this was during a period of a few years when it was allowed to leave the flagstick in on a putt) and didn't drop but also didn't go several feet past as it would have. He was still one behind, now with just two holes to play.

On the 17th, Palmer thought he hit a perfect eight-iron approach, but it checked up 25 feet short of the hole. He backed away from the putt twice, distracted by spectator movement behind the hole. Finally, he stroked it and watched as the ball crept to the hole—and barely toppled in over the front edge. The gallery favorite leaped in the air and did a dance; he was now tied for the lead.

1960		
1	Arnold Palmer	67–73–72–70—282
2	Ken Venturi	73–69–71–70—283
3	Dow Finsterwald	71–70–72–71—284
4	Billy Casper	71–71–71–74—287
5	Julius Boros	72–71–70–75—288
T6	Walter Burkemo	72–69–75–73—289
T6	Ben Hogan	73–68–72–76—289
T6	Gary Player	72–71–72–74—289
T9	Lionel Hebert	74–70–73–73—290
T9	Stan Leonard	72–72–72–74—290

Palmer struck another solid approach to 18, this one landing pin high two feet right of the hole and spinning sideways to finish six feet left of it—nearly the same spot that Venturi missed from. Palmer knocked it in the hole for a second straight birdie and his second Masters title. He had closed with a 70 and became only the second player to lead outright after every round (Craig Wood, 1941), though it didn't exactly feel like a wire-to-wire victory.

Sitting in the clubhouse hoping his score would hold up, Venturi cautioned newsmen that "I haven't won it yet." When it was over, the runner-up could look back on many frustrations as a Masters title had slipped away from him for a third time in a relatively young career—the 42 on Thursday, the missed two-footer on Saturday, the lackluster back nine and missed putt on 18 on Sunday. In the end, though, it was the heroic finish by Palmer that took it away from him.

At the awards ceremony, Palmer told Venturi that while he was glad to win, "I'm truly sorry it had to be this way."

For the second year in a row, not to mention many other times going back to Gene Sarazen, a fast finish won the Masters. Augusta National, with its potential for birdies but bogey danger lurking, was proving to be the perfect setting for drama. And where the game's greatest players shined most brightly.

Palmer's 1960 victory put him in that class, with *Golf World* saying he was in position to dominate the game like Hogan, Snead, Walter Hagen, and Bobby Jones before him, and Jack Williams of the *Atlanta Constitution* calling him the new Mr. Golf.

It was a signature moment for Palmer, followed by another at the U.S. Open, where he charged from behind in the final round to take the title. He would win eight times during the year and would go beyond Mr. Golf to become known as The King.

A Costly Penalty

Dow Finsterwald knew that practice putting after completion of a hole wasn't allowed under a local rule in force at PGA events, but he thought it was OK at the Masters, which wasn't run by the PGA. He hadn't noticed that the local rule was printed on the back of the scorecard. When fellow competitor Billy Casper stopped him from taking a practice putt on the first hole of the second round, Finsterwald saw PGA official Ed Carter standing by the green and asked about it. Carter couldn't tell him for sure right away (apparently, he hadn't read the back of the scorecard, either), and went to check. Finsterwald was on the eighth hole when Carter got back to him to confirm that the local rule was in effect. On the 11th hole, Finsterwald told a Masters official that he had taken a practice putt during the first round. On the 14th hole, committee co-chairman John Ames told Finsterwald that he would at least be penalized two strokes, and possibly disqualified for an incorrect first-round scorecard. With that hanging over him, Finsterwald managed to complete a second-round 70. Around the time he finished 18, the committee announced that the disqualification would be waived, as the infraction didn't affect the play of his ball, but the two strokes retroactively added to his first-round score knocked Finsterwald from the 36-hole lead. As fate would have it, Finsterwald finished the tournament two strokes behind the winner.

1961

Once again, the Masters would come down to a duel between the players regarded as Nos. 1 and 2 coming into the event. The finish would again be highly dramatic, but this time not at all heroic.

One of the players, of course, was defending champion Arnold Palmer, who had won eight times in 1960 and already added three titles in 1961. However, he didn't come in as the tour's leading money winner, a distinction owned by 25-year-old Gary Player of South Africa.

This was the first time Player was playing a full schedule in the U.S. Previously, the earliest he had started was the end of March. He had won his first tournament in South Africa at age 19 and been invited to his first Masters in 1957 at 21 after finishing fourth in the previous year's British Open. In 1959, he won the British Open, establishing himself as a force to be reckoned with on the international scene.

Player had won twice in the U.S.—albeit in limited appearances—from 1957 to 1960. Now making a full run at it, he had two wins, a second, three thirds, and a fourth already heading into the second week of April.

The young South African gave a warning signal on Wednesday when he played a 14-hole practice round in six-under, walking in at that point because the course closed at 2:30 to prepare for the final round. Palmer was less than satisfied with his practice rounds, but he was ready when the bell rang, shooting a 68 in the first round to tie for the lead with Bob Rosburg.

Notably, Palmer played the first round with 21-year-old amateur Jack Nicklaus, who had won the 1959 U.S. Amateur and would capture it again later in 1961. Nicklaus said he'd never been as nervous as he was on the first hole, but he went out and shot a 70 for fourth place even while missing 13 putts inside 15 feet. "He could have been 67 or better," said an impressed Palmer, who would see plenty of Nicklaus in the future, probably more than he preferred to.

Player was very much in the picture with a 69 and touted his distance off the tee. "Last year I simply couldn't reach these par fives in two and I went to work and now I can reach all of them. I'm 25 yards longer now than I was," said the 5-foot-7, 150-pounder, with a degree of exaggeration. The work referred both to Player's physical regimen—he was doing 70 finger pushups each day—and an improved swing featuring better balance.

The next day Player and Palmer reversed their 68 and 69 to tie for first at 137, pulling away from the field as nobody else managed better than 141. Player finished in style with a 30-foot putt from the fringe on 18 for his fifth birdie of the day. He could have had one more, but his tee shot on the 12th hit the cup on the fly and bounded 15 feet away as he settled for a par.

Player said he would continue with his aggressive style. And why not? It seemed to work well for Palmer. "I just play my game. If it comes off, it does. If it doesn't, well, I'm just 25," Player said.

And the South African, already becoming known for his dogged determination, made a promise. "I am not going to choke. If I play badly, it's not because of the pressure."

Palmer had 28 putts for the second straight day as he was scrambling more than he would like, but said he was a bit more satisfied than he was after the first round.

Arnold would be anything but satisfied after a third round that started with great promise with birdies on the first two holes before rapidly deteriorating as he finished with a 73. He was in second place, but four behind Player, as his streak of six straight Masters rounds with at least a share of the lead came to an end.

"Where is the casket?" he asked as he entered for his post-round media interview. "I never got the right club in my hand all day. I just never had my concentration.… I felt I couldn't get myself up all day. Oh, well, tomorrow's another day. This one was a mess."

Player shot a 69 to make him the first to shoot the first three rounds in the 60s at the Masters—and his 12th straight round in the 60s on tour. He started after Palmer and was well aware that Palmer's birdies on the first two holes had put him behind—but proceeded to birdie the first two holes himself. Player would bogey the 11th, 12th, and 13th holes, but rebounded with birdies on 15—where a spectator behind the green stopped his second shot with his hand and apparently accidentally batted it onto the green—and 16. "I was feeling so good about my play that I just kept attacking."

A day after Palmer oddly came out flat, Player strangely seemed to have lost some confidence the morning before the scheduled final round, telling writers, "The way I feel about it is that many great players have shot bad rounds here after leading the tournament. If I shoot one today, I won't be the first."

Player did OK on Sunday, but lost some ground to Palmer—which turned out not to matter because the round was canceled before it was finished, and would

1961

I	Gary Player	69–68–69–74—280
T2	Arnold Palmer	68–69–73–71—281
T2	Charles Coe	72–71–69–69—281
T4	Tommy Bolt	72–71–74–68—285
T4	Don January	74–68–72–71—285
6	Paul Harney	71–73–68–74—286
T7	Jack Burke Jr.	76–70–68–73—287
T7	Billy Casper	72–77–69–69—287
T7	Bill Collins	74–72–67–74—287
T7	Jack Nicklaus	70–75–70–72—287

be replayed in its entirety on Monday. Player was even par through 11 holes and Palmer two under through nine, to cut the margin from four strokes to two, when a downpour that had started in earnest about 45 minutes earlier showed no signs of relenting, making play impossible.

The idea of suspending play and continuing the next day from the point it stopped was not yet in vogue—in fact, it was not even thought about as a possibility. It was either finish the round or wipe it out and start again the next day.

There was no debate about whether the round could have continued under the conditions. "There was no other choice," said Palmer, even though he was now four strokes behind again instead of two.

Without prompting, Player returned to one of his themes for the week, saying, "I played well and proved to myself I'm not a choker. This gives me added confidence for tomorrow."

Monday dawned with thankfully nice weather. In a reversal of the third round, Player was off a half hour earlier and birdied the first two holes to get the jump on Palmer, going six ahead before his rival even made it to the first tee. Palmer got those two strokes back with birdies on Nos. 2 and 6 while Player was completing the front nine with a two-under 34. Things started to get interesting when Palmer birdied the eighth while Player was making a bogey on 10.

It was the beginning of an awful finish for Player, who hit only two greens in regulation on the back nine. He managed to save par on 11 and 12, then disaster struck on the 13th. He hit his drive so far into the trees on the right that his best escape was into the parallel 14th fairway. But it was taking so long to clear the gallery from his intended line to the 14th that he gave up and decided to play toward the 13th. Player punched a two-iron through an opening, but it rolled too far and ended up in the creek to the left of the fairway. After a penalty stroke, he hit a three-iron to the back edge of the green 35 feet away and took three putts from there to make a double bogey on what is normally a birdie hole.

Player compounded his troubles with a bogey on the other par-five on the back nine, the 15th. After laying up in two, his wedge approach sucked backward off the green but not into the pond in front. He chipped to three feet—and missed the putt.

While his long game continued to abandon him, Player showed his grit on the final two holes. His nine-iron approach went over the green on the 17th, leaving a very difficult pitch shot, but he ended up holing a 12-foot putt for a par. After a poor drive on 18, he hit a four-iron into the right bunker, blasted to five feet and made the putt for another par save. It was a small consolation as he trudged off the 18th green with a stunned, dejected look after a 40 on the back nine for a 74.

Palmer found himself making up ground as he strung together pars on the back nine, including an unlikely save on the 12th, where he went way over the green and rolled his recovery shot with a putter through a bunker to two feet. That was about the time Player bogeyed the 15th, so now Palmer led by one in his bid to win a second straight Masters and third in four years. He hit the green in two on 13, some 80 feet away and three-putted for a par. Birdie also escaped him on 15, where he had to lay up and ultimately missed a 30-footer. By now, Player had finished and Palmer knew that three pars would do it.

He got the first two and hit a strong drive on the 18th. Now it was Palmer's turn for disaster. He pushed his seven-iron approach into the same bunker Player had found, but Arnie, taking little time, bladed his bunker shot over the green into the gallery, bent over and grabbed his knees in anguish. Now he needed to make a tough up-and-down just to force a playoff. Using a putter to roll the ball up the slope to the green, he went 15 feet past. When he missed that one, he had a double bogey and a 38 on the back nine for a 71, and the title belonged to Player.

"I thought sixes only happened to other people," Palmer was heard to mutter as he walked off the green.

To the assembled press, Palmer said of his play over the closing holes, "For the first time in my life I got overconfident. I never felt I was going to do anything but win. Once I got ahead, I forgot there's more to it than that. You've got to finish."

In later years, Palmer pinpointed a key moment in his concentration lapse. After his drive on 18, a friend in the gallery, teaching pro George Low, called Palmer over and said, "Nice going boy. You won it." In his autobiography, *A Golfer's Life*, with James Dodson, Palmer wrote that he lost his concentration, and on his approach shot thought about getting the ball on the green instead of about his swing. He compounded the error by rushing his bunker shot.

The struggles of Player and Palmer almost allowed 37-year-old Oklahoma amateur Charles Coe, an Augusta National member, to come from nowhere and steal the title. Playing with Palmer, Coe shot a 34 on the back nine for a 69 and a tie for second, one stroke behind the winner. The 1949 and 1958 U.S. Amateur champion, and runner-up to Nicklaus in a thrilling 1959 final in that event, narrowly missed an eight-foot birdie putt on 17 and couldn't convert from 20 feet on 18 or the Masters might have had its first amateur champion.

Instead, it had its first international winner in Player, who was the second youngest to claim the title. (Byron Nelson, also 25, was four months younger in 1937.)

Player was asked afterward if he had choked in the final round. "No, I didn't choke, believe me," he said. Perhaps the bad back nine was indeed just a poorly timed coincidence. Certainly, Player had showed his mettle with the up-and-down pars on the last two holes. Anyway, it didn't matter, for, in the end, Player got to don the green jacket.

1962

Starting in 1958, Arnold Palmer had alternated years winning the Masters or blowing it when he should have won. He was also in the midst of a long period of dominance on the PGA circuit, with 20 wins from 1958 to 1961 and two more early in 1962 (on the way to eight for the year). It's only natural that all eyes were on Palmer as the Masters approached. If he followed the pattern, it was his year to win.

Palmer arrived the Thursday before Masters week and played four consecutive practice rounds with Jack Nicklaus, the winner of the 1959 and 1961 U.S. Amateur, and a rookie pro in the 1962 season. Keeping an eye on a challenger to the throne, perhaps?

Nicklaus also attracted plenty of attention in the pre-tournament buildup—he reportedly outscored Palmer in all four practice rounds. Defending champion Gary Player, it seemed, was the forgotten man. The South African had led the money list in 1961 yet hadn't won a tournament since the last Masters, and his results so far in 1962 were mediocre at best.

"I must admit I am a bit surprised to see the experts counting me out so quickly," Player said on Tuesday. "However, I cannot say I am not pleased. I play better when I am underrated."

Player blamed his slow start to the year on poor putting, saying he was happy with his tee-to-green game. Before heading to the first tee on Thursday morning, he spent an hour on the practice green and decided to go back to the putting stroke he had used at the last Masters.

It worked: Player made four putts of 10 feet or longer as he shot a 67 to take the lead on a damp, chilly day. Julius Boros was second at 69, with Palmer one of four players at 70. The tournament favorite was two-over after 11 holes, but rallied with birdies on 12, 13, 15, and 18, the latter with a 25-foot putt.

"I'm mad at that hole, and I want to get even," said Palmer of the 18th. He could have said the same thing about the 12th, where he also drained a 25-footer.

Arnie was even better on the back nine in the second round, touring it in 31 strokes on the way to a 66 and the 36-hole lead at 136. After a three-birdie, two-bogey front nine, he was blemish free on the back with a birdie on 10 and four in a row from 13 to 16. Player was second, two strokes behind, after a 71 that consisted of 16 pars, one bogey, and an eagle on the 15th. Gene Littler (68) was third at 139, which meant that the reigning champions of the British Open (Palmer), Masters (Player), and U.S. Open (Littler) were 1–2–3.

A fourth player joined the fray on Saturday, with Dow Finsterwald shooting a 65 to move into second place, two behind Palmer. Finsterwald, known at the Masters for his unfortunate two-stroke penalty and third-place finish in 1960, was trying to emerge from a slump. The Ohio native ranked in the top four on the money list from 1956 to 1960 and won the 1958 PGA Championship before falling outside the top 30 players in a winless 1961.

Finsterwald went out in 32 and came back in 33, preserving a bogeyless round with an escape from deep in the forest on the 18th, where he lofted an eight-iron over trees to 65 yards short of the green and ended up making an eight-foot par putt.

Palmer continued his slow start/fast finish pattern, following a front-nine 37 (eight pars, one bogey) with a 32 on the back. This time the birdies came on Nos. 10, 12, 15, and 18. His 205 total for three rounds matched the tournament record of Ben Hogan in 1953, giving him a chance at Hogan's 72-hole record of 274. "Sure, I'm going to try for the record," he said. "But the tournament comes first."

Player was in third place at 209 with a 71 that included a bogey on the 13th hole. He told himself he wouldn't go for the green in two this year on the tempting par five, which had given him trouble the year before. But a good drive tempted him to go for it. He could have reached the green with a three-iron, he lamented after the round. Instead, he tried to cut a four-wood from a sloping lie and wound up hitting into the water. Littler also had a 71 for a 210 total; with nobody else better than 213, it looked to be a four-man race.

And a wild race, as it turned out, one in which Palmer let the others back into it with some shoddy play then came up clutch at the end.

Things began to get weird on the par-five second hole, where Palmer missed an 18-inch birdie putt. Later admitting that he "kinda got shook" by the miss, he proceeded to hit his tee shot into the woods on the third hole and hit a tree with his next shot. While he recovered to make a par four there, he hit a fat one-iron from the tee at the par-three fourth that plopped down 50 yards short of the green. A bogey there was followed by two more at Nos. 5 and 7.

Palmer made the turn with a 39 to stand at eight-under, creating a three-way tie for the lead. Player, who was paired with Palmer, had been six strokes behind just six holes earlier after bogeys on two of the first three holes. He went on to birdie Nos. 5, 6, 8, and 9 around a bogey at the seventh for a 35 on the front nine. Finsterwald birdied the second to get to 10-under, bogeyed the fourth and fifth and treaded water after that.

Arnie's Army let out a gasp on the 10th hole, where their hero three-putted from 20 feet for a double bogey to go five-over for the round. Player appeared to take control when he rifled a three-iron to three feet on the 11th for a birdie that gave him the lead by one over Finsterwald and three over Palmer.

Soon, though, Player bogeyed the 12th and Finsterwald birdied 13; now, it was Dow in front by one. Palmer couldn't seem to make up any ground. He went for both back-nine par fives in two, but couldn't get up and down on either and was stuck at six-under.

Finsterwald, playing about two holes in front of the Palmer-Player pairing, slipped up on the 17th, where his second shot went over the green and he missed a six-foot par putt after a mediocre chip. Now he and Player, who was on his way to parring the last six holes, were tied at eight-under.

Palmer, two strokes behind, hit his tee shot on the par-three 16th to the right back fringe and faced a devilish downhill chip that would be tough to stop near the hole. He heard Jimmy Demaret, doing television commentary, say that he would be lucky to get up and down. "This shot will perhaps put Arnold Palmer out of contention for the Masters championship," Demaret intoned.

1962		
1	Arnold Palmer	70–66–69–75—280*
2	Gary Player	67–71–71–71—280
3	Dow Finsterwald	74–68–65–73—280
4	Gene Littler	71–68–71–72—282
T5	Jerry Barber	72–72–69–74—287
T5	Jimmy Demaret	73–73–71–70—287
T5	Billy Maxwell	71–73–72–71—287
T5	Mike Souchak	70–72–74–71—287
T9	Charles Coe	72–74–71–71—288
T9	Ken Venturi	75–70–71–72—288
*Palmer (70) won playoff over Player (71),		
Finsterwald (77)		

Instead, Palmer's deft chip followed the slope straight down into the cup, banging against the flagstick for a stunning birdie. With a gallery roar and a Palmer celebration, he was back in it.

What happened next surprised no one. Palmer hit his approach within 15 feet on the 17th and he holed the birdie putt to tie for the lead. Even on a day when he started out of sorts, Palmer had summoned a late charge.

A birdie on the 18th would have been too much to ask, though, and when he and Player two-putted for pars on the closing hole it set up a three-way Monday playoff along with Finsterwald with all finishing at 280.

Palmer admitted he was fortunate to be in a playoff after a final-round 75. "I played so badly I couldn't have made the Podunk Open," he said. Neither Player (71) nor Finsterwald (73) burned it up. But the back-and-forth parrying and thrusting had led to another riveting Masters final round. As Alfred Wright wrote in *Sports Illustrated*, "The finish of the Masters has become, year after year, a piece of fiction—characters by Saki, plot by Hitchcock."

The plot was thick in the 18-hole playoff, too. Though Finsterwald was Palmer's best friend on tour, he still hungered to get back at Arnold for 1960. Palmer had his own score to settle by avenging his loss to Player in 1961, and joining Demaret and Sam Snead as a three-time Masters winner. Player, meanwhile, had his eyes fixed on his own prize: becoming the first to win back-to-back Masters.

Finsterwald bogeyed the first hole and was shaken up when his tee shot on the second hole hit a woman spectator in the face. He shot 40–37 and was never a factor.

Palmer's troubles with the front nine continued, going out in 37 with eight pars and a bogey on the seventh. Player jumped in front with birdies on the first two holes and, with a bogey on five and a birdie at six, shot a 34 to take a three-stroke advantage to the second nine.

That part of the property belonged to Palmer this week, and the playoff was no different. The turning point came on the 10th hole, when Arnold sank a 30-foot birdie putt and Gary's five-foot par putt hung on the lip. The margin was down to one.

Palmer birdied the 12th with a seven-iron to four feet, while Player three-putted from 55 feet for a bogey. Now Palmer was up by one. A solid one-iron second shot to the 13th green produced a birdie for Palmer while Player made a par. The patented Palmer charge continued with a birdie from 16 feet on the 14th, where Player made his third bogey in five holes. It was the third two-shot swing on the back nine. In one of the reversals that Augusta National seems to produce more than any other course, Palmer had gone from three behind to four ahead in just five holes.

Player would birdie the 15th and 18th, but it was too late. Palmer got a birdie of his own at 16 and parred the other incoming holes for a 31 on the back nine and a 68 to Player's 71. Over the course of five rounds, Palmer played the front nine in five over and the back nine in an extraordinary 17 under. On the two holes that had cost him the Masters in 1959 and 1961, he was three-under on the 12th and two-under on the 18th.

After going back and forth between blowing the Masters and winning it in a four-year stretch, Palmer had somehow managed to do both in the same year.

1963

Jack Nicklaus was only in his second year as a professional, but he was already looming large heading into what would be his fifth Masters appearance. He played in three as an amateur, finishing T13 in 1960 and T7 in 1961 after a missed cut in his 1959 debut.

Bobby Jones took a great interest in Nicklaus. Late in 1961, he wrote Jack a letter urging him to remain an amateur. The note from the greatest amateur to play the game gave Nicklaus pause, but he ultimately decided to turn professional. In his rookie season of 1962, he finished a somewhat disappointing T15 in the Masters. However, he quickly established himself as a force in the game when he outdueled Arnold Palmer to win the U.S. Open at age 22.

In fact, Nicklaus, Palmer, and Gary Player were already being called the Big Three.

They earned that label by sweeping the four majors in 1962, Palmer winning the Masters and British Open, Nicklaus the U.S. Open, and Player the PGA Championship. So far in 1963, they had accounted for six wins (Palmer three, Nicklaus two, Player one) and were 1–2–3 on the money list (Player-Palmer-Nicklaus).

Some observers were saying the Big Three were even money against the field. There was considerable pushback against that notion from other players. Jimmy Demaret called it ridiculous; Billy Casper said it was crazy; and Tommy Bolt said, "The Big Three—strictly a publicity gimmick!"

For that matter, the Big Three didn't sound all that optimistic themselves.

Nicklaus had been slowed by a case of bursitis in his hip since late January. He had played in four events in the two months since then, winning one, but didn't hit any practice balls other than a limited number to warm up before a round. The hip was now better, and just before the beginning of Masters week Nicklaus had gotten clearance from the doctor to practice. On Monday, he said, "I'm not ready to play the tournament. The short irons aren't what they should be. When you don't practice, that's what goes first."

Despite his three victories, Palmer didn't feel like he was playing as well as his eight-win season of the year before. At 33, Arnie lamented that he must be getting old, because the young fellows were hitting it past him while he seemed to be losing distance.

Player, who had five runner-up finishes along with his one victory in the first three months of the season, nonetheless said he felt less confident than he ever had coming into the Masters. "I have a strange premonition that the tournament this year is going to be won by somebody else—somebody besides Palmer, Nicklaus or myself."

Palmer, holding no ill will to the young rival to his throne, played a nine-hole practice round with Nicklaus on Wednesday. "Jack has been playing terrific," said Palmer after watching Nicklaus shoot a 32 on the back nine. Palmer didn't feel any better about his own game.

Neither was happy after the first round, both shooting 74. Palmer was rolling along nicely at two-under through 13 holes on a day when wind and hard, baked greens made scores soar, but his performance down the stretch was just the opposite of his superb showings of a year earlier. He played the last five in four-over with a double bogey on 15, where he chunked his third shot into the water. Nicklaus simply had a blah round.

The co-leaders were 40-year-old Bo Wininger and Mike Souchak at 69. Wininger led his press conference by asking, "Whatever happened to the Big Three?"

One of the Big Three wasn't far behind: Player shot a 71 that he was as happy with as the 67 he had opened with a year earlier, considering the conditions. The 1961 champion put in a request that the greens be watered.

The outlook brightened considerably for Nicklaus on Friday, when he took advantage of more benign conditions to fire a 66 for a 140 total to move within one of the lead held by Souchak. Young Jack said it was probably the best round he had ever shot, as he didn't have a bogey and lipped out several birdie putts before playing the last seven holes in four-under. Player moved backward with a 74 for 145 and Palmer stagnated at 73—147.

His experience in four previous Masters had taught Nicklaus that playing his usual fade off every tee wasn't the best way to attack Augusta National. He headed into 1963 determined to develop a reliable right-to-left draw shot to use at the Masters. Even without much practice time, he seemed to be managing it.

In the third round, Nicklaus had more to worry about than hitting a draw. For him and the rest of the field, it became a matter of surviving miserable weather and a soggy course, as it rained overnight and for most of the day Saturday. Nicklaus coped better than most. He shot a 74 that was good enough to move into the lead by one stroke over 46-year-old Ed Furgol, the 1954 U.S. Open champion.

Nicklaus went through eight gloves; even so, he had the club slip in his hands on his tee shot on the 11th hole, almost leading to disaster. His ball hit a tree about 150 yards off the tee on the right side, but he wasn't sure where it ended up. Walking toward the trees on the right, he wondered if he would find it. Suddenly, a lone policeman on the left side of the fairway—where spectators weren't allowed—called out, "Is this yours?" The ball had ricocheted across the fairway, and it was lucky the patrolman had seen it. Even better, Nicklaus escaped with a par four when he pounded a three-wood just short of the green, chipped on, and made an eight-footer.

There were other tribulations, notably a pair of missed putts from two feet or less early in the round ("putts my 18-month-old could have made," Nicklaus told reporters). But with pars on the last 11 holes, Nicklaus put himself in the driver's seat heading to the final round.

Souchak, playing with Nicklaus, shot a 79, and erstwhile contenders Wininger and Jay Hebert fell back with 77 and 81—Hebert leading the tournament through nine holes before a horrid 45 on the back nine.

The *Augusta Chronicle* reported that conditions were as bad as they ever had been in a round that wasn't called off. Casual water was a problem, especially in low areas like the 13th hole, where Nicklaus and Souchak hit their drives within iron distance of reaching the green in two, but had to move so far back in taking relief from casual water that they had to lay up.

Many players felt the round should have been called off, but the committee apparently wanted to avoid the situation of canceling and replaying the third round, as they had done in 1961. Fortunately, it stopped raining around 4:20 p.m. and players were able to slog on, even if they didn't want to.

The low round was 71 by three players, including Julius Boros, who moved into third place two strokes back at 216. In good position to make a run in the final round were three-time champion 50-year-old Sam Snead and Tony Lema, playing in his first Masters at age 29. Both shot 74 to stand at 217. Player (74) was five strokes off the lead at 219, with Palmer (73) at 220—just close enough that a charge wasn't out of the question.

Palmer opened Sunday with birdies on the first two holes—the charge was on! Except it wasn't. Arnie went one-over the rest of the round, shooting a 71 that left him tied for ninth. It was the first time since 1957 he hadn't come to the last couple of holes with either the lead or a chance to win.

Nicklaus parred the first seven holes of the final round, making it 18 pars in a row, then bogeyed the eighth when he flubbed a shot from a greenside bunker. He went to the back nine holding a precarious one-stroke lead.

Developments came quickly and furiously in a 15-minute span starting when Nicklaus was on the 11th green and heard a loud roar from Snead rolling in a long birdie putt on the 14th to tie him. In his autobiography *My Story*, Nicklaus recounts being unnerved as he walked to the 12th tee that he heard not only cheers for Snead's birdie being posted on the leaderboard but also some in the gallery rooting against him. That may have contributed to his hitting a seven-iron into the front bunker on the 12th. Nicklaus blasted from a half-buried lie over the green, chipped on, and faced a nine-foot bogey putt.

Meanwhile, Player holed a 10-foot birdie putt and did a dance on the 15th green as he went to four-under for the round and joined Snead at one-under for the tournament while Nicklaus was staring at a bogey putt he needed to make to stay one behind them at even par. Adding to the drama, Boros, playing with Nicklaus, made a 12-foot birdie putt to get to even par himself.

1963		
1	Jack Nicklaus	74–66–74–72—286
2	Tony Lema	74–69–74–70—287
T3	Julius Boros	76–69–71–72—288
T3	Sam Snead	70–73–74–71—288
T5	Dow Finsterwald	74–73–73–69—289
T5	Ed Furgol	70–71–74–74—289
T5	Gary Player	71–74–74–70—289
8	Bo Wininger	69–72–77–72—290
T9	Don January	73–75–72–71—291
T9	Arnold Palmer	74–73–73–71—291

Nicklaus, in the early stages of building a reputation as the best clutch putter ever to play the game, holed the bogey putt. "It was a very big putt," he told the media after the round.

Still, the challenges from other contenders continued to mount. Lema birdied the 13th hole to get to even par, tied with Nicklaus. And Snead birdied the 15th to take the lead alone, two ahead of Jack.

Nicklaus gathered himself to hit a good drive on 13 and reached the green with a two-iron. Two putts from 60 feet, the second one a testy five-footer, gave him a birdie—finally, his first of the day. Just as importantly, Player and Snead fell back just as quickly as they had risen.

Player bogeyed 17 and 18 to drop to one-over for the tournament. He lamented that his final-round 70 could have been much better if not for some missed short putts. "I hit the ball poorly the first three rounds, but today I played so well I could hardly believe it."

Snead three-putted from 50 feet for a bogey on the 16th, missing a four-foot putt. Now he was tied with Nicklaus for the lead. He was playing remarkable golf for a 50-year-old, but could he pull off a fourth Masters title? The gallery wanted to see it. At the encouragement of the 18th-green announcer, they gave Sam a three-minute ovation as he reached the final green. Unfortunately, he had hit his four-iron approach into a bunker. After blasting out to eight feet, he couldn't make the putt. The fans groaned as the bogey dropped Snead to even par after a closing 71.

Nicklaus got a break on 15 when his second shot stopped in mud just short of water long and left, from where he got a free drop, hit a great third shot, but missed a four-foot birdie putt. Walking to the 16th green, he saw that he was now ahead by one since Snead had bogeyed 18. Nicklaus made it a two-stroke margin by holing a 13-foot birdie putt on 16.

Up ahead, Lema faced a downhill, big-breaking 25-foot birdie putt on 18 to get to one-under. He rolled it in ("prettiest thing I ever saw," Lema would say) and hurled his ball back down the fairway in celebration.

After four lackluster years on tour, Lema had come into his own with two victories in 1962 and had eight straight top-10 finishes coming into his Masters debut. He played all of his practice rounds with fellow Northern Californian Ken Venturi, and said that he got advice equivalent to playing the course for five years. "Most of the credit goes to Venturi, who has a lot of tough luck here," said Lema.

On the 17th fairway, Nicklaus heard the roar for Lema and knew he needed two pars to close out a victory. He got the first one with two putts from the front fringe on 17. Not wanting to flirt with trees on the right on 18, he pulled his tee shot to the left, finishing behind the ropes in mud trampled by spectators. He again got a free drop, selected a six-iron, and hit it 30 feet past the hole, leaving a downhiller to get down in two.

Nicklaus thought the first putt was in, but it slipped by the edge and trickled three feet past the hole. The short putt for the win looked like it might break out of the hole, but barely caught the left edge and dropped. "It looked like 86 feet," Nicklaus said at the media conference of the final putt. "I didn't see it go in; I just closed my eyes."

Lema watched on television as his chance at a playoff slipped away with Nicklaus' par. On the way to the awards ceremony to accept runner-up honors, Lema was met by Venturi (who had finished 34th) for congratulations and commiseration—both had tears in their eyes.

Nicklaus made only 11 birdies in the tournament but only nine bogeys on a week when the weather gods were capricious. His final-round 72 and 286 total were good enough to make him the youngest Masters champion—and prove that the Big Three were worthy of the nickname. He would go on to add the PGA Championship title later in the year.

Crowd Capacity Reached

In its coverage of the 1962 final round, the *Augusta Chronicle* ran a photo of a sea of humanity on the course with the headline, "Mob Scene in 26th Masters Tournament." Estimates of the weekend crowds ranged from 40,000 to 60,000 in various publications. While Augusta National, then, as now, didn't release attendance figures, it moved in 1963 to limit ticket sales for the first time to keep crowds at a manageable level. Based on parking capacity and advance ticket sales, tournament chairman Clifford Roberts announced that 5,000 tickets would be available at the gate on Thursday and Friday and 3,000 on Saturday and Sunday. Previously, walk-up ticket sales had been unrestricted. Augusta announced the following February that the policy would stand, with the amount of tickets available at the gate subject to the number sold in advance.

1964

Arnold Palmer arrived in Augusta in a slump—at least, that's what the press was calling it, given that he hadn't won a tournament since the previous October. It was the first time since 1956 Palmer had entered the Masters without having already posted a victory on the year. Also, while winning seven tournaments in 1963, he had been shut out in the majors for the first time since 1959.

Palmer was tired of reading and hearing about it. "It seems that everyone wants to tell me what's wrong with my game," he said on the eve of the tournament. "I've had slumps before. I'm not unduly alarmed about my game. Naturally, I'm not pleased."

The general assumption was that his victory drought was caused by a lack of focus and drive brought on by distracting business interests. Arnold pointed to something else as the reason for his slow start to 1964—quitting smoking in January had given him the jitters. He felt that he had gotten over it by now, though.

It should be clarified by what was meant by a Palmer "slump." He had gone all of 11 tournaments without a victory, 10 of them in 1964, while finishing second once and third twice. He ranked fourth on the money list. Such are the high standards he had set while winning 29 tournaments from 1960 to 1963.

Defending champion Jack Nicklaus was the favorite, though he had lost the third-round lead at the Greater Greensboro Open the week before with a final-round 73 for a T4. (He hadn't yet started his routine of skipping tournaments played immediately before major championships.) Gary Player was a huge question mark, having come down with tonsillitis upon arrival in Augusta. With a temperature of 101 on Monday of Masters week, he was prescribed penicillin by a local doctor and scheduled to have his tonsils out the Monday after the tournament.

Palmer and Player proved to be in fine form and health when the tournament began on Thursday, shooting 69s to head a quintet of players tied for the lead. The others were Bob Goalby, Australia's Kel Nagle, and "an unknown club pro from Charlotte, North Carolina," Davis Love Jr.

The 29-year-old Love, who qualified for the Masters by finishing T14 in the 1963 U.S. Open, told reporters that his wife was expecting their first child any time. That child, Davis Love III, would be born the day after the tournament, and would go on to leave his own mark on the Masters.

Palmer hit 17 greens and said his round was "pretty uninteresting" but that he would take three more like it. With greens softened by Wednesday rains, Nicklaus hit all 18 of them in regulation or better, so was disappointed with an opening 71 that included two-putting the first 17 greens, followed by a three-putt bogey from 15 feet on the 18th. (As with all reported greens hit and putt totals from before official stats began in 1980, it's possible that putting from the fringe was counted as a green hit.)

During the second round, a small plane flew overhead trailing a banner that said, "Go Arnie Go." Arnie's Army now had added an Air Force. Palmer didn't know who had arranged for the plane, and was a bit sheepish about it, but it was a day when he really did "go," building a four-stroke lead with a 68.

He finished with one of his trademark Augusta flourishes, collecting birdies on four of the last six holes. The round could have been even better, as he missed seven birdie or eagle putts of 12 feet or less, including a two-footer for birdie at No. 8 and a five-footer for eagle at 13. He termed it one of his best tee-to-green rounds ever.

Player was second at 141 after a ho-hum 72 that included 16 pars, while Nicklaus was in a 12-way tie for ninth at 144. Looking ahead to the weekend, Nicklaus said, "It all depends on Arnold. If he has a normal round, anybody at par or better can catch him. But if he keeps playing like this, forget it."

Palmer didn't give the field any openings in the third round, cruising around with a 69 for a 206 total. Even when he appeared to stumble with an approach shot into the water on the 11th, he recovered with a 60-yard pitch to within an inch of the hole to escape with a bogey. At just level par through 13, he birdied the next three holes to open a comfortable margin heading into Sunday. Bruce Devlin of Australia was second at 211, followed by Dave Marr, who made the field on a vote of past champions, at 212, and Player at 213.

1964		
1	Arnold Palmer	69–68–69–70—276
T2	Dave Marr	70–73–69–70—282
T2	Jack Nicklaus	71–73–71–67—282
4	Bruce Devlin	72–72–67–73—284
T5	Billy Casper	76–72–69–69—286
T5	Jim Ferrier	71–73–69–73—286
T5	Paul Harney	73–72–71–70—286
T5	Gary Player	69–72–72–73—286
T9	Dow Finsterwald	71–72–75–69—287
T9	Ben Hogan	73–75–67–72—287
T9	Tony Lema	75–68–74–70—287
T9	Mike Souchak	73–74–70–70—287

The biggest excitement on Saturday was stirred up by 51-year-old Ben Hogan, who rekindled memories of old glories with a 67 that included a 32 on the back nine. The gallery gave him a rousing ovation at the 18th green as he completed his second lowest round ever at the Masters.

Arnie's Air Force was back in the sky on Sunday, this time with a banner that said, "Arnie Go For 67." That was the score Palmer needed to break Hogan's record 274 total for 72 holes set in 1953. Arnie admitted he had the record in his sights at a couple points on the back nine, but he didn't quite get there as he settled for a 70 and a 276 total to win by six. He also just missed being the first player with four rounds in the 60s—a feat that wasn't accomplished until 2020 when Cameron Smith did it.

The day wasn't completely devoid of suspense. Devlin birdied the first two holes to pull within three strokes before falling back with a 73 to place fourth. Marr shot a 33 on the front nine, and he got within three when Palmer bogeyed the 10th. Anyone who was around in 1961 or 1962 knew that Palmer didn't have the tournament locked up at that point. However, Marr quickly bogeyed 11 and 12 to end his bid.

One more threat remained. Nicklaus eagled the 13th, where his second shot hit the flagstick, and birdied the 15th to pull within four. After rounds of 71–73–71, he was on his way to a 67. Shortly after the Nicklaus birdie on 15, Palmer birdied the 14th and added another at 15. Now it really was over.

Palmer had wrapped up a fourth Masters championship, and it was the first time he came to the 72nd hole with a comfortable lead so he could enjoy the walk up to the green and bask in the adoration of the crowd without tension. Still, the 18th green produced excitement. Marr, playing with Palmer, holed a 25-foot birdie putt for a 70 to tie Nicklaus for second place at 282. And Palmer finished in appropriate fashion by sinking a 15-footer for a birdie to earn a final roar.

"I guess this is the most exciting victory I've ever had," said Palmer, referring to the overall experience rather than a thrilling climax, and admitting, "When I teed off the first day, the question mark was as big in my eyes as anyone's."

While not reining in his aggressive style, Palmer was very pleased with a week in which he made only six bogeys. "It seems to me I waste a couple of shots every week I play—careless shots and careless putts. It seems to be the way I am. This week I decided not to be careless. I hit some shots that were not too good, but they weren't careless shots. I actually feel that I did not waste a shot."

Very few would have predicted at the time that it would be the 34-year-old Palmer's last major championship title. While coming to perhaps a premature end, his total of seven major victories included four at the Masters, where Augusta National proved the ideal setting for the game's most dynamic player to flourish.

Hat Trick

Arnold Palmer typically played without a hat, but felt he needed protection from the sun at the Masters this year due to a skin condition on his face. He tried a different hat each day in the last two practice rounds and the first round but didn't like any of them—and neither did his wife, Winnie. Before the second round, she handed him a visor to wear. He found that to be more comfortable; what's more, he shot a 68 to take a four-stroke lead, so he stuck with the visor the rest of the way.

1965

Recognizing the importance of preparation for the Masters, Jack Nicklaus initiated a new routine in 1965. The game's young star increased his focus on the year's first major by coming to Augusta the week before the tournament and playing six practice rounds through Saturday (in future years, four rounds would be the norm). He then left town, returning Monday evening for a final tune-up Tuesday and Wednesday.

Those pre-tournament sessions showed Nicklaus was ready for a run at a second Masters title—he was 19 under par in the six early practice rounds and added a 67 on Tuesday of Masters week. "I'm in a much better frame of mind this year," he said that Tuesday. "Last year I was tense."

Defending champion Arnold Palmer came into the tournament in something more like a slump than his purported slump the year before. He hadn't won since the previous May, and in the six tournaments he entered before the Masters he had finished better than ninth only once. "My game is not quite what I like it to be," he admitted, but added, "I always feel better in Augusta. Maybe I'm a little more confident here." Four victories at a place will do that for you.

The weather was perfect on Thursday, with very little wind, and players took advantage as 33 of them broke par—far surpassing the record of 20 at the time. The assault was led by Gary Player with a 65, one stroke off the tournament record. "I really was trying to shoot 64," said the South African battler, noting that he had done that in a practice round in 1959. Doing it in the tournament is a different matter. Since Lloyd Mangrum shot his 64 in 1940, only two players had even managed 65s—Cary Middlecoff in 1955 and Dow Finsterwald in 1962. Player came close to the record with four birdies on the front nine and three on the back in a bogey-free round.

Nicklaus wasn't free of tension at the start, hooking his drive on the first hole into the trees, but he had an opening, hit an eight-iron to eight feet, and made a birdie. Four-under through eight holes, he slowed down a bit but still was in good position with a 67 that put him in a four-way tie for second.

Palmer complained of his putting entering the week and had more cause for concern after not making a putt longer than three feet in shooting a 70, with his four birdies coming on the par fives.

Arnie changed putters in the second round, and immediately holed a 15-foot putt for a birdie on the first hole. But he pointed to chipping, not putting, as the reason for his second-round 68 that included a chip-in birdie on the third hole and a couple of other chips within inches.

The 68 was the low score on a day when the wind picked up and the greens were baked by the sun, making it hard to hold approach shots. Another factor, the players said, was a set of harder-than-usual pin positions. The positions were, perhaps not coincidentally, chosen on the day after low scoring. Only four players broke par in the second round.

Conditions were such that Player pronounced himself quite happy with a 73. Nicklaus weathered an awful three-hole stretch when he bogeyed the 11th and 12th with poor chip shots and bogeyed the 13th with an ill-advised three-wood second shot from pine needles that found the water. He recovered with birdies on 15 and 16 for a 71.

The Big Three all sat on 138 totals and were in a three-way tie for the lead. The stage was set for a battle of the titans on the weekend.

As it turned out, there was only one titan this week. The anticipated drama among the three never unfolded. Instead, there was sheer awe at the performance turned in by Nicklaus. The kid from Ohio overpowered the course and blew away the field with a third-round 64 to surge into a five-stroke lead.

The young Nicklaus possessed such length off the tee that he made Augusta National look small. He had given a sign of things to come in 1964 when he reached the 15th green with a seven-iron second shot after a drive estimated at 370 yards during his final-round 67. This time he reached the 13th and 15th with five-irons and the uphill eighth with a three-iron. But it was a recovery from a poor tee shot at the other par five, the second, that lit the fuse for his record-tying round.

He was deep in the trees to the right of the fairway with almost no way out. Yet, he somehow managed to spy a narrow opening and threaded a three-iron through it. Nicklaus then hit a pitching wedge from 105 yards to 23 feet and made the putt for an unlikely birdie. More birdies followed at the fourth (18 feet), sixth (22 feet), seventh (two feet after a pitching wedge approach), and eighth (two-putt from 75 feet) for a 31 that tied the record for the front nine.

On the back nine, Nicklaus' two-putt birdie at 13 was routine, his birdie at 15 less so after finding a couple of trees in his way after a drive to the left. His five-iron second shot didn't draw enough and finished to the right of the green, from where he pitched to two feet. His eighth birdie of the day came at the 16th on a six-iron to eight feet. There were no bogeys, with the only missed green coming at 17, where

1965

1	Jack Nicklaus	67–71–64–69—271
T2	Arnold Palmer	70–68–72–70—280
T2	Gary Player	65–73–69–73—280
4	Mason Rudolph	70–75–66–72—283
5	Dan Sikes	67–72–71–75—285
T6	Gene Littler	71–74–67–74—286
T6	Ramon Sota	71–73–70–72—286
T8	Frank Beard	68–77–72–70—287
T8	Tommy Bolt	69–78–69–71—287
10	George Knudson	72–73–69–74—288

his eight-iron spun back to the front fringe and he got up and down with no problem.

In his book *My Story*, Nicklaus wrote, "I have never before and have never since played quite as fine a complete round of golf in a major championship.... I drove the ball great distances, hit it virtually dead straight with the irons, putted the eyes out of it, never fumbled a strategy decision, never was nervous, felt all the while as though golf was one of the simplest human activities, wanted to go on murdering par forever and a day, and had an absolute ball."

Finally, somebody had matched Mangrum's 64 of 25 years earlier. The round boosted Nicklaus to the 54-hole record with a 202 total.

Player shot a fine score, a 69, but it was hampered by a couple of bogeys and found himself five strokes behind in second place at 207—the only player closer than eight strokes. Palmer missed putts of two feet and 18 inches on the first six holes and ended up with a 72 for 210 and a tie for third with Dan Sikes. "It was all putting. I got very disgusted with myself today," said Arnold.

Theoretically, Jack Burke Jr.'s comeback from eight strokes behind in 1956 could have given Palmer a sliver of hope entering the final round, but the chances of a Nicklaus collapse were slim. Player was the only one with a realistic—but small—chance. He birdied the second hole before Nicklaus teed off, but then bogeyed Nos. 3, 4, and 5. And that was it.

In any case, Nicklaus didn't fall back. Quite the contrary: He posted the day's best round with a 69 for a 271 total that was three strokes better than Hogan's 72-hole record of 1953. His victory margin was a record nine strokes over Player (70) and Palmer (73).

Nicklaus got around the front nine in 35 and saw he was comfortably ahead. After a birdie from 25 feet at the 12th, he knew he had the victory wrapped up and began thinking about Hogan's record, which he could beat by two by parring in. For a change, he didn't birdie either the 13th or 15th, with his only three-putt green of the tournament coming on the latter hole. Nicklaus got one last birdie when he nearly holed a nine-iron at the 17th and enjoyed the accolades of the crowd on the closing hole.

"It was the most enjoyable round of golf I've ever played in my life," he said afterward. "Completely relaxed."

Saying that Augusta National and the Masters were his favorite course and tournament, Nicklaus voiced his satisfaction at the way he had won it. "Two years ago, I felt that several players let me win when they faltered. But this time I was in control all the way."

For the week, he hit 62 of the 72 greens in regulation, had 22 birdies and only five bogeys. He demonstrated more than just power; in fact, he won the tournament on the par threes, where he was seven-under for the week compared to Player at four-over and Palmer at five-over.

At the awards ceremony, Bobby Jones called it "the greatest tournament performance in all of golfing history" and later in the evening told a group of writers that Nicklaus "plays a game with which I am not familiar."

The victory was special to Nicklaus for another reason. Up to that point in his career, the crowds hadn't warmed to him; indeed, they often openly rooted against him when Palmer was in the picture. That changed in 1965 at Augusta, where the crowds were won over by his outstanding play and appreciative demeanor, providing shouts of encouragement as well as birdie roars.

"I was at last beginning to emerge from the shadow of Arnold, and was becoming a golfer people could enjoyably follow and yell and holler and whoop for," Nicklaus wrote in *My Story*. "I had hit the shots in Augusta that week, but the ten or twenty or thirty thousand people who had watched them were more responsible for the way those shots came out than they will ever know."

1966

After Jack Nicklaus won in 1965, defending champion Arnold Palmer said to him after the green jacket ceremony, "We've got odd and even years sewn up here so I expect you to put the green coat on me next year." The two had alternated victories, Palmer in 1962 and '64 and Nicklaus 1963 and '65. Nicklaus responded, good-naturedly, "I hope I can end that string."

Nicklaus did indeed end it, as well as the hex on defending champions, but it came about in a much different fashion than his triumph of the previous year.

After feeling stale at the end of the 1965 season, Nicklaus decided that for the sake of longevity he should cut back his schedule. He played only four events before the Masters in 1966 and understandably didn't feel tournament sharp. On the Saturday before the tournament, Nicklaus played a practice round with Ben Hogan, and it was reported that the 53-year-old legend outscored the 26-year-old star, 68–72. Hogan hadn't finished better than sixth since 1955, but sounded a warning that he might be a threat this time. "I'm here to win, not just to show up," he said. "I'm playing well. In fact, I'm playing better than I have in 10 years."

Nicklaus received tragic news on Wednesday evening—four close friends (two couples) had died in the crash of a small, private plane headed from Ohio to Georgia for the Masters. With that weighing on his mind, Nicklaus nonetheless went out and shot the best round of the day Thursday, a 68 that gave him a three-stroke lead on a windy day.

He hit what was becoming his traditional duck-hook off the first tee, this time going through the trees into the ninth fairway, from where he hit a four-iron to 25 feet and made the putt for a birdie. That was the catalyst to a 33 on the front nine.

The only player to go without a bogey on the day, Nicklaus added a birdie at the 13th for his four-under round.

The stage seemed set for another runaway for the Golden Bear, but this is where the plot took a decidedly different turn. Nicklaus wasn't himself on Friday, shooting a 76, matching his highest Masters score, one that he had turned in as a 19-year-old amateur. He hit the ball reasonably well, but his putting was downright inept—five three-putts, three of them from within 15 feet, and seven putts missed from five feet and less. "I missed a few to the right and made a slight adjustment. Then I missed a few to the left," said a shell-shocked Nicklaus after the round.

Paul Harney took advantage of an early tee time to shoot a 68 for a 143 total that didn't attract much attention when he finished, but he ended up tied for the lead with England's Peter Butler (71) after the wind picked up in the afternoon. The field was so bunched that leading didn't mean much, especially with five players one stroke back, including Nicklaus, Palmer, and Doug Sanders, the hottest player in golf with wins in the last two tournaments. Hogan, making good on his pre-tournament proclamation, was a threat, shooting a 71 with 17 pars and a birdie at 18 to stand at 145.

Saturday produced a round of volatility, with some notable surges forward and even more movements backward, often by the same player at different points in the round. At the end of the day, nobody was under par for 54 holes, with Nicklaus and Tommy Jacobs tied for the lead at 216.

Jack surged ahead with a 33 on the front nine before coming to grief at the 12th hole with a double bogey from a plugged lie in the back bunker. He then took three from the fringe and failed to birdie the 13th and more than negated a birdie on 15 with an uncharacteristic finish of bogeys on 17 and 18 for a 72.

"It's kind of silly. I've had two opportunities to run away from the field and blown them both," Nicklaus said. "And the field's had two opportunities to run away from me and blown them both. Maybe nobody wants to win."

Conversely, a round pivoting from woefulness to brilliance was turned in by Gay Brewer, who was four over through 10 holes (six over for the tournament at that point) and birdied the next four, all on putts of between 10 and 25 feet. A 33 on the back nine gave him a 72 and a 218 total that put him very much in the hunt.

A massive gallery followed the pairing of Palmer and Hogan—the first time they had ever played together in a tournament. They fit right in with the up-and-down pattern. The duo combined for five three-putts on the front nine, Hogan shooting a 38 and Palmer a 37, before both unleashed some fireworks on the inward nine and then slipped up again at the end. Hogan chipped in for a birdie on 10, holed a 30-foot putt for a birdie on 11, and reached the 13th green in two for another birdie to pull within one of the lead. He bogeyed 15 and 17, finishing with a 73 for 218. Palmer fell to three-over for the round when he bogeyed the 13th with a second shot in the creek for the second straight day, fought back with birdies on 14 and 15, then three-putted for a bogey on 16 and shot a 74 for 218.

Hogan, in a rare appearance in the press room (usually he was interviewed at his locker), sitting beside Palmer, said, "I want to apologize to Arnie for being so jittery on the greens."

Gene Littler took the cake on this day of extremes, going out in 42 and setting a record on the back nine with a 30. Anyway, he was out of it at 224.

The steadiest round was turned in by co-leader Jacobs, and he spiced up a 15-par round with a 40-foot eagle putt on the 13th. His 70 matched the best round of the day.

The high scoring was most likely due to the poor condition of the fairways and greens following an unusually rough winter. In order to preserve the grass, the fairways weren't cut as low as usual, making it more difficult to hit crisp, controlled approach shots to very firm greens.

The numbers on the leaderboard remained green on Sunday, with the exception of one player. Brewer got a red "1" beside his name when he birdied the ninth for a 33 on the front nine and a string of red "1s" as he parred the first eight holes on the back nine. Brewer's second shot on 18 went 60 feet beyond the hole. His downhill putt rolled seven feet past, and his second putt hit the hole but spun out. With other contenders still on the course, Brewer, wearing a look of utter dejection, could only wait to see if his score of 288 would hold up.

He had already beaten his playing partner, Palmer, who was tied for the lead at even par for the tournament through eight holes before Brewer's ninth-hole birdie. Arnie went out in 34. His putter failed him as he missed five putts under 10 feet on the back nine. Two strokes behind coming to the 18th, he fired at the pin in an effort to get the birdie that would have given him a chance to tie Brewer, but he found a bunker and made a bogey for a 72 and a 290 total.

Next came Jacobs, playing in the following twosome. He fell to two over for the round and tournament with a bogey on the 10th, three off the lead. Birdies on 13 and 15 got him back to even par, and Brewer's bogey put him in a tie for first. Jacobs' tee shot on 18 was mishit and squirted to the right, hitting a tree. It caromed into the fairway, but a long way from the green, from where he hit an outstanding four-wood to 20 feet and made a par.

Various would-be contenders fell by the wayside with too many bogeys along the way, including Sanders, Harney, Don January, and Ray Floyd.

Finally came Nicklaus, paired with Hogan in the marquee final-round twosome in very different circumstances than their practice round together eight days earlier. Under the pressure of the final round, Hogan's age caught up with him, and he faded out of the picture with a 77. Nicklaus dug himself a hole by playing the first 10 holes in two over with four bogeys and two birdies, falling three behind.

Things were looking grim when he didn't birdie the 13th. His drive hit a tree on 14 and bounced back into the fairway, still leaving him a healthy distance from the green. Jack hit what he called his best shot of the week, a three-iron to six feet, and he made the birdie putt. On 15 his drive veered left, leaving a couple of trees on a direct line to the green. Figuring it wasn't a time to lay up, he hit a hook with a two-iron that came off perfectly, leading to a two-putt birdie to get to even par.

Nicklaus hit another great iron on 17, leaving a birdie putt from three-and-a-half feet. Brewer had made his closing bogey by that point, so Nicklaus would surely make the putt for the lead and walk away with the victory, right? Not this week. He

1966

1	Jack Nicklaus	68–76–72–72—288*
2	Tommy Jacobs	75–71–70–72—288
3	Gay Brewer	74–72–72–70—288
T4	Arnold Palmer	74–70–74–72—290
T4	Doug Sanders	74–70–75–71—290
T6	Don January	71–73–73–75—292
T6	George Knudson	73–76–72–71—292
T8	Raymond Floyd	72–73–74–74—293
T8	Paul Harney	75–68–76–74—293
T10	Billy Casper	71–75–76–72—294
T10	Jay Hebert	72–74–73–75—294
T10	Bob Rosburg	74–71–73–77—294

*Nicklaus (70) won playoff over Jacobs (72), Brewer (78)

pulled the putt so badly it didn't even come close.

On 18, Nicklaus had a birdie putt from 40 feet, a shorter version of Brewer's down-hiller. Judging the speed and line almost perfectly, Nicklaus missed by an inch and tapped in for a 72 to set up a three-way playoff the next day.

Looking back on the week, the defending champion mused, "I don't know how I'm still in the tournament. But I don't intend to blow it again."

While Nicklaus felt fortunate to be in the playoff, Jacobs was happy to be there for a different reason. The 31-year-old was a four-time winner on the PGA Tour, but his game had deteriorated in 1965 and he contemplated getting a club job. In the midst of fiddling with his swing, he didn't have a top-25 finish on the year. The 34-year-old Brewer, on the other hand, was coming on strong, having won four times since the previous fall.

However, it was Brewer who fell flat in the 18-hole playoff, as he struggled to a 78 while Nicklaus and Jacobs fought a tight battle.

Jacobs holed a 30-foot birdie putt on the first hole; Nicklaus answered with a three-wood second shot that hit the flagstick to set up a birdie four at the second. Both played the first eight holes in two-under and bogeyed the ninth for 35s on the front nine.

The pivotal holes were 10 and 11. Both missed the 10th green to the left; Jacobs hit a weak chip and bogeyed while Nicklaus saved par. While Jacobs was studying a 12-foot birdie putt at the 11th, Nicklaus jolted him by holing a 25-footer for a birdie. When Jacobs couldn't match, the margin was two. The pair made the same score on every remaining hole, with bogeys on the 12th and birdies on the 15th, Nicklaus holing a clutch 12-footer there to match Jacobs' two-putt birdie.

There was still some suspense on the 18th hole, where Nicklaus drove left and pulled his approach shot into the gallery left of the green. With Jacobs putting for a birdie from 25 feet, there was still a chance for a two-stroke swing, especially as Nicklaus faced a tough lie on bare ground. Choosing a putter, he deftly ran the ball up the slope and onto the green five feet from the hole. Jacobs missed and Nicklaus made, giving him a 70 for a two-stroke margin and a third Masters title in just five starts as a pro.

The first win by a defender created a dilemma at the awards ceremony, where the previous year's champion traditionally puts the green jacket on the winner. The solution: Nicklaus put the jacket on himself.

It's a Sellout

On March 15, three weeks before the start of the tournament, Masters chairman Clifford Roberts announced that series badges were sold out. In fact, orders exceeded supply. Those whose orders were unfulfilled got first crack at advance daily tickets, which were sold out by March 29. In 1965, advance series badges had sold out the day before the tournament, and advance daily tickets for weekend rounds were gone before the weekend arrived. This situation resulted in would-be spectators being turned away, because there were no gate sales on Saturday and Sunday. This year—as in all future years—there would be no tickets available at the gate on any of the four tournament days. In 1967, Roberts, while not announcing a number, said that there was a 10 percent reduction in the number of badges sold, presumably for the purpose of keeping the crowd at a more manageable number.

1967–1973

The Darkhorse Era

This was a stretch of years when relatively unheralded players ruled, while Arnold Palmer was exiting his prime, Jack Nicklaus turned in some uncharacteristically mediocre showings, and Gary Player never quite scaled the leaderboard. For five of the seven winners in this era, the Masters was their only major championship victory. Billy Casper, the 1970 champion, owned two U.S. Opens and ultimately 51 tour victories; however, throughout his career he found himself in the shadow of the Big Three. Nicklaus did win in 1972, but that year produced one of the dullest final rounds in tournament history with high scoring and little suspense. Another instance of events not following the script came in 1968, when Roberto De Vicenzo missed what should have been a playoff when he signed a scorecard showing a score one stroke higher than he actually made.

Nevertheless, the tournament's growth continued unabated. The television blackout that had been imposed within 225 miles of Augusta on what proved to be the unfounded fear that TV coverage would hurt ticket sales was lifted in 1969. Demand for tickets continued to grow to the extent that sales for season badges were limited to a mailing list of past patrons, and that list was closed in 1972 when a waiting list was started. To provide the unprivileged masses a chance to walk the Augusta National grounds, practice round tickets were still sold at the gate.

1967

The word "three-peat" hadn't yet entered the English lexicon, but all eyes were on Jack Nicklaus as he tried for a third straight Masters. He didn't come in on a roll, with his only win on the year coming in his first start, and said that his pre-Masters week practice sessions had not been as successful as those in previous years.

The other member of what was now being referred to as the Big Two in Masters previews, Arnold Palmer, was feeling good. He already had two victories, three additional top-three finishes, and a spot atop the money list. "For the first time in some years, I find myself at Masters time without having to worry about one aspect of my game," he said.

Did anybody else have a chance after five years of Nicklaus or Palmer at the top? Sure, said 1966 U.S. Open champion Billy Casper. "It's not a closed corporation."

One player who felt he had a chance was Gay Brewer. In his previous start, two weeks before the Masters, he opened 66–64–61 at the Pensacola Open, winning with a 26-under 262 total. The 35-year-old had let the Masters slip away with his three-putt on the 72nd hole the previous year but, coming off his Pensacola performance and some excellent practice rounds, he said on Wednesday, "I feel real good. My confidence is up. I want the Masters—I think I can win it."

The golf course featured a pair of new fairway bunkers on the left side of the 18th, the area where Nicklaus had habitually bashed his tee shot, because it lacked trouble. Now, he said he was thinking of hitting a one-iron off the tee to stay short of the first bunker.

For the second year in a row, players were complaining about relatively long grass in the fairways making it hard to control iron shots. That difficulty and shifting winds contributed to only one sub-70 round being posted on Thursday, a 67 by Bert Yancey, playing in his first Masters. The 28-year-old attended the United States Military Academy at West Point before being discharged in his senior year when he suffered what was termed a nervous breakdown (he was later diagnosed with bipolar disorder). He recovered and joined the pro tour in 1964 and came into his own in 1966 with three victories.

Julius Boros, second on the money list at age 47, was tied for second at 70 with Casper and amateur Downing Gray. Nicklaus had a ho-hum 72, saying, "I'm not particularly concerned," while Palmer had only one birdie in a 73.

Brewer had a golden opportunity for a low round when he birdied Nos. 6 and 7 and eagled 8 to shoot a 33 on the front nine. He came crashing down with a four-putt from 20 feet to double bogey the 12th and a second shot into the water on the 13th on the way to a 40 on the back for a 73. Yet *Golf World* reported that Brewer, a relatively mild soul who was not known for cockiness, said that day: "I'm playing better than anyone out there."

The Kentuckian backed it up the next day, hitting every green in regulation and shooting a 68 with four birdies and 14 pars to stand one shot out of the lead at 141. He lamented the mistakes on 12 and 13 the previous day, but said he felt "more confident, calmer than last year."

Yancey stayed in front at 140 with a wild 73 that included six birdies and seven bogeys, two of the stumbles coming on the last two holes. Joining Brewer at 141 were Boros, Bobby Nichols, and 22-year-old Englishman Tony Jacklin.

The biggest news of the day, however, was Nicklaus shockingly shooting a 79 to miss the cut with a 151 total. "Everything I tried went wrong," he said. "I've had good luck in this tournament. Maybe I'm due for something bad." Palmer had a second straight day with only one birdie, but at least he was still in the field with another 73 for 146.

Arnie finally got it going in the third round at four-under through 16 holes to shoot up the leaderboard. Then he three-putted from 20 feet to bogey the 17th and drove into one of the new fairway bunkers to bogey the 18th, finishing the day four strokes out of the lead with eight players in front of him.

The story of the third round was Ben Hogan. The 54-year-old legend birdied the first four holes of the back nine, causing fans to flock to his gallery and welcome him to every green with heartfelt cheers and applause. It was a stirring march to the clubhouse as Hogan added a birdie at 15 and dramatically holed a 25-foot birdie putt at 18 for a record-tying 30 on the back nine and a 66. For the second straight year, he sat two strokes out of the lead through 54 holes.

The round was all the more remarkable, considering that upon receiving his Masters invitation, Hogan had told Bobby Jones he wouldn't be able to play because of a shoulder ailment. Jones encouraged him to at least come and tee off. Ultimately, Hogan decided to get cortisone shots and felt well enough to compete.

"I said I could come but that I hadn't played any golf and didn't think I could play well," Hogan said. Of course, there was the matter of putting, where Hogan was highly uncomfortable—he missed two 18-inch putts in the first two rounds.

"Once I have the putter behind the ball, sometimes I can move and sometimes I can't," he admitted. "But I conquered it out there today."

A trio of players were tied for the lead at 211—Yancey (71), Boros (70), and Nichols (70). In a turnaround from the day before, Yancey was steady with two birdies and one bogey. As a Masters first-timer, he was expected to succumb to the pressure of leading, but it hadn't happened so far. "Nothing has gotten the better of me yet," he said. "I know I should feel differently, but I don't."

Boros was the one with the up-and-down round, hitting into the water to double bogey the 12th and ultimately chipping in on the 18th for his sixth birdie of the day. In terms of personality, though, the laid-back Boros always stayed on an even keel. He relaxed on Saturday morning before his round by fishing on the pond at Augusta National's Par 3 Course.

Nichols, playing with Boros, double bogeyed the 17th when forced to hit a left-handed shot out of the trees, then earned a share of the lead with an 18-foot birdie putt at the 18th. "I'm playing as well as I ever have in my life," said the 1964 PGA champion.

Just as he had done on Thursday, Brewer squandered an opportunity to lead. Two-under through 10 holes after a birdie at 10, he double bogeyed the 11th after a chunked pitch and bogeyed 18 from finding one of the fairway bunkers and settled for a 72 and 213 total, two behind.

Brewer and Nichols played together on Sunday, a comfortable pairing for two Kentuckians who had become good friends on tour. Both played college golf on football scholarships magnanimously given out by coach Bear Bryant—Brewer at the University of Kentucky and Nichols at Texas A&M, where Bryant had moved by the time Bobby came along four years later.

"We talked to each other out there a lot, and we were both hoping that one of us would get in," said Nichols after the round.

Among other contenders, Palmer shot a 69 that only got him a fourth-place finish. Hogan was spent after his great performance of Saturday and shot a final-round 77, just as he had done the year before. He underwent shoulder surgery later in the year and never played another Masters, retiring from competition altogether except for a three-tournament farewell run in 1969.

1967		
1	Gay Brewer	73–68–72–67—280
2	Bobby Nichols	72–69–70–70—281
3	Bert Yancey	67–73–71–73—284
4	Arnold Palmer	73–73–70–69—285
5	Julius Boros	71–70–70–75—286
T6	Paul Harney	73–71–74–69—287
T6	Gary Player	75–69–72–71—287
T8	Tommy Aaron	75–68–74–71—288
T8	Lionel Hebert	77–71–67–73—288
T10	Roberto De Vicenzo	73–72–74–71—290
T10	Bruce Devlin	74–70–75–71—290
T10	Ben Hogan	74–73–66–77—290
T10	Mason Rudolph	72–76–72–70—290
T10	Sam Snead	72–76–71–71—290

Yancey and Boros were in the twosome immediately behind Brewer and Nichols, and there was a four-way tie between that quartet early on the back nine, Brewer at two-under for the day and the others at even par. Boros dropped back with a bogey on 11, where he hit his second shot in the water and one-putted, and a double bogey on 12, where he didn't hit his tee shot in the water but three-putted. He ended up with a 75 and finished fifth.

Brewer took control at the 13th, hitting the green with a four-iron second shot and two-putting for a birdie, while Nichols knocked a four-wood second into a greenside bunker and made a par. When Yancey three-putted for a par behind them, Brewer was a stroke ahead.

Nichols hit his approach shot to six feet at the 14th only to watch his friend hole a 20-footer for birdie before he made his. It was much the same at 15. Nichols hit the green in two and made an easy two-putt birdie, while Brewer knocked a four-wood over the green, chipped to 10 feet, and made the putt for a third straight birdie to stay one ahead.

Yancey tried to hang in there as he birdied the 15th, but bogeys on 16 and 17 left him with a 73 and third place. It was up to the Kentucky duo now.

Routine pars at 16 were followed by a Brewer drive that struck a tree and bounced backward on 17. It was then that dark thoughts of the previous year crept into Gay's mind. He gave himself a pep talk, "but I can't tell you what it was," he said after the round. It worked, as he saved par with a four-wood that nearly got to the green, a fine chip, and a four-foot putt.

At the 18th, Brewer resolved not to get above the hole, as he had done in 1966. This time he hit his approach onto the very front of the green. When Nichols missed a 20-foot birdie putt, Brewer made sure not to knock his 18-footer past the hole, leaving himself an uphill putt from a foot-and-a-half for the win. He tapped it in, erasing the year-old demons. "Experience counts for something here," he said of his strategy on 18.

Nichols could only admire what his buddy had done. "I said I would be happy with a 70 and that's what I shot, but it simply wasn't good enough," said the runner-up.

It would have been good enough on many days, but not on this one when Brewer shot a 67 that he called "the greatest round of golf I've ever played."

Rare Bird

Bruce Devlin spiced the opening round with a double eagle on the 530-yard eighth hole, the first double eagle at the Masters since Gene Sarazen's on the 15th hole of the final round in 1935. While that one had propelled Sarazen to a victory, Devlin's perfect strike with a four-wood up the hill to a blind green was a lone highlight to a first-round 74. "It really was the only decent shot I hit all day," said the 29-year-old Australian, who was recovering from infected blisters in his feet and said his practice rounds were "pathetic." The double eagle ultimately helped him post a T10 finish.

1968

The Greater Greensboro Open, which preceded the Masters on the schedule, ended up with a 36-hole finish on the Monday of Masters week due to a Friday rainout and Sunday being a national day of mourning for the assassination of Martin Luther King Jr. That meant little practice time at Augusta National for Greensboro competitors, especially with rain on Tuesday afternoon (except for Arnold Palmer, who flew his private jet to and from Augusta on Sunday for a day of practice).

It didn't bother Billy Casper, who won at Greensboro and declared, "I've never felt better about my [Masters] chances. I hope this is my year."

Casper's Masters record wasn't exactly bad—five times T11 or better in 11 starts. But with no finish better than fourth, it wasn't quite commensurate with the overall record of a 36-year-old who was well on his way to 51 PGA Tour victories. One of the best putters in the game at most venues, he mysteriously seemed to struggle on the greens at Augusta National.

His Augusta fortunes took a turn for the better on Thursday as Casper grabbed the first-round lead with a 68, holing a 55-foot putt on the 17th, continuing to strike an optimistic tone, saying he had a new-found "inner peace."

Five players were one stroke back at 69, including Roberto De Vicenzo, a globe-trotting Argentinian who won the 1967 British Open. He never played a full season in the U.S., though he performed well in part-time appearances through the 1950s. He rarely played in America in the early 1960s, then made a partial return with six U.S. starts in 1966 (with a win) and nine in 1967 (a second and a third). Still going strong, he would celebrate his 45th birthday on Sunday. "I hope to see you right here [Sunday]," he said in the press interview room. "If I win, I buy everybody big Coca-Cola."

Also at 69 was Jack Nicklaus, the tournament favorite despite going winless in six events on the year. "This is the first tournament I've been ready for," he said before it started.

Bob Goalby bogeyed the 18th to just miss out on the second-place tie, finishing with a 70. The 39-year-old could take no encouragement from his Masters record (eight appearances, only two previous subpar rounds, and a best finish of T25) nor his recent form (previous six tournaments: T45, cut, T59, T54, withdrew after 78, cut). Coming off a strong year in 1967, when he finished 10th on the money list, Goalby nonetheless decided to make a swing change to combat a hook that had plagued him throughout his career. Sticking with it despite the disheartening results, the adjustment began to click during Masters practice rounds, where he shot 67–66–67 on Monday to Wednesday.

It wasn't Casper's year after all. Feeling sick from something he ate at breakfast—"probably the sausage," he said—Billy shot a 75 on the way to a T16 finish. Palmer was even worse, missing the Masters cut for the first time with rounds of 72–79 that duplicated Nicklaus' scores of the previous year.

Those high scores were especially surprising coming on a day of favorable conditions. Don January (68) and Gary Player (67) assumed the lead at 139, January chipping in for an eagle at 15 a day after a chip-in eagle at 13. Player said he wasn't taking anything for granted. "Augusta National is such a humbling course that one couldn't relax even if he had a 10-shot lead with nine holes to play."

Frank Beard had the best round of the day, a 65, saying he struck the ball about the same as his opening-round 75. He figured five strokes of the difference was accounted for by the lack of wind and another five by better putting. He was tied with Nicklaus (71) and Goalby (70) at 140.

The five players at 142 included Bruce Devlin (73), who was six-under for the tournament through nine holes before missing a short par putt at 10 and making a quadruple bogey at 11. He hit his second shot in the pond there, took a penalty drop, and his next shot finished in the tall grass that then grew on the green side of the water. He took a swing and barely moved the ball before getting out with his next swipe.

De Vicenzo also was at 73—142. The good-natured Argentinian said he played "like a monkey" on No. 8, where he went from the right trees to the left trees and "like a duck" on No. 15, where he hit his second shot in the water and made a par.

The third round was headed for a six-way tie for the lead at five-under as Player lined up a downhill 30-foot putt on the 18th green. When the South African holed the double-breaking putt it moved him to six-under, one ahead of five players who had already finished. The long putt was one of the few highlights on the greens for the 1961 champion, who had three three-putts in a 72.

January would have been six-under if he hadn't missed a three-foot birdie putt on the 18th. He also hit a long putt off the green into the hazard on 13; he was able to play from the bank but ultimately went putt-chip-putt-putt for a bogey. Devlin would have been the leader if not for his quadruple bogey of the day before; he had a 32 on the back nine Saturday for a 69 and five-under 211 total. Also at 211 were 25-year-old Ray Floyd (69), Beard (71), and Goalby (71).

Goalby headed to the practice tee after the round to try to fix the hook that leaked back into his game in the middle of the round. He was able to scramble for a par on the eighth, bogeyed the 10th, and got away with a big hook on the 13th, where he unintentionally drove it around the corner of the dogleg to set up a two-putt birdie.

De Vicenzo was one of three at 212 after a mostly uneventful round of 70, unable to buy a putt until a 10-footer for birdie dropped on the 18th, making up for a bogey on 17 with a miss from two feet.

Nicklaus was four strokes back at 214 after a disappointing 74 that included four three-putts and bogeys on 15 (second shot in the water) and 18 (left his second shot in the fairway bunker when it caught the lip). He remained optimistic that he could make a move on Sunday, which he did with a 67. It got him nowhere, however, with his score bettered by three players who started out ahead of, or even with, him.

The final round produced the lowest scoring average in the history of the tournament by nearly a stroke at 71.29 (the old record was 72.19 in 1963, lowered temporarily to 72.02 on Saturday). With greens that were a comfortable speed and holding approach shots, combined with little wind and generous pin placements, 30 of the field of 52 broke par.

It's hard to imagine a better start than De Vicenzo had. He holed a 135-yard nine-iron for an eagle on the first hole, then came within inches of eagles on the next two. After a second shot over the green, he chipped close on the par-five second, and hit his approach within inches of the hole on the third. By playing the first three holes in four-under, De Vicenzo took the lead from Player before Gary had even teed off.

"After first three holes, I think maybe I make 17 birdies and eagle," Roberto said after the round. He didn't quite do that, but he did birdie the eighth with a chip and a tap-in for a 31 on the front nine.

Devlin was hot at the start, too, with birdies on the first three holes to get to eight-under and tie De Vicenzo until Roberto birdied the eighth. A string of 11 straight pars by Devlin wasn't enough to move forward on this day, and, with birdie-bogey on 15 and 16, he finished with a 69 and fourth place.

Goalby had been runner-up in two majors, the 1961 U.S. Open and 1962 PGA Championship. The southern Illinois native attended the University of Illinois on a football scholarship and ended up playing mostly on the baseball team there. After a stint in the service, he concentrated on golf, got a job as a club pro, and hit the tour in 1958 at the age of 28. Goalby won six times from 1958–62, then not again until once in 1967.

Trying to reestablish himself after his slow start in 1968—and make another bid at a major in the process—Goalby parred the first four holes of the final round before birdies at the fifth (six feet), sixth (18 feet from the fringe), and eighth (12 feet) got him to eight-under and in the thick of things with a 33 on the front nine.

Player didn't disappear entirely, countering an early bogey with birdies at Nos. 7 and 8 to get to seven-under. On a day when he said his putting was "pathetic," he couldn't get to eight-under until a birdie at 15, and even that was a missed opportunity as he couldn't convert a 10-foot eagle putt. Bogeys on the last two holes left him with a 72.

One more player thrust himself into the leading pack. Bert Yancey, who finished third in his Masters debut in 1967 and avowedly wanted to win the Masters more than any other tournament, started at four-under and shot a 33 on the front nine. Birdies at 13, 15, 16, and 17 shot him to nine-under to pull within one stroke of the lead. Yancey saved par from 12 feet at the 18th for a 65, but outstanding rounds by De Vicenzo and Goalby rendered his nine-under moot, placing him third for the tournament.

De Vicenzo handled the 12th with aplomb, making a birdie from 10 feet to get to 10-under and ahead by two. A 12-foot birdie putt on 15 restored the margin to two at 11-under shortly after the CBS telecast began. Goalby, meanwhile, kept himself from dropping back by chipping close for pars on 11 and 12. He had to lay up with his second shot on 13, then lofted a sand wedge to eight feet and birdied to go nine-under. When Goalby answered De Vicenzo's birdie on 15 with one of his own from 18 feet on 14, he was back within one.

De Vicenzo stayed ahead in what was now a two-man battle with a deft pitch from a tough spot on 16 to save par. It was going to take something special to catch him, and Goalby produced it with a three-iron second shot on 15 that cleared the water and landed softly enough to stop within 10 feet of the hole. Probably unaware, De Vicenzo nonetheless answered with an approach shot to four feet on the parallel 17th. The two hit their putts within a second of each other, CBS showing a split screen as De Vicenzo birdied and Goalby eagled to both reach 12-under.

As brilliant as they had been to this point, both players now made mistakes down the stretch. De Vicenzo hooked a four-iron long and left on the 18th, and, with spectators dancing to avert it, the ball rolled deep into the crowd. It wasn't all bad, having also rolled back toward pin high, where he wouldn't have to contend with the downhill slope of the green on his next shot. He was still left with a nasty hardpan lie, so he pulled out his putter and ran it six feet from the hole. The putt, which would have not only have kept a share of the lead but also given him a course record-tying 64 (or so it seemed), barely grazed the right lip. De Vicenzo trailed by one.

Goalby gave him a reprieve with a three-putt bogey from 40 feet on 17—his only three-putt of the week—to fall back to 11-under himself. Fearing a return of his hook, Goalby had taken a three-wood off the 17th tee and flared it to the right. He did the same thing on 18, hitting a tree and bounding into the fairway but leaving a long second shot. Goalby was up to the challenge. He cut a two-iron to the green some 45 feet from the hole.

As Goalby played the 18th, the television camera kept cutting to De Vicenzo sitting and watching from the scorer's table. That was odd, since Roberto had finished two twosomes ahead of Goalby and had already left the table only to return a few minutes later. It was also peculiar that De Vicenzo's playing partner, Tommy Aaron, was still at the table.

Goalby stroked his downhill putt to four feet left of the hole. With TV going back and forth between shots of Goalby and a glum-looking De Vicenzo, Bob lined up the par putt that the scoreboard showed he needed to make a playoff. With a firm stroke, he knocked it into the hole.

The two remaining twosomes finished their rounds, with announcer Pat Summerall repeatedly reminding viewers that CBS would broadcast the final holes of the 18-hole playoff the next day at 5:00 p.m. Then, as the last player was about to putt out, Summerall changed his tune. "Be sure you stay with us. We might have something of great importance to report to you.... There is a possibility there is some problem, some question, and we believe it might be with the manner in which [De Vicenzo] signed his scorecard."

Indeed, it was. When De Vicenzo and Aaron finished, they belatedly caught up with marking each other's scorecards, Roberto filling in Aaron's last five holes and Tommy marking De Vicenzo's last two. Unfortunately, Aaron wrote a 4 and a 5 instead of the 3 and 5 De Vicenzo had made. Roberto, in a daze because he thought he'd just lost the Masters with a bogey on the last hole, took a quick look at the card without checking it hole by hole, and signed. The scorer's table was in the open, with spectators only feet away. Adding to the confusion, an official was asking Roberto to come to the Butler cabin for a television interview.

He left the table but was called back from the cabin before he made it to the interview. Aaron had glanced at De Vicenzo's scorecard lying on the table and noticed the total 66. He was certain Roberto had shot a 65. Neither player had filled in the box for total; this was unnecessary, since the hole-by-hole scores were what was official once a player signed. A committee member at the table had added the scores and written in the 66. Aaron saw the offending "4" and knew that he had to point out the error.

Aaron was hoping that something could be done to rectify the situation. But he knew, and the officials knew, that under the Rules of Golf if a player signed for a score higher than he actually shot, the higher score would stand (if he signed for a lower score, he would be disqualified). There was no need to consult with the USGA. Masters Rules Committee chairman Isaac Grainger was a former USGA president and one of the foremost authorities on the Rules of Golf. Just to be sure, Grainger and other officials went to Bobby Jones, who was unable to leave his cabin because of his syringomyelia condition. All agreed there was no other choice. De Vicenzo would be stuck with the 66, a 10-under total, and second place.

"What a stupid I am," said a shell-shocked De Vicenzo, who handled the situation with grace. "We are professionals. We have to know rules. I sign wrong card, it is my fault.... I know Aaron feel like I feel. He probably feel worse."

As he was making a quick exit from the locker room, Aaron told reporters, "As soon as I took another look at the card, I knew it was wrong and I told the committee to get Roberto back. I thought the fact that I was still there might make a difference, but..."

Goalby said, "I'm very happy to have won the tournament. I'd be a liar if I told you anything else. But I sincerely regret this had to happen to Roberto, who is a wonderful guy.... I'm sorry I didn't have a chance to win the title outright in a playoff tomorrow."

That was the rub. Goalby unfortunately came out looking like a tainted champion, even though he might well have ended up the winner had there been a playoff. The fact that De Vicenzo was such a popular guy —"Everybody loves Roberto," announcer Henry Longhurst said during the telecast—just added to the angst of what seemed an unjust ending, especially to those unfamiliar with golf's rules.

1968		
1	Bob Goalby	70–70–71–66—277
2	Roberto De Vicenzo	69–73–70–66—278
3	Bert Yancey	71–71–72–65—279
4	Bruce Devlin	69–73–69–69—280
T5	Frank Beard	75–65–71–70—281
T5	Jack Nicklaus	69–71–74–67—281
T7	Tommy Aaron	69–72–72–69—282
T7	Raymond Floyd	71–71–69–71—282
T7	Lionel Hebert	72–71–71–68—282
T7	Jerry Pittman	70–73–70–69—282
T7	Gary Player	72–67–71–72—282

Telegrams poured into Augusta National that evening and the next day and, needless to say, they were overwhelmingly critical. Chairman Clifford Roberts defended the decision as unavoidable under the rules, but the Tuesday morning *Augusta Chronicle* published news that the club was considering ways to shield players from the distracting activity around the 18th green while checking and signing scorecards—a tacit admission of a degree of fault. The next year, a tent was erected to give players a quiet space and room to focus before attaching signature to score—sadly, a move one year too late for De Vicenzo.

1969

Billy Casper led the tour in earnings in 1968, winning six times; however, his Masters prospects were questionable in 1969, not only because of his relative lack of success in Augusta but also because of a freakish allergic flare-up. Two weeks earlier in practice rounds for a tournament in Miami, he had a violent reaction to pesticides applied to the turf. His arms and legs swelled up so badly he withdrew after two rounds, and didn't touch a club for a week.

After some good practice rounds, Casper came flying out of the gate on Thursday, grabbing the lead with a 66. Billy said the ends of his fingers were still numb, but "if I can keep 'em numb and play like this..." He had six birdies, no bogeys, and displayed a fine touch on the greens with nine one-putts. Bruce Devlin, recovering from a bout with pneumonia, shot a 67 and was joined at that number by George Archer, who complained of an intestinal upset.

Archer said he was surprised by his score, because he didn't feel he was playing that well. "I missed some shots, but they stayed on the greens." Not exactly brimming with optimism, the lanky Californian said, "I'm going to play each day and hope for the best. There's a long way to go."

Jack Nicklaus, the tournament favorite despite a relatively lackluster year in 1968 with only two victories, was in good shape with a 68 thanks to a three-hole burst of birdie-birdie-eagle on 13–14–15. Arnold Palmer, who made news with a 63 in a practice round the Saturday before the tournament, finished with a 73 on a day when 23 players broke par.

After a day of low scoring, the players were greeted on Friday by pin positions that some called the toughest ever and greens that were firming up. Casper, for one, had several approach shots land on greens and bounce over the back. Fortunately, his short-game touch hadn't abandoned him, and he had seven one-putt pars and only one bogey in a 71 that gave him a share of the 36-hole lead at 137. He confirmed to reporters after the round that he had opted not to have sausage at breakfast this year.

Devlin gained a tie for first with a 45-foot birdie putt at the 18th for a 70. It was three strokes back to the next players at 140, Archer and Dan Sikes. Archer's round was the opposite of Thursday's. This time, he felt he hit the ball well but had three three-putts in shooting a 73. Considered one of the best putters on tour, Archer said his weakness on the greens was long putts, and that he was having trouble with the severe slopes on Augusta's greens.

Next came a pack of nine players grouped at 142. They included Charles Coody, who had the only round in the 60s with a 68, and Tom Weiskopf, with a second straight 71 coming off a runner-up finish in a playoff at Greensboro. The 26-year-old Weiskopf had come into his own in 1968, his fourth year on tour, with two victories and a ranking of fourth on the money list. He then went on a five-month stint in the Army Reserves that September and only came back on tour at the beginning of March.

Weiskopf followed Nicklaus as a golfer at Ohio State, and the two were paired on this Friday. While over his career Weiskopf would be overshadowed by Nicklaus, he got the better of Jack this time. Nicklaus did very little right, going backward with a 75 for a 143 total.

Casper went back in front himself on Saturday with a second straight two-birdie, one-bogey 71. He wasn't sharp on the front nine, saving par on three of the first six holes and making a bogey on the seventh. Birdies on nine and 10 righted the ship and he parred in, continuing his strategy of laying up on the back nine par fives as he had done every day. Casper said he arrived at that plan because he had wasted strokes by gambling and losing on 13 and 15 in past years. He said his strategy on Sunday would depend on his position in the tournament—if he was behind, he would go for it on those holes if he was in range.

Archer moved into second place, one stroke back at 209, with a 69 thanks to a 32 on the back nine highlighted by a 35-foot eagle putt at the 15th and a 12-footer to birdie the 18th. He was nine-under on the par fives through three rounds, "not bad for a short hitter."

Despite his 6-foot-6 frame, the San Francisco native was indeed relatively short off the tee, though he made up for it with accuracy and his short game. Archer didn't play college golf and was taken under the wing of wealthy Californian Gene Selvage, who hired George to work on his ranch in the town of Gilroy 80 miles south of San Francisco, giving him afternoons off to play golf. Eventually, Selvage funded Archer's foray onto the pro tour in 1964.

Archer quickly found success and continued to develop to the point where he won three times in 1968 and added another at the Bing Crosby National Pro-Am in early 1969. By now, the 29-year-old had a small ranch of his own. Known as the "Gilroy cowboy," Archer was quick to point out that his days as a ranch hand consisted mostly of menial jobs like painting and cleaning out the cow barn. "I wasn't good enough to be a first-class cowboy…one who rides horses."

He was playing in his third Masters, having finished T16 and T22, and said of his approach to the final round, "I have no strategy. I just try to go out there and do the best I can."

Miller Barber was in third at 210 after the best score of the day, a 68, while Coody and Weiskopf both had 69s for 211. Devlin found the water on 11 (bogey) and 16 (double bogey) on the way to a 76 and was five strokes behind.

Nicklaus was seven strokes back after a 72 and could be described as on the fringe of contention. Jack wasn't himself Sunday, shooting a 76 with eight bogeys to finish T24 while Palmer was 27th. They would be long gone by the time of the green jacket ceremony where they once had been annual participants.

"Whatever happened to the Masters we all knew and loved?" wrote Dan Jenkins in *Sports Illustrated*, calling the group of contenders on Sunday "a ragtag group of escapees from some distant Citrus Open on the regular professional tour."

That was probably unfair to two-time U.S. Open champion Casper, but Billy played like anything but a star on the first 10 holes of the final round, going five-over while hitting only two greens. "I've played with 14-handicappers who hit the ball better than I did through 10 holes," he said.

While lacking in superstar power, this Masters did produce plenty of suspense down the stretch, with five players locked in a tight battle. With so many players dealing with major championship pressure for the first time, it was ultimately decided more by bogeys than birdies.

Archer had a three-stroke lead at the turn at eight-under, but later admitted he didn't feel secure. Coody, a steady money winner in his five years on tour but with only one career victory, was the first challenger. After pars on the first 10 holes, he birdied the 11th and moved within one when Archer bogeyed the 10th.

Coody leapfrogged Archer with an eagle on the 13th, where he hit a two-iron second shot to 25 feet. George squared it with a birdie on 13, where he was just off the green in two and chipped within inches. Unable to stand that prosperity, both bogeyed the 14th to slip to seven-under and let others back in it.

Casper rallied after his horrible start, posting birdies on 11, 13, and 15—going for the green in two on the par fives. That got him to six-under, and, in the twosome ahead of him, Weiskopf (playing with Archer) birdied 13 and 15 to get to seven-under.

Archer preserved his seven-under standing thanks to a saved par on the 15th, where he went for the green with a four-iron second shot only to find the water. Undaunted, he pitched to 13 feet and made the putt. On a hole where he had gone birdie-birdie-eagle in the first three rounds, a final-round par was just as important.

1969

1	George Archer	67–73–69–72—281
T2	Billy Casper	66–71–71–74—282
T2	George Knudson	70–73–69–70—282
T2	Tom Weiskopf	71–71–69–71—282
T5	Charles Coody	74–68–69–72—283
T5	Don January	74–73–70–66—283
7	Miller Barber	71–71–68–74—284
T8	Tommy Aaron	71–71–73–70—285
T8	Lionel Hebert	69–73–70–73—285
T8	Gene Littler	69–75–70–71—285

Playing just ahead of Archer and Weiskopf, Coody had gone ahead at eight-under with a tap-in birdie on 15 after chipping close. "I knew I was in the lead," Coody said later. "I'd like to say it didn't affect me, but on No. 16 I hit a bad shot," pulling it into a bunker. He didn't get up and down, and, when Weiskopf birdied 15 moments later, it was a three-way tie.

A fifth contender suddenly joined the party. Canada's George Knudson had been hanging around all week with rounds of 70–73–69 and was even par through 14 holes of the final round. He birdied the 15th, then holed a 20-foot birdie putt on the 16th for a two-stroke swing on playing partner Coody and was within one at six-under.

Coody unraveled with a bogey on 17, where he missed to the right with an eight-iron and hit a weak chip, and another bogey on 18, where he drove way left, the three closing bogeys leaving him at five-under with a 72.

Now it was just Weiskopf and Archer at seven-under. "I've never experienced pressure like that before," said Weiskopf, whose drive on 17 sailed to the right and bounced off a TV camera cart. He was fortunate to have a decent lie and a clear shot, but hit a nine-iron heavy and into the front bunker. Weiskopf blasted out to 12 feet, and couldn't convert the putt, nor could he birdie 18 as he closed with a 71 to finish at six-under. Knudson didn't birdie 17 or 18 and he also was in the clubhouse at six-under after a 70.

Archer was in a bad spot off the tee at 17, in the right trees and well behind Weiskopf. George managed a crucial par, punching a low four-iron onto the green and two-putting from 60 feet, making a five-footer. Then he almost birdied the 18th, leaving a 12-foot putt just short. It was a 37 on the back nine and a 72 for Archer, good enough for the victory unless Casper could birdie 18.

Billy was to the right of the green with his approach on 18. His chip came close, but didn't drop, with the par handing Casper a 74 and a tie for second with Weiskopf and Knudson after leading or sharing the lead through the first three rounds.

"I don't think I've ever been scared for so long," Archer said of the back-nine tension. "There were nine other players who could've won, and I'm fortunate nobody got hot."

The one player who did get hot was Don January with a final-round 66, but he started too far back and tied Coody for fifth place, two strokes behind, as Archer was able to claim his first—and only—major title in a career that would ultimately yield 13 victories.

"I never thought of winning the Masters or the Open," said Archer. "That's like aiming at the moon."

End of the Blackout

The Masters had been televised since 1956, but if you lived too close to Augusta you weren't able to watch it—a TV blackout was imposed within a 225-mile radius of the tournament's host city. The blackout was put in place to protect ticket sales. Yet, even after the event became such a hot ticket that it sold out every year, the restriction remained justified by the assumption that a lifted blackout might hurt the gate in future years. Or, as Bobby Jones said, it would be "a breach of faith" to those who had already bought tickets and had not been given, at the time, the alternative of watching the event on TV. Unrest with the blackout grew and, in 1967, state legislation was proposed in Georgia to ban blackouts of events where tickets were sold out. The blackout was lifted for Columbus, Georgia, located on the other side of the state, in 1967, and the following year Charlotte, North Carolina, and Florence, South Carolina, were added to the exemption. Finally, in January of 1969, noting that ticket sales hadn't diminished in Charlotte or Florence and were only slightly down in Columbus, the club announced that there would be no blackout. Even with everybody able to watch on television, the Masters remained the hottest ticket in sports.

1970

Billy Casper came into the Masters feeling fresh after taking five weeks off before playing in Greensboro the week before Augusta. "Some players make the mistake of playing too much to get ready for a big tournament," the 38-year-old veteran said on Monday. "That way, you can get mentally tired. The game of golf is played with your mind."

Casper had some more reasons for optimism. For a couple of years now, he had become comfortable hitting a right-to-left draw more suited to Augusta National than the fade he used to employ. He also had a new driver that he said gave him 20 or 30 extra yards off the tee. And once he got close to the hole, he felt good about having his caddie, Matthew Palmer, read the greens for him, which he had started to do a year earlier when he nearly won. "Last year was the first year I putted well here. The greens here are subtle. He has good local knowledge and he helped me a lot."

Gene Littler took six weeks off before playing in Greensboro, but he wasn't so confident. Quite the opposite, in fact. He said he took a breather because he was hitting the ball so poorly at Tucson, where he shot a final-round 77. On Monday of Masters week, he told a reporter, "I'm a basket case." On Wednesday, he said, "I still haven't found the answer."

Bert Yancey left Greensboro after a poor first round so he could come to Augusta and work on his putting. Asked if he was sick at Greensboro, Yancey replied, "No, I was obsessed with the Masters."

Yancey had finished third, third, and T12 in his first three Masters appearances, and nobody wanted to win at Augusta more. Yancey stayed each year at a house owned by the appropriately named J.B. Masters, only a few hundred yards from the Augusta National property. There his landlords fixed up a special room for him with Masters memorabilia, newspaper clippings from past years, and a miniature green jacket made by Mrs. Masters. Yancey also had made clay models of every green at Augusta National.

"I never feel like playing golf until I get here. Everything before the Masters is just shadow boxing," Yancey said.

Yancey's obsession appeared to be paying off in the first round when he shot a 69 marred only by a missed birdie putt from 18 inches on the 17th hole. It cost him what could have been a share of the lead with Tommy Aaron, another man with a strong Masters track record and an affinity for the course. "I enjoy playing here more than any course on tour," said Aaron, who shot a 68 despite a bogey on the 18th. The Georgia native finished T8–T7–T8 in the last three Masters.

Littler wasn't such a fan of Augusta National, at least in how it fit his game, but he managed an opening 69. "The course favors the guy who hits the ball a long way in the air. I don't hit a long ball in the air," said the 39-year-old, who was playing in his 17th Masters with a best finish of fourth in 1962. Nor did he think he had fully solved his problems with ball-striking, attributing his score mostly to putting.

Casper was four strokes back at 72, expressing satisfaction with his round and surprise that 10 players broke par considering the firmness of the greens. Gary Player, coming off a victory in Greensboro, had a 74 and also claimed he was comfortable with his position.

On Friday, Casper and Player proved correct in not writing themselves off, both shooting 68. Casper made three putts of 25 feet or longer, while Player had a 32 on the front nine. Aaron went four over on the first four holes and did well to recover for a 74. With the door to the lead opened, Yancey and Littler took advantage with solid, if unspectacular, rounds of 70 to share first position at 139.

Littler birdied the first two holes and merely held his ground the rest of the way with his putter not as sharp as in the first round. "I'm still not hitting the ball what I would call well. I admit it's better," said the man whose silky swing was the envy of his tour brethren and whose consistency throughout his career earned him the nickname "Gene the Machine."

Yancey met after the round with PGA Tour Commissioner Joe Dey, who fined him $150 for skipping out on Greensboro. It was good news for Yancey, since that was the minimum punishment. Dey later explained to the press that Yancey had thought he was given permission by the tournament sponsor to withdraw.

Early action in the third round included such theatrics as 1969 leading money-winner Frank Beard making birdies on five of the first six holes, Aaron continuing his roller-coaster ride with a 31 on the front nine, and Charles Coody making birdies on the first four holes of the back nine.

By the end of the day, the same players formed the leading group, in a different order. Casper was now on top with a 68 for a 208 total—the very same score he led with through 54 holes the previous year.

Perhaps sensing challenges coming his way, Casper explained that he "threw caution to the wind at 13 today" and went for it from 245 yards. His four-wood found the green for a two-putt birdie, then he returned to his more cautious strategy by laying up at 15—and made a birdie there, too, after a wedge to 14 feet. Another birdie followed at the 16th.

Littler gained the lead with a 33 on the front nine, then tossed it away with bogeys on 11 and 12 and a three-putt par on 13, missing two-foot putts on the latter two holes. He ended up with a 70 for 209 to trail by one.

Player fired a second consecutive 68 for 210 and promised to stay aggressive in the final round. "I have two seconds here and nobody remembers it," said the 1961 champion. "I've made up my mind to go for it. I'm going to try to birdie every hole."

Yancey shot a 72 for a 211 total, tied with Aaron (69) and Coody (67), who both carded 67s. Yancey's three-stroke deficit was chalked up to a triple bogey at the 12th, where he didn't hit enough club and found the water and then missed the green with his pitch. Still, he was proud of himself for battling back to play the last six holes in two-under.

As usual, Yancey walked to the course from the Masters house on Sunday, no doubt contemplating how much a victory would mean to him. He made a strong start with birdies on Nos. 2, 3, and 5 to pull within one of the lead and turn the Masters into a tight four-way battle with Casper, Littler, and Player. From that point until the conclusion, the quartet would remain within two strokes of each other.

Casper gave away the lead at the eighth hole. A drive into a fairway bunker led to a five-iron third shot to the par five, which he pulled badly, the ball rolling down a hill to a treed area, where it settled on a maintenance road. His fourth shot caught a branch, finishing short of the green, leading to a double bogey.

Littler, playing a twosome ahead, had made his second birdie of the day on the eighth hole to get to nine-under, as Casper slipped to seven-under with his double (he had birdied the fourth). Billy quickly recaptured a share of the lead by holing a 20-foot birdie putt at the ninth, where Littler had bogeyed. They were joined in a three-way tie at eight-under by Yancey, who toured the front nine in 33, with Player one behind after a 35.

In only two instances on the back nine did anyone take the solo lead, Littler doing so both times, but only fleetingly. He got to nine-under with a birdie on 13 only to be tied by Player, who birdied 12 and 13 in the following group. Littler went to 10-under with a birdie on 15, where he hit a four-wood over the green and chipped to three feet. He quickly gave the stroke back with what he called a "terrible, half-skulled" tee shot into a bunker on the par-three 16th and resulting bogey.

Casper was two behind after a bogey at 11, so he again gambled on the 13th. "Normally, I wouldn't have gone for it because I had a bad lie. But I needed the birdie. It was a remarkable shot," he said of his four-wood that carried over the creek and set up a two-putt birdie from 35 feet.

The 15th hole had been lengthened, and a series of mounds installed on the right of the fairway. Only five players in the field went for the green in two in the first round, but, with a following wind on Sunday, all of the contenders decided to go for it. Casper hit his second shot into the right bunker, blasted to four feet, and made the putt to get to nine-under.

All Yancey could do was string together pars as he frustratingly stayed at eight-under, missing birdie putts of five and six feet on 13 and 14 and catching a bad lie in the greenside bunker with his second shot at 15. He hit what he thought was a good approach at 18 but had under-clubbed and splashed into the front bunker. He needed to hole out from there to have any chance; instead, he took three to get down for a 70 and a seven-under 281. "I played the best rounds of my life the last two days," he lamented, referring to his ball-striking and not his scores, which were harmed by the mis-clubbing on 12 Saturday and 18 Sunday and putts that wouldn't fall.

Player bogeyed 14, taking three putts from the fringe, and got back to nine-under with a nine-foot birdie at 16. True to his plan of trying to birdie every hole, he fired at the flag on 18, figuring that playing partner Casper had a chance to birdie the hole and beat him. The shot plunged into a buried lie in the front bunker, from where he hit an outstanding shot to eight feet.

Casper, meanwhile, hit a six-iron approach to 10 feet. His putt for the victory looked good all the way before hitting the lip and staying out. He had also narrowly missed a six-foot birdie try at 17.

Now Player had a putt to make it a three-way playoff. Distracted by a whirring movie camera on a greenside platform, he stepped away. The camera whirred again as he hit the putt, which missed. "It wasn't just the 18th," Player said minutes later. "I putted so badly the whole round." Echoing Yancey, he said, "This is the finest golf I've ever played to lose a tournament."

Neither Casper nor Littler had lost it yet—they had made enough putts to stay alive. The two had grown up in the San Diego area and competed in junior golf. Littler, 11 months older, usually had the upper hand then. They went on to play together for the golf team at the Naval Training Center, and still lived just 20 miles apart.

The matchup was reminiscent of the 1942 playoff between Byron Nelson and Ben Hogan, accomplished players who grew up in the same city. Casper and Littler were two of the premier players of their generation, with 44 and 22 victories, respectively, at the time, on the way to career totals of 51 and 29. Both had won U.S. Opens—Casper two and Littler one—but no other majors. Truthfully, neither was seen as a dynamic personality or player. They let their clubs do the talking and didn't overpower courses. Neither had seen as much success at the Masters as they had achieved elsewhere, despite numerous attempts at Augusta. Littler was playing in the event for the 17th time and Casper the 14th. Another major would go a long way in securing their legacy, but only one would come away with it.

Asked for his strategy in the playoff, Casper said, "I'll just tee it high on the first hole and let it fly."

Littler, not known for his quips, came up with one, responding, "I'll tee it low and let it go."

Littler vacated his rented house Sunday night because the owners had returned, and he found accommodation at an Augusta National member's cottage adjacent to the 10th fairway. Unfortunately, he lost his game somewhere along the way, or maybe it was the return of his early-week problems.

Casper jumped ahead in the playoff by picking up a stroke on his rival on each of the first four holes, making birdies on the first (six feet) and third (35 feet) while Littler bogeyed the second and fourth. The par-five second hole was pivotal. Casper hooked his tee shot and was fortunate not to end up in a creek. He lofted a nine-iron over some tall trees and hit a 175-yard third shot just over the back of the green. Littler was close to the green in two. Shockingly, Gene dumped a relatively simple 30-yard pitch shot into a bunker and bogeyed while Casper chipped close and made a par.

1970		
1	Billy Casper	72–68–68–71—279*
2	Gene Littler	69–70–70–70—279
3	Gary Player	74–68–68–70—280
4	Bert Yancey	69–70–72–70—281
T5	Tommy Aaron	68–74–69–72—283
T5	Dave Hill	73–70–70–70—283
T5	Dave Stockton	72–72–69–70—283
8	Jack Nicklaus	71–75–69–69—284
9	Frank Beard	71–76–68–70—285
T10	Bob Lunn	70–70–75–72—287
T10	Chi Chi Rodriguez	70–76–73–68—287
*Casper won playoff, 69–74		

A birdie on the seventh and an exchange of pars on the other front-nine holes left Billy five ahead as he turned in 33, having needed only 12 putts.

Casper bogeyed the 10th, still gaining a stroke when Littler double bogeyed after taking two shots to escape the woods. The lead became seven when Casper birdied the 11th. CBS television was due to air soon, and its personnel were lamenting the lack of suspense in their upcoming broadcast. "Well, is it safe to say Littler is a shoo-in for second?" somebody in the TV truck asked. "He may finish third," was the reply.

Few knew better than Casper that he didn't quite have it sewn up yet. After all, he had made up seven strokes on the back nine to tie Arnold Palmer in the 1966 U.S. Open before winning a playoff. Littler did indeed make Casper sweat, creating some TV drama. He made up a stroke on Casper on four straight holes, with birdies on 13 and 15 and Casper bogeys on 12 and 14.

Suddenly, Casper's advantage was down to three strokes with three holes to play. Littler hit his tee shot to 30 feet on the 16th and Casper later admitted to feeling the pressure. "I knew I needed to make a good swing," and he did with a five-iron to eight feet. The putt was true, and now the victory really was locked up. With a birdie on 17 for good measure, the final tally was 69–74.

Casper had two people to thank in his post-round interview. "I want to thank Gene for helping make it easier with a bad start," he said.

The other was his caddie, Matthew Palmer. "Matthew is responsible for me being here. He has an exceptional talent for reading the greens."

Asked why he only started using Palmer (Matthew, that is) to read the greens last year in his sixth year as his caddie, Casper said, "I'm just a hard-head I guess."

Better late than never, and finally the owner of a green jacket.

Structure Comes to Pairings

This was just the second year that the Masters sent the leaders off in the last tee times on the weekend, with pairings based on their scores. In the early days, the leaders were spread throughout the field instead of all going off last. After television began in 1956, the tournament began to put the leaders toward the end of the field, but with pairings still at the whim of the committee instead of by scores. Starting in 1969, the committee started automatically putting the players in first and third place in the last twosome, second and fourth place in the next to last, etc. It worked out nicely in 1970, with the last four players staging a tight battle on the final nine.

....

1971

Jack Nicklaus arrived in Augusta in pursuit of the Grand Slam, his avowed goal of winning all four major championships in the same year. That could be said about any year in his prime, but even more so in 1971, because he already had a major in his pocket.

The PGA Championship was held in February that year at PGA National Golf Club in South Florida in order to avoid the August heat. So, for once, the Masters wasn't the first major. When Nicklaus won the PGA, the Masters took on even greater meaning.

"I'm ready. It's no secret I'd like to win 'em all," he said on the eve of the Masters.

Arnold Palmer was also confident, enjoying a resurgence at age 41. He had won twice so far and led the money list. His prospects appeared strong to reverse recently disappointing Masters showings.

The headliners took a back seat in the first round to Charles Coody, who vaulted into a three-stroke lead with a 66. While not a star, Coody was hardly unknown at Augusta, having blown the lead in 1969 with bogeys on the last three holes and dropping from contention in the final round in 1970 with a 77 after a 67 the previous day.

The 33-year-old was a consistent player, inside the top 35 on the money list for the last five years. Yet, he had managed only two career victories: one in his rookie season of 1964 and the other in 1969. He was neither a charismatic personality, nor a fashionable dresser—the yin to an Arnold Palmer yang. In an era when striped and plaid plants, and colorful outfits, were coming in vogue, Coody remained conservative. His wife, Lynette, would get him to wear striped pants on occasion, but it would last only a day. "Honey, let's face it, I'm drab," he would tell her. "Furthermore, I like white."

The 6-foot-2 Texan managed to make his opening 66 look almost routine, with relatively easy birdies on all four par fives and nary a bogey on the card on a day when tough pin positions kept anyone else from going low despite fair weather. He was asked in his press conference about the Masters that got away in 1969.

"You really know how to hurt a guy," Coody responded, but he knew that would be a hot topic so long as he remained at or near the top of the leaderboard.

Five players were grouped at 69, with only 25-year-old Hale Irwin, looking for his first tour victory, and 41-year-old Don January destined to hover in contention.

Nicklaus shot a respectable 70, which could have been better if not for missed birdie putts of five feet on 15 and four feet on 18 and a second shot in the water on 13. Palmer had a 73, missing an eight-inch putt to double bogey the fifth hole and not striking the ball very well either, calling it his worst round of the year. He would end the tournament T18 and would never post a top-10 finish in any future Masters (his last was 1967).

Coody forfeited his advantage plus another stroke as he struggled to a 73 in the second round. His 139 total left him one behind January (69) and tied with Bob Murphy. The lowlight for Coody was the sixth hole, where he used his putter four times en route to a double bogey. The first attempt was from the front right fringe, which rolled up short of the hump in the green then did a U-turn, rolling back to the front fringe, roughly where it had begun its circuitous journey. From there, it took three more strokes to get in the hole. That came on the heels of bogeys on the fourth and fifth, and he made the turn in 39.

The 12th could have been another disaster, as he left one in the bunker, but Coody one-putted for a bogey there. Four-over to that point, he rescued his round and his tournament prospects with birdies on 13, 15, and 16, then saved par from a bunker on 18.

"It was one of the worst rounds I've ever played," said Coody. "I was fortunate to get a 73."

Nicklaus, on the other hand, voiced frustration that his 71 could have been better. He again missed two short birdie putts (four and three feet), hit into the water with his second shot on 15, and went over several greens with wedges. He said he felt like he'd wasted 10 shots in the first two rounds. "Sure, I'm getting impatient. I really want to win this one. It's all I've been thinking about, but I have to make some putts to get going," he said. "And I can't hit one in the water every round."

Jack was three strokes behind January, the 1967 PGA champion playing in his 13th Masters with a best finish of T4 in 1961. On Saturday, the lanky Texan lost the lead with a 73, saying he didn't hit his approach shots close enough to the hole. Nicklaus finally got it going with a 68 and shared first place with Coody at 209.

Coody got off to a brilliant start and led by four strokes after playing the first 13 holes in five-under. Then he bogeyed the 14th with a missed five-footer, could only par the 15th after a bad drive, and bogeyed 16 and 17 for a 70. Now the tall Texan who didn't have the winning knack on tour or at the Masters was tied with the best player and biggest winner in the game.

The pro J.C. Snead once said of going up against Nicklaus, "He knows he's going to beat you, you know he's going to beat you, and he knows that you know he's going to beat you."

Coody knew the task was daunting. "Subconsciously, you try to put the guy out of your mind. But you always know he's there." Still, he said, "I look at it confidently. I have a good chance of winning. I feel like I'm playing well."

Nicklaus was happy with his third round after two days of "piddling around." There was still some piddling on Saturday; a ball in the water on 11 (he saved a bogey), a missed three-foot par putt on 14, and a bogey on 18. This time, though, he offset those moments with seven birdies. It was quite an adventurous round, with not a single par after the 10th hole (five birdies, three bogeys).

Coody may have been helped on Sunday by the 1–3, 2–4 pairing system in effect. He didn't have to go head-to-head with Nicklaus; instead it was Coody and Tom Weiskopf in the next-to-last pair, followed by Nicklaus and January.

It didn't turn out to be a two-man battle. January couldn't quite get into the thick of it, finishing with a 72, nor could Weiskopf (72) or Irwin (76), who started three strokes back. Instead, the challenge came from 23-year-old Johnny Miller, who began four behind after rounds of 72–73–68.

With an affinity for striped pants, white belts, and garish colors, Miller was named the flashiest dresser on tour by the Men's Fashion Association of America. He was also showing signs of being a flashy player. In 1970, his second year on tour, Miller shot the lowest round of the season with a 61 at the Phoenix Open, though he was still looking for his first victory.

For a while, it appeared that breakthrough would come on the major-championship level at the Masters. Miller birdied the third hole from 12 feet, the fourth from 30 feet, and the eighth from two feet for a 33 on the front nine. He wasn't finished. "I'm a streak player," he had said after his Saturday round, and his final-round streak continued with a birdie on the 11th from 10 feet and didn't stop even when he hit his tee shot into the front bunker at the 12th. He holed out from there for a birdie to jump up the leaderboard to a tie for first with Nicklaus and Coody.

Miller grabbed the outright lead with an approach to six feet and a birdie on the 14th. The lead became two strokes when Coody bogeyed the 14th behind him, Nicklaus already having made a bogey on the 12th.

"After 14 was the first I thought about winning. I had just been trying to make birdies. It was like a practice round," Miller said. Then, walking down the 15th fairway he said, "I was thinking about how that green coat would look on me."

Miller boldly went for the green with a three-wood on the 15th and cleared the water, landing in the right bunker. He came out to six feet and missed the putt, settling for a par.

His inexperience beginning to show, Miller's mindset changed. "Now I was thinking about how not to get any bogeys," he said. Bogeys are just what he got, though. His tee shot on 16 was pushed into a bunker and his seven-foot putt for a par lipped out. On the 18th, he drove to the left, missed the green to the right, and two-putted from 18 feet for another bogey, giving him a 68 and a seven-under 281 total.

Coody was seven-under through 14 holes, with two birdies and two bogeys on the day. "I'm not in the class of a charger or gambler or anything like that, but I had to get birdies," he would say. He fired at the green on the 15th, settling for a par after his second shot went to the right and he missed a nine-foot birdie putt. Now he headed to the part of the course that had cost him the 1969 Masters.

On the 16th tee, caddie Walter "Cricket" Pritchett told him that a par there would be good. Coody put his arm around the caddie's shoulder and said, "Cricket, I'm going to birdie this hole." That's just what he did, with a six-iron to 15 feet and a birdie putt.

In retrospect, a par on 17 proved just as vital. Coody snapped his tee shot so far left that he ended up in a greenside bunker on the adjacent seventh hole. His second shot was short of the green—there was no way he could reach it from his position—but he chipped to three feet and walked away with a par. A routine par on 18 brought him in with a 70 for nine-under 279. With Nicklaus still stuck on seven-under behind him, that did it.

1971		
1	Charles Coody	66–73–70–70—279
T2	Johnny Miller	72–73–68–68—281
T2	Jack Nicklaus	70–71–68–72—281
T4	Don January	69–69–73–72—283
T4	Gene Littler	72–69–73–69—283
T6	Gary Player	72–72–71–69—284
T6	Ken Still	72–71–72–69—284
T6	Tom Weiskopf	71–69–72–72—284
T9	Frank Beard	74–73–69–70—286
T9	Roberto De Vicenzo	76–69–72–69—286
T9	Dave Stockton	72–73–69–72—286

Nicklaus parred 18 for a 72 and a tie for second with Miller, and almost couldn't believe it. "I might have been overconfident. I never felt I wasn't going to win," he said.

While one might wonder why he was so confident after an erratic first three rounds, perhaps that was the very reason for his confidence—despite giving away so many shots, he was still in position for a win that would match Palmer's four Masters titles and put him halfway to a Grand Slam.

His confidence stoked by a birdie on the first hole, Nicklaus went the wrong way with three-putt bogeys on Nos. 4 and 5. Birdies at the sixth and eighth brought him back into a tie for the lead and he still felt sure he would win. Then the 12th hole grabbed him. His eight-iron hung out to the right and finished on a sandbar next to Rae's Creek at the bottom of the slope. For the fourth straight day, he had hit a shot into a water hazard. This time he was able to play out, but the ball didn't clear the bank ahead of him and he had to try again. He got that one to 12 feet and made the putt for a bogey.

"I knew 13 and 15 were ahead. I wasn't concerned," Nicklaus said. But he didn't get a birdie on either of those par fives, three-putting from 60 feet on the 13th and going over the green in two and chipping well past on the 15th. Nor could he birdie anywhere else, finishing with a string of pars, unlike the previous day.

Instead of the technicolor Miller or history-seeking Nicklaus, it was unassuming Charles Coody who got to put on the green jacket—over a white shirt, of course.

1972

Jack Nicklaus was a heavy favorite going into the 1972 Masters among pretty much everyone—except maybe himself.

The trouble started during his pre-Masters week practice when rain kept him off the course for three days after his arrival. He finally got to play on Saturday and found himself spraying his driver and hooking his irons. Originally scheduled to depart for his Florida home on Saturday, he delayed it by a day to get in a practice round on Sunday.

Back in Augusta after a quick visit with the family, Nicklaus shot a 73 in a Tuesday practice round. "I'm just fiddling around, trying to make things happen. I'm not particularly happy," he said. "I don't like to depend on artificial methods to hit shots."

Earlier signs had been positive: Nicklaus was the first player ever to earn more than $100,000 before the Masters, having won twice and finished second twice.

Overall, the biggest threat to Nicklaus' No. 1 status in golf at this point was Lee Trevino, who swept the U.S., British, and Canadian Opens in 1971. But Trevino had stayed away from the Masters for the last two years, having decided after his first two appearances in 1968 and 1969 that the course didn't suit his game. High iron shots and the ability to draw the ball were considered advantageous at Augusta, while Trevino hit the ball low and always with a fade. The Mexican-American from humble origins didn't seem comfortable with the Augusta National atmosphere, either. He changed shoes in the parking lot and didn't go into the clubhouse.

The news on course condition was grim. Augusta's Bermuda grass greens had been invaded by Poa annua, a faster growing strain of grass that made the greens bumpy, especially late in the day. To smooth the greens, they were cut especially close, which made them very fast. Add in their firmness and the greens now made approach shots devilishly difficult to judge and control.

Only five players broke par in the first round. One of them was Nicklaus, who led the way with a 68. Two-over par after a bogey on the 10th, things suddenly clicked and Nicklaus played the next six holes in six-under, with pars on 17 and 18 giving him a 31 on the back nine.

The turnaround came on the 11th hole, where Nicklaus normally aimed for the right side of the green for safety from the pond on the left. Thinking to himself that it was time to make something happen, he instead took dead aim at the flag, hit a five-iron to 10 feet, and sank the birdie putt. That was quite a bold decision for someone who had been hooking his irons. He followed with a 25-foot birdie putt at the 12th and an up-and-down from a bunker to birdie the 13th after a six-iron second shot.

Nicklaus had birdied his way around Amen Corner, and he wasn't through. After a par on 14, he ripped a one-iron second shot over the water on 15 and holed a 30-foot eagle putt. For a capper, he sank a 22-footer for birdie on the 16th.

"I think the worst part of my problems is over," he said, while still not convinced that his swing was hitting on all cylinders since a hot putter had played a major role in his back-nine scoring. "I'm still not swinging the way I'd like to, but I'm improving every day. I'll play better tomorrow, for sure, although I can't promise I'll score this well."

The leaderboard was spiced by an appearance of a visitor from yesteryear, as Sam Snead was in second place with a 69. Just a month away from turning 60, the two-time Masters champion was now putting with a side-saddle style in an often-losing effort to overcome his woes on the greens. Another legend was in third place, Arnold Palmer shooting a welcome 70 after having blown the Greater Greensboro

Open the previous weekend when he triple bogeyed the 16th hole of the final round and missed a playoff by one stroke.

Charles Coody had a stretch nearly as spectacular as Nicklaus, but also a spectacular fall. The defending champion aced the sixth hole to go four-under for the round, and on the very next hole took four strokes to get out of a greenside bunker before holing a 10-foot putt for a triple bogey. Who said Coody was a dull golfer? He finished with a 73.

Nicklaus stayed in front with a 71 in the second round for a 139 total, finishing with a one-stroke lead that could have been larger. Two-under through 14 holes, he felt some wind in his face in the 15th fairway and hit a three-wood second shot only to see it clear the green on the fly and bound into the pond along the 16th hole. He double bogeyed there and missed a four-foot birdie putt on 17, though he recovered with a birdie on 18 and said afterward that he played better from tee to green than on Thursday.

Snead birdied the second and third holes to get to five-under for the tournament before reality set in and he shot a 75. Palmer also had a 75 with a near reprise of his 1958 ruling situation, except this time the verdict went against him. Denied relief from a depression made by a chair next to the ninth green, he played a second ball after taking a drop. Told on the 12th tee that the score with the original ball counted, costing him a stroke, an unhappy Palmer proceeded to make a triple bogey on that hole. Neither Snead nor Palmer would be a factor the rest of the way.

Their places as closest pursuers of Nicklaus were taken by 42-year-old Paul Harney at 140 and nearly perennial Masters contender Bert Yancey at 141, both with 69s.

Trevino barely made the cut with rounds of 75 and 76, then added a desultory 77 and said in a post-round interview that he expected to go for a 78 to 80 in the final round. Masters chairman Clifford Roberts, wanting to clear the air, invited him into his office, where they just talked golf rather than addressing any specifics. Upon emerging, Trevino said Roberts was a "nice man" and now said, "I may even shoot even par tomorrow [he did]," and "I'll be back again next year."

Nicklaus threatened to turn the tournament into a rout, leading by four strokes or so for most of the round. Then he uncharacteristically bogeyed the 17th and 18th holes for a 73 and ended up only one stroke ahead of Jim Jamieson, 212 to 213.

Waiting for Jamieson to finish his press interview before he could start his own, Nicklaus, disgusted with his ball-striking down the stretch, saw darkness approaching and ducked out for a quick practice session that kept the writers waiting. Upon his return, he said of his post-round practice, "It was terrible when I started, but I finished pretty good." That was positive spin, though. In his autobiography *My Story*, he would write that he came out of the session unsure he had solved the problem of trying to get more leg action in his swing, something he'd been working on without great success since the previous week.

Still, the tournament favorite was in the lead, and his pursuers weren't exactly a murderer's row. Jamieson had yet to post a victory in his three-plus years on tour, having qualified for the Masters by finishing in the top eight of the PGA

1972

1	Jack Nicklaus	68–71–73–74—286
T2	Bruce Crampton	72–75–69–73—289
T2	Bobby Mitchell	73–72–71–73—289
T2	Tom Weiskopf	74–71–70–74—289
T5	Homero Blancas	76–71–69–74—290
T5	Bruce Devlin	74–75–70–71—290
T5	Jerry Heard	73–71–72–74—290
T5	Jim Jamieson	72–70–71–77—290
T5	Jerry McGee	73–74–71–72—290
T10	Gary Player	73–75–72–71—291
T10	Dave Stockton	76–70–74–71—291

Championship. He compiled his opening rounds of 72–70–71 with a hodge-podge bag of clubs; irons made by four different companies, woods made by another, and a putter bought at a department store, earning the label "the department store pro." The 5-foot-10, 210-pounder had an engaging personality, and said to the assembled writers, "Does my nervousness show? No, except my hands and insides shake a little."

It was two strokes further back to Harney and Tom Weiskopf, the latter expected to be the biggest threat. Weiskopf had shot a 70 that he reported could have been several shots better, and said of Nicklaus, with whom he would be paired Sunday, "He's not invincible."

Australia's Bruce Crampton, owner of nine tour titles at age 36 but with no top-10s in the Masters, led a group at 216 thanks to a sizzling finish of five-under on the last six holes. He was joined by Bobby Mitchell, Homero Blancas, and Jerry Heard.

The Sunday of the 1972 Masters was a rare one in that it was practically free of gallery roars. Nicklaus aptly described it after winning with a final-round 74 and total of 286. "Nobody was doing anything. Nobody was making a move and nothing was happening."

With hard greens and Poa annua making approach shots and putting into hit-and-hope guessing games, the best rounds of the day were 71s by Bruce Devlin, Gary Player, and Dave Stockton, who all started far back and only nudged their way into the top 10. Among the 10 players within five strokes of the lead through 54 holes, none shot better than 73.

Nicklaus played the best golf of anyone on the front nine, carding a 35 while the other contenders were all at least two over, Weiskopf shooting himself out of it early with bogeys on three of the first four holes and others having assorted troubles. Ultimately, Crampton and Mitchell, a 29-year-old playing in the second of what would be only three career Masters, shot 73s and Weiskopf a 74 to tie for second three strokes behind.

It only got that close because Nicklaus bogeyed 11 and 14 with three-putts and 15 with a badly pulled four-iron and pitch shot that missed the green. There was only one moment of something like drama when Nicklaus bunkered his approach at 17 and had a 10-foot putt for par. Crampton and Mitchell had finished and weren't threats at this point, three strokes behind, but Weiskopf, four behind, had a birdie putt inside of Nicklaus' par effort. A Nicklaus miss and Weiskopf make would cut it to two with one to play. Nicklaus didn't miss, and strolled up the 18th with his fourth Masters title in hand.

While Nicklaus completed a wire-to-wire victory in relatively dull fashion on Sunday, he really won the tournament with a brilliant stretch of golf on Thursday. After that, it was a matter of holding on against Poa annua and a swing that never felt quite right. Fortunately for him, the rest of the field had their own troubles.

Ticket Crunch

In 1968, Augusta National had begun giving first chance to order tickets to those on its mailing list, which comprised previous ticket purchasers and those having requested to be added to the list. With demand for tickets continuing to surge, that patrons' list was closed in 1972 and a waiting list started. With little attrition among previous ticket buyers, only a small fraction of the waiting list would be able to get tickets in future years, and the waiting list kept swelling to such an untenable length that it was closed in 1978.

1973

Jack Nicklaus followed his 1972 Masters victory with the U.S. Open title at Pebble Beach, his Grand Slam quest ending when Lee Trevino edged him at the British Open. The Slam was again on the agenda in 1973, though for a second consecutive year rain and uncertainty about his swing impacted Nicklaus' pre-tournament practice.

Nicklaus hadn't played well in his last two Florida starts, so he canceled a planned business trip to Spain and entered the New Orleans Open two weeks before the Masters. Jack won there, joining Trevino and Bruce Crampton as multiple winners on the year, though in typical fashion he still wasn't completely satisfied with the way he was swinging, nor did he seem convinced after his Masters practice, calling his preparation just "OK."

Nicklaus showed on Thursday that his swing was fine, shooting a 69 to trail leader Tommy Aaron by one. Nicklaus was the only player in the field to clear the water with his second shot on the 15th, which played into a headwind, needing only a one-iron to do it. He put it into the right bunker, then nearly holed out to secure his fourth birdie of the day.

Aaron's position at the top was a surprise considering that he hadn't played well so far in 1973, having to take two breaks from the tour to be with his wife during serious operations. He played poorly in practice rounds, and wasn't feeling good on the range before the first round until, near the end of his warmup, fellow competitor Gary Cowan told him that his swing looked too fast.

Unsure that the tip would work, Aaron headed to the first tee thinking only about trying to make the cut. His prospects brightened with a good drive and approach to 15 feet on the first hole, where he birdied, and two good shots to the vicinity of the par-five second green for an easy up-and-down birdie. It led to a 32 on the front nine on the way to a 68 and his second 18-hole Masters lead following 1970.

The 36-year-old native and resident of Gainesville, Georgia, north of Atlanta, had a good Masters record, finishing in the top 10 every year from 1967 to 1970 and six top-15s in eight appearances. "My natural hook is probably an advantage here," he said, "but I can't always control the hook the way I would like to."

The biggest story in the second round wasn't at the top of the leaderboard, where four players tied for the lead. Rather, it was Nicklaus struggling to a 77 with a 40 on the front nine. The game's No. 1 player looked hopeless with a putter in his hands, three-putting five times and accumulating 39 putts. The only good news for Nicklaus was that nobody could pull away at the front of the field, and his 146 total was only five out of the lead.

The front-running position was shared by Aaron, Gay Brewer, J.C. Snead, and Bob Dickson. Aaron bogeyed the first two holes with drives into fairway bunkers, the opposite of his first-round start, and was happy to survive with a 73 thanks to birdies on 13 and 14. Realistically, it was anybody's ballgame at this point, with 26 players within five strokes. That included University of Texas junior Ben Crenshaw, who played with Nicklaus and led the tournament after a 32 on the front nine before a 40 on the back for a 144 total.

The final two rounds would be played on Sunday and Monday after two-and-a-half inches of rain were dumped on Augusta on Saturday morning. There was no prospect of playing 36 holes on Sunday, because most of that morning would be needed for the grounds crew to get the course in shape.

Six players led or shared the lead during the third round, but, by the end, 24-year-old Peter Oosterhuis opened a three-stroke lead with a 32 on the back nine for a 68. The 6-foot-5 Englishman had led the European Tour Order of Merit the last two years, but was little known in the U.S., having played the two previous Masters with little distinction and five events so far in 1973 with a best of T15.

Aaron had a wild first nine with no pars after the first hole, where a promising start with birdies on Nos. 2 and 3 dissolved in a sea of bogeys as his swing and short game both went awry. He bogeyed Nos. 4 and 5, enjoyed a brief respite with a birdie at the sixth, then double bogeyed the seventh after a drive into the trees, bogeyed the eighth with another bad drive, and bogeyed the ninth. To his credit, he righted the ship with a 35 on the back nine but his 74 left him at 215, four strokes behind.

J.C. Snead, Jim Jamieson, and 1968 champ Bob Goalby were tied for second at 214. Snead went out in 34 to go in front by two at the turn, then promptly bogeyed 10, 11, and 12 on the way to a 73, apparently unable to withstand the thin, rarified air of leading the Masters. "All of a sudden I felt completely exhausted. I flat ran out of gas," he said.

Nicklaus had a good chance to stay in hailing distance of the lead but blew it with a triple bogey at the 15th for a 73. He didn't make solid contact with a three-wood second shot, which plunged into the pond, his penalty drop ended up in a small depression, and he dumped his pitch shot into the water. Eight strokes behind at 219, the tournament favorite was now a longshot.

Oosterhuis was strongly challenged by three players as the final round played out—Aaron, Snead, and Nicklaus.

Aaron's track record didn't stamp him as a likely winner, though maybe if he mounted a charge he might finish second. That would be a familiar position for the bespectacled Georgia native, who in his 11-plus seasons on tour had compiled 13 runner-up finishes against only one victory, the 1970 Atlanta Classic close to home. He also cracked the winner's circle at the 1969 Canadian Open, though as Aaron's luck would have it that wasn't considered an official PGA Tour event despite drawing many tour players in its field.

Some observers felt that his swing was loose, others that he lacked grit. Surely bad luck and unfortunate timing must have been part of it, but the lack of victories was glaring for the man who became known as the tour's bridesmaid.

Jesse Carlyle Snead was the nephew of three-time Masters champion Sam, and was just coming into his own after a late start as a pro. He joined the tour in 1968 at age 27 after playing minor-league baseball, and didn't crack the top 100 money winners in his first three seasons before blossoming in 1971 with two victories. J.C. didn't see his uncle Sam much growing up, but once he got heavily into golf, Sam was a big help. Now J.C. was trying to add a second Snead name to the Masters trophy, while receiving advice from Sam, who was staying in the same rented house.

Nicklaus would need a red-hot start to be a legitimate contender, and that's what he got. Five birdies on the front nine against one bogey gave him a 32 to move him into red figures for the tournament at one-under. He was four strokes back and drawing a flock of spectators.

Oosterhuis birdied the third hole, then suffered a couple of bogeys to make the turn in 37. By that time he had fallen behind Aaron and Snead, who started strongly. Aaron birdied the first three holes, going one better than his first-round start, and added another at the eighth for a front-nine 32. Snead birdied the fourth and eighth for a 34, and joined Aaron at five-under, one ahead of Oosterhuis.

All had their troubles on the next three holes and were down to three-under when they finished the 12th. Aaron bogeyed 10 and 11, Oosterhuis bogeyed 12, and Snead made the classic Augusta National mistake when he hit his tee shot into the water at 12, later lamenting that he switched from a six-iron to a seven-iron. Why did he change? "Just stupid, I guess," he said after the round.

The trio all birdied the 13th to get to four-under. Up ahead, Nicklaus had birdied both back-nine par fives, though he blunted his charge with a bogey at 14. Needing to make something happen at 18, he overcame a tee shot into a fairway bunker by holing a 30-foot putt from the fringe for a birdie and a 66 to get to three-under—a red three on the leaderboard that drew the attention of the contenders behind him.

Aaron was walking down the 15th fairway at four-under when Nicklaus finished, and knew that any mistake could lead to yet another runner-up finish or worse. This time was different. Aaron steeled himself, cleared the pond with his second shot to the back fringe, chipped to four feet, and made the birdie putt. Tommy remained solid with three finishing pars for a 68 and waited on the twosome of Snead and Oosterhuis. Snead only managed a par on 15 after laying up in two, while Oosterhuis made a bogey six after going for the green and hitting his shot way to the right from where his pitch didn't reach the green.

1973

1	Tommy Aaron	68–73–74–68—283
2	J.C. Snead	70–71–73–70—284
T3	Jim Jamieson	73–71–70–71—285
T3	Jack Nicklaus	69–77–73–66—285
T3	Peter Oosterhuis	73–70–68–74—285
T6	Bob Goalby	75–69–71–73—288
T6	Johnny Miller	75–69–71–73—288
T8	Bruce Devlin	73–72–72–72—289
T8	Masashi Ozaki	69–74–73–73—289
T10	Gay Brewer	75–66–74–76—291
T10	Gardner Dickinson	74–70–72–75—291
T10	Don January	75–71–75–70—291
T10	Chi Chi Rodriguez	72–70–73–76—291

Oosterhuis parred in for a 74 to tie for third at three-under with Nicklaus and Jamieson, who made a late birdie for a 71. Snead kept hope alive by saving par from a bunker on 17, holing a 10-foot putt. His approach to the 18th left a 20-foot birdie putt from right of the hole to try to force a playoff and send an already long tournament to Tuesday. With Aaron watching on television, the putt narrowly missed, and Snead was second after a closing 70.

Nicklaus could only ponder what might have been. "I gave it away with the eight on 15 yesterday," he said. Even then, he might have come all the way back without two three-putt bogeys that kept his last round from being even better.

Aaron, naturally, was on top of the world. Of all the tournaments that could have finally yielded a victory to him, the Masters was on top of the list.

"This one makes up for a lot of those I didn't win. I dreamed of winning this tournament as a boy," said the man who grew up as the son of a Georgia club professional.

Aaron was asked if this got rid of the bridesmaid tag. "It should, don't you think?" he responded. "It's been overplayed. It's no crime to finish second.... Everybody has failures, but I have never lost confidence in myself."

The victory didn't open up the floodgates for Aaron. In fact, he never won again on the PGA Tour, nor did he ever finish in the top 60 money winners after 1973, as back troubles diminished his game. But at least he had a green jacket.

Good Catch

While Tommy Aaron had a good track record at the Masters, he was best remembered for writing the wrong score on Roberto De Vicenzo's scorecard in 1968. Ironically, in the 1973 final round fellow competitor Johnny Miller put him down for a five on the 13th hole instead of the four that Aaron made. Fortunately, Aaron caught the mistake, signed a correct scorecard, and claimed the Masters title.

1974–1982

Return of the Elite

The big names were back, and order was restored. Nearly all Masters champions over this nine-year span also won at least one other major during their career. The one exception was 1982 champion Craig Stadler, but he was Player of the Year that year. Gary Player and new star Tom Watson each won twice and Jack Nicklaus and another new star, Seve Ballesteros, each donned a green jacket once during this time frame. Even the runners-up were of the highest order as big names battled for the title, with Johnny Miller and Tom Weiskopf losing to Nicklaus in a 1975 shootout, Nicklaus finishing second twice to Watson, and Watson himself also a two-time runner-up.

Scores continued to descend in the mid- to late-1970s, Ray Floyd matching the tournament record 271 total in 1976. With the greens all Bermuda grass (no longer overseeded with rye), the putting surfaces had slowed down since the mid-1960s. Was Augusta losing its teeth? If there were any doubts, tournament officials moved to dispel them. To do that, they restored slicker greens—along with the fear they foster. Before the 1981 tournament, the greens were changed to bentgrass to make them speedier and to make putting and approach shots more demanding. It worked handily. Winning scores went up: From 1971–80 the average was 278.1; from 1981–90, even with equipment improvements leading to lower scores on tour overall, it was 280.9.

The tournament's aura and popularity continued to rise, propelled even further by the excitement of golf's superstars staging battles for the title, with 1975 a classic example. Television ratings were annually the highest of the four majors, and the waiting list for tickets was closed in 1978—with hardly anybody giving up their valuable tickets, the waiting list had kept growing. By this time, a Masters badge had become one of the most prized tickets of any sports event, rivaling the World Series, Super Bowl, and Kentucky Derby.

1974

Three players loomed large heading into the 1974 Masters—Jack Nicklaus, Johnny Miller, and Tom Weiskopf.

Nicklaus, of course, was in his prime and had won seven events in 1973. The 26-year-old Miller was the hottest player in golf, having swept the first three tournaments of the 1974 season and added a fourth victory at the Heritage Classic two weeks before the Masters. Weiskopf had ruled the tour for a large part of 1973, winning five times (including the British Open) in a stretch of eight tournaments while finishing second, third, and fifth in the other three.

The confident Miller coyly remarked he wouldn't predict he would win, especially with Nicklaus in the field, but added, "I will say one thing, I'll be surprised and disappointed if I don't win." Weiskopf was downgraded slightly due to a hand injury suffered at Phoenix early in the year and was 28th on the money list; however, he did have three top-10s in his last four starts and reported that the hand was on the mend.

Not receiving much attention was 38-year-old 1961 champion Gary Player, who was given 20-to-1 odds at Ladbrokes compared to 3-to-1 for Nicklaus. In any case, he was glad to be back after missing the 1973 Masters due to surgery.

Augusta had planted a new strain of grass on the fairways in the past year, allowing them to be mown shorter after years of players complaining about flyer lies. That helped scoring, as did the lack of wind.

Jim Colbert led nine sub-70 scorers with a 67 highlighted by a chip-in birdie on 12 and a birdie on 13 from the 14th fairway. Hale Irwin, now age 28 with two tour wins to his credit (soon to add his first of three U.S. Open titles in June), set a tournament record with five straight birdies starting on No. 12, none with a putt longer than 10 feet. He shot a 68 along with Hubert Green, another 28-year-old making a name for himself. Nicklaus was reasonably satisfied with a six-birdie 69, though unamused with a bogey on the 18th. Weiskopf was at 71 and Miller came in with a disappointing 72, but said, "If this is my worst round, I think I'll win the tournament."

It wasn't his worst round; Miller followed with a 74 in the second round and, despite playing better on the weekend (69–70), finished T15.

Dave Stockton moved to the front with a 66 on Friday, including a 13th-hole eagle, for a 137 total. The 1970 PGA champion was known as one of the tour's best putters and scramblers, as he demonstrated in this round with only 26 putts and surviving four trips into the woods.

"I call it enjoyable golf [rather than scrambling]," he said. "I turn up in some funny places, but it makes the game interesting."

Stockton pointed out to the writers that he had recently improved his swing and was hitting more greens. The next day he admitted that, while having thought he'd played solidly, he changed his mind after walking out of the interview and called his father—a former teaching pro—for emergency swing advice.

Irwin and Green both shot 70, Green with a 32 on the back nine, and were at 138, with Colbert (72 with four birdies, an eagle, and six bogeys) and Frank Beard at 139. Weiskopf moved forward with a 69 and along with Nicklaus was one of five at 140.

Nicklaus eagled the 13th hole before giving it back with a bogey on 15, where he hit his second shot in the water. Player eagled the 15th to briefly get on the leaderboard at four-under, promptly dropping off it with bogeys on 16 and 17 for a second straight 71.

Player returned to the leaderboard in a big way on the back nine of the third round. Two days after Irwin birdied the 12th through 16th holes to become the first ever with five consecutive birdies, Player matched the feat—and did it on the same holes.

The South African was one-under through 11 holes, thanks to a birdie at the second, when his streak began with a seven-iron within a foot of the hole on the 12th. He reached a greenside bunker in two on 13 and made a 15-foot birdie putt, holed a six-footer on 14, two-putted 15, and sank another six-footer to complete the streak on 16. Two finishing pars gave him a 66 and a 208 total, one behind leader Stockton, and some needed relief after a frustrating first two rounds.

"I never felt as depressed as I did last night. I never played better than I did the first 36 holes.… I was missing every three- and five-footer I had and three-putting all over the place," Player said on Saturday.

Stockton's third round was framed by a pair of pitching-wedge third shots to par fives, with polarized results. He holed out from 80 yards for an eagle on the second hole and, when he added a birdie at the third, he built a four-stroke lead. Still three-under for the day coming to the 15th hole, where he laid up in two, Stockton found his ball sitting on a replaced divot. Failing to make solid contact, the shot came up short and plunged into the pond. He managed to save a bogey with an excellent pitch to three feet after a penalty drop and finished with a 70.

Entering the final round, Stockton was one in front of Player and Colbert, two ahead of Bobby Nichols and Phil Rodgers and three clear of Weiskopf and Irwin.

"I'll bet a lot of the players like seeing me up here instead of Nicklaus," said Stockton. Not that he felt they should be too reassured. "I've got everything together. If I play tomorrow like I know how to play this course, everybody will be in trouble."

Nicklaus was five strokes back after a dispiriting 72 that he said felt like an 80 due to the prime scoring conditions and a sloppy finish after playing the first eight holes in three-under.

The conditions were ripe for scoring in the final round, too, as England's Maurice Bembridge demonstrated early. A 30-foot putt on the 18th hole gave him a 30 on the back nine and a record-tying 64 for an ultimate T9 finish. Arnold Palmer, who had opened with a 76, matched his best Masters score ever with a 67 to move into T11, giving his still faithful army something to cheer about.

None of the leaders would tear it up in that fashion, which led to a tight, multi-player battle. At one point midway through the back nine, six players were within one stroke of each other at the top of the board.

In the final pairing of Player and Stockton, the ninth was a critical hole. Player's approach shot cleared the front bunker by inches, rolled through the fringe, and finished six feet from the hole. Stockton's birdie putt was from 20 feet. He had left a number of putts short while parring the first eight holes; determined not to make the same mistake, he knocked this one three-and-a-half feet past. Player made his birdie, Stockton missed the short one, and the two-stroke swing left Gary two strokes ahead at 10-under, having posted a 34 on the front nine to Stockton's 37.

Among the contenders, Weiskopf and Nicklaus shot 33s on the front nine, Weiskopf getting to nine-under and Nicklaus seven-under. As usual, the 10th through 12th holes took their toll, Nicklaus playing them one-over and Player, Stockton, and Weiskopf all going two-over in that three-hole stretch.

Now it was time for Nicklaus to make a statement to the rest of the contenders anxiously watching the leaderboards for the numbers next to his name. He did just that with a 30-foot eagle putt at the 13th to pull within one of the lead. Surprisingly, he gave one of those strokes right back with a three-putt from the fringe on 14, missing from five feet.

Nicklaus fired at the green in two on the 15th, but he didn't quite make it. The ball hit near the top of the bank and rolled back down, coming to rest on some mud at the edge of the water. Jack took off his right sock, rolled his pants leg up, put his shoe back on for traction, stepped knee deep in the water, and blasted out of the muddy lie. The ball finished inches from the hole!

The birdie very briefly pulled Nicklaus into a four-way tie for the lead before Player birdied the 13th. The mud shot would have become legendary if Nicklaus had gone on to win. Alas, he followed by hitting his tee shot into a bunker on 16 and making a bogey. He would finish with two pars for a 69 and a seven-under total that was unlikely to be good enough.

Weiskopf birdied the 13th and 15th holes to get to nine-under, tied for first with Player. Tom promptly blew it by hitting a fat five-iron short and left into the water on 16. He scrambled for a one-putt bogey and lipped out birdie putts in the 20-foot range on the last two holes to finish at eight-under with a 70. His 33–37 final round was typical of his week—he played the back nine in even par compared to eight-under on the front.

Irwin rallied after playing the first seven holes in two-over, collecting birdies on Nos. 8, 12, 13, and 16 to get to eight-under. He, too, fell back, making a bogey on 18 when he missed from six feet. Colbert's troubles came early; he would finish with a bang by holing a 142-yard eight-iron for an eagle on the 18th, but all it got him was a 73 and a seven-under total.

It was down to the last twosome of Player and Stockton, who were hitting the ball nicely but not taking advantage of it. "We missed so many putts, it was ridiculous," said Stockton, whose feel on the greens abandoned him at the worst of times as he had trouble judging the speed of the surfaces.

His only birdie in a final-round 73 came on a two-putt on the 13th hole. That put him at eight-under, but he stayed there when he failed to convert a 10-foot birdie putt at 15. Player missed a four-footer for birdie there to stay at nine-under, and he and Stockton both parred 16.

Player struck the winning blow at the 17th with a nine-iron from "exactly 140 yards," he said. That's exactly how far it traveled, coming to rest six inches from the hole. Upon hitting the shot, Player immediately tossed his club to his caddie and said he wouldn't have to putt that one. He heard the gallery roar, but the approach at 17 is slightly uphill, so he couldn't see how close the ball was to the hole. As he walked to the green, he gestured to the crowd, holding his hands about three feet apart, then narrowing them as he was getting signals back from the spectators, finally holding them six inches apart.

1974

1	Gary Player	71–71–66–70—278
T2	Dave Stockton	71–66–70–73—280
T2	Tom Weiskopf	71–69–70–70—280
T4	Jim Colbert	67–72–69–73—281
T4	Hale Irwin	68–70–72–71—281
T4	Jack Nicklaus	69–71–72–69—281
T7	Bobby Nichols	73–68–68–73—282
T7	Phil Rodgers	72–69–68–73—282
T9	Maurice Bembridge	73–74–72–64—283
T9	Hubert Green	68–70–74–71—283

The tap-in birdie and a par at the closing hole gave Player a 70, a total of 278, two strokes better than Stockton and Weiskopf, for a second Masters title coming a record 13 years after his first. It was nice to win with a brilliant shot instead of bene-fitting from a fellow competitor's double bogey, as in 1961.

"You know that I'm inclined to exaggerate at times," Player admitted to the assembled press, before saying, "My tee-to-green play was far superior in this tour-nament than in any major championship. But I putted like a dub."

He wasn't really *that* bad on the greens but, after missing two four-foot putts on the back nine, Player was undoubtedly thrilled that his approach on 17 settled a few inches from the hole rather than a few feet.

Deuces Wild

Art Wall was a soft-spoken man with a flair for the spectacular on the golf course. He birdied five of the last six holes to win the 1959 Masters, and 15 years later he was at it again. This time the 50-year-old, in the field on a lifetime invitation from his victory, went 2–2–2 on three consecutive holes in the first round. He sank a 35-foot putt on the tough par-three fourth, holed a 220-yard four-wood for an eagle on the par-four fifth, and hit his tee shot to four feet and converted the birdie on the par-three sixth. The unprecedented burst was the impetus for a 32 on the front nine, though he finished with a 70. Wall went on to finish T37—but he did make another eagle, on the eighth hole of the third round.

1975

A headline in the *Augusta Chronicle* on the Sunday before the tournament read "Masters Could Reach New Heights This Year." The story below the headline covered the many intriguing storylines and scenarios that could play out to make this one of the greatest Masters ever. The tournament proved to be perhaps even better than anticipated.

The same three players were at the forefront of pre-tournament speculation as favorites for the second straight year—Jack Nicklaus, Johnny Miller, and Tom Weiskopf.

Nicklaus was coming off a year that wasn't up to his usual standards in 1974, but that was forgotten as he came into the Masters red hot with finishes of 3–3–1–1 in his last four tournaments. "My swing pattern is the best it's been in two or three years," he said.

Many thought that Nicklaus' hot streak was ignited by talk that Miller was on the verge of supplanting him as the best player in the game. The younger blond won eight tournaments in 1974 and started 1975 with a display of par-breaking that had never been seen before. He won the first two events of the tour season in Phoenix and Tucson by 14 and nine strokes, shooting a 61 in each tournament and finishing a combined 49-under par. When he added a win at the Bob Hope Desert Classic in his fourth start, he landed on the cover of *Newsweek*.

Throughout the spring, Nicklaus was constantly being asked about Miller and Miller about Nicklaus. "My best is as good as his best at times," said Miller on Tuesday of Masters week. "His worst is better than my worst. I think he's a lot better performer, more consistent." Nicklaus didn't want to get into any comparisons. When asked about Miller, he said, "Golf is a bigger game than any individual," and went on to say that he felt Gary Player had a better year than Miller in 1974 because he won two majors, adding the British Open to his Masters title, while Miller was shut out in the big ones.

Weiskopf had been in the background after a winless 1974, but thrust himself back into the conversation by finishing second to Nicklaus at the Heritage two weeks before the Masters and leading wire-to-wire to win in Greensboro the following week. Already a three-time runner-up in Augusta at age 32, Weiskopf had the Masters on his mind when he spoke with reporters following his Greensboro victory. "There's no reason I can't go to that final hole in Augusta with a chance to win," he said. "I'm not saying I'm going to win—nobody can do that. But if it doesn't happen this year, I'm confident it will happen some year."

Not so confident was Lee Trevino, but at least he was back after declining his invitation the previous year. Still skeptical of his Augusta chances, he returned because his 1974 PGA Championship victory meant that a green jacket would complete a career Grand Slam. "Now I've got to play," he said.

Another player was groundbreaking heading into this Masters: Lee Elder was about to become the first Black golfer to play in the tournament's 39-year history. The absence of African-American competitors had stood out conspicuously. This was especially true given the club's all-White membership and its location in the Jim Crow South, where racial segregation had been the norm up into the 1960s and efforts at integration widely opposed and slow to take root.

Indeed, the optics weren't good, but, until Elder, no Black golfer had met any of the qualifications for an invitation. Professional golf had been shamefully slow in opening to African-Americans, the PGA's Caucasian-only clause not eliminated until 1961 (some Black professionals had played in a limited number of tour events before then, but couldn't play a regular schedule nor join the PGA).

There were only a handful of African-American tour players in the 1960s, with Pete Brown the first to win a tournament in 1964 and Charlie Sifford claiming victories in 1967 and 1969. At the time, a tournament win wasn't one of the qualifications for the Masters. Through the late 1960s and early 1970s, the club expanded its qualification criteria in a general effort to make sure that quality pros didn't slip through the cracks, with the effect—intentional or not—of making it more likely a Black player would qualify. First, the number of otherwise unqualified players getting in from a points list was increased from four to six in 1968 and eight in 1971. Then, in 1972, it was announced that winners of PGA Tour events would be invited (with the points list being eliminated).

By then, it can fairly be said that Masters officials were hoping a Black player would qualify, if only to relieve the criticism. "The sooner we have a Black golfer, the happier we are going to be," Masters chairman Clifford Roberts said in 1971. "Sooner or later, we'll have a Black golfer in the Masters and we'll have a Black golfer as Masters champion."

In 1973, Congressman Herman Badillo wrote a letter to Roberts, urging him to invite Elder to the Masters, but Roberts declined, saying it would be "reverse discrimination." Elder made a name for himself by losing to Nicklaus in a playoff at the 1968 American Golf Classic in his rookie season and had been a regular in the top 40 on the money list. However, he hadn't managed to win a tournament, finish in the top 16 in the U.S. Open, or top eight in the PGA Championship, the main avenues to Masters qualification.

Finally, in 1974, the week after the Masters, Elder won the Monsanto Open in Pensacola, Florida, to qualify for Augusta. There would be a 51-week wait, during which Elder was inundated with interview requests from the press, television, and even talk shows. Finally, the time arrived. In his Tuesday interview, Elder said he shouldn't be compared to Jackie Robinson or other pioneers. "I really don't feel like a great man in history," he said.

That may have been true, but he certainly wasn't just another first-time Masters competitor. With heightened security—on hand just in case—Elder made his way to the first tee on Thursday and proceeded around the course to a warm reception on every green. Under the scrutiny, he shot a respectable 74, which was T39. However, a 78 the next day meant he missed the cut.

A light rain fell through most of the first round, keeping the greens soft and receptive. Bobby Nichols, the 1967 runner-up, led with a 67. Nicklaus was hovering at 68 after a nearly flawless ball-striking round, and noted that he hit all four par fives in two and every other green in regulation. He made a five-footer for a birdie at the third, three-putted the eighth for a par, and two-putted everywhere else. He didn't have many birdie chances on the par threes and fours, hitting a lot of approach shots in the 15- to 25-foot range in a round he said was unintentionally conservative.

Weiskopf had a similar round, though he bogeyed the 18th for a 69. He hit 16 greens, birdied all of the par fives, and had 34 putts, saying he left many putts short, unable to adjust to greens that were slower than usual.

Miller's putting problems were worse. He missed three par putts in the three- to five-foot range to go three-over through the first four holes and finished with a 75 while hitting 15 greens. Looking back on it decades later, he would tell Gil Capps for the book *The Magnificent Masters*, "I was over amped. I was over my comfort zone before the tournament started.... I just wanted to win it too badly."

Trevino, by contrast, got off to a great start, going four-under through seven holes. He said he was aided by learning to hook the ball within the last year—a shot he had employed in winning the 1974 PGA—and by soft conditions that helped his low approaches into greens, though he ultimately settled for a 71.

Nicklaus threatened to run away and hide in the second round with a 67 for a 135 total that tied the 36-hole record and a five-stroke lead, also tying the record. "It was the easiest 67 you've ever seen," said Jerry Heard after playing with Nicklaus, whose impeccable ball-striking continued.

Jack had to settle for pars on both front-nine par fives, but he hit iron shots to within seven feet for birdies on Nos. 6 and 7. He finally made a long putt, a 28-footer for birdie on 11, added a seven-foot birdie on 12, and seemingly routine two-putt birdies on 13 and 15 to go six-under for the day before making his first bogey of the tournament at the 18th, where he missed the green to the left.

Many felt that the tournament was essentially over. "Nobody can catch Nicklaus with a lead like that," said Bruce Devlin, a comment echoed by several other players.

While saying that he was playing "probably better than I ever have in my life," Nicklaus sought to dampen the notion that he had the tournament in the bag. "I've been coming to Augusta for many years. I've seen many strange things happen. I've blown five-stroke leads before and I've come from five behind before."

There was an interesting trio five strokes behind at 140. Forty-five-year-old Arnold Palmer (69–71) and 43-year-old Billy Casper (70–70) were trying to rekindle old glories while 25-year-old Tom Watson (70–70) was seeking to make a name for himself. Watson, who at that point owned one tour victory and had blown the 54-hole lead at the 1974 U.S. Open, played with Palmer and had an eagle on 13 from three feet. Palmer, wearing glasses at this stage of his career, was showing signs he wasn't through, having finished third at the Hawaiian Open earlier in the year. He took the lead early in the second round until bogeys at 11 and 12, along with the play of late-starter Nicklaus, dropped him back.

Weiskopf, who was in a six-way tie at 141 (including Nichols and Trevino), also had a disappointing back nine in shooting a 34–38—72, with bogeys on both par fives on the inward nine. His drive on the 13th came to rest next to a pine cone, which he didn't touch out of fear of causing the ball to move, and his second shot hit a tree. His drive on the 15th finished on the upslope of one of the fairway mounds, and he hit a one-iron fat and into the water. "That's like throwing four shots away—or at least three," he said of the twin bogeys.

Miller's putting and score were slightly better than the first round, but still not great, as he shot a 71 for a 146 total, 11 strokes behind Nicklaus.

Kenneth Denlinger in the *Washington Post* wrote, "Hey, Johnny Miller. Let me tell you something. All those 61s at Tu-nix, or whatever, and all that money don't mean much unless you win some tournaments the big guys want, too. Get yourself some more majors, kid, then maybe I'll get excited."

Winning this event was a longshot, but, on Saturday, Miller at least showed he could go low at Augusta National. The tour's streakiest player ran off six straight birdies from the second to seventh holes with a combination of ball-striking and a putter that finally warmed up. It started with a bunker shot to tap-in range for a birdie at No. 2, followed by putts of 14, 10, and 14 feet on the next three holes, a five-iron to a foot on the sixth, and a 35-foot putt from the fringe on No. 7. Miller broke the record of five straight birdies set last year by Player, whom he happened to be paired with, and Hale Irwin. Miller also set a record for the front nine with a 30.

Miller had stormed to a 63 in the final round to win the 1973 U.S. Open at Oakmont. Could he shoot a course-record 63 at Augusta? "I was more interested in the record than the tournament," said Miller, who figured he was too far back to have much of a chance at contention. His effort came up short when he made just one birdie on the back nine (a pitch to six feet from the bank of the creek on 13) and eight pars for a 65, with a birdie miss from six feet on 17.

With Nicklaus in the midst of a mediocre round, Miller realized when he finished that he might have a chance to win after all—and revealed his signature cockiness. "He [Nicklaus] had better not make a mistake. I'm certainly not going to choke. I could blow him right out of the box," Miller said.

Nicklaus was paired with Palmer in a match-up of the two four-time Masters champions—not necessarily good news for either of them, since they seldom played well when paired, perhaps because they were too wrapped up in trying to beat each other. The huge gallery watched Nicklaus shoot a 73 and Palmer scramble to a 75 on a day when he hit only six greens in regulation. Dan Foster of the *Greenville (S.C.) News* wrote that it was like watching "two guys staging a fistfight while their boat was sinking."

Nicklaus bogeyed the first from a bunker, birdied the second, then went to two-over on the day with three-putt bogeys on 10 and 11. A birdie on 12 helped, but a three-putt par on 13 slowed him and he parred in from there. His not-so-good day became even worse when Weiskopf wrapped up a round of 66, which meant Nicklaus went from five ahead to one behind.

"I didn't say, 'Gee whiz, Jack's won the tournament,'" said Weiskopf, who credited his round to better putting. Even par through five holes, Tom birdied Nos. 6, 8, 10, 13, 16, and 18, making a 30-footer on the 10th and 15-footers on 16 and 18 to take the lead, more than making up for a missed birdie putt from three feet on 15.

It was pointed out to Weiskopf that two weeks earlier at the Heritage, he made up six strokes on Nicklaus in the third round (68–74) to tie for the lead, and Jack ended up winning by three. "I hope it doesn't turn out like that tournament," Tom said.

Through 54 holes, the three consensus favorites were 1–2–3, with Weiskopf at 207, Nicklaus 208, and Miller 211. The only other player within five strokes was Watson at 212. Trevino fell back to 215 on the way to a T10 finish that he would never better at Augusta (he matched it in 1985).

The stage was set for a stirring final round, with Weiskopf and Miller in the final twosome in the 1–3 pairing scheme, and Nicklaus and Watson paired ahead of them in a preview of major championships to come. Watson wasn't a factor on Sunday, except for playing an unwanted supporting role in the round's key moment.

One other player deserves mention: Irwin, tying the tournament record with a 64 in the final round. It earned him a tie for fourth with Nichols, five strokes out of third place in what was the Nicklaus-Weiskopf-Miller show.

Nicklaus was uncharacteristically nervous at the start of the day, heading to the practice range in his street shoes before his caddie, Willie Peterson, pointed out to him that he needed to change. Jack went on to have a warmup where, he said, "I couldn't get with it. I couldn't get my tempo and my timing wasn't right." It carried over to the first tee, where he hit his tee shot way to the right, caroming off a tree and leading to a bogey.

Fortunately, the 35-year-old veteran of many majors realized what he was doing wrong—swinging too fast, with too short a backswing—and corrected it by the second hole. He birdied the second and third holes, each from three feet, to temporarily tie Weiskopf and initiate a back-and-forth front nine.

Weiskopf didn't have a birdie chance on the second after a poor drive, but he answered Nicklaus' birdie on No. 3 with one of his own from 18 feet to go back ahead by one. Nicklaus tied it again thanks to a five-iron to four feet on the fifth; Weiskopf made a birdie on the sixth (eight feet) to regain the lead. Finally, Nicklaus had a birdie that Weiskopf didn't have an answer for, sinking a nine-foot putt on the ninth for an outgoing 33 to Weiskopf's 34, leaving them tied at 11-under.

Miller went birdie-bogey on Nos. 2 and 3 to trail by five at that point. Birdies on the fourth (six feet) and sixth (14 feet) gave him a lifeline, and two more on the eighth (two-putt) and ninth (18 feet) catapulted him to a 32 on the opening nine and in serious contention two strokes off the lead. For the weekend, he played the front nine in 62 strokes.

The 11th hole was a setback for the final twosome. Weiskopf aimed his second shot at the right side of the green but came over the top of it and the ball hit left of the green and bounded into the water. Allowed to take a penalty drop directly on the other side of the pond (instead of a longer shot from the drop zone), Weiskopf hit an excellent pitch to three feet, salvaging a bogey. Miller found the green with his approach, 30 feet from the hole, but three-putted for a bogey, missing from just inside three feet.

Neither Nicklaus nor Weiskopf could birdie the 13th, Nicklaus pulling his second shot and hitting a poor chip and Weiskopf forced to lay up after a drive to the right. Miller made up a stroke with a two-putt birdie, and now it was Nicklaus at -11, Weiskopf at -10, and Miller at -9.

The action really began to get interesting at the 14th hole. Nicklaus came up short with his approach. Using a putter from the front fringe, he knocked it all the way to the back fringe, 20 feet past the hole, to set up a bogey. Weiskopf followed with a birdie thanks to an eight-iron to six feet; the two-stroke swing put him ahead by one. Miller made a crazy par. He hooked his tee shot, hit a tree on his second shot with the ball dropping straight down, then pulled off a brilliant eight-iron shot, hitting the flagstick to make a par from two feet.

Ahead on 15, Nicklaus hit a short (for him) drive in the fairway, leaving himself 245 yards from the hole. He pulled a three-wood out of the bag, but really wanted to hit a one-iron despite the distance being at the upper limit for that club. He waited for the wind to die down, then snatched the one-iron and hit a magnificent shot, nearly hitting the flagstick on the first bounce and settling 18 feet past the hole. The shot was so good that he celebrated it with raised arms walking down the fairway. Two putts later, he had a birdie and a tie for the lead.

Nicklaus hit a disappointing five-iron tee shot on 16, finishing 40 feet short of the hole. Behind him, Weiskopf hit a one-iron second shot over the green on 15, leaving a tough pitch that went 15 feet past the hole. Meanwhile, Nicklaus was in a waiting mode while playing partner Watson hit his tee shot on 16 into the water, walked up to the green to see if he could drop it there, but had to walk back toward the tee, dropped, then hit another shot in the water. After another penalty drop, he finally hit one onto the green—short of Nicklaus' ball and on the same line so Jack could watch how Tom's putt broke.

While Nicklaus was standing on the 16th green, Weiskopf holed his 15-foot putt to go back ahead by one. "That will be evil music ringing in Jack Nicklaus' ears," CBS announcer Ben Wright said of the gallery roar. Nicklaus was anything but rattled. "I had a feeling about that putt. 'I think I can make this,' I said to myself," he told the press after the round. From 40 feet uphill to the back-right hole location, he did make it, setting off a celebratory jog across the green as Nicklaus was now tied for the lead again.

Because it took so long for Nicklaus and Watson to play the 16th hole, Weiskopf and Miller (who two-putted for birdie on 15 to stay within two) were standing on the tee when Nicklaus holed his putt. "Back on the tee, Weiskopf has to take it this time, having dished it out on the hole before," said Henry Longhurst, calling the action on the 16th hole.

"I knew Tom was going to have a tough time playing the hole after watching me make two," said Nicklaus. Indeed, he did. Changing clubs from a six-iron to a five-iron, Weiskopf tried to make an easy swing and instead made a bad one, catching the turf behind the ball and coming up short on the front fringe more than 100 feet from the hole. He used a putter from there, but the position of the ridge he had to climb made it an almost impossible shot, and the slope took the ball 15 feet left of the hole. That one didn't fall, and the bogey dropped Weiskopf one behind. For the second time in three holes there was a two-stroke swing, this one in the opposite direction.

1975

1	Jack Nicklaus	68-67-73-68—276
T2	Johnny Miller	75-71-65-66—277
T2	Tom Weiskopf	69-72-66-70—277
T4	Hale Irwin	73-74-71-64—282
T4	Bobby Nichols	67-74-72-69—282
6	Billy Casper	70-70-73-70—283
7	Dave Hill	75-71-70-68—284
T8	Hubert Green	74-71-70-70—285
T8	Tom Watson	70-70-72-73—285
T10	Tom Kite	72-74-71-69—286
T10	J.C. Snead	69-72-75-70—286
T10	Lee Trevino	71-70-74-71—286

The steely Nicklaus wasn't going to make a mistake down the stretch. He made a routine par at 17 and hit a nice approach to 11 feet at the closing hole. While he was waiting to putt, Weiskopf missed a 20-foot birdie putt on 17, and Miller elicited a roar with a birdie from 15 feet to pull within one for the first time all day. Again, Watson putting first helped Nicklaus, this time giving him a chance to see on the scoreboard which player had birdied 17. Noticing he still held a one-stroke lead, he hit a conservative putt and tapped in for a par and a 68.

Miller carved a drive into the fairway, aiming at the bunkers and hitting a big fade. Weiskopf had been going with a three-wood off the tee for most of the day and had hit a three-wood or one-iron on the 18th in the first three rounds. He decided to go with a driver on the 72nd hole and unleashed a monster tee shot, flying over the corner of the dogleg and finishing 46 yards ahead of Miller's ball. It was the best drive anyone had ever seen on the 18th.

With the pin on the left side of the green, Miller decided to aim his seven-iron to the right of the flag. "That's the only regret I have about the whole tournament," he said, as his shot went where he aimed it, finishing 18 feet from the hole, to the right and past it. Weiskopf covered the flagstick with his nine-iron approach, giving himself a birdie chance from eight feet behind the hole.

The scene was drenched with drama as two of the most talented players of the era—each owning only one major but currently challenging for supremacy in the contemporary scene—had putts to tie the greatest major champion of all time. Miller went first, and his putt broke below the hole. Now it was Weiskopf. He rapped his putt a little too firmly, and it took the break only after passing the hole. Nicklaus was the champion of the Masters for the fifth time, surpassing Palmer.

In the immediate aftermath, Weiskopf struggled to describe the feeling on the 18th green as the missed putt gave him a 70 and a fourth runner-up finish at Augusta. "Someone once said you can't explain pain," he said.

Miller wasn't as crestfallen. "I was just fighting my guts out trying to catch those guys," he said. "I had 131 for two days here [with a 66 in the final round]. I would say that's not too shabby."

Nicklaus said, "I had the best feeling of control over the golf ball for a stretch of four days that I can remember. This is the best I've played ever."

The greatest player in the history of the game played his best golf, and yet won by only one stroke over his two top current rivals. No wonder nearly every magazine and newspaper account called it the greatest Masters ever. Nicklaus concurred.

"In all the time I have played golf, I thought this was the most exciting display I had ever seen," he said after the round.

....

A Playoff Switch

On the Monday morning after the Masters, Augusta was hit with nearly an inch of rain. That would have been the day of an 18-hole playoff had the tournament finished in a tie; it's uncertain whether it could have been completed that day. The PGA Tour had long gone to sudden-death playoffs to decide ties, but the four major championships all held to the 18-hole format. Masters chairman Clifford Roberts decided that the downsides of waiting an extra day to determine a champion outweighed the perception that a full-round test was needed to break a tie in a big tournament. Before the 1976 tournament, he announced that a tie in the Masters would be settled in a sudden-death playoff. The PGA Championship followed suit a year later and held the first sudden-death playoff in a major in 1977, while no playoff was necessary at the Masters until 1979.

....

1976

Ray Floyd burst onto the tour in 1963, showing great promise by winning the St. Petersburg Open at age 20. He seemed to be well on the way to fulfilling that promise when he won the PGA Championship and two other tournaments in 1969.

However, Floyd was also developing a reputation as a partier. Over the next few years of winless mediocrity golf seemed to take a back seat to having a good time. That changed in 1973 when he met and married a woman named Maria, whom he credited with getting him on the right path and dedicating himself to golf again.

Floyd returned to the top 20 on the money list in 1974, and, in 1975, claimed his first victory in six years when he captured the Kemper Open. Still, he wasn't seen as a major force in golf. In the annual *Augusta Chronicle* poll of sportswriters and local pros, 18 players were mentioned as either a 1–2–3 pick or a dark horse. Floyd got zero mentions.

In the first round, Floyd showed that he was now a force to be reckoned with, leading an assault on par with a 65. His not-so-secret weapon was a five-wood that he put in the bag to enable higher second-shot approaches to Augusta National's par fives and to better handle sidehill lies. The club replaced a one-iron, which, upon reflection, Floyd realized he had hardly used in his nine previous Masters.

Floyd employed the five-wood on three par fives, hitting the green on all three occasions for two-putt birdies. "I'm tickled to death with that club," said Floyd, who also used a three-wood second shot to set up a chip-and-putt birdie on the other par five. Floyd surged home with four straight birdies starting at the 13th, giving him eight birdies against a lone bogey at the 12th.

Seven players broke 70, including Andy North, who was second with a 66 but destined for an 81 the next day. The main threat was Jack Nicklaus, who managed a 67 despite not making a putt longer than five feet—an eagle on 15 helped. Larry

Ziegler, a long-hitting journeyman, also had a 67 with a birdie-eagle-birdie streak on Nos. 13 through 15 in unconventional fashion, the eagle coming with a holed eight-iron on the par-four 14th.

Nicklaus teed off relatively early in the second round with a chance to put some pressure on, but it was playing partner Ben Crenshaw who got off to a flying start. The 24-year-old Texan, who shot a 70 on Thursday, started birdie-eagle-birdie on the first three holes to pull within one of Floyd before the leader teed off. While Crenshaw cooled off to shoot another 70, Nicklaus joined the chase. Even par through six holes despite an eagle on the second, Nicklaus holed a 95-yard sand wedge shot for an eagle on the par-four seventh—his third eagle in a span of 11 holes.

Twice on the back nine, on 13 and 15, Nicklaus momentarily caught Floyd on the leaderboard, but Ray, still on the front nine, quickly made a birdie of his own each time. Nicklaus bogeyed the 16th and headed for the press interview two strokes behind with a 69. He wouldn't stay that close for long, as Floyd had plenty of holes remaining to do some damage.

Following a 33 on the first nine with three pars, Floyd had an anxious moment with his five-wood on the 13th, which fortunately just cleared the water and ended up just inside the hazard line with a good lie. He took advantage with a pitch to eight feet and a birdie, then he holed a 25-foot birdie putt on the 14th.

Floyd needed a three-wood for his second shot on 15 instead of his trusty five-wood. It was a bit of a gamble from 245 yards, but it paid off beautifully. The shot soared high in the air, landed softly 10 feet short of the hole, and looked like it might find the cup for a double eagle before settling three feet away. The resulting eagle put Floyd seven-under for the round with a chance to duplicate his opening 65. A three-putt bogey from 90 feet on the 17th prevented that, but a 10-foot par putt on 18 got him home with a 66.

The 33-year-old North Carolinian was the son of a club pro, L.B., who taught him the game, but in the last couple of years he had been working with Nicklaus' teacher, Jack Grout. Floyd was so dialed in that he said he was not only hitting fairways but specific points he was aiming at. He was nine-under on the par fives through two rounds. Not to mention his putter—he didn't miss a putt inside 15 feet on Friday.

Floyd's 131 total for 36 holes was a record by four shots, surpassing Henry Picard (1935), Byron Nelson (1942), Ken Venturi (1956), and Nicklaus (1975), and giving him a five-stroke lead on Nicklaus. Hubert Green was next at 137 thanks to a 66 of his own.

Green was red hot with wins in his last three starts heading into the Masters. The man who complained early in his career about a lack of attention, as most of the eight wins in his first five years came in low-profile events, now said he was getting too much attention. Perhaps trying too hard, Green shot himself out of it with a 41 on the back nine of the third round for a 78, his round turning in the wrong direction when he gambled to make birdies to catch Floyd and instead made bogeys.

With greens firming up and pin positions on the diabolical side, Augusta National parried against low scoring on Saturday. Only two players broke 70, both of whom starting too far back to be factors: Hale Irwin with a 67 and Lee Trevino enjoying a rare respite from his Augusta woes with a 69 after barely making the cut.

In those circumstances, Floyd's third-round 70 was almost as good as his opening rounds, boosting his lead to a record-smashing eight strokes (nobody had ever led by more than five through 54 holes). He continued making birdies look routine on the par fives, where his four birdies put him a remarkable 13-under on the week through 12 holes.

It all wasn't flawless. Floyd overcame some adversity during the round, namely a double bogey on the 11th, where he hit his second shot in the water to slip to one-over on the day with his lead down to four strokes. On the 13th, Floyd decided that staying in attack mode would produce the best results this week. His drive strayed to the right, leaving him with a sidehill lie on bare ground with 219 yards to clear the water. He elected not to lay up, he said, because there was little chance of birdie playing it that way with the pin so close to the hazard.

Floyd pulled out (what else?) his five-wood. "If I would have missed it just slightly, I would have been in the hazard," he said. He didn't miss, of course; in fact, he hit it so solidly he surprised himself by reaching the bunker on the far side of the green. He blasted to three feet for a birdie that righted the ship, followed with a routine birdie on the 15th (five-wood second shot, two putts), and closed the round with a birdie from eight feet on 18.

"It was quite an enjoyable day," said Floyd, who checked the leaderboards frequently as he strolled around the course. "Every time one of the leaders got a bogey, I had another shot in the lead."

Indeed, the struggles of the other contenders helped make it a runaway. Nicklaus was three-over through 10 before birdies on 13 and 14 brought him a 73 and second place eight behind at 209. Ziegler stayed the closest for a while with a 34 on the front nine, then he was birdie-less on the back for a 38 and 72—210.

If one tried hard enough, a scenario could be imagined in which Floyd could possibly lose—only because it was Nicklaus who was closest. Clearly, nobody else had a chance, but if Jack shot a 65, well…

It didn't take long on Sunday to see that a comeback wouldn't materialize. Nicklaus didn't get the birdie he needed on the par-five second, then he bogeyed the third and shot a 37 on the front nine. Nicklaus being Nicklaus, he still didn't think he was out of it. "If I could shoot a 30 on the back nine and put some pressure on," he thought to himself as he made the turn; instead he shot a 36 for a 73 and a T3 finish with Ziegler (72).

There was so little happening of import in the final round that two sports-writers were sleeping and snoring in the press tent in the final round, while others were watching television—of the NBA playoff game on an adjacent screen to the closed-circuit Masters broadcast.

1976

1	Raymond Floyd	65–66–70–70—271
2	Ben Crenshaw	70–70–72–67—279
T3	Jack Nicklaus	67–69–73–73—282
T3	Larry Ziegler	67–71–72–72—282
T5	Charles Coody	72–69–70–74—285
T5	Hale Irwin	71–77–67–70—285
T5	Tom Kite	73–67–72–73—285
8	Billy Casper	71–76–71–69—287
T9	Roger Maltbie	72–75–70–71—288
T9	Graham Marsh	73–68–75–72—288
T9	Tom Weiskopf	73–71–70–74—288

Finally, Crenshaw injected some life into the day. Starting out at 212, the young mophead with the long swing and pure putting stroke eagled the 13th, birdied the 14th from the trees, and splashed a shot out of the water hazard to par 15, finishing with a 67, one of only three Sunday rounds in the 60s. "I was just playing for second. I was free-wheeling it," he said. "Yes, I definitely think in the future I'll have my year here."

The only suspense was whether Floyd would be able to beat or match Nicklaus' 72-hole record of 17-under 271, needing a 70 to tie it, not an easy target on this day. He made only one bogey, on the fourth, and birdied Nos. 5, 12, and 15 for a 70 and a share of the record, though his eight-stroke victory margin was one shy of Nicklaus' in 1965.

He broke one record by going 14-under on the par fives, the previous best being Jimmy Demaret's 13-under in 1950. Floyd managed only to par the first three par fives on Sunday and laid up on the 15th, not from conservative play but rather due to a relatively short drive. It was the first time all week he didn't go for a par five in two, an indication of how well he was driving the ball. He got this birdie in different fashion with a sand-wedge approach and 15-foot putt.

As for the 72-hole record, Nicklaus said, "I really am surprised to see the record tied. I thought it would stand for a long time."

Floyd hoped that in addition to making Masters history, his performance would mark a turning point in his career.

"People might say I *was* a great player," he said, referring to the fast start to his career. "I want to *be* a great player. I had the talent. I knew it was there. I just had to go get it. I'm tired of being a mediocre player.... I want to win a lot of tournaments."

The Masters marked his seventh victory at age 33. He would go on to win 15 after that, including the 1981 PGA Championship and 1986 U.S. Open.

1977

Tom Watson had two victories in 1977 coming into the Masters and was the leading money winner by a healthy margin. He was also being called a choker.

The label was first hung on Watson early in his career when he lost third-round leads at the 1973 Hawaiian Open and World Open and 1974 U.S. Open with rounds ranging from 75 to 79. He seemingly escaped it by claiming a major title at the 1975 British Open. However, he had blown leads in his last two tournaments entering the 1977 Masters, closing with a 77 at the Players Championship and a 74 at the Heritage Classic, losing a four-stroke 54-hole advantage at the latter event.

So, questions from the press were warranted. Watson got them early in the week, and they only intensified as he stayed in contention through the first three rounds. Some of the questions were rather blunt, including, "Do you choke?"

Watson blamed his recent final-round woes on swing issues, noting that he felt he was swinging well early in the year when he won the Bing Crosby Pro-Am and San Diego Open but wasn't so comfortable in the last month or so. "I just didn't have a swing I could believe in," he said. "When you get under pressure, it's difficult to feel confident when you don't trust your swing."

Watson also said that he was a "jumpy person" and that his swing sometimes got too fast, so he needed to try to walk slowly and waggle slowly in order to carry over to his swing.

The 27-year-old worked with his mentor Byron Nelson during the week to try to solve his swing problems. Nelson, always in town for the Masters as the 1937 and 1942 champion, was essentially Watson's swing coach at this time, and the two headed to the range at nearby West Lake Country Club for a session on Tuesday, working on swing fundamentals and tempo.

Watson had a satisfactory start with a 70 in the first round, good for a tie for fourth on a day marked by tricky winds. Hubert Green birdied four of the last six holes for a 67 and a two-stroke lead over 47-year-old Don January and 24-year-old Billy Kratzert. Jack Nicklaus, in his annual role as favorite, shot a 72 and lamented his putting—he said that with an average day on the greens it would have been a 68.

Green had 11 wins to that point in his career but was still looking for his first major. "It's the majors where the greats stand up. I've always sat down," he admitted. Alas, Green took a seat, or at least a step backward, with a 74 in the second round while Watson and Rod Funseth moved into a tie for the lead at 139. Neither of them exuded confidence heading into the weekend.

"I wasn't very happy with the way I played. I didn't hit the ball solid," said Watson, noting that he hit a lot of iron shots thin. He was happy to get everything out of the round that he could, with birdies on all four par fives in a 69 marred by a bogey on the final hole. On the one hand, it was a good sign to be leading after what he considered a mediocre ball-striking round. However, considering his comments about a general lack of confidence in his swing, and his troubles of the last few weeks, perhaps it was a day that didn't portend well for the weekend.

Funseth had the best round of the day, a 67, scoring consecutive birdies on holes 7–10. He frankly didn't expect his position at the top of the leaderboard to last. "I couldn't imagine myself as Masters champion.... It's only one good round," he said, in either a display of honesty or an attempt to lower expectations. The 44-year-old owned only two tour victories (he would end his career with three), but had set or tied several course records along the way, demonstrating an ability for "one good round" while rarely being able to put four of them together.

Nicklaus was in a tie for eighth at 142 after a 70 that was only a slightly better putting round than his first—he made a couple of putts longer than 10 feet, though he missed three in the four-foot range. Jack finally putted better in the third round, but didn't hit the ball as well and some of the putts he made were for pars. With a 70 he remained three strokes behind and now in a tie for fourth.

Watson had a 70 and again held a share of the lead, this time with Ben Crenshaw, who had a 69 for a matching 209 total. While Watson was now well established, Crenshaw had the flashier amateur record and a victory in the fall of 1973 in his first event as a PGA Tour member. The University of Texas product was winless in 1974 and 1975 before breaking through with three victories in 1976, a comeback of sorts at age 24.

Crenshaw was known for his velvety putting stroke, making him a good fit for Augusta National. He needed his putting and short-game prowess on the first six holes on Saturday, as he saved par after missing four of the greens. Ben got his game under control after that, collecting birdies on three of the next seven holes.

Asked about the presence of Nicklaus lurking behind, Crenshaw gave him respect, but spoke for the tour's young lions when saying, "We're not as scared of him as we used to be."

Watson wasn't happy about misjudging the wind on four approach shots, though he emerged with pars on three of those holes. Birdies on 15 and 18, the latter after a six-iron to five feet, enabled him to join Crenshaw at the top.

Rik Massengale, a 30-year-old who won the Bob Hope Desert Classic early in the year, made the day's biggest move with a 32 on the front nine to temporarily take the lead. He promptly bogeyed 10 and 11, though he did recover with three birdies on the way in for the day's best round, a 67, to sit one stroke off the lead. It was two strokes further back to Nicklaus and Jim Colbert.

The 1–3 pairing format split Watson and Crenshaw, Watson going in the last twosome with Massengale while Crenshaw drew the assignment of playing with Nicklaus just ahead of them. Perhaps he wasn't scared, but Crenshaw played like he was uncomfortable, bogeying the second and third holes and spiraling downward to a 76 and a T8 finish.

Watson and Massengale threatened to turn the tournament into a two-man race on the front nine. Massengale birdied the second to tie for the lead, then the pair put on a show starting on the difficult par-four fifth, where both birdied. Watson went one ahead with a 15-foot birdie putt on the sixth. Massengale hit his second shot to four feet on the seventh, and so did Watson. Two more birdies. Both also birdied the eighth, Massengale with a two-putt and Watson holing a 15-footer after hitting his three-wood second shot well to the right. It was four straight birdies for Watson, three of them matched by Massengale.

Nicklaus had a fine front nine of his own with birdies on the first, second, and eighth holes for a 33. As he walked to the 10th tee, he was surprised to see he had actually lost a stroke and was now four behind.

It didn't take long for the situation to change. Nicklaus birdied the 10th hole with a beautiful four-iron to five feet. As he had done a day earlier, Massengale bogeyed the 10th and 11th; this time he didn't make any more birdies and was on his way to a 70. Watson bogeyed the 10th, missing from four feet. Was this the start of a back-nine collapse?

Meanwhile, up ahead, Tom Kite was making a move. With the rare feat of consecutive birdies on Nos. 10–12, he went to five-under on the day and eight-under for the tournament, two behind leader Watson and tied with Nicklaus.

Nicklaus held his ground thanks to a 12-foot putt for par

1977		
1	Tom Watson	70–69–70–67—276
2	Jack Nicklaus	72–70–70–66—278
T3	Tom Kite	70–73–70–67—280
T3	Rik Massengale	70–73–67–70—280
5	Hale Irwin	70–74–70–68—282
T6	David Graham	75–67–73–69—284
T6	Lou Graham	75–71–69–69—284
T8	Ben Crenshaw	71–69–69–76—285
T8	Raymond Floyd	71–72–71–71—285
T8	Hubert Green	67–74–72–72—285
T8	Don January	69–76–71–69—285
T8	Gene Littler	71–72–73–69—285
T8	John Schlee	75–73–69–68—285

on the 11th, gained a stroke with a 12-footer on the 12th for a birdie, and another with a two-putt birdie on 13. Standing in the 13th fairway, Watson saw Nicklaus look back and give a wave after his birdie. Tom thought the gesture was directed at him, as in laying down a challenge, and became momentarily angry. After the round, Nicklaus assured him that he was merely waving at the gallery; in any case, a fired-up Watson hit a two-iron to the fringe and chipped to three feet for a birdie to regain the lead.

Nicklaus barely missed a 15-foot birdie putt at the 14th. Minutes later, Watson made a bogey there when he left his approach short of the big hump in the green and three-putted from 45 feet, missing a five-footer.

Again, Watson watched from the fairway as Nicklaus birdied a par five, this time nearly holing a chip from behind the 15th green that would have been an eagle—and this time taking the lead. For the second time on the back nine, Watson answered with a well-struck two-iron over the water to the back fringe and a birdie.

Was this the same Watson who had blown the lead in his last two tournaments? As he strode the fairways and swung with confidence, it didn't seem so. Still, victory was a 50–50 proposition at best, as he went to the last three holes tied with the game's dominant player. (Kite was out of it, with a birdie on 15 offset by a bogey on 16 to finish at eight-under with a 67 while Watson and Nicklaus were 10-under.) The possibility of a playoff loomed large.

Watson missed a 15-foot birdie putt on 16 and thought to himself, "I have to birdie one of the last two holes." He struck a nine-iron approach to 20 feet on 17 and sized up a right-to-left slightly downhill putt. The man who made more long putts than anyone at this stage of his career struck it perfectly and leaped in the air when it dropped into the hole.

Standing in the 18th fairway contemplating his approach shot, Nicklaus heard the gallery roar and now knew he was one behind. Originally planning to hit a six-iron approach to the center of the green, past the pin, now he figured he had to fire at the flagstick but later admitted "my mind wasn't ready" for the change in strategy. He didn't think a seven-iron was enough, so he tried a soft six-iron and wasn't able to execute it, the ball falling into the front bunker. The resulting bogey enabled Watson to win by two with a par at the last hole.

Nicklaus had fired a 66, yet at the end it was Watson who struck the killer blow and Nicklaus who blinked. The need to stay aggressive in the face of Nicklaus' charge served Watson well.

"I knew I couldn't make pars and beat Jack," said the new champion, who shot a 67 for a 276 total that had been bettered only three times in Masters history. Despite the excitement of the day, Watson said he was able to resist going too fast with his pace or his swing, except on the first tee where he hooked his tee shot into the trees and still emerged with a par.

At Watson's post-round press conference, a writer asked a question that was perhaps inevitable but would never need to be asked again: "Does this mean an end to the choker image?"

"What do you think?" Watson replied. "I'll let you answer that question."

....

Familiar Position

Hale Irwin posted his fourth straight top-five finish in the Masters, though for the third straight time he wasn't in the title hunt on Sunday. Irwin's only real chance at victory was in 1974 when he began the final round three strokes out of the lead and shot a 71 to finish T4, three strokes behind. He came from well back with a closing 64 to finish T4 in 1975, six strokes back of the winner, was 14 strokes behind in a T5 when Ray Floyd ran away from the field in 1976, and six strokes off Tom Watson's winning score in finishing fifth with a closing 68 in 1977. The three-time U.S. Open champion went on to post three more top-10 finishes, in 1978, 1983, and 1991, none in the top five.

....

1978

Gary Player was irked during the Greater Greensboro Open the week before the Masters when the local paper referred to him as a "fading star." The 42-year-old hadn't won on the PGA Tour since 1974, but felt he deserved credit for winning several times in his native South Afrrica during that time.

One star who definitely wasn't fading was 38-year-old Jack Nicklaus. Though outdueled by Tom Watson at both the Masters and British Open in 1977, Nicklaus recovered and came into this Masters with finishes of 2–1–2–1 in his last four tournaments.

Nicklaus and Player shot 72s and Watson a 73 in the first round, while the leader was John Schlee with a 68. Schlee had mostly quit the tour to take a club job in the fall of the previous year, but he had a Masters invitation thanks to a T8 finish at Augusta in an otherwise poor 1977 season. He would follow with three rounds of 75 or worse to finish T42.

The most notable figure on the first-round leaderboard was Lee Trevino in a tie for third with a 70, including a 32 on the back nine. Trevino had missed the 1977 Masters due to back problems related to surgery in the fall of the previous year (not because of declining an invitation as he had done in the past). Oddly, Trevino said the after-effects of that back surgery gave him more hope at Augusta National. He had been forced to change his swing, and now said he was hitting the ball higher, could hit a draw as easily as a fade, and was longer off the tee.

The new-found ability to hit a long draw around the corner enabled Trevino to hit a six-iron second shot to the par-five second in the second round, setting up a birdie that was the catalyst for a 69 and a share of the lead. Needing a Masters victory to accomplish a career Grand Slam, the Merry Mex said, "If I win here Sunday, I wouldn't know about it until Thursday. We'd probably have the damnedest party on that Par 3 Course that you've ever seen."

For the second consecutive year, Rod Funseth was tied for first with a 139 total with a great second round, going one better than a year earlier with a 66. He sounded slightly more positive this time. "If I could have two more rounds like today, I'd have no problem."

Another repeat from 1977 was Hubert Green sitting at 141, two strokes off the lead, this time moving forward in the second round with a 69. Having finally captured his first major at the 1977 U.S. Open, Green was focused on winning: "I don't want to finish second or third here."

Watson was also at 141 thanks to a 68 that he felt could have been even better considering how close he hit the ball to the hole. Nicklaus had a 73 for a 145 total and wasn't happy with the relatively slow pace of the greens—"membership speed," he called it.

Scoring improved on the weekend, Green going the lowest on Saturday with a 65 for a 206 total and a three-stroke lead. The Alabama native, who said he wanted to win the Masters more than any other tournament, played the first eight holes in five-under for a 31 on the front nine and did some scrambling on the back, including a seven-foot par putt that wiggled in on the 18th.

Green was bolstered by the fact that he had held onto the 54-hole lead in winning the U.S. Open the previous summer. "I would rather be three ahead than three behind," he said. "I'm the guy that can lose the tournament; the others have to win it."

While a three-stroke lead was a nice cushion, Watson was a formidable contender to hold off after a 68 for 209. Tom was two-over through six holes, when he said he got angry after a second three-putt green and turned his fortunes around. He finally got the putter working—along with everything else—to play the last 12 holes in six-under, including a par save at 18. He was tied for second with Funseth, who hung in there with a solid 70.

Trevino's hopes were dealt a severe blow when he triple bogeyed the fifth hole, courtesy of a three-iron approach that flew over the green into some bushes. He was proud that he managed to come back for a 72 for 211 to trail by five, but admitted that "I think any green jacket went out the window." He would follow with a 74 and finish T14.

Nicklaus had a 33 on the back nine for a 69 that left him eight strokes off the lead at 214. His frustration came out when a writer asked him how it felt to keep hitting the ball close to the hole and not make putts. "It drives you absolutely up a tree!" he responded. A final-round 67 on Sunday was too late—and not even the best round of the day—as Nicklaus finished seventh.

Not receiving any attention from the press through 54 holes was Gary Player, who quietly birdied the 13th, 14th, and 15th for a 69 on Saturday, went to the locker room, and fell asleep. He had opened with 72–72 and was tied for 10th, seven strokes behind.

On Sunday morning, Player's 16-year-old son, Wayne, told him, "Dad, if you putt well, you'll shoot 64." Gary had switched a week earlier from his usual "pop" putting stroke to a longer stroke as employed by many younger players. He wasn't comfortable with it in Greensboro or the first three rounds at Augusta, but something clicked on Sunday and he putted lights-out.

His birdie at the second was a tap-in, and that was followed by a 30-foot birdie putt at the fourth. A bogey at the seventh was a setback, and at one-under on the day and four-under on the tournament through eight holes, he still barely registered as he was six behind. The determined South African, his eyes burning with intensity, proceeded to play the last 10 holes in seven-under to match the course record 64.

Player birdied the ninth from 12 feet and holed a 25-footer to birdie the 10th. He nearly chipped in for a birdie on 11, laying on the ground and kicking his feet in the air in a display that showed he felt he was very much in the race. He followed with a 15-foot birdie putt at the 12th and another birdie at the 13th, where he left his 15-foot eagle try on the lip.

After his second shot on 13, Player said to the other member of his twosome, future Masters champion Seve Ballesteros, "Seve, I want to tell you something," and waved his club at the spectators. "These people think I can't win anymore, but I'm going to show them they're wrong."

Now Player was eight-under and would get within one of the lead when, behind him, Green hit in the water on the 11th and managed a bogey with a nice pitch shot. That was Green's third bogey of the round against two birdies to that point—a lackluster start that left him in a four-way dogfight that was as taut as any the Masters had seen.

The 45-year-old Funseth, still the owner of just two career wins, was making a game effort against his more illustrious foes and managing to ignore whatever negative thoughts he might have had. A six-foot birdie putt at the tough 10th got him to two-under for the round, nine-under overall, and tied for the lead when Green bogeyed 11.

Watson birdied the second and otherwise had all pars through the 12th, including a couple of nice saves. On the 13th, he rifled a two-iron to 20 feet and drained the putt for an eagle that got him to 10-under, leapfrogging into the lead.

It soon became a four-way tie. Up ahead Player had two-putted for a birdie at 15 after a full-bore three-wood to the green and now he holed a 15-foot birdie putt at 16. Behind Watson, Green and Funseth, playing together in the last twosome, both birdied 13 to get to 10-under.

On this volatile day, it wouldn't stay tied for long. Watson hurt his cause with a blunder on the 14th, where he missed a slick six-foot birdie putt, and then missed the two-and-a-half-foot comebacker and made a bogey. "I hit a good putt that didn't go in, and a bad putt that didn't come close," said Watson.

1978		
1	Gary Player	72–72–69–64—277
T2	Rod Funseth	73–66–70–69—278
T2	Hubert Green	72–69–65–72—278
T2	Tom Watson	73–68–68–69—278
T5	Wally Armstrong	72–70–70–68—280
T5	Billy Kratzert	70–74–67–69—280
7	Jack Nicklaus	72–73–69–67—281
8	Hale Irwin	73–67–71–71—282
T9	David Graham	75–69–67–72—283
T9	Joe Inman	69–73–72–69—283

Minutes later, Funseth also three-putted, missing a three-footer from nearly the same spot as Watson. To their credit, Watson and Funseth both recovered with birdies at the 15th to get back to 10-under.

Player, with a chance to set a target score, hit a six-iron approach 15 feet past the hole on the 18th. Experience and his red-hot, new putting stroke both worked in his favor. He remembered the eight-foot putt he had missed on the same line in 1970 that would have gotten him into a playoff, a putt that didn't take the expected break. This time he played it straight and rolled the putt into the hole—the sixth putt of 12 feet or longer Player made during the round, one that gave him a 30 on the back nine. Following a fist pump and a hug from 21-year-old Ballesteros, Player retired to watch on television as three players tried to match his 277 total.

Two of them had already reached 11-under by the time Player got to the TV room. Watson holed a 15-foot putt at the 16th and Green tapped in for a birdie on 15 after narrowly missing from 20 feet for eagle.

Like a year earlier, Watson was tied for the lead coming to 17. He didn't get a birdie there this time, and he put himself in trouble on the 18th when he hooked his four-wood tee shot into an area of newly planted small pine trees. His planned slice with a four-iron didn't come off and his approach bounced down a hill into the gallery to the left of the green. Facing a tough recovery, he used a putter to roll the ball up the slope to 12 feet from the hole. The putt didn't fall, and the bogey enabled Player to dodge one challenger.

Green slipped to 10-under with a three-putt bogey from 15 feet on 16, missing a three-footer. As he and Funseth walked up the 18th fairway, Green pointed out to his fellow competitor that they were in the identical situation as Weiskopf and Johnny Miller had been in 1975: needing birdies to force a tie.

Just as Weiskopf and Miller had done, both rose to the occasion on their approach shots—Funseth a good one to 20 feet behind the hole and Green a great one with an eight-iron from 137 yards to three feet.

Funseth went first and barely missed, leaving him with a 69 and 10-under total. Now all Green had to do was hole his three-footer and force sudden-death. It was a prospect Player admitted he dreaded—he was 1–8 in sudden-death playoffs on the PGA Tour (3–10 overall including 18-hole playoffs). Green lined up the putt, stood over it—and stepped away. He had heard CBS radio announcer Jim Kelly in the booth next to the green say that he needed this putt to force a playoff.

Green got into his hunched-over stance again, stroked the ball, and reacted with dismay as the putt missed to the right. Player was the champion, and the title Green wanted so badly had slipped through his grasp.

"I have no one to blame but myself," said Green, referring not just to the putt but to other mistakes along the way. "Gary Player shot a fine round, make that a great round, but if I shoot a 70 it doesn't matter."

A shaken Green returned to the 18th green after the interview and tried the three-footer five times, making four (he missed the second attempt).

Putting truly determined the outcome of this Masters, not just the ones Player made but the ones others missed. Watson, Funseth, and Green all missed from three feet or less over the last five holes—Green twice.

Player, of course, would take it any way he could get it, and with a 64 he certainly earned his third Masters title. At 42 years, five months he became the oldest Masters champion, and just to prove that he wasn't fading, he went out and won the next two weeks on the PGA Tour to make it three in a row.

....

13 on 13

Japan's Tsuneyuki Nakajima (he would later become known as Tommy) wasn't going to make the cut after an opening 80, but he had a good second round going until he reached the 13th hole and proceeded to make a 13. He drove into the creek on the left, took a penalty drop, hit his third down the fairway, and dumped his fourth into the creek by the green. This is where it got weird. He tried to play out of the hazard, but the ball popped up and hit his foot when it came down for a two-stroke penalty. Nakajima tried to give his club to his caddie for cleaning, but in doing so the club touched the ground in the hazard for another two-stroke penalty. He then played out of the hazard, the ball flying into a bunker on the other side of the green. A blast and two putts later, he had a 13 on his scorecard, making his second-round 80 somewhat respectable under the circumstances. In describing the hole to a group of writers Nakajima's translator said, "He lost…" and then hesitated. "Lost confidence?" he was asked. "No, lost count."

....

1979

Defending champion Gary Player spoke at the Augusta Golf Association's annual dinner on Sunday night, and the headline in the *Augusta Chronicle* the next day was "First-timer won't win, says Player."

Player wasn't exactly going out on a limb. No player had won the Masters in his first try since Gene Sarazen in 1935, the second year of the tournament. There were a couple of intriguing Masters rookies this year in Fuzzy Zoeller and Lon

Hinkle, both long hitters who ranked third and fourth on the money list with victories already on the season. But they weren't high on anyone's list of picks to win the Masters.

For the first time since 1965, Jack Nicklaus wasn't atop the list of favorites. At age 39, he had played in five events so far in the season with no top-10 finishes, though he said his game was "in fine shape" after ironing a few things out. Tom Watson was the strong favorite after 11 PGA Tour wins since the start of 1977, and a victory and runner-up finish in Augusta the last two years.

Watson (68) and Nicklaus (69) were among 10 players shooting in the 60s in the first round. Nicklaus said he was "delighted" with his round, finally admitting that he was apprehensive coming into the tournament. Watson appeared headed for the lead when he birdied five of six holes starting at the eighth to get to five-under and had a six-iron second shot to the 15th—only to hit that approach into the water and make a bogey six.

Bruce Lietzke, a 27-year-old with four victories to his credit, led the way with a 67. The group of four at 68 included Ed Sneed, who didn't have a bogey and was feeling good about his game after finishing second to Watson at the Heritage Classic.

Craig Stadler, who a year earlier won the satellite Magnolia Classic in Mississippi during Masters week, birdied five of the last six holes for a 69. He proceeded to birdie four of the first five holes in the second round for an astounding streak of nine birdies in 11 holes. The 25-year-old former U.S. Amateur champion, who was in his third year on tour with moderate success so far, shot a 31 on the front nine and finished with a 66 for a 135 total.

That only earned him a tie for the lead with Sneed, who continued to strike the ball with machine-line efficiency in another bogey-free round. One-under through 12 holes while missing several birdie putts in the 12-foot range, Sneed birdied four of the last six with two-putts on both par fives and a 45-foot putt on the 17th to post a 67.

Sneed finished just before what turned into a two-hour delay for a rainstorm. Lietzke, an admitted "fair weather player" had to play 10 holes after the resumption. Troubled with iron shots from wet lies and adjusting to the speed of the greens, the first-round leader was four-over on those holes for a 75.

Leonard Thompson (70) and Ray Floyd (68), who had just won in Greensboro, were closest to the co-leaders, three back at 138. Watson was at 139 after a 71 marred by a poor finish, with bogeys on 14 and 17 and a saved par on 15 after a second shot in the water for the second straight day. Nicklaus started badly with a 39 on the front nine but recovered with 32 on the back to stand at 140.

The third round brought complaints—or at least comments—from players that the hole locations were closer to the edges and hazards than usual. Sneed wasn't bothered as he shot a 69 that was good enough to move into a commanding five-stroke lead as 36-hole co-leader Stadler slipped to a 74 and nobody shot better than 68.

Sneed finally made a bogey, his first of the week, at the fifth hole, but that was the only dropped shot against four birdies as he was seldom in trouble, missing only two greens. The low-key but witty and well-spoken 34-year-old was in his 11th year on tour with only three victories to his name. Still, he didn't seem surprised to be leading and was confident in his game, his fluid swing having recently been tweaked by former tour pro George Fazio.

"I've been playing well all year," he had said on Friday. "I've been saying for a year and a half that my best golf is ahead of me.... I have the game to win."

His fellow competitors at the Masters agreed. Watson, tied for second with Stadler five strokes behind after a 70, said, "That's a helluva lot of shots to make up.... Ed is swinging very well. He's going to be tough to beat."

"The tournament is pretty well over as far as who is going to win. It looks like the year Ray Floyd won," said Thompson, tied for sixth at 211. Nicklaus wasn't conceding, but even he knew his chances were slim from eight strokes back at 212 following a 72.

Lietzke and Zoeller were tied for fourth at 210, Zoeller playing the first eight holes in four-under to get within two of the lead before Sneed gained ground and Fuzzy stalled to post a 69 and end up six behind.

Frank Urban Zoeller's nickname came from his initials, and the resulting "Fuzzy" was somehow particularly apt, given that he was one of the free spirits on tour, chatting with the galleries while displaying a happy-go-lucky attitude. He got a good break on Thursday, when, for his first-ever Masters round, he was paired with the wisecracking, equally jocular Lee Trevino. "I laughed all the way around," said Zoeller, who had a 70 that day with an eagle on the eighth and a double bogey on the 12th.

Zoeller, 27, was in his fifth year on tour and just learning to harness his power off the tee by holding back a little bit for the sake of accuracy. He claimed his first career victory in January in San Diego.

In the second round, Zoeller shot a 71 while paired with Sneed. "I've never seen anything like it," marveled Fuzzy on Saturday. "He hit it right at the flag all day." Add Zoeller to the list of players feeling they didn't have much chance of winning on Sunday.

That feeling changed when Sneed proved shaky over the first 10 holes of the final round, his iron play far less crisp. Missed greens on the fourth, sixth, and 10th led to bogeys. A three-putt par at the second didn't help Sneed's cause, as he stumbled to three-over for the round through 10.

Suddenly, several players were back in the ballgame. That didn't include Stadler, who played a stretch of eight holes starting at No. 7 in six-over despite an eagle on the 13th and shot a 76.

The onset of wind made it a difficult day for charging from behind with a low number. There were only two rounds in the 60s, and the average score was 74.47. But one player managed a charge—and, no surprise, it was Nicklaus. A birdie on the 13th got him to three-under for the day and within two of Sneed, who had just bogeyed the 10th.

Nicklaus drove to the left on 15 and had to lay up. His sand wedge third shot came up short, rolled down the bank and settled just in the water. He staged a sequel to his 1974 blast out of the hazard, this time finishing 15 feet away and sinking the putt for a crowd-pleasing par save to keep his hopes alive.

Those hopes swelled when he holed a big-breaking 18-footer on 16 to pull within one of Sneed as Nicklaus appeared to be on the cusp of an epic comeback. Nicklaus figured he still needed another birdie on the last two holes and fired at a hole location on the back of the 17th green. He caught a flyer from the right rough, though, and his ball bounded down a bank behind the green, leading to a two-putt bogey from 12 feet. A par on 18 gave him a 69 for a seven-under total.

Tom Kite, who always seemed to be lurking at Augusta, pulled within two by playing the first 13 holes with two birdies and 11 pars to get to seven-under for the tournament. His challenge ended with a tee shot into the water on the 16th for a double bogey as he closed with a 72. Tom Watson was the closest to Sneed throughout, with birdies at the second and third and a bogey at the fourth making him eight-under, where he stayed during a long stretch of pars.

Sneed gathered himself and put together a stretch of holes that reestablished his command. He saved par from a bunker on 12, birdied 13 after a chip to four feet, saved par with a 10-foot putt on 14 after a drive into the trees, and birdied 15 with a pitch to six feet after laying up. Now, he was back to 11-under and three ahead of Watson, who bogeyed 14 and birdied 15.

What about Zoeller? He had never gotten closer than three strokes, playing the first 12 holes in one-over with bogeys on Nos. 4 and 12 and a birdie on 8. He got a two-putt birdie at 13 and, trailing by four, gambled on 15 with a three-wood from 235 yards that fought through a headwind to reach the green and set up another two-putt birdie. He was such a bit player at this point that the shot wasn't shown on the television broadcast.

As the saying goes, it was Sneed's tournament to lose on the last three holes—and that's just what he did, not with any terrible shots but in slow-motion fashion with shots that weren't quite good enough and short putts that didn't fall. He hit a safe tee shot to the right side of the 16th green, away from the water on the left, and missed a second putt from six feet. Bogey. His approach to the 17th bounded to the back fringe, and he used a putter from there to within four feet, then missed that. Bogey. Now his lead was one with one hole left.

Zoeller suddenly became more than a bit player now, thanks to a birdie from 14 feet on 17 where Watson failed to reprise his 1977 heroics, missing a 10-foot birdie try. Zoeller was looking over a par putt of eight feet on the 18th when Sneed's bogey on 17 went up on the adjacent leaderboard. Fuzzy needed the putt to stay within one of Sneed (and tied with Watson), and he drilled it.

Needing a par on 18, Sneed pushed his seven-iron approach, which finished in an awkward lie an inch outside a bunker. Under the circumstances, he hit a nice pitch shot to six feet, leaving an uphill putt for the victory. It hung on the left edge and refused to fall, even as Sneed walked up to it, bent over, and gazed at the ball in a mix of anguish and disbelief.

Now it was a sudden-death playoff with Sneed, Watson, and Zoeller, but we should spare a moment for Nicklaus. He finished one shot behind and would have made it a four-way playoff if not for a bogey on 17. One could fairly speculate that he might have played it safer and not bogeyed there if he had known eight-under

1979		
1	Fuzzy Zoeller	70–71–69–70—280*
T2	Ed Sneed	68–67–69–76—280
T2	Tom Watson	68–71–70–71—280
4	Jack Nicklaus	69–71–72–69—281
5	Tom Kite	71–72–68–72—283
6	Bruce Lietzke	67–75–68–74—284
T7	Craig Stadler	69–66–74–76—285
T7	Leonard Thompson	68–70–73–74—285
T7	Lanny Wadkins	73–69–70–73—285
T10	Hubert Green	74–69–72–71—286
T10	Gene Littler	74–71–69–72—286
*Zoeller won on second playoff hole		

would tie for first. As it was, it was yet another Masters where Nicklaus left himself behind after three rounds and staged a rally that came up just short, just as he had done in 1973, 1974, 1977, and 1978.

The tournament's first sudden-death playoff began on No. 10, one of the toughest at Augusta National, but the participants made it look easy. All hit good drives, Sneed and Watson hit their approaches to about 10 feet, with Zoeller later quipping, "I didn't know if there was room for my ball." He planted his approach about 11 feet behind the hole. All missed, Watson going third after a measurement with a flagstick and envelope determined he was slightly inside Sneed.

Sneed's approach on the second extra hole, No. 11, found the back bunker, while Watson hit his to 18 feet. Zoeller had ripped a long drive, leaving just an eight-iron, and it was a very good one to eight feet. Sneed very nearly holed his bunker shot and Watson barely missed, leaving the stage to Zoeller. When his putt dropped into the hole, Zoeller leaped and tossed his putter high into the air in celebration of a victory even he never expected.

"Hell, I wasn't supposed to win, never really challenged all day, and I thought Ed was going to win. I was just trying to keep up with Tom," said Zoeller, who only caught up to Watson on the 17th hole and Sneed on the 18th.

A downcast Sneed couldn't really figure out what had happened. "I can't explain it. I don't feel like I lost my composure. I didn't feel tight," he said. It's hard to assess what effect the Masters setback might have had, but, in any case, he would win only one more tournament in his career.

Watson could look back on a bogey at the 14th costing him the tournament for a second straight year, though he still had a putt to win on the first playoff hole. "I thought I would win it on the 10th, but I hit a bad putt," said Watson. "It was just a terrible round of putting."

So, a Masters rookie won for the first time since the tournament's infancy. It helped Zoeller that his Masters debut happened just as he was coming into his own. While there was some truth to the conventional wisdom that it takes several years of experience to learn Augusta National, Zoeller said he had a secret weapon in veteran Augusta caddie Jariah Beard, who read every putt for him.

"He knew every blade of grass out there," said Zoeller. "I was like a blind man with a seeing eye dog."

....

A Three-Act 64

Miller Barber tied the course record with a 64 in a second round that occurred in three parts. He played one hole before a two-hour rain delay and 14 more before play was halted by darkness. Wearing his prescription dark glasses, Barber couldn't see the hole on his 80-foot chip shot on No. 15 just before the suspension. He nonetheless chipped in for an eagle to get to seven-under. Returning to the course at 8 a.m., Barber birdied the 17th and parred 16 and 18 for the record-tying score. His other three rounds were 75, 72, and 76, leading to a T12 finish.

....

1980

Seve Ballesteros turned 23 the day before the first round of the 1980 Masters, yet he already had quite an impressive resume. He led the Order of Merit on the European Tour in 1976, 1977, and 1978 and owned 10 victories on that growing circuit. He finished second in the 1976 British Open as a precocious 19-year-old and claimed his first major championship at that event in 1979 at Royal Lytham & St. Annes. He won the 1978 Greater Greensboro Open just before his 21st birthday in only the third tournament he ever played in the United States.

Add in dashing good looks and a swashbuckling style that reminded observers of a young Arnold Palmer, and the young Spaniard was a star in the making. With his prodigious length off the tee and extraordinary touch around the greens, he appeared to be a perfect match for Augusta National. Already playing in his fourth Masters, Seve had improving finishes of T33, T18, and T12.

Ballesteros posted one of three 66s on Thursday for a share of the lead, making seven birdies despite not reaching any of the par fives in two. His par-five tee shots weren't especially wild, just far enough off to be blocked out by intervening trees, and, with his exquisite short game, Seve made birdies on three of them.

In winning the British Open the previous summer, Ballesteros hit only two of Lytham's narrow fairways in the final round but made pars and birdies from everywhere, including a birdie from a part of the course grounds used as a parking lot during the championship.

Ballesteros tried to push back on his reputation for spraying the ball off the tee. In his post-round interview on Thursday, he said that 1979 was a bad year of driving for him and previously he was a long and straight hitter. A bad back had caused the problems in 1979, and he had now cut down on his swing to put less strain on his back.

Joining Seve at 66 were 1979 PGA Championship winner David Graham of Australia and unheralded American Jeff Mitchell. Australia's Jack Newton probably should have joined them. He was five-under through seven holes thanks to a wild start of birdies on Nos. 1–3, a bogey at the fourth, and birdies on the next three before finally making his first par of the day at the eighth. An eagle at the 13th was yet another highlight, but bogeys on the ninth, 14th, and 18th left him with a somewhat disappointing 68. "You look at the four bogeys and they were from basi-cally nowhere," said Newton, reflecting on two three-putts and two relatively easy chips. "I was never really in trouble."

Ballesteros, on the other hand, was a player who could turn trouble into birdies, pulling off three Houdini acts in Friday's second round. The most dramatic came on the 17th hole, where Seve hooked his tee shot so badly it rested on the green of the adjacent seventh hole. Graham and Andy North were playing No. 7 when they saw a third ball on the putting surface 15 feet from the hole as they walked up to the green, with Ballesteros standing and waiting for them.

"You have a putt for an eagle if you want it," said Graham, who then asked Seve if he wanted to play through. Ballesteros waited for Graham and North to putt out, then took a free drop off the green as required by the rules. It was a blind shot to the 17th green from there, so Ballesteros used a scoreboard as a marker and aimed to the right of it. His seven-iron flew straight at the flag, finishing 15 feet behind the hole. When Ballesteros made the putt, he flung his hat into the air in celebration of a most unlikely birdie.

His other two wildly hooked drives had also led to birdies. On the par-five second his tee shot hit a tree and kicked into the fairway, from where he hit a one-iron and then a sand wedge to 10 feet. On the 14th, his tee shot landed well to the left but bounded down a hill almost to the fairway, leading to a pitching wedge approach to 20 feet and another birdie.

"I played very good yesterday. Today, a little inconsistent," said Ballesteros of a six-birdie, three-bogey round of 69 that was good for a three-stroke lead at 135. His back nine was an adventurous 33 with birdies on 10, 13, 14, 15, and 17 and bogeys on 11 and 16.

Ballesteros was able to open up a nice cushion, with the four other players who shot 66 or 68 in the first round all going over par—Graham 66–73, Mitchell 66–75, Newton 68–74, and frequent Masters contender Hubert Green 68–74. Tying Graham for second was Rex Caldwell with reverse rounds of 73–66.

Tom Watson, the Player of the Year three times running and a winner or runner-up in three straight Masters, managed a 69 for 142 and figured he would need a couple of 67s to catch the leader. Instead, he shot a pair of 71s for a T12.

Ballesteros gave the field some hope with a shaky start on Saturday. He played the first four holes one-over (two bogeys and a birdie), then hit a horrible hook off the fifth tee way down the hill toward the sixth green in an area where few players had ever ventured. "It was one of the worst shots I've hit anywhere," he said.

Ahead of him was a tree-covered steep uphill slope back to the fifth hole. There were too many trees to find an opening, and the height required to get over them was extreme. The shot looked impossible to most observers. Not to Seve, who pulled out his pitching wedge, swung with all his might, and lofted the ball over the intimidating pines into the fifth fairway within 100 yards of the green. From there, he hit a sand wedge to 20 feet and two-putted for a bogey that felt like a save.

His lead down to two shots, Ballesteros got back to playing the type of golf that put him ahead in the first place. He hit a pitching wedge to two feet for a birdie on the seventh hole and followed with a shot that was a timely reminder of the talent the young Spanish star possessed—a 245-yard three-iron second shot uphill to within five feet of the hole to set up an eagle on the eighth.

Ballesteros continued to pull away on the back nine with two-putt birdies on 13 and 15 (he was five-under on the par fives in the round) and birdies on 14 and 18 against a bogey at 16. It added up to a 68 for a 203 total, two higher than Ray Floyd's 54-hole record, and a seven-stroke lead. "I have a seven handicap for tomorrow," said Seve.

Maybe even more than that, since second-place Ed Fiori (69 for 210) wasn't considered a strong threat. The group eight strokes back included Newton, with a 32 on the back nine for a 69 that got him into the final twosome with Ballesteros on Sunday, and Graham, who came from four strokes behind to win the 1979 PGA.

The question hanging over the Masters was which route Seve would take on Sunday. Would he do a Floyd/Nicklaus and make a run at the scoring record or a Venturi/Sneed and fall back toward the rest of the field? The answer was that, somehow, he did both.

The front nine had all the makings of a romp as Ballesteros birdied the first (10 feet), third (four feet), and fifth (25 feet), and for good measure made a par out of the woods on the eighth (which could now be called "doing a Seve"). With a 33, he was 16-under for the tournament, needing a 35 on the back nine to tie the scoring record. He was a whopping 10 strokes clear of second place.

Then came one of those wild swings of fortune that Augusta National produces more often than any other course. It started innocently enough when Ballesteros three-putted the 10th from 25 feet for a bogey. More worrisome, he failed the test at the 12th when he aimed his six-iron at the center of the green but pushed it badly into Rae's Creek for a double bogey. Newton had picked up a stroke on each of the 10th and 11th by going par-birdie, now he gained three strokes on the 12th with a birdie from 12 feet. In three holes, the 10-stroke lead had been cut in half. And there was more to come.

Seve's apparent disintegration continued on the 13th when he hit a fat three-iron into the creek guarding the green and made a bogey while Newton two-putted from 20 feet for a birdie. Suddenly, Ballesteros was only three ahead with five to play. Going into the round, Seve seemed more likely to hold up to pressure than the typical 23-year-old, based on his track record. Yet now, all bets were off.

Meanwhile, another pursuer threatened. Gibby Gilbert, a 39-year-old with three career tour wins, started the round nine strokes behind after a third-round 68. Nobody paid attention when he shot a 34 on the front nine Sunday, but the Tennessean made everyone take notice when he reeled off four straight birdies starting at the 13th hole. The last one came on a seven-foot putt at the 16th to reach 10-under, just two behind.

By that time, Ballesteros had parred the 14th thanks to a six-iron over the trees after a drive to the left and was standing in the 15th fairway with just a four-iron to the green. With the tournament in the balance, he struck a beauty over the fronting pond to 20 feet. Newton, still three behind, knocked a downhill, 25-foot eagle putt

1980		
1	Seve Ballesteros	66–69–68–72—275
T2	Gibby Gilbert	70–74–68–67—279
T2	Jack Newton	68–74–69–68—279
4	Hubert Green	68–74–71–67—280
5	David Graham	66–73–72–70—281
T6	Ben Crenshaw	76–70–68–69—283
T6	Ed Fiori	71–70–69–73—283
T6	Tom Kite	69–71–74–69—283
T6	Larry Nelson	69–72–73–69—283
T6	Jerry Pate	72–68–76–67—283
T6	Gary Player	71–71–71–79—283

eight feet past the hole and missed that one. Ballesteros, learning from Newton's putt, gently rolled his 20-footer to tap-in range for a birdie.

The crisis averted, Ballesteros was now three ahead of Gilbert and four clear of Newton. While it wasn't quite over at that point, Seve made sure of things with three routine pars coming in for a round of 72 and a 275 total. Not a record and not a fourth round in the 60s, but good enough.

Gilbert bogeyed 18 for a 67 and a tie for second at 279 with Newton, who came home with a 33 for a 68. The 30-year-old Australian, a playoff runner-up to Watson in the 1975 British Open, regretted two front-nine bogeys on Sunday and even more so the four bogeys in the last five holes of his second-round 74. "That was the tournament right there," he said.

Ballesteros admitted after the round that he had to overcome a crisis of confidence. "I was comfortable. [Leading by] 10 strokes is a lot…. Then I was uncomfortable. I'm in trouble. I was thinking I was about to lose the tournament. I say I must try hard, and finally I start playing well."

The Spaniard was only the second non-American to win the Masters, joining Gary Player, and the youngest ever winner, four months younger than Nicklaus in 1963—pretty good company. Firmly established as one of the best players in the world, he hadn't shaken his reputation for wildness off the tee, as his escapes from trouble were more memorable than his many great shots from the fairway.

"This week I didn't drive very bad. This year I drive very good," he insisted, and then quipped, "The more you go into the woods, the more practice you get."

13 on 12

Two years after Tommy Nakijima took 13 on the par-five 13th hole for the highest hole score ever in the Masters, Tom Weiskopf matched the 13 and went even further over par on the par-three 12th. After a tee shot into Rae's Creek, Weiskopf chunked four balls into the water from a muddy drop area. "I was determined to keep trying 'til I did it right," said the four-time runner-up after finding a new kind of frustration at Augusta.

1981

Over the last decade or two, players had noticed the greens getting slower. Officials saw it, too, and, after the 1980 tournament, announced that the greens would be switched from Bermuda grass to bentgrass, a type that produces faster surfaces. Bentgrass was harder to maintain in hot weather, and, at the time, was rarely used on courses in the South. But new strains of bent were more adaptable and Augusta National had the resources necessary to make it work (it helped that the course was closed in the summer).

While somewhat softer than the Bermuda surfaces, the speed, combined with the slopes of the greens, made downhill putts something to truly fear and significantly changed the complexion of the course. Hord Hardin, who took over as chairman in 1980, said of the greens, "We could make them so slick we'd have to furnish ice skates on the first tee."

The weather was perfect in the first round, with little wind, yet nobody shot better than 69. There were four players at that figure: Johnny Miller, Greg Norman, Curtis Strange, and Lon Hinkle. Jack Nicklaus was among seven players at 70; Tom Watson in a group of six at 71.

Miller, the one-time golden boy, was on the comeback trail. He had fallen from the heights of 1973–76 when he won 13 times including two majors, to the depths of going winless in 1977–79 and not even cracking the top 75 money leaders in two of those years. Things began to look up in 1980 (one win), and he roared back early in 1981 with victories in his old stomping grounds of Tucson and Los Angeles. "My game is now good enough to enjoy," he said before the start of the Masters.

Now it was Norman in the young blond role. Still little known in the U.S., the 25-year-old Australian was making a name for himself internationally with several wins in his homeland and a ranking of second on the 1980 European Tour Order of Merit. He missed a chance to lead outright when he made his only bogey of the day on the 18th hole.

Nicklaus thought he should have been leading instead of one behind, having missed five birdie putts from inside 12 feet. The new greens had a lot to do with it. "I had so many putts where I was afraid I'd have four or five feet coming back," he said.

The second round was a different story, as Nicklaus made three putts of 15 to 20 feet on the way to a 65 that would be the best of the week by three strokes and gave him a four-stroke lead at 135. Those putts came consecutively on the last three holes of a run of four straight birdies from Nos. 4–7. There were a couple of hiccups— misses of birdie tries from three feet on the eighth and 15th. On the plus side were par saves thanks to excellent chips on 10, 11, and 12 that enabled him to play a bogey-free round, and approaches within four feet for birdies on 14 and 16.

The 41-year-old Nicklaus was coming off a year when he answered the doubters following his worst year ever in 1979 by winning both the U.S. Open and PGA Championship. It was agreed he would be tough to catch, though the task wouldn't be impossible. After all, he had lost a five-stroke 36-hole lead in 1975 before rallying to victory.

Watson, Norman, Hinkle, and Bruce Lietzke were tied for second at 139. Watson, who piled up 22 wins in 1977–80, hadn't found the winner's circle in his first seven 1981 starts but wasn't too concerned. After opening rounds of 71–68, he said, "I'm halfway up an up cycle."

Miller was considerably less confident after a 72 left him six back at 141, his only three birdies coming from inches away—two of them after approaches to par fours. "If I was outside a foot, I didn't have a chance," he said. "These greens are too tough for my act."

The third round of 1981 was one of the prime examples of the volatility Augusta National's back nine can wreak on leaderboards, with huge swings in opposite directions in a little over an hour. Nicklaus headed to the 12th hole two strokes ahead of Watson and, as he walked down the 15th fairway, he had fallen four strokes behind. By the time Nicklaus teed off on the 17th hole, the two were tied.

First, the preliminaries. Nicklaus birdied the second, then bogeyed the seventh and ninth to play the first 11 holes in one-over. Watson had three birdies and two bogeys over the first 11 holes to cut his deficit from four strokes to two.

As Nicklaus stood on the 12th tee, he heard a roar when Watson's second shot to the 13th finished four feet from the hole. You wouldn't expect Nicklaus to get rattled, but perhaps his game wasn't sharp on this day. For whatever reason, he hit his tee shot into the water on 12 and made a double bogey. Watson missed his short eagle putt on 13; still, he took a one-stroke lead with his birdie.

Soon, Watson was ahead by three when he birdied the 14th from four feet and Nicklaus found the water for the second consecutive hole with his second shot on 13, leading to a bogey. When Watson two-putted for a birdie on 15, he was up by four.

"Well, we've gone from four up [at the start of the round] to four down," Nicklaus said to his caddie. "We'll just have to go out and get them back."

He did—and quickly. Nicklaus two-putted for a birdie on 15 and hit the flagstick with his tee shot on 16, making a four-foot putt for birdie. In the twosome ahead, Watson hit a pitching wedge into a greenside bunker on 17, blasted out to eight feet, knocked his first putt four feet past, and missed that one. Double bogey, and a tie for the lead.

"I had a hot streak going and then the 'hammermitts' took over," said Watson. Known as one of the finest putters in the game, Tom was nonetheless having occasional trouble with his touch on the newly slick greens.

In a final twist, Nicklaus bogeyed the 18th, missing a three-foot par putt to post a disappointing 75 while Watson took a one-stroke lead with a 70 for 209. Norman had an up-and-down 72 with four each of birdies and bogeys to sit two back at 211.

The confident Aussie said of the upcoming final round, "There's no pressure on me. I might set things on fire." He also told the assembled writers about shooting sharks when fishing off the coast of Australia, and soon was tagged with the nickname "The Great White Shark."

Miller was in a seven-way tie for 10th, five strokes behind, after another frustrating day on the greens and a 73. Heading to the course on Sunday morning, Miller felt he didn't have much of a chance, but after encouragement from a couple of friends, he had second thoughts: "I thought maybe I do have a chance. I might as well go for it.… I was shooting at the pin on every hole."

He birdied the first hole from three feet and added another birdie at the second. His charge stalled with three-putt bogeys at Nos. 4 and 6, then revived with a birdie on the eighth and, finally, a long putt dropping at the ninth from 25 feet, and stalled again with a bogey at 10 that left him four strokes off the lead.

Watson and Nicklaus both played the first six holes in even par; Watson with a birdie on the second and bogey on the sixth. Nicklaus made six pars but wasn't on his game. He was in the left woods with his second shot at the second and made a 15-foot par putt for a bunker save at the fourth.

John Mahaffey thrust himself into the thick of things with a birdie at the seventh to go two-under on the day and pull within one, while Nicklaus bogeyed from a bunker to fall two behind. Nicklaus bogeyed the ninth as well, three-putting from a long distance to make the turn in 38.

Watson went ahead by two with a birdie at the eighth. His approach at the ninth was strong, finishing on the back fringe. During the course of the week, several players had putted off the green as the downhill slope was now treacherous on the slick-as-ice bentgrass. Watson used a putter from the fringe only to watch the ball roll and roll and roll, past the flagstick and all the way down into the fairway. The "hammermitts" had struck again, though he managed to save a bogey with a chip and a four-foot putt.

Watson's lead was quickly restored to two over Mahaffey and Norman when the former bogeyed the 10th. Mahaffey also bogeyed the 11th on the way to a 40 on the back nine. Norman, after a 36 on the front nine, hooked his tee shot deep into the trees on the 10th and made a double bogey. When he missed birdie putts of 12 and eight feet on the next two holes, his challenge was done.

Now it was Miller's time to make a move, which he did with birdies on the 13th and 14th to get to five-under and within two. The second of those birdies was a highly unlikely one on a 20-foot downhill, sidehill putt from the fringe with a huge break, perhaps making up, at least a little, for his many misses on the greens during the week. He couldn't convert an eight-foot birdie try on the 15th, but cashed in on a 14-footer at 17 to get to six-under and within one of Watson, who was then on the 12th, where he made an eight-foot second putt for par.

Watson's lead was in danger when his four-iron second shot on the 13th was pushed to the right and landed in the creek. He escaped with a par with a pitch from the drop area to five feet.

Miller parred the 18th for a 68 and a six-under total. Watson missed an eight-foot birdie chance on the 14th, then gave himself another opportunity with a four-wood second shot to 40 feet on 15. The putt was a downhiller that Watson said he hit as if it were an eight-foot putt. This time the touch was more velvet than hammer, as the putt eased stealthily down the slope, halting a foot from the hole for a birdie.

Meanwhile, Nicklaus had finally made his first birdie of the day at the 13th and given it right back with a bogey on 14. where he missed from three feet. Jack mustered a final challenge with a birdie from 10 feet on the 15th and a 25-foot uphill birdie putt on 16, evoking memories of his even longer birdie in 1975. That got him to six-under just as Watson was about to tap in his birdie on 15 to go eight-under.

Watson had a flash of trepidation when, for the second straight day, he hit a pitching wedge approach into the bunker on 17. "Holy mackerel, Watson, what are you

1981

1	Tom Watson	71–68–70–71—280
T2	Johnny Miller	69–72–73–68—282
T2	Jack Nicklaus	70–65–75–72—282
4	Greg Norman	69–70–72–72—283
T5	Tom Kite	74–72–70–68—284
T5	Jerry Pate	71–72–71–70—284
7	David Graham	70–70–74–71—285
T8	Ben Crenshaw	71–72–70–73—286
T8	Raymond Floyd	75–71–71–69—286
T8	John Mahaffey	72–71–69–74—286

doing?" said Miller, watching the telecast in the locker room, previewing his coming days as a TV commentator.

Unlike the previous day on 17, Watson recovered nicely to four feet and saved par. He parred 18 for a 71, a 280 total, and a two-stroke victory over Miller and Nicklaus, who settled for a 72. It was Miller's third runner-up finish at Augusta without a victory and Nicklaus' fourth (matching Tom Weiskopf for the most) to go with five victories.

The final-round action wasn't nearly as stirring as in 1975, yet this ranks as a classic Masters due to the elite quality of the leading players. For Watson, his dominance of the tour in 1977–81 was reflected in his performances at Augusta. In the five-year span, he had two wins—outdueling Nicklaus both times—a playoff loss and a second-place finish one stroke behind.

Paired Off

Jack Nicklaus was surprised and annoyed that he wasn't paired with Tom Watson in the final round, as they were 1–2 in the standings through 54 holes. Nicklaus had apparently forgotten or not noticed that the Masters had used a 1–3, 2–4, etc. pairing system in the third and fourth rounds since 1969. When the Masters went to that structure, the PGA Tour was using a 1–3–5, 2–4–6, etc. system for its threesomes on the weekend rounds. The Tour had since switched to a 1–2–3 system, and the USGA paired 1–2 in the U.S. Open, as Nicklaus had experienced the previous summer when he played the final round with closest competitor Isao Aoki. Here, though, second-place Nicklaus ended up with John Mahaffey, while Watson was with Greg Norman in the final twosome. The next year, the Masters changed to a 1–2, 3–4, etc. format.

1982

In Year 2 of the bentgrass greens, it was expected that they would be firmer than they were in 1981 and probably even faster. Still, players weren't prepared for what they found in early-week practice rounds.

"Treacherous doesn't begin to describe it. These greens are about impossible now," defending champion Tom Watson warned. "We'll have a lot of four-putts and three-putts."

When Thursday came, scores did soar sky-high, but the speed of the greens was only one factor. The weather was as miserable as anyone could remember for the

Masters, or any tournament, with temperatures ranging from 40 to 48 degrees and a steady drizzle that only slightly slowed the pace of the greens.

It was so tough that when a bedraggled Jim Thorpe came into the locker room after shooting an 88, he predicted that someone would score higher. Not long afterward, Frank Conner posted an 89. Both were tour regulars, not inexperienced amateurs or aging past Masters champions.

Play was halted at 4:30 p.m. when the rain turned harder. Of the 58 players who finished their rounds, the leader was Fuzzy Zoeller with a 72. Among the 36 players on the course when play was suspended, Watson and Craig Stadler were the best at one-under through nine holes. (There were several groups on the 10th tee due to delays caused by casual water on the fairway.)

The players who completed their first rounds on Friday morning at 7:30 a.m. didn't get a break—the temperature was still in the 40s and the course wet. In fact, Watson skied to a 42 on the back nine with a triple bogey-bogey-bogey finish and Stadler had two double bogeys on the way to a 40. The only movement forward was by Jack Nicklaus, who played his eight morning holes in three-under for a 33 on the back nine and a 69 and a three-stroke lead, with Zoeller and Jack Renner the only ones at par 72. The carnage produced by the conditions included a 77.32 scoring average for the field and 17 rounds in the 80s.

The weather was nicer in the afternoon for the second round, but the course was soppy and playing long, with the par fives not so reachable in two. While not quite as fast as they had been on Tuesday, the greens were still quick, with pin positions that were so close to slopes they turned putting (and sometimes approach shots) into an adventure.

Before the tournament, Nicklaus praised the move to faster greens, saying it made the course play like Bobby Jones intended. He also noted that as greens slowed down over the course of the past 15 years or so, pin positions had gotten "less sensible" in order to maintain the challenge. Unfortunately, many of those hole locations were used in the second round of 1982. Nicklaus was one of the chief victims, shooting a 77 with five three-putts. For the second consecutive year, he had lost a Masters lead, a surprising development even if he was now north of 40. He would continue to slide to a T15 finish.

At the end of the long day, Stadler and Curtis Strange, who both played 27 holes, were tied for the lead at even-par 144. Strange rallied from five-over through 12 holes of the first round to shoot 74–70, while Stadler bounced back from his back-nine 40 in the morning with a 69 that included approach shots on the ninth and 10th holes inside two feet.

The 28-year-old Stadler was coming into his own, with three wins in 1980–81 and another in Tucson in 1982, along with six top-10s on the year entering the Masters. Known for his mercurial temper, Stadler admitted that he still got angry and might bang a club on the ground, but that now he was able to get over it more quickly. "I put the bad shots behind me. That wasn't the case two years ago," he said.

Another player riding high was Tom Kite, the 1981 leading money winner and No. 2 on the list so far in 1982, just ahead of Stadler. Known for his week-to-week consistency and for piling up top-10s, Kite moved into position at 145 with a wild second-round 69 that featured eight birdies, three bogeys, and a double bogey. The third player to match the low second round of 69 was defending champion Watson, who reversed Nicklaus' start with 77–69, joining Jack two strokes off the lead. Kite would shoot 73–69 on the weekend for one of his typical T5 Masters finishes, where he would be joined by Watson (70–71).

Masters chairman Hord Hardin admitted that the hole locations were harsh in the second round. The tournament committee went in the other direction on Saturday. With beautiful weather and little wind, red numbers flowed onto the leaderboards, though not for Strange, who fell back with a 73.

At the end of the round, Stadler emerged as the leader with a 67, showcasing his new-found resiliency. He got off to a shaky start with a double bogey on the second hole, where he hooked his drive into a creek. The man nicknamed the Walrus for his round build and droopy mustache, clawed his way back to even par with approach shots to tap-in range at the par-four fifth and ninth along with a couple of par saves for a 36 on the front nine.

He proceeded to hole a bunker shot for a birdie on the 10th and sink a 10-foot birdie putt on the 12th. Stadler more than made up for a failure to birdie either of the back nine par fives by making putts of 15, 40, and 30 feet for birdies on the last three holes and a 31 on the back nine.

Seve Ballesteros was in the interview room recounting a 69 that put him at 214 for 54 holes when Stadler's final birdie was posted on the leaderboard. "Birdie, birdie, birdie—that's consistent," he responded with a grin when asked to comment on Stadler's finish.

Noting Stadler's three-stroke lead, and speaking from his own 1980 experience, the Spaniard hopefully added, "There's a lot of pressure on you when you're ahead. It's easier to win from behind."

Ballesteros was tied for second with Jerry Pate, the tour's leading money winner, who three weeks earlier had won the Players Championship and dived into the pond next to the 18th green at TPC Sawgrass. The celebration reprised a dive into a pond following a 1981 win in Memphis that ended a two-year victory drought. Pate shot a 67 on Saturday to move into contention at Augusta, prompting the question of what he would do if he won the Masters. "Probably accept the trophy gracefully like everybody else," he said, then joked that he might donate his prize money for Augusta National to install a pond for any future victories.

The most sensational scoring feat of the day was by Dan Pohl, who collected back-to-back eagles at the 13th (10-foot putt) and 14th (118-yard pitching wedge) followed by birdies at 15 and 16 to go six-under for a four-hole stretch and shoot a 67. The fourth-year pro owned no victories on the PGA Tour, having qualified by finishing third at the 1981 PGA Championship. He came into the tournament "a little less confident than normal" with a bad shoulder that contributed to a shaky start to the season and bothered him in cold weather, contributing to his opening rounds of 75–75. While he was a nice story for Saturday, Pohl didn't figure to be a factor in the final round, which he started six strokes behind the leader.

Pohl exceeded expectations with a 33 on the front nine on Sunday—but Stadler also had a 33, and it didn't look like he would let anybody into the tournament. Craig birdied the second (two-putt), sixth (20 feet), and seventh (15 feet) along with a couple of par saves, and led by six.

As Stadler walked down the 11th fairway, he thought to himself, "This is easy," and wondered how much he was going to win by. The golf gods, and Augusta National's back nine, punished him for those presumptive notions.

1982		
1	Craig Stadler	75–69–67–73—284*
2	Dan Pohl	75–75–67–67—284
T3	Seve Ballesteros	73–73–68–71—285
T3	Jerry Pate	74–73–67–71—285
T5	Tom Kite	76–69–73–69—287
T5	Tom Watson	77–69–70–71—287
T7	Raymond Floyd	74–72–69–74—289
T7	Larry Nelson	79–71–70–69—289
T7	Curtis Strange	74–70–73–72—289
T10	Andy Bean	75–72–73–70—290
T10	Mark Hayes	74–73–73–70—290
T10	Tom Weiskopf	75–72–68–75—290
T10	Fuzzy Zoeller	72–76–70–72—290
*Stadler won on first playoff hole		

Stadler had gone 28 holes without a bogey, but now he missed the green on the 12th and failed to convert an eight-foot par putt. He tried to bogey the 13th as his four-iron second shot found the hazard, but the ball skipped out of the water onto the bank and he made par. The 14th was a bogey when he wasted a good recovery from the trees by three-putting. A disappointing par on 15 was followed by a bogey at 16, where he hit his tee shot into the back-right bunker and a seemingly good effort from there trickled down off the top plateau where the pin was located.

A back nine that started as a walk in the park had now turned into a harrowing minefield. Stadler was now five-under, with Pohl waiting on the practice putting green at four-under after a second consecutive 67, having birdied 12 and 13, bogeyed 14, saved par with a six-foot putt after a second shot in the water at 15, and birdied 16 with a tee shot within a foot.

Ballesteros was about to finish three-under, shooting a 71 with birdies on 15, 17, and 18 that were too little and too late after bogeys on 10 and 12. Still in the hunt at three-under, playing with Stadler, was Pate, who trailed by eight after a front-nine 38 and fought back with birdies on 10, 15, and 16.

The outcome was still uncertain on the 18th green, with the hole in the back, and Stadler and Pate facing uphill birdie putts of 30 and 20 feet, respectively. In a week when players were used to stroking the ball gingerly, these were putts that were deceptively slow. Pohl had left his birdie try short on the same line. Stadler, just wanting to two-putt, left his effort six feet short. Pate somehow left his putt short, too, even knowing he had a chance to get into a playoff if he made it and if Stadler missed. Now Stadler had a six-foot putt to win the Masters. It never had a chance, missing to the left as Stadler slumped over.

Stadler had played with Ed Sneed in the final twosome three years earlier when Sneed blew the Masters down the stretch and lost in a playoff. Now Stadler knew what Sneed felt like, while Pohl was looking eerily like 1979 champion Fuzzy Zoeller—a long-hitting (Pohl had led the tour in driving distance the last two years) Masters rookie who never even shared the lead until the 72nd hole.

On the way to the 10th tee for the playoff, a shell-shocked Stadler received a pep talk from his wife, Sue, and hit a good drive and a six-iron to the green, 40 feet from the hole. Pohl's seven-iron was pushed to about the same distance but off the green to the right. Pohl was away and, using a putter, left the shot six feet short. Stadler putted up close and secured his par. Pohl's putt to stay alive didn't drop, a rather anticlimactic finish that left Stadler standing there for a few seconds before it sunk in that he was the Masters champion.

Stadler became the second player to win a green jacket with a 40 on the back nine of the final round, joining Gary Player (1961). "I'll take 'em any way I can," said a relieved Stadler, who not only escaped the Sneed stigma but went on to the best year of his career, winning four times to take Player-of-the-Year honors.

....

Nightmare Finish

Mark Hayes had one thing on his mind as he prepared for an eight-foot birdie putt on the 18th green in the second round—making it to get into a tie for the lead. "I never even considered that it might roll down the hill," he said. The downhill slope started about three feet past the hole, and when Hayes hit the putt a bit too hard it caught the slope and trickled 35 feet past. The nightmare wasn't over. He didn't hit the next putt hard enough, and it rolled back down to him, some 35 feet away once again. He ended up making a four-footer for his fourth putt and a double bogey to trail by three, the most dramatic victim of the slicker greens.

....

1983–1996

The European Age

Spain's Seve Ballesteros heralded the coming European storm in 1980, and it began in earnest with Seve's second Masters victory in 1983. Ballesteros was just one of a group of world-class Europeans who emerged in the late 1970s and early 1980s shortly after the birth and early growth of the European Tour.

Bernhard Langer of Germany followed Ballesteros into the Augusta winner's circle in 1985, then came a flood starting in 1988 with Scotland's Sandy Lyle, England's Nick Faldo (twice), and Wales' Ian Woosnam making it four in a row. Add a second green jacket for Langer in 1993, a first for Spain's Jose Maria Olazabal in 1994, and a third for Faldo in 1996, and it was seven European wins in a nine-year span. (Olazabal would add a second Masters in 1999.)

There's no question Europe produced an exceptional crop of players in this period. But there was something about the Masters and Augusta National that brought out the best in them. The six Europeans who accounted for 11 Masters victories combined to win exactly zero U.S. Opens and PGA Championships (they won seven British Opens). The explanation is necessarily speculative, but with such a dramatic difference in the outcomes it most likely was that the Europeans benefited from the lack of rough at Augusta National compared to the penal long grass at the other two U.S. majors.

The European winners had different styles of play, some long hitters and some not so long. Yet all had a high degree of creativity, especially around the greens, which Augusta allowed them to display more than they could on the more constrictive courses and setups at the U.S. Open and PGA Championship. Indeed, Augusta National practically demands creativity and imagination when playing to its slick, undulating putting surfaces.

Prior to Ballesteros' first win, the only foreign player to capture the Masters was South Africa's Gary Player, three times. So, it was quite a dramatic shift from pre-1980 to the 1980s onward, coinciding with golf at the highest level becoming a more international game. The Masters began to invite more foreign players in this period, though it was only later the tournament took the biggest step in that direction when it began to invite the top 50 on the World Ranking in 1999.

Another foreign player with a big impact in the 1980s and '90s was Australia's Greg Norman, with three seconds and two thirds in the 14-year period covered in this chapter, making for a heartbreaking tale of near misses for the man who never earned a green jacket. Americans weren't *completely* absent in this time frame. All their five victories were noteworthy in some aspect—Jack Nicklaus winning for a sixth time, Larry Mize ending a playoff with one of the most dramatic shots in Masters history, Fred Couples affirming his No. 1 status at the time of his win, and Ben Crenshaw claiming a pair of jackets.

1983

The Masters was the last tournament to require players to use club caddies, a policy that ended in 1983. Over the previous couple of decades, a corps of regular tour caddies had emerged and players increasingly chafed at not being able to bring their familiar sidekicks to Augusta National. In making the players' case, Tom Watson asked Masters chairman Hord Hardin, an attorney by profession, how he would feel going into the most important trial of his life without his top legal secretary.

While many of Augusta National's bag-toters had the advantage of local knowledge, particularly in reading greens, others had regular jobs and caddied only Masters week. A general deterioration in quality had been noted, and the final straw came in 1982, when a number of caddies failed to show up in time for the 7:30 a.m. Friday completion of the suspended first round.

The first round of 1983 almost spilled over into a second day, too, as the last twosome finished just before dark, with play having been halted for 45 minutes by rain. Thursday's highlight was a 68 by 53-year-old Arnold Palmer, who noted that this was a round where his gallery swelled during the round instead of shrinking.

There was some hope that the man who was old enough to play on the relatively new senior tour could stick around as a contender. He had shown signs of a revival by leading the Los Angeles Open with nine holes to play in January, and, when asked after the round whether he thought he had a chance to win again, Arnie answered, "Damn right!" It was too much to ask, though, as Palmer finished with 74–76–78.

The Los Angeles Open that Palmer threatened to win was captured by Gil Morgan, the second of his two wins to start the year. The 36-year-old, who now owned six career victories, topped Palmer on this day, too, shooting a 67 with no bogeys thanks to a 35-foot putt for a par on 18. He was tied for first with Ray Floyd and Jack Renner, who had six straight 3s starting at the 12th hole—two eagles, two birdies, and two pars.

Ten players shot in the 60s on a windless day when players could fire at pins on greens softened by rain on Wednesday night and a shower in the afternoon. The most noteworthy of the others were 1980 champion Seve Ballesteros, the Spanish scrambler who once again pleaded for fans and writers to "remember my good shots as well as the bad ones," with a 68 and defending champion Craig Stadler with a 69.

Rain arrived in full force on Friday, washing out the entire day and threatening the weekend. The hope was to play the second round on Saturday and 36 holes on Sunday, an uncertain proposition with the second round not starting until 11 a.m. due to the time needed to prepare the course.

The players slogged and splashed their way around the course on Saturday. A persistent drizzle and a period of rain that led to a 33-minute delay oversaturated the course. Even after play resumed, the grounds crew had to squeegee casual water off the greens. Tom Watson quipped that he missed a putt "because I couldn't read the flow."

The squeegeeing was needed so often on the 13th hole that the later threesomes found four groups on the tee when they got there, leading to rounds that ended six-and-a-half hours after they began. Play was halted by darkness with two threesomes still on the course. Since they would have to finish on Sunday morning, and pairings could be made only after the cut was determined, that meant just 18 holes on the rest of Sunday and a Monday finish.

At the end of the day Saturday, Morgan was leading at seven-under through 16 holes, having followed an eagle at the 15th with a three-putt bogey at the 16th. Ballesteros was at six-under through 17 thanks to birdies on 13, 14, and 15, and Floyd five-under through 16. That trio made nothing but pars in the Sunday completion of the round, so it was Morgan leading at 137 with Ballesteros at 138, both with 70s. Jack Nicklaus was out of the tournament, withdrawing with back spasms just before the start of the second round on Saturday after a 73 in Round 1.

Sunday was mercifully clear, but the wind arrived and made it a tough day, producing six rounds in the 80s and only one in the 60s. The latter was recorded by Stadler with a 69 to move into a tie for the lead, finishing with a 30-foot birdie putt at 17 and a seven-footer to save par at 18.

He was joined at the top at 210 by Floyd, whose 71 was highlighted by a seven-iron to three inches for a birdie on the 12th. Ballesteros wasn't particularly sharp, but he was only one stroke back at 211 after a 15-foot birdie putt on 18 gave him a 73. Watson was at 212 after a 37–34—71 and very much in it despite saying he wasn't hitting the ball crisply nor putting well.

Morgan having fallen back with a 76, it would be Watson-Ballesteros and then Stadler-Floyd in the last two twosomes in Monday's final round. That was a strong quartet accounting for five of the last seven Masters titles.

The Stadler-Floyd matchup was particularly intriguing. Stadler had defeated Floyd in a playoff at the 1982 World Series of Golf that determined which one would be Player of the Year, each already owning three wins including a major coming into that event. Floyd turned the tables, beating Stadler at the big-money Sun City Classic in South Africa in December and a $300,000 first prize (for perspective, Floyd was second on the 1982 money list with $386,809 for the entire PGA Tour season).

1983

1	Seve Ballesteros	68–70–73–69—280
T2	Ben Crenshaw	76–70–70–68—284
T2	Tom Kite	70–72–73–69—284
T4	Raymond Floyd	67–72–71–75—285
T4	Tom Watson	70–71–71–73—285
T6	Hale Irwin	72–73–72–69—286
T6	Craig Stadler	69–72–69–76—286
T8	Gil Morgan	67–70–76–74—287
T8	Dan Pohl	74–72–70–71—287
T8	Lanny Wadkins	73–70–73–71—287

Both promised to play the course—and not each other—in the final round. As it turned out, neither had the other to worry about. Just ahead of them, Ballesteros grabbed control of the tournament right out of the starting gate. He never let go.

Two days after celebrating his 26th birthday, the Spanish conquistador hit a seven-iron to eight feet at the first hole and made it for a birdie. He hit a beauty of a four-wood on the second over a greenside bunker, stopping it on the green 15 feet away, and made the putt for an eagle. After a par on the third, he hit another beauty on the fourth, a four-iron that settled two feet from the hole for a birdie that put him four-under through four holes.

"It was like he was in a Ferrari and everyone else was in Chevrolets," said Tom Kite.

Floyd and Stadler, at even par for the day, were now already three behind. Floyd would drop further back with bogeys at Nos. 5 and 6, and wouldn't make a birdie until the 17th en route to a 75. Stadler would remain even par through 10 and within three until he bogeyed 11, 12, 14, and 16 for a 76.

It was left to Watson to challenge Seve, and he did just that by hitting a driver from the fairway for his second shot to the eighth and holing a 25-foot eagle putt to get to three-under for the day and pull within two. The challenge was short lived. The 1977 and 1981 champion took himself out of it with consecutive bogeys on Nos. 9–11, with two three-putts and a bad tee shot, finishing with a 73.

Ballesteros birdied the ninth from 12 feet for a 31 on the front nine and a four-stroke lead. As in 1980, things got shaky from there as he bogeyed the 10th and 12th and hooked his tee shot left of the creek and into the trees on the 13th. He punched out and hit the green with a three-iron to initiate a string of pars to the clubhouse, including a chip-in on the 18th for a 69 and an eight-under 280 total.

That was plenty good enough with Watson, Stadler, and Floyd all shooting over par. Kite and Ben Crenshaw passed that trio to claim a tie for second, but started too far behind to challenge for the title, finishing at 284 with 69 and 68, respectively. Crenshaw dug himself too deep of a hole with a first-round 76, and Kite's play was lackluster other than shooting 32 on the back nine in both the first and fourth rounds.

After the third round, Ballesteros had said, "This is my favorite place in the world to play right here." Now, it was even more so.

Lost Cause

Scott Simpson began the final round five strokes out of the lead and made a move with a 32 on the front nine—the only player to come close to keeping pace with Seve Ballesteros' 31. The future 1987 U.S. Open champion, at this time a 27-year-old, one-time PGA Tour winner, found the water on the 11th hole for a double bogey. On the 12th, he misjudged the wind and watched his six-iron tee shot fly over the green onto a bank covered with bushes and flowers. After a five-minute search, the ball wasn't found; Simpson had to walk back to the tee for a stroke-and-distance penalty and ended up with a triple bogey. "You lose a lot of balls at the Masters," Simpson remarked sarcastically after the round. A 41 on the back nine gave him a 73 and an 11th-place finish when a par 36 would have put him in second place.

···

1984

At the age of 32, Ben Crenshaw was already playing in his 13th Masters. The onetime young phenom had five top-10s in Augusta and two runner-up finishes but was hampered by perennially slow starts. He had never broken 70 in the first round and was over par eight times.

The costliest instance was in 1983 when Crenshaw opened with a 76 and then shot 70–70–68 to tie for second, four strokes back. Crenshaw started playing his way into the Masters at the Greater Greensboro Open in 1981 instead of taking the week off to arrive in Augusta early. It hadn't worked so far. This year he shot a final-round 67 at Greensboro to tie for third, so he at least came into Augusta on a good note.

Whether it was momentum from Greensboro or just simply overdue, Crenshaw shot out of the gate at the Masters with a 67 to take the lead with the only bogey-free round of the day. He didn't even need his putting wizardry to do it, making only two putts of six feet or longer—a six-footer for a par on the 10th and 12-footer for a birdie on the 12th. His other birdies came on a wedge to two feet on the third, a chip close on the eighth, a two-putt from 15 feet on 13 and a two-putt from 12 feet on 15.

"It could have been a 62 or 63," said Crenshaw. "But I'm not complaining. It was a comfortable round, and I've had some funny-looking opening rounds."

Another player making his 13th Masters start also posted his first opening round in the 60s—44-year-old Lee Trevino with a 68 for solo second place. Trevino would fall back to a 43rd-place finish. Crenshaw also slipped in the second round, but not too far, with a 72. He made five birdies, just like the first round, but had five bogeys, including a three-putt from the fringe on the 18th. "I just gave some shots away and you can't do that on a day when conditions are perfect," he said.

Mark Lye, an excitable 31-year-old playing in his first Masters, took fullest advantage. "Are you guys as surprised as I am?" the 103rd-ranked player on the money list asked the writers after a 66 for a 135 total and a three-stroke lead. Lye holed a bunker shot for an eagle on the second hole and added three birdies for a 31 on the front nine. Tom Kite claimed second place at 138 with a 68 thanks to birdies at 13, 15, and 16, with Crenshaw one stroke further back.

The third round was not completed on Saturday due to two rain delays. When play was halted by darkness, Lye held on to the lead by only one stroke after a three-putt double bogey at the ninth left him at nine-under. With a suspension for darkness looming, he made sure to hit his tee shot on the 12th before the horn sounded. Kite, in the same twosome and in second place at eight-under, hit his shot into the front bunker.

They didn't finish the hole, but, up ahead, Crenshaw exercised his option to hole out on the 13th after the horn. He had an 80-foot eagle putt and didn't want to wait until morning when he wouldn't be certain of the green speed. Crenshaw got the long putt within two feet for a birdie that put him seven-under, two behind. Earlier, he had holed a bunker shot for a birdie at the ninth.

Larry Nelson, who opened with a 76, finished the third round before the suspension on Saturday with a 66 to get to five-under. He was threatening to pull off a repeat of his 1983 U.S. Open victory, where he stormed from seven strokes behind with a 65–67 weekend.

When play resumed at 8 a.m. on Saturday morning, Kite got up and down from the bunker at 12 and tied for the lead when Lye three-putted from 20 feet. After some back and forth, they were tied again going to 18. From the edge of the tree line, Kite hit a five-iron to 10 feet and made a closing birdie for a 69 and a one-stroke lead at 207 with Lye at 208 after a 73. Crenshaw, with a birdie at 15, a bogey at 16, and a lipped-out birdie putt from 10 feet at 18 had a 70 and was at 209 with 26-year-old Englishman Nick Faldo and two-time major champion David Graham. Tom Watson, recovering from a birdie-less 74 in the first round with 67–69, was at 210.

The 34-year-old Kite was on an extraordinary run at the Masters with four straight finishes of fifth or sixth followed by a second-place tie with Crenshaw in 1983 (he also had a third and a fifth in earlier years). Most of those top-sixes had been accomplished through the back door with final rounds in the 60s; he had never entered the last round closer than four strokes out of the lead. Not a long hitter, Kite nonetheless was comfortable at Augusta, where his touch around and on the greens served him well.

Kite was paired with Lye in the final round and would also need to keep an eye on Crenshaw in the twosome ahead. Tom and Ben grew up together in Austin, Texas, both taught by Harvey Penick, and attended the University of Texas, where they shared the 1972 NCAA individual championship. While Kite had a fine amateur career, he was overshadowed by golden-boy Crenshaw, who captured two additional NCAA titles and won his first event as a PGA Tour member in 1973.

Kite's pro career didn't get off to quite that fast a start, but by the early 1980s he had become the tour's most consistent money earner (he led the money list in 1981) though only claiming five victories so far. Crenshaw had nine wins to that point; however, he'd had some down periods, particularly in 1982 when he fell to 83rd in earnings. His long, sometimes loose swing had come in for criticism and he had tinkered with it. Heading into 1983, Ben was persuaded by Penick to revert to his old swing. It worked, as he claimed his first win in three years and climbed back into the top-10 on the money list. One thing the two Texans *did* have in common— neither had yet won a major championship.

In the final round, Kite birdied the second hole, bogeyed the fourth, and made pars for the rest of the front nine. From Nos. 4–7, he was one ahead of Crenshaw, who birdied the second and made pars through No. 7. For most of the front nine, eight players were within three strokes of the lead before Crenshaw grabbed control with three straight birdies starting at the eighth. He wedged to eight feet for his birdie on No. 8 and made a 10-footer at the ninth to take a one-stroke lead over Kite.

1984		
1	Ben Crenshaw	67–72–70–68—277
2	Tom Watson	74–67–69–69—279
T3	David Edwards	71–70–72–67—280
T3	Gil Morgan	73–71–69–67—280
5	Larry Nelson	76–69–66–70—281
T6	Ronnie Black	71–74–69–68—282
T6	David Graham	69–70–70–73—282
T6	Tom Kite	70–68–69–75—282
T6	Mark Lye	69–66–73–74—282
10	Fred Couples	71–73–67–72—283

The killer blow came on the 10th, where Crenshaw's approach came up 60 feet short. From there, he did the almost impossible, hitting the monster putt on just the right line with just the right speed to dive into the cup. Kite and Lye had to watch from the fairway.

"When we saw that putt go in on 10, it took the life out of us," said Lye. "You could see the look on Tom's face. It hit him."

Kite, who had hit a short drive, missed the green with a wood and made a bogey on 10. His Masters essentially ended at the 12th, where he hit a seven-iron into the water and made a triple bogey when he nearly found the hazard again after a penalty drop. He ended up with a 75 and tied for sixth—upstaged by Crenshaw again. Lye suffered a similar fate. He had birdied Nos. 8 and 9 to recover from a double bogey at the fifth but bogeyed the 10th and 11th on the way to a 74 and a T6.

Up ahead, Nelson was making a move with a 33 on the front nine and a birdie on the 11th to get to four-under for the round and nine-under for the tournament. He strode to the 12th tee one behind Crenshaw, who hadn't yet birdied the 10th.

"I got so excited by the response I got after making birdie on 11 that I just couldn't settle down," said Nelson. "I wasn't ready to hit, but I had to." He hit a six-iron so fat that it splashed in the middle of the creek, not even coming close to the bank on the other side, and he double bogeyed. Nelson birdied 13 and was hanging around in a tie for second three strokes behind when he made a double bogey on 17, this one with a three-putt from short range. A birdie on 18 gave him a 70 and fifth place.

Crenshaw bogeyed the 11th with an approach to the right, then birdied the 12th from 12 feet to take a three-stroke lead. With that cushion, he elected to lay up on the back-nine par fives, parring 13 and making a 15-foot birdie putt on 15. While considering what to do with his second shot on the 13th, Crenshaw thought he saw Billy Joe Patton in the gallery (it turned out Patton wasn't there). A golf history buff, Crenshaw remembered what happened to Patton in 1954 and wasn't going to bring the water into play.

Two more long putts played a big role on the second nine. Crenshaw reached the back left of the green from tree trouble on 14, and the flag was on the front right 70 feet away, downhill and with a huge break. Fearing putting off the green, as he had done in a practice round, Crenshaw instead hit it too softly and came up 15 feet short—then nailed that one to stay ahead by three. The birdie on the 15th put him ahead by four, and he preserved that margin with a velvet touch on a downhill 35-footer on 16 that he hit as gently as a six-foot putt and coaxed within tap-in range.

Gil Morgan and David Edwards shot 67s to get to eight-under, which was not enough to threaten Crenshaw. Watson took too long to get going, though birdies on 13 and 16 put him in the group at eight-under and another at 18, combined with a Crenshaw bogey on 17, brought him within two. That's how they finished: Watson second and Crenshaw first with a routine par at 18 and a closing 68.

Crenshaw had been second in five major championships. The two at the Masters weren't close, but he had lost a playoff at the 1979 PGA Championship and blown the 1975 U.S. Open and 1979 British Open with double bogeys on the 71st hole. After those experiences, Ben admitted, "You start wondering if you can hold yourself together."

The man they called Gentle Ben felt the gallery pulling hard for him to finally get that first major. "If there was one thing going on in my mind out there it was that I didn't want to let everybody down again." He didn't.

....

Cut-line Drama

Defending champion Seve Ballesteros missed the cut by one stroke in most unfortunate fashion. He was penalized two strokes on the 13th hole for taking a practice swing, and thereby grounding his club, when he didn't realize he was inside the hazard short of the green. Jack Nicklaus made the cut in a most unlikely manner when he birdied the last three holes of the second round, chipping in on the 18th hole, for the 146 total that was needed to make it to the weekend. He ultimately rose to a T18 finish.

....

1985

Three weeks before the Masters, Curtis Strange won the Las Vegas Invitational for his second victory of the year to move to No. 1 on the money list. The 30-year-old had emerged from a 1981–82 stretch where he was in the top-10 money winners without a victory, and now owned three wins in the past seven months.

Bernhard Langer of Germany was coming off a 1984 campaign when he won four times on the European Tour and led the Order of Merit, which still didn't earn him much attention heading into the Masters. Seve Ballesteros had won twice in Augusta and Nick Faldo had made somewhat of a mark in the U.S. while playing semi-regularly in the past three years and winning the 1984 Heritage Classic. Still, the quality of the new crop of elite players from Europe wasn't fully appreciated.

That Strange and Langer would be headliners on the weekend didn't seem likely on Thursday evening. In Strange's case, it didn't seem possible. The tour's hottest player shot a first-round 80 and made a reservation for a flight home to Virginia at 2:50 p.m. on Friday for a quick getaway after the second round. Langer had a quiet 72.

Only three players broke 70 on opening day, Gary Hallberg with a 68 and Tom Watson and Payne Stewart with 69s. Watson had warned on Wednesday that the greens were as fast as he had ever seen them, and that if they weren't slowed down it could get "ridiculous." They were indeed a bit slower on Thursday, but the pin positions were harsh, David Graham calling them "downright rude." Most of the troubling placements were on the front nine, and Watson ended up blitzing the back nine for a 31 with an eagle on the 13th and three birdies.

With cable television broadcasting the first two rounds in the afternoon (as started in 1982), pairings for the second round were made by scores. That turned out to be a break for the high scorers from Thursday who went off in calm conditions before the wind picked up considerably in the afternoon. Sandy Lyle went 78–65 and Strange improved by 15 strokes with 80–65. The former NCAA champion from Wake Forest holed an eight-iron for an eagle at the third and collected four straight birdies starting at the 11th to go eight-under through 14. His threat to the course record fizzled with a three-putt bogey at 15 and three pars; still, he had gone from oblivion to relevance—and gladly canceled his plane reservation.

Of the six scores in the 60s, five came from the first 21 players to tee off, who shot 76 or worse in the first round, and the other was a 67 by Craig Stadler, who opened with a 73. The 1982 champion birdied five of the last eight holes, two of them after tee shots into the gallery, to tie for the lead at 140 with Stewart and Watson, who both shot 71. Watson bogeyed 16 and 17, expanding the number of players who made the cut under the 10-shot rule to 60 in the field of 77. Surprisingly, perennial contender Tom Kite was one of the 17 who went home on the weekend.

The churn from top down and bottom up continued in the third round. The Saturday scores of the four top players through 36 holes were: Watson 75 with four three-putts, Stadler 76, Stewart 76, and Hallberg 75. Hallberg started the third round one behind and surged into a three-stroke lead with a 33 on the front nine and then nosedived to a 42 on the back with a triple bogey at 16.

The lead remained four-under at the end of the day for the third straight round, Ray Floyd taking over first place with a 69 for 212. "At 15, I looked up at the scoreboard and said, 'My goodness, I'm in the lead.' I was shocked," said Floyd. The 1976 champion had a game plan for every hole that he had written out on Monday evening, saying it kept him from being overly aggressive. "I'm going to play intelligently, even if I feel like I'm playing defensively."

Strange continued his rebound with a 68 to stand just one stroke out of the lead, and had researchers scrambling to find the last time anyone had won a major championship with a round in the 80s (it was George Duncan at the 1920 British Open). "I think I have a good chance to win, and yes I'm surprised as hell," he said after a round that included a lone bogey at the first hole and five birdies.

Two strokes behind were Ballesteros, going quietly along at 72–71–71, and Langer, who carded a 68 on Saturday to move up from the middle of the pack after a 72–74 start. Langer was two-over for the day through six holes and still not much of a factor at even par through 12. That's when an admitted "bad gamble" paid off thanks to a dose of luck. From a bad lie in the right rough on the 13th, Langer decided to go for the green in two even though he figured his three-wood shot from there would end up in the water seven out of ten times. "I was two-over [for the tournament] at the time, so I was in no position to play safe. I'm playing this week to win." His shot landed *short* of the creek guarding the green—and bounced over it, finishing 18 feet from the hole.

The 27-year-old German sank the putt for an eagle, made a birdie from 12 feet on the 14th, and added another birdie with a chip close on the 15th after a six-iron second shot. From two-over to two-under just like that, and suddenly very much in the picture.

Floyd's reputation as a great front-runner had taken a hit from his retreat at the 1983 Masters and another one the week before this Masters, when he shot a 78 at Greensboro after leading through 54 holes. On this Sunday, he found that a game plan couldn't help him if his ball-striking was inaccurate. He hit only three greens in shooting a 38 on the front nine; an eagle on the 15th helped him shoot a 72, but it wasn't good enough. Ballesteros had an uncharacteristically uneventful round of 16 pars and two birdies for a 70—also not good enough.

Strange grabbed control of the tournament with a flawless front nine, hitting every green and making birdies on Nos. 2 (four feet), 4 (15 feet), 7 (six feet), and 8 (four feet) for a 32. The man who shot a first-round 80 now had a four-stroke lead over Langer and Ballesteros heading to the back nine of the final round. Reporters were already brainstorming how they would lead their stories, but Strange knew there was plenty of golf left. Aware that one of his challengers could make a charge, Curtis told himself to stay aggressive.

Strange bogeyed the 10th with a three-putt, but got the stroke back at the 12th with a 20-foot birdie. Langer, playing with Ballesteros in the twosome ahead of Strange and Floyd, also birdied the 12th and when he birdied the 13th with a five-iron and two-putt from 22 feet he was within two. Back in the fairway, Strange contemplated a second shot from 208 yards. Unlike Ben Crenshaw a year earlier, he decided to go for the green in two with a four-wood.

The distance wasn't a problem. However, the shot drifted to the right and landed in the hazard on that side of the green. It was playable, barely in the water, and Strange splashed it out, but the shot only made it partway up the bank. From there, he pitched to eight feet and missed the putt. Now he led by one.

Up ahead, Langer hit a strong drive on the downwind 15th and reached the green with a five-iron for another two-putt birdie (he played the 13th in five-under and the 15th in four-under in the tournament). Strange's lead was gone. Now it was a tie.

Strange faced a second shot of 200 yards to the 15th and pulled out a four-iron, the same club he had used to hit the green from a similar spot the day before. This time it landed halfway up the bank of the pond in front of the green and rolled back into the water. When he couldn't get up and down after a penalty drop, Strange trailed by one.

The two par fives had produced a difference of four shots between the two main protagonists, and that determined the outcome. Langer gave himself a cushion with a birdie on 17 and bogeyed 18 from a bunker for a second consecutive 68. Strange's approach to 18 was mishit and finished in front of the green; his 45-foot chip to force a playoff didn't go in; and, when he missed a 12-foot par putt, he had a back-nine 39 for a 71 and a tie for second with Floyd and Ballesteros.

The Masters had its second champion from continental Europe, and from a most unlikely place—Germany had never produced anything like a world-

1985		
1	Bernhard Langer	72–74–68–68—282
T2	Seve Ballesteros	72–71–71–70—284
T2	Raymond Floyd	70–73–69–72—284
T2	Curtis Strange	80–65–68–71—284
5	Jay Haas	73–73–72–67—285
T6	Gary Hallberg	68–73–75–70—286
T6	Bruce Lietzke	72–71–73–70—286
T6	Jack Nicklaus	71–74–72–69—286
T6	Craig Stadler	73–67–76–70—286
T10	Fred Couples	75–73–69–70—287
T10	David Graham	74–71–71–71—287
T10	Lee Trevino	70–73–72–72—287
T10	Tom Watson	69–71–75–72—287

class golfer. Asked who was the best golfer ever to come out of Germany before him, Langer responded, "Probably Toni Kugelmuller," producing only blank stares.

The victory was a major advance from Langer's Masters debut in 1982 when he missed the cut with 11 three-putts in two rounds. Now he was putting cross-handed from inside 20 feet, with a conventional grip on longer putts. If it worked well enough to win on Augusta's devilish greens, Langer could rest assured it would work anywhere.

Strange naturally faced questions about following in Billy Joe Patton's footsteps by losing the Masters with water balls on 13 and 15. "I didn't think about not going for it because the shots were so short," he said, adding that the shot to 15 was the one that confounded him, because he was sure he hit it well. "I may have trouble with this for a while, but I hope not. I would have had more trouble if I backed off and lost."

1986

Jack Nicklaus shot a 69 in the final round of the 1985 Masters to finish T6 and called it his best ever ball-striking round at Augusta National, hitting all 18 greens and two par fives in two. That round showed he could still play in his mid-40s; however, at age 46, he came into the 1986 Masters on a decidedly downward trend.

In seven starts on the year, he missed three cuts, withdrew once, and had a best finish of T39 to rank a very un-Nicklaus-like 160th on the money list. In his Sunday preview of the Masters surveying the contenders, *Atlanta Constitution* golf writer Tom McCollister wrote, "Nicklaus is gone, done. He just doesn't have the game anymore. It's rusted from lack of use. He's 46, and nobody that old wins the Masters." Nicklaus' friend and housemate for the week, John Montgomery, taped a clipping of the article onto the refrigerator door, knowing that it would provide Jack with motivation.

McCollister's *Constitution* colleague Glenn Sheeley piled on Wednesday, writing of Nicklaus that "it's time for Carnegie Hall and he's having trouble hitting all the right notes at the town band shell." CBS-TV analyst Ken Venturi was quoted as saying, "Jack's got to be thinking about when it's time to retire."

Actually, Nicklaus was thinking about what he needed to do to repair his golf game. He had a session a few weeks earlier with his lifelong teacher Jack Grout, who told him to get rid of the excessive hand action in his swing. It was taking a while to make the adjustment, but he was beginning to see progress even as he was missing the cut in the Players Championship. He finally got the feel on the Friday before the Masters while practicing at Augusta National, telling his wife Barbara, "I finally found that fellow I used to know on the golf course."

Nicklaus' poor results also were a function of a relative lack of focus on his golf game. He had become more involved with his business since personally taking over the operation the previous September. It was rumored that the business was in dire financial straits because of a couple of bad real-estate deals, which Nicklaus would later confirm. Also, he was less motivated by week-to-week PGA Tour events.

"Golf hasn't been the number-one priority. But with Masters and major championship season, golf is the number-one priority now," he said on Wednesday, talking to a small gaggle of writers. For the first time in years, he hadn't been requested to appear at the media center for a pre-tournament interview.

Could he win? "My chances are better than they were a week or two ago," he said. "I didn't think too much of my chances then."

His chances didn't look good after a first-round 74, though they weren't completely gone. Nicklaus was in a tie for 25th, six strokes off the lead, after a windy day putting on greens that players said were the fastest they had ever seen. "I'm amazed that guys are making any putts out there," said Nicklaus, who was three-over through 12 holes before making his only birdie of the day at the 13th.

Billy Kratzert and Ken Green were on top at 68, with T.C. Chen and Gary Koch at 69, but more noteworthy were Tom Kite, Tom Watson, and Greg Norman at 70 and Seve Ballesteros at 71.

Ballesteros moved ahead on Friday with a 69 in the second round to lead at 140. He came to Augusta embroiled in controversy, having been banned from the PGA Tour for 1986 for playing less than the required 15 events the year before (he had joined as a member in 1984). The Spaniard could play the majors, because they weren't run by the PGA Tour. He was allowed to play in New Orleans three weeks before the Masters as defending champion (he missed the cut). Seve planned to tee it up in five mini-tour events in Florida to get ready for the Masters, though he ended up playing in only one due to the illness and death of his father.

On the Sunday before the tournament, Ballesteros told a British TV crew that the Masters "is mine," a quote that was widely reported in the days before the tournament. After his Friday round, he denied saying that he would win and that he had been misinterpreted. His big blow in the second round was an eagle from 25 feet on the 15th. That made up for a failed gamble on the 13th, where he tried a three-wood from amongst the trees in the right rough that bounced into the hazard guarding the green (though he did manage to play it out and make a par). Other than that, he said his round was "nothing very dynamic" as he concentrated on keeping his approach shots below the hole on the treacherous greens.

The very first Official World Golf Ranking (then called the Sony Ranking) had come out on the Sunday before the Masters, with Ballesteros ranked No. 2, barely behind Germany's Bernhard Langer, who won six tournaments worldwide in 1985 to Seve's five. Defending champion Langer had a 68 to jump into a tie for fourth at 142. For the second straight year, he switched putters during the tournament, this time switching to a lighter one for the second round. Norman was also at 142 after a 72 that would have been better if not for a four-putt on the 10th hole.

Nicklaus improved to a 71, still six shots out of the lead. The *Augusta Chronicle*, showing more optimism about his chances than the *Constitution*, headlined its Nicklaus story, "Golden Bear lurks in the shadows, ready to pounce."

Nicklaus, who was often being called the Olden Bear these days, said he putted a little better in his three-birdie, two-bogey round than the first day, making four of 12 putts inside 15 feet after just one of 11 on Thursday. "When you have the ball that close that many times, you have to make more putts," he said. "I've played my best two rounds of the year and haven't scored."

Saturday was an easier day for everyone. "They did something to the greens to slow them up," said Nicklaus. Combined with a lack of wind and relatively generous pin positions, scoring plunged from an average of 74.68 for the difficult first two days to 70.98 in the third round—the lowest scoring day ever in the Masters to that point.

Nobody took more advantage than Nick Price, who broke the course record of 64 originally set be Lloyd Mangrum in 1940 and matched by five players—including Nicklaus—between 1965 and 1979. The 29-year-old from Zimbabwe bogeyed the first hole and reeled off 10 birdies the rest of the way.

Birdies on Nos. 2, 5, 6, and 8 gave him a 33 on the front nine, and then he really got hot on the toughest stretch on the course with birdies on 10 (four feet), 11 (15 feet), and 12 (20 feet—his longest made putt of the day). He added a fourth straight birdie on 13, where he had to lay up after a drive to the right and hit a sand wedge to six feet. "The course record is on. Let's go!" he said to his caddie on the 14th fairway.

Price settled for a par on 14 and had to lay up on 15 but hit a sand wedge to four feet to get to eight-under for the round without hitting any of the par fives in two. He moved to nine-under with a five-iron tee shot that trickled down the slope to within three feet on the 16th. Not settling, Price came very close to a 62 or even a 61. He narrowly missed a 15-foot birdie putt at the 17th and recovered from a bad drive to the left by hitting a four-iron to 25 feet on 18. It matched the longest birdie putt he'd left himself since the fourth hole, but he nearly made it, the ball hitting the hole and spinning halfway around it before popping out.

"I think Bobby Jones held up his hand from somewhere and said, 'That's enough, boy,'" said Price.

The performance was quite a contrast to his first round, a 79 in which Price said he had six three-putts. Following the path of Curtis Strange a year earlier, Price fought back into contention through 54 holes, in his case with 69–63 for a 132 total that was a Masters record for the middle 36 holes. Through that point in his career, he was a solid money earner but had only one victory on the PGA Tour and two on the European Tour, and was best known for losing the 1982 British Open after leading by three with six holes to play. Now he had another chance in a major, sitting at 211, one stroke out of the lead.

The top position at 210 was held by Norman, who fired a 68 thanks to a 32 on the back nine, where he birdied 11, 12, 13, and 17. Even with the more benign conditions, he said a key to his best showing since his 1981 debut, when he finished fourth, was a more conservative approach. "I've tended to play too aggressively in the past," he said.

Ballesteros yielded the lead with bogeys on the last two holes, with a three-putt at 17 and poor drive on 18, to fall one behind. It was a mostly uneventful round with just two birdies and the two late bogeys for a 72 on a day ripe for scoring, Seve saying he struck the ball well but failed on a number of birdie putts inside 20 feet.

Joining Price and Ballesteros at 211 were Langer with a no-bogey 69 and Donnie Hammond with a 67. A pair of Toms, Watson and Kite, were at 212 after matching 70–74–68 scores, joined by Japan's Tommy Nakajima. Watson lamented a triple bogey at the 12th in the second round, while Kite's biggest frustration was a missed two-foot par putt at 18 on Saturday. There was nobody at 213, and Nicklaus headed a group of seven at 214 after a 69.

The good news for Nicklaus was that he birdied Nos. 8, 9, 11, and 12 to get to four-under on the day. Unfortunately, he hit a two-iron second shot into the water and bogeyed the 13th and only made a par on the 15th. Birdies on the two back-nine par fives would have put him within one of the lead. Still, he had improved his position from 25th to 17th to ninth over the first three rounds. Could he advance farther on Sunday?

"If I can play as well as I've been playing and make a few putts, I might scare somebody," he said.

Norman, 31, had only joined the PGA Tour in 1984 after mostly playing on the European circuit. He won twice in 1984, then had a down year in 1985 with no victories in the U.S., though he did capture the Australian PGA and Australian Open in November. He only had one top-25 finish in seven starts so far in 1986 but was feeling better after a mysterious respiratory ailment had finally been diagnosed and treated with antibiotics.

His pursuit of a first major got off to an erratic ball-striking start, but his short game bailed him out with par saves from tough spots on the first, second, and fourth holes. Langer birdied the second and was tied for the lead when CBS came on the air with the last twosome on the fifth hole, but the defending champion soon ran into trouble and dropped clear out of the top 10 with a 75. There were eight players within two strokes on that first television leaderboard, including Jay Haas, who shot a 31 on the front nine to get to five-under and within one of the lead. He would stall with an even-par back nine for a 67.

Nicklaus wasn't on that leaderboard, as he was sputtering through the front nine at even for the day and two-under overall. He birdied the second, punching out after a drive into the trees and hitting a 100-yard pitching wedge to eight feet. Jack gave that one back with a three-putt bogey on the fourth, missing a second putt from five feet, and added another short miss at the sixth when he couldn't convert a four-foot birdie putt. At this point, he wasn't scaring anyone.

The round almost took a worse turn on the eighth, where he drove into the trees for the second time on a par five. Figuring he was at a point he needed to make something happen, Nicklaus gambled by trying to thread a three-wood through a narrow gap to get close to the green. Aiming to the left of the closest tree ahead of him, he pushed the shot to the right of that tree—and made it through an even narrower gap. He ended up missing a 10-foot birdie putt, but disaster had luckily been averted.

Nicklaus set himself up with another 10-foot birdie putt on the ninth hole. Before Nicklaus putted, a roar arose from the eighth green, where Kite had just holed an 81-yard shot for an eagle to get to five-under after a lackluster start. Less than a minute later, another roar from the eighth—Ballesteros had holed a 40-yard shot for an eagle to take the lead at eight-under (Norman was seven-under after a birdie at the sixth). That roar prompted Nicklaus to step away from his putt and say to the gallery, "OK, let's see if we can get a roar up here." He got that roar by sinking the putt, but it only got him to three-under and five strokes off Seve's lead.

Since earlier in the spring, Nicklaus had been using a new putter model from his equipment company, MacGregor, one with a very oversized head. The results had been spotty so far, but he was beginning to feel more comfortable with it. During the first three rounds of poor-to-mediocre putting at Augusta, he had been told by several people that his problem was moving his head on putts rather than keeping it still during the stroke—his wife, Barbara; a friend, Bob Hoag; and CBS analyst Tom Weiskopf all gave him that tip. Suddenly, everything clicked into place at just the right time.

As Nicklaus looked over a 25-footer for birdie on the 10th, he had a feeling he would make the putt—and he did. "We won't count him out on this back nine," CBS announcer Bob Murphy said. "How many times has he played it in next-to-nothing to win."

The five-time Masters champion followed by sinking a 22-foot birdie putt on the 11th, again celebrating the successful effort with his signature raise of the putter skyward with his left arm. He was now five-under for the tournament, just two strokes behind Norman and Ballesteros, who drove up against a tree on the ninth and bogeyed. The Nicklaus charge stalled on the 12th, where he hit his tee shot long and left, pitched to eight feet, and missed the putt.

The setback only served to inspire him. "That was the hole that got me going. I got aggressive after that," he said after the round.

Nicklaus made a textbook birdie on the 13th with a three-wood tee shot around the corner, a three-iron to 30 feet, and two putts. He had to save par after going over the green on 14 and did just that with a delicate chip to within a foot.

There was plenty of action elsewhere. Payne Stewart made a cameo on the leaderboard with a birdie on 15 to pull within two strokes at five-under (he would bogey 17). Kite birdied the 11th to reach six-under. Norman came a cropper at the 10th hole yet again. He had made a double bogey there to ruin his 1981 bid and another in the second round this year. Now he hooked a drive, which hit a tree and kicked into the fairway. He wasted the break, hooking a four-iron well to the left next to two trees, leaving a difficult punch shot. The attempt scooted across the green into a bunker and three strokes later Norman had yet another double bogey, falling two behind at five-under.

Two twosomes ahead of Nicklaus, Corey Pavin and Mark McCumber both eagled the 15th to technically pull within one and two strokes of the lead at six- and five-under. However, Ballesteros was already set up for an eight-foot eagle putt on 13, which he made. His second eagle of the round put Seve nine-under, two strokes ahead of Kite, who made a two-putt birdie on 13.

In short order, Pavin badly hooked his iron tee shot into the pond on 16, leading to a double bogey—the second straight day he went eagle-double bogey on 15 and 16. McCumber faded away with two bogeys coming in.

Nicklaus was unaware of Seve's eagle on 13, which left him four behind with four to play. Still, he sensed he needed an eagle on 15 anyway. The flag was in a relatively generous position near the middle of the green, and three of the four players in the two preceding twosomes had made eagles (Koch joining Pavin and McCumber). Nicklaus fired his four-iron straight at the flag, a magnificent shot that landed a couple feet from the hole and finished 12 feet away. Remembering that he had a similar putt in 1975 and didn't hit it firmly enough, Nicklaus made an aggressive stroke and knocked the ball into the hole for an eagle. The gallery roar dwarfed the sound Ballesteros had produced for his eagle on 13; the crowd was fully behind Nicklaus as they sensed a career-capping triumph in the making for the best golfer of all time.

As Nicklaus walked to the 16th tee, Rick Reilly wrote in *Sports Illustrated*, "One had the feeling of being indoors at, say, an overtime Kentucky basketball game, yet all the while being outdoors. That's loud."

Nicklaus selected a five-iron for his tee shot on 16 and sent it on a perfect line just to the right of the flag. "Be right!" said his son, Jackie, who was his caddie on this momentous day. "It is," said Jack as he bent down to pick up his tee while the ball was still in the air, knowing that he wouldn't be able to see where the ball ended up anyway. The crowd told him. The distance was indeed perfect, the ball coming within a couple inches of the hole as it rolled down the slope and settled three-and-a-half feet away.

Behind him, Nicklaus' old major foil, Watson, was making a run of his own. The man who beat Nicklaus at the 1977 Masters and British Open, 1981 Masters, and 1982 U.S. Open had birdied 13 and 14 and now had an 18-foot eagle putt on 15 to join Nicklaus at seven-under. Perhaps in a rush to putt before a Nicklaus putt at the nearby 16th, which could create disquieting pandemonium, Watson missed and settled for six-under. Nicklaus made his putt to get to eight-under, within one stroke of Ballesteros, who was in the 15th fairway at nine-under.

Seve had a four-iron second shot of his own to the 15th, which should have been a chance to increase his lead. Instead, he caught the turf behind the ball for a fat smother-hook that dived midway into the pond. Ahead on the 17th tee, Nicklaus heard what he called a "funny sound" made by the gallery in reaction to Seve's shot. It was a combination of groans and murmurs mixed with a greater amount of somewhat subdued cheering and applause, as the Nicklaus-favoring gallery couldn't quite contain their schadenfreude over Ballesteros' misfortune.

Ballesteros finished the 15th with a bogey after a penalty drop, a pitch, and two putts from 15 feet. Kite made a two-putt birdie to create a three-way tie for the lead at eight-under.

Nicklaus pulled his tee shot to the left on 17 and mostly escaped tree trouble, except he had to be sure to keep his pitching wedge approach just low enough to miss a branch ahead of him. He executed it perfectly, finishing 11 feet from the hole. It was a tricky putt to read, with two subtle breaks that canceled each other out. As the ball approached and fell into the hole, CBS announcer Verne Lundquist called out, "Maybe...yes sir!" Nicklaus had played his last nine holes in seven-under—with a bogey!—and was in the lead.

It wasn't over yet. There was still some work left on the 18th hole, and some sweating out of the action behind him. The flag was on the back portion of the 18th green, and Nicklaus' five-iron approach didn't carry over the upslope, rolling back down to 50 feet short of the hole. The reception as he reached the 18th green was called by veteran announcer Venturi "the most emotional and largest ovation I've ever heard."

Nicklaus said there were several points during the round that he had tears welling up in his eyes and had to remind himself there was still golf to play. This was one of them. The putting touch that had suddenly descended upon him on the back nine didn't go away, as he rolled the long putt within a few inches of the hole for a par, a back-nine 30, a 65, a nine-under 279 total, and a hug with 24-year-old son Jackie.

Ballesteros and Kite both saved par on 16. Seve's chances were extinguished by a three-putt bogey on the 17th, where his first putt raced 15 feet past. Kite parred 17 and headed to 18 needing a birdie to tie. He gave himself a great chance with a second shot 12 feet to the right of the hole. The putt looked good until the last instant, when it dived to the left of the cup. Kite was left with a 68 that wasn't quite good enough. It was another near miss, but at least, Kite said, he didn't feel like he had lost it like he did in 1984.

The final twosome of Norman and Price were forgotten men midway through the back nine, mostly abandoned by the gallery and playing in eerie near silence while roars reverberated ahead of them. After one of those roars, Norman turned to his playing companion and said, "Let's let these people know we're still here."

Price was within two strokes after the 10th hole and within three after the 15th, but his final-round 71 left him in a supporting role and fifth-place finish. When Norman failed to birdie the 13th, staying at five-under, his chances appeared to be gone. The Australian had a rally in him, though. He birdied the 14th from 12 feet, the 15th with a two-putt, and the 16th from two feet to reach eight-under.

1986

1	Jack Nicklaus	74–71–69–65—279
T2	Tom Kite	70–74–68–68—280
T2	Greg Norman	70–72–68–70—280
4	Seve Ballesteros	71–68–72–70—281
5	Nick Price	79–69–63–71—282
T6	Jay Haas	76–69–71–67—283
T6	Tom Watson	70–74–68–71—283
T8	Tommy Nakajima	70–71–71–72—284
T8	Payne Stewart	75–71–69–69—284
T8	Bob Tway	70–73–71–70—284

Norman was in trouble on 17 after hooking his drive into the seventh fairway. Forced to play a low punch shot between trees and under branches, he pulled it off beautifully, the ball running up onto the green and stopping 12 feet from the hole. When he made the putt, he was tied for the lead—the 54-hole leader and the comeback kid all in the same crazy day.

Norman used a three-wood off the tee on 18 to avoid the fairway bunkers and ended up with a similar distance to the hole as Nicklaus, who also hit a three-wood. Seeking to reach the back plateau and give himself a chance for a winning birdie, Norman hit a four-iron. He made a bad swing, flaring the ball terribly to the right about 10 deep into the gallery. With little chance to get a pitch close from the packed-down earth, he played a reasonably good bump-and-run to 15 feet. When the putt slipped by the hole for a final-round 70, Nicklaus was the champion by one over Norman and Kite and two over Ballesteros.

In a way, it was a tale of three four-irons. Ballesteros didn't go to the media center after the round, but the *Constitution*'s Thomas Stinson buttonholed him as he was about to leave the course. "Hard to know what happened," Seve said of the shot on 15. "I wasn't nervous. I think I tried to hit a four-iron too easy. I should have hit a five-iron." Norman said an insufficient weight shift caused him to leave the clubface open and block his approach to 18. Nicklaus, on the other hand, hit a pure four-iron to deliver the eagle he knew he needed on 15. He always was known as the game's best long-iron player in his prime. This wasn't his prime, of course, but it was a reawakening. A sixth Masters title was a reminder that the kid who came out of Ohio to earn his first green jacket 23 years earlier had gone on to build a legacy as the greatest to ever play the game.

Nicklaus called out McCollister in the press conference, saying that he was motivated by being written off as a contender. "Glad I could help," the writer responded.

Without explicitly eating crow in print, McCollister summed up Nicklaus' charge to a sixth Masters title in his lead story in Monday's paper: "Like a man possessed, seeking that one last hurrah, he made time stand still."

1987

Scoring was predicted to be high, as players noted in the practice rounds that the bentgrass greens had finally achieved the desired firmness and were as fast as ever. Sure enough, only two players shot below 71 in the first round, and they happened to be in the same twosome—John Cook with a 69 and Larry Mize with a 70.

Mize was a native son, born in Augusta. His family moved back and forth a couple times between Augusta and Columbus, Georgia, when he was growing up, and Mize now lived in Columbus. He attended high school in Augusta and worked on the scoreboard at the third hole at ages 14 and 15, so he felt an intimate connection to the Masters.

His home course in his high school years was Augusta Country Club, which directly borders Augusta National behind the National's 12th green and 13th tee. Mize had a couple of chances to play Augusta National while he was in high school, but declined in favor of earning his way there one day at the Masters. He qualified for the first time in 1984, finishing 11th. In 1986, he shot a 65 in the final round to finish T16.

Mize and Cook had relatively early tee times, which helped since the wind picked up in the afternoon not only causing havoc to balls in the air but also drying out the greens even more. They were hand watered at the end of the day, making them a bit more playable, though still challenging for Friday play.

Roger Maltbie took advantage with a 66, 10 strokes better than his opening round, with four birdies on the last six holes. The 35-year-old was enjoying a career revival, qualifying for the Masters in 1986 for the first time since his only two appearances in 1976 and 1977.

Conditions again became tougher in the afternoon, and there were no low numbers from the first round's lead pack. The 36-hole leader was Curtis Strange at 141 after a wild 70 that included an eagle hole-out with a six-iron on the fifth hole, five birdies, and five bogeys. Two years removed from letting the Masters slip away on the final nine, the determined Virginian said, "Whatever tournament you blow, you want to come back and win. Obviously, to me, this is the one tournament I'd like to win."

In addition to the 1985 disappointment, Strange went backward after holding the lead on two other occasions. He shared the lead through 18 holes with a 69 in 1981 and followed with a 79, then co-led through 36 holes in 1982, following with a 73 and going on to a T7 finish. This time he shot another third-round 73, a round where he was in fine shape until playing the last six holes in three-over. The water got him again when he hit a two-iron into the pond for a bogey on 15 and he was a victim of a slick green as he three-putted 16, his first putt from 12 feet and his second from 40. That left him at 214, two behind Maltbie and Ben Crenshaw and one behind Greg Norman and Bernhard Langer.

Crenshaw, who shot a 75 in the first round, surged into his share of the lead with a 31 on the back nine for a 67, reeling off four straight birdies starting at the 12th and another on the 18th.

Norman went one better with a six-birdie, no-bogey 66, only one of the birdies from longer than eight feet. Having led all four majors through 54 holes in 1986, winning only the British Open, he was now one back and ready for yet another go at a major Sunday. Lurking rather quietly at 214 was perennial contender Seve Ballesteros (73–71–70), who, unlike Strange, didn't embrace the revenge theme.

"I remember the good things. I just don't remember anything from last year," the two-time champion insisted early in the week.

Mize appeared headed toward being only a local angle—and not much of one at that—when he was three-over on the day and one-over on the tournament through 12 holes. Then he heated up with birdies on 13, 16, and 18 for a 72, joining Ballesterors and Strange at two off the lead, and gaining confidence from hitting the ball better than in the first two rounds.

"Everybody is expecting Norman and all those guys to do everything and nobody is expecting for me to do too much. Maybe I can slip right in there," said the 28-year-old.

Winning a major would certainly be a surprise for the sixth-year tour pro with one victory—that in 1983—and a reputation for coming up short on Sunday. He lost four-stroke 54-hole leads at the 1985 Kemper Open and 1986 Players Championship and lost a playoff to Greg Norman at the 1986 Kemper Open among four runner-up finishes in the last two years. Some were calling him Larry DeMize.

There were 16 players within five strokes of the lead through 54 holes, and it stayed bunched on Sunday, with gusty winds and slick greens preventing anyone from shooting low enough to pull away. At one point, shortly after the last twosome made the turn, there were nine players within one stroke, three at three-under and six at two-under.

Three of those players shot their way out of it with 40s on the back nine—Strange, Langer, and T.C. Chen. Another was Jodie Mudd, who, as a tour rookie in 1983 (in the field from a top-24 finish as an amateur in 1982), entered the final round two strokes out of the lead and shot an embarrassing 86. Now back in the Masters for the first time in four years, the thin Kentuckian was five back through 54 holes and jumped into contention with a birdie-eagle-birdie start to get to three-under overall. His charge stalled: Over the last 15 holes he bogeyed the 12th and parred the rest. Mudd's two-under was very much in the hunt down the stretch; he just couldn't get the late birdie he needed.

Only one player reached four-under on the back nine, and that was for only one hole. Mize got there with a two-putt birdie on the 13th in an up-and-down round that included five birdies and three bogeys to that point and also featured a 20-foot, par-saving putt on the 11th after missing the green to the right (remember that). He followed with a 20-foot birdie putt on 12 and a two-putt birdie on 13.

The see-saw ride continued, Mize losing the lead with consecutive bogeys on 14 and 15. The first came on a poor chip and a missed 10-footer; the second was a potential killer when he overclubbed on a four-iron second shot to the 15th and bounded all the way into the 16th-hole pond. After two routine pars, Mize came to the 18th hole one behind and made a clutch birdie with a nine-iron to six feet for a 71. Now he waited to see if his three-under 285 would hold up.

Next came Ballesteros, having a grind-it-out kind of day. He was two-under for the tournament through the 15th, where he two-putted from the fringe for his second birdie of the day against two bogeys. He had a 15-foot birdie putt on the 16th that looked in all the way until a cruel lip-out. The Spaniard successfully got to three-under with an approach to four feet for a birdie on the 17th. He almost let it slip away on 18, hitting his second shot into the right bunker, but came out nicely to four feet and he saved par.

Norman followed, and he was having a very different kind of round. He matched Mize's six birdies, but made one more bogey (six) for a 72. Starting at three-under, he twice got to four-under on the front nine before a bad stretch with bogeys on Nos. 6, 7, 10, and 11 that dropped him all the way to even par. The blond Australian gamely battled back with birdies at 12 (four feet), 13 (two-putt), and 15 (chip to three feet), stumbled with a bogey at 16, and returned to three-under by ramming home a 25-foot birdie putt on 17. He intentionally bashed a drive *over* the fairway bunkers on 18 into the open area on the left that Jack Nicklaus favored in his younger days, approached to 20 feet, and hit a putt he thought was in before it dove away in the final inches.

Finally came the last twosome of Maltbie and Crenshaw. Maltbie led through nine holes at four-under, but fell back with bogeys at 10, 11, and 14. He became the third contender to birdie the 17th; his only getting him to two-under, however. He couldn't get a tying birdie on 18, and shot a 74 for 286.

Crenshaw tried mightily to scramble his way to the title on a day when his approach shots were off, whether it was from misjudging the wind or a swing that was slightly off-kilter. He missed six of the first seven greens, but got away with it for a while with a birdie at the second, a fantastic pitch to four feet at the third, and a 15-foot par save at the fourth. Bogeys at the sixth and seventh, though, dropped him to three-under, and that's where he stayed for nine holes with a couple more par saves from 10 to 15 feet and no real birdie chances.

Ben held the lead at three-under through the first seven holes of the back nine, often by himself, but in a four-way tie by the time he got to the 17th. That's where his luck and touch ran out. One of his more well-struck iron shots bounced over the green on 17 when he hit a nine-iron, not the pitching wedge his caddie, Carl Jackson, recommended. A downhill chip from 20 feet to the back pin trickled five feet past. Ben's putter finally ran out of magic as he made a rare bad stroke. When he missed a 20-footer from nearly the same spot as Norman had missed on the 18th, Crenshaw was saddled with a 74 to tie Maltbie and Mudd at 286, one stroke out of the playoff.

As the extra-hole trio arrived at the 10th tee, Mize seemed out of place. The other two were established as among the best players in the game—arguably the top two at that point—and both carried themselves with an air of bravado. Mize was a nice player with a nice swing who went unnoticed unless he was losing a tournament on the back nine somewhere.

To his credit, Mize felt he belonged. "I was pretty nervous standing with those two boys, but I was not intimidated," he said.

Mize hit the best approach on the first playoff hole, a seven-iron to 12 feet, while the other two were on the back fringe 20 to 25 feet away and missed their birdies. Mize's uphill putt for the victory came close, but lost steam at the end. Ballesteros' putt from the fringe had rolled five feet past, and he missed coming back. Just as in 1986, it became a Masters for Seve to forget—literally.

1987

1	Larry Mize	70–72–72–71—285*
T2	Seve Ballesteros	73–71–70–71—285
T2	Greg Norman	73–74–66–72—285
T4	Ben Crenshaw	75–70–67–74—286
T4	Roger Maltbie	76–66–70–74—286
T4	Jodie Mudd	74–72–71–69—286
T7	Jay Haas	72–72–72–73—289
T7	Bernhard Langer	71–72–70–76—289
T7	Jack Nicklaus	74–72–73–70—289
T7	Tom Watson	71–72–74–72—289
T7	D.A. Weibring	72–75–71–71—289

*Mize won on second playoff hole

Mize's five-iron approach to the second playoff hole, the 11th, was so far to the right, he turned away in disgust. Norman's seven-iron finished on the fringe some 35 feet from the hole. In regulation, Mize hit a relatively poor pitch to 20 feet—and made the putt on the same line as the 30-yard pitch he had now. When he was in high school, Mize used to practice pitch shots in the yard of his family's home not far from Augusta National. Now, he took out a sand wedge and kept the trajectory low enough for the ball to take two bounces short of the green and begin rolling like a putt—right into the hole!

The gallery exploded with a roar and prolonged cheering while Norman looked crestfallen—he had lost the preceding major, the 1986 PGA Championship, when Bob Tway holed a bunker shot on the 72nd hole. What were the odds of the same player being beaten by shots holed from off the green on the concluding hole of two straight majors? Astronomical. However, that was the result when Norman couldn't hole his putt from the fringe.

On Saturday evening, Mize, speaking of his boyhood Masters dreams, had said: "I've dreamed of winning it a lot of times. Somewhere along the way, I won it going away and coming from behind. I guess in my dreams I've won it about every way I could."

In Sunday's aftermath, Mize admitted he'd never dreamed of winning the Masters with a chip-in to beat two of the greatest players in the world—and have the green jacket draped over his shoulders by defending champion Jack Nicklaus, the greatest in the history of the game. The Augusta kid had not only achieved his dream. He exceeded it.

How Far Was It?

Many reports of the 1987 Masters said that Mize's playoff chip-in was from 140 feet, a "fact" that has been picked up in subsequent stories. But it was actually much shorter. In the pre-laser measuring days, reporters generally went with putt and chip distances estimated by the players, or occasionally using their own estimates from watching on television or in person. In his post-round interview, an overwhelmed Mize, still processing all that had happened, said he didn't know how long the shot was. The 140-foot number had originated from shell-shocked eyewitness Greg Norman.

Not everyone went with 140 feet. The Associated Press report simply said it was from far right of the green. Thomas Boswell in the *Washington Post* called it 100 feet, and *Golf World* in its report said 27 yards. A look at a recording of the CBS telecast shows that *Golf World* and Boswell were closer to the truth. Mize went up to the green to assess the shot. His walk back to the ball showed him to be some 18 paces from the edge of the putting surface. The distance the shot rolled on the green was slightly less than Norman's putt from the fringe, which Greg estimated at 30 feet, but appears longer. Using a round number, since it's not a precise measurement, 30 yards is a fair estimate for Mize's historic shot.

....

1988

Sandy Lyle came into the Masters fresh off a victory at the Greater Greensboro Open, his second PGA Tour win of the year. While Australia's Greg Norman and Spain's Seve Ballesteros were hailed as the leading international stars, the low-key Lyle was playing as well or better than anybody in the game. The Scotsman—he was born, raised, and lived in England but considered himself Scottish because his parents were from Scotland—won the Players Championship in 1987 and led the money list so far in 1988 thanks to wins in Phoenix and Greensboro.

The 1985 British Open champion had also won in Greensboro in 1986, going on to finish T11 in Augusta that year, paired with champion Jack Nicklaus in the final round. The 30-year-old was playing in his seventh Masters, where his main trouble was rocky first rounds. Lyle's scoring average was an abominable 75.67 in the first round, but with a 71.56 average over the other three rounds, he managed to make five of six cuts and post three top-25 finishes.

This time, though, Lyle finally got off to a good Masters start. His opening round of 71 was better than the number suggests. On a day Nicklaus called "one of the most difficult days I've ever seen here," with wind gusts up to 30 mph and crusty greens, Lyle was tied for third despite a bogey on the 18th, where his three-foot putt was deflected by a spike mark. Eighty in the field of 91 shot over par, 20 of them 80 or higher.

The co-leaders were Larry Nelson and Robert Wrenn at 69, neither of whom were destined to stick around near the top. One player who would remain a factor all week was Mark Calcavecchia, who recovered from playing the first seven holes three-over to shoot a 71.

Lyle moved to the front on Friday with a 67 for 138, playing the par fives in three-under for the second straight day. A bogey on the first hole was followed by four birdies on the front nine, while four-iron second shots and up-and-downs led to birdies on 13 and 15.

Calcavecchia was next, two strokes back after a 69. He once again struck the ball poorly on the first seven holes, surviving this time thanks to four par saves, all from difficult spots and two on putts of 15 and 18 feet. "I felt like I was semi-cheating the course," he said after settling down for a three-birdie, no-bogey round.

The headlines, though, went to Fuzzy Zoeller, and not just because he had the day's low round of 66. The 1979 champion spent nearly the entirety of his post-round interview blasting the condition of the greens, saying he was tired of watching good shots bounce over greens and downhill putts that wouldn't stop. "It would be nice if they gave us some decent putting surfaces to play on. I hate for golf to be tricked up," he said.

That the criticism came from someone who had scored so well meant it wasn't just a case of sour grapes, though in fact Zoeller had also been steaming after a first-round 76—his fine second round just gave him a forum and a mass audience.

Zoeller wasn't alone in his thinking; even Arnold Palmer chimed in. "They either need to redesign some of the bentgrass greens or go back to Bermuda," said the four-time champion. Curtis Strange four-putted the ninth green and said, "There ain't a blade of grass on it."

Nicklaus saw some validity in the complaints, but added, "They will put a little water on the greens and they will be fine tomorrow."

That's pretty much what happened, as 29 of the remaining field of 46 shot par or better on Saturday. Still, it wasn't a day when the leaders produced a lot of roars. Lyle and Calcavecchia both shot even-par 72, yet managed to hold onto the 1 and 2 spots through 54 holes.

Lyle temporarily opened a four-stroke lead with a 34 on the front nine, but couldn't get a birdie on the back and bogeyed 13, where he drove into the creek, and 16. Calcavecchia's lone highlight was an eagle on the 15th, where he hooked a four-iron around a tree to 12 feet. "I guess I should consider myself pretty lucky to be only two strokes behind the way I played, "he said. "It was such a relief when I walked off the 18th green. I said, geez, let me out of here and I'll start over tomorrow."

Ben Crenshaw was the prime mover in the third round with a 67 capped by birdies on 17 and 18 from 30 and 12 feet, earning a tie for second with Calcavecchia at 212 and a spot with Lyle in Sunday's final twosome. Next came Zoeller, Fred Couples, and Bernhard Langer at 214.

Norman hadn't been heard from since a back-nine 41 on Thursday led to a first-round 77. There was finally a Shark sighting on Sunday when he tied the front-nine record with a 30 and went on to shoot a 64 that was too late to get him in real contention but earned him a tie for fifth at 285, where he was joined by Couples.

While Norman started too far back, that wasn't necessarily true of Craig Stadler. Beginning the day five strokes behind, the 1982 champion birdied the second and seventh and holed a 30-foot putt for the only eagle of the week on the eighth for a 32 on the front nine.

Stadler only made up a couple strokes on Lyle, who continued his trend of strong starts. The Scotsman demonstrated both his length off the tee and his short-game touch, two key attributes at Augusta, on the first four holes. He needed only a seven-iron second shot on the second hole to set up a two-putt birdie from 12 feet. The key hole was the fourth, where Lyle turned a potential bogey into a birdie by chipping in from 60 feet. Then he made up for a bogey on the sixth hole with a birdie on the ninth, where he hit a seven-iron to tap-in range. The two-under 34 put Lyle eight-under for the week on the front nine. Now he headed to the back, where he was only even par so far.

Crenshaw briefly threatened by going one-under through three holes, but he bogeyed the sixth and seventh and couldn't get anything going after that, ultimately shooting a 72 for fourth place.

Calcavecchia also bogeyed the sixth and seventh to go two-over for the day, but quickly rallied with birdies on the next two holes for a 36 on the front nine. The 27-year-old, known

1988		
1	Sandy Lyle	71–67–72–71—281
2	Mark Calcavecchia	71–69–72–70—282
3	Craig Stadler	76–69–70–68—283
4	Ben Crenshaw	72–73–67–72—284
T5	Fred Couples	75–68–71–71—285
T5	Greg Norman	77–73–71–64—285
T5	Don Pooley	71–72–72–70—285
8	David Frost	73–74–71–68—286
T9	Bernhard Langer	71–72–71–73—287
T9	Tom Watson	72–71–73–71—287

for his aggressive play and deft short game, was contending in a major for the first time and he was hanging in there, not a total surprise since he had cracked the top 10 money winners on tour in the previous season.

Lyle led by three or four strokes from the fourth hole through the 10th, yet it took only two holes for him to give it away. He missed the 11th green to the right, hit a weak putt from the fringe, and missed from 10 feet. Then he committed the cardinal sin of shooting at a back right hole location on the 12th hole, bringing the water into play if he came up short, which is just what he did. With the resulting double bogey, he was suddenly tied with Calcavecchia at five-under—and soon with Stadler, who birdied the 14th from 15 feet.

Calcavecchia, who had trailed by five through seven holes, jumped into the lead with a two-putt birdie at the 13th. Stadler joined him by chipping close to birdie the 15th, but dropped a stroke behind with a bunkered tee shot and bogey at 16.

Lyle said on Saturday night that patience would be "the 15th club in my bag" in the final round. That patience was sorely tested as he let three straight birdie chances slip away while trailing by one. He hit huge drives on both par fives, but hit too much club on both, going over the 13th green with a seven-iron into a back bunker, where an up-and-down was almost out of the question, and leaving a delicate pitch on the 15th, where he ended up missing a five-foot birdie putt. In between, he missed a 10-footer for birdie on 14.

The man who Calcavecchia called "99 percent unflappable" hurled his visor to the ground when his eagle chip lipped out on 15. Lyle collected himself after the disappointment of the birdie miss to hit a fine tee shot 15 feet behind the hole on the 16th. His patience was rewarded, as he finally converted a birdie try to tie for the lead.

Up ahead, Stadler narrowly missed 20-foot birdie putts on the final two holes to finish at five-under after a 68. Calcavecchia gamely stayed at six-under with par saves from eight and 10 feet on 15 and 16 and a chip to six inches on 18 for a 70. He then waited to see what Lyle would do on the home hole.

Things looked good for Calcavecchia and not-so-good for Lyle when Sandy's one-iron tee shot found the first of two fairway bunkers on the left side, leaving a shot of just over 140 yards uphill. "I thought it was all over," said Lyle. "I didn't think I would have a chance of getting it out of that bunker and getting it on the green."

He felt a little better after seeing the ball sitting in a good lie on the upslope, and a lot better when he clipped his seven-iron shot perfectly and watched the ball sail on its intended line. He couldn't see the result, but heard the reaction from the crowd as the ball landed some 25 feet past the hole, just enough below the back plateau to take the downslope toward the front hole location, settling 10 feet away. The birdie putt was straight down the hill, and Lyle's putt was true, making him the first British player to win the Masters. The water ball at the 12th was forgotten. Instead, the 1988 Masters would be remembered for a magnificent—and very long—sand save.

....

Putt-Putt-Putt-Putt

Legend has it that when asked in his post-round interview to describe his four-putt on the 16th green in the first round, Seve Ballesteros replied, "I miss, I miss, I miss, I make." His actual response was concise, but not quite that pithy. "35 feet, went four feet past, I missed the hole, I missed the hole again," said the two-time champion, who shot a 73 that day and went on to finish T11. He wasn't the only one to four-putt the green on Thursday. Mark O'Meara gently tapped a downhill 10-foot putt only to watch the wind and slope carry it 60 feet past the hole, from where he took three more.

Such shenanigans were one reason Fuzzy Zoeller lambasted the condition of the greens after the second round. While many players supported Zoeller, Tom Watson publicly disagreed, saying that the greens were fair. Told after the third round that Watson four-putted 16 that day, Zoeller said, "I hope he enjoyed every one of them."

....

1989

England's Nick Faldo finished second, third, and fourth in the last three major championships of 1988 in a follow-up to winning his first major at the 1987 British Open. In five appearances at the Masters, though, the 31-year-old had never finished better than T15.

A solidly built man of 6-foot-3 height, Faldo nonetheless was only a medium-length hitter, building his game more on precision. Nor was he considered a great putter, though he certainly wasn't a bad one. So, the jury was still out on how well Augusta National suited him.

Coming into the Masters, Faldo decided to give his putting game a jolt by switching to a Bullseye style putter for the first time as a professional. It worked nicely in the first round, as he holed a couple of 20-footers and a 12-foot eagle putt on the 13th in a round of 68, one of only three sub-70 rounds on a windy day. That was one stroke better than Scott Hoch, who had an eagle of his own from 60 feet on the 15th.

They trailed surprising first-round leader Lee Trevino, who at the age of 49 turned in his best career round at the course he didn't love, shooting a 67. This from the same man who shot 81-83 the previous year, and as a parting shot said, "I hope to God they don't invite me back."

Actually, an invitation was a foregone conclusion as his victory in the 1984 PGA Championship gave him a five-year pass. Trevino overcame his Augusta angst and was taking his game more seriously than in recent years as he wanted to be ready for the senior tour when he turned 50 in December. He made five birdies and no bogeys on Thursday.

A no-bogey round was out of the question on Friday. The morning brought rain and cold, with a wind chill of 35 degrees. The rain stopped in the afternoon and it warmed up a little, but the wind picked up, too, gusting up to 30 mph. "My brains are gone," said Augusta veteran Ben Crenshaw after battling the wind.

Faldo and Trevino tied for the 36-hole lead at 141, Faldo jumping ahead with a 34 on the front nine before a 39 on the back while Trevino did the opposite with 38-36. "I knew it was going to be a tough day, so I hung in there," said Trevino. "Par was about 75."

Only seven players posted under-par totals for 36 holes. By the end of another miserable weather day on Saturday, just one player would stand at under par for the tournament when play was suspended with 14 players not completing the third round. Crenshaw played his 13 holes in three-under to get to four-under overall, while the next best were Faldo, Hoch, and Mike Reid at even par, all through 12 or 13 holes.

Play was suspended at 3:30 p.m. for a lightning and rain delay of one hour, 40 minutes. When it resumed, players fought a mostly losing battle against wet conditions and impending darkness, with Reid the only player under par during that time. Seve Ballesteros was particularly bothered, with bogeys on 11, 12, and 13—his last three holes—dropping him from even par to three-over.

Trevino fell out of it on Saturday, playing his 12 holes in seven-over, blaming his eventual 81 more on poor putting than the conditions. Scoring wasn't impossible in the third round, Greg Norman shooting a 68 to vault into contention at one-over after opening rounds of 74–75.

Norman was becoming the tournament's "nearly man" with runner-up finishes in particularly anguishing fashion in 1986 and 1987 followed by a fifth in 1988. Ballesteros' frustrations were also growing with runner-up finishes in 1985 and 1987 and a fourth in 1986 that also counted as a squandered opportunity, though at least he could look back on two earlier Masters titles to salve his wounds. Both would make their moves on Sunday—and continue their roles as tragic heroes.

Interviewed on Saturday evening when leading by four strokes, Crenshaw said, "I need a bigger lead than I have, because I know what can happen around here. I'm trying my dead level best to build on the lead I've got."

Instead, the lead shrank when the third round concluded Sunday morning. Ben played his last five holes in one-over for a 70 and a 213 total, only one ahead of Hoch and Reid, both of whom moved forward in the morning. Also moving in a positive direction was Ballesteros, who birdied 14, 15, and 17 to recover to a 73 and 216 total.

Seve's move became a surge when the fourth round started, which he opened with a blitz reminiscent of his race to the title in 1983. He stiffed his approach to two feet for a birdie on the first hole, then began connecting from long range. After dumping a pitch shot into a bunker on the second, he holed out for a birdie from the sand. He followed by sinking birdie putts of 40 feet on the fourth and 35 feet on the fifth to go four-under for the round (and seven-under on his last 10 holes). A more conventional birdie from six feet on the ninth gave him a 31 on the front nine, just like 1983. The brilliant nine shot him into the lead, as it did in 1983, though this time he was only ahead by one instead of by four heading into a back nine that always seemed to be filled with land mines for him.

With the greens softened by rain and nothing falling from the sky (not yet, anyway), good scoring was possible for the first time all week. Another who took advantage was Faldo, but he was five strokes behind after a third-round 77, which would have been even worse if he hadn't made a birdie putt estimated at somewhere between 90 and 100 feet on the second hole.

Failing to take advantage of good conditions on Sunday morning, going two-over in his six-hole windup of the third round, the Englishman was so disgusted with his putting that he took a half-dozen putters with him to a 45-minute session on the practice green. The new Bullseye was ditched in favor of a TaylorMade model. The switch worked like a charm, as Faldo sank birdie putts of 17, 12, 15, and 20 feet in shooting a 32 on the front nine, bringing him to two-under, three back of Ballesteros and Reid, who also had a hot hand.

The slender Reid, one of the shortest hitters on tour and known as "Radar" for his accuracy, was in his 13th year on tour and playing in only his third Masters, having missed the cut in the other two with no rounds better than 75. A consistent top-60 money earner, Reid finally broke through for his first two tour wins in 1987 and 1988. Nobody expected him to be a factor in the Masters, but there he was following rounds of 72–71–71 with a 33 on the front nine Sunday with birdies on Nos. 6, 8, and 9 to get to five-under and a share of the lead.

Right behind him on the course was Hoch, who also birdied the ninth to wrap up a mistake-free front nine of 33 to join the tie at five-under. Like Reid, Hoch was a steady performer ranking in the top 40 on the money list in seven straight years. But he was not a big winner—the last of his three wins in nine-plus years on tour was in 1984. In five Masters starts, his best finish was T27.

Ballesteros, Faldo, Reid, and Hoch would all hold or share the lead at some point on a wild back nine, as would Crenshaw and Norman, with a backdrop of spectator umbrellas as the rain, naturally, returned.

Seve was the first to falter, hooking his tee shot into the trees at the 10th and making a bogey to drop to four-under. He shot himself out of it with a tee shot into the water on the par-three 16th, a too-late birdie on 18 giving him a 38 on the back nine for a 69 and fifth place. In the long view, it was the back-nine par fives that cost him the tournament. Not only did he fail to birdie them in the final round, he was one-over for the week on both the 13th and 15th. He bogeyed 13 on Thursday when he tried to play out of the hazard next to the green and failed to get out, and made another bogey as darkness closed in on Saturday. And he double bogeyed 15 in the second round when he four-putted, two of the misses from three feet.

Reid grabbed the solo lead with a chip-in birdie from 20 feet on the 12th. His underdog bid came crashing down when he missed a three-foot par putt on 14 and hit his third shot into the water for a double bogey on the par-five 15th. A bogey on 18 left him with a 72 and sixth place.

1989		
1	Nick Faldo	68–73–77–65—283*
2	Scott Hoch	69–74–71–69—283
T3	Ben Crenshaw	71–72–70–71—284
T3	Greg Norman	74–75–68–67—284
5	Seve Ballesteros	71–72–73–69—285
6	Mike Reid	72–71–71–72—286
7	Jodie Mudd	73–76–72–66—287
T8	Chip Beck	74–76–70–68—288
T8	Jose Maria Olazabal	77–73–70–68—288
T8	Jeff Sluman	74–72–74–68—288

*Faldo won on second playoff hole

Faldo bogeyed the 11th with a poor drive to slip to one-under. Undaunted, he hit an outstanding second shot to the 13th for a two-putt birdie from 15 feet and a fine approach to the 14th for a five-foot birdie. Then his putter took over again. First, he holed a big-breaking 18-foot putt from the back fringe on the 16th—nearly the same putt Lyle had made a year before. Next he drained a 45-footer at the 17th as the new putter continued to work its magic. He almost added yet another birdie at 18, but his 15-foot effort slid just under the hole, leaving him with a 65 and a posted five-under 283 total for the others to try to beat or tie.

Norman somehow matched Faldo's streak of four-under on five holes starting at the 13th, changing the location of the lone par to the 14th. He had to make a 25-foot putt on 13, where he laid up after his drive hit a tree, blasted from the bunker to within a foot on 15, canned a 30-footer on 16, and staked an approach to two feet on 17 to get to five-under and tied for the lead. He wasn't up to the task on 18, though. Norman hit a one-iron off the tee to stay short of the fairway bunkers. Choosing a five-iron for his second shot, he came up short, chipped up, and missed a 12-foot par putt. Just like 1986, a bogey on 18 left him one behind. Oddly, he said his approach shot was "the most perfect five-iron I ever hit," while also denying that he mis-clubbed.

In the final twosome, Hoch continued to play the steadiest golf of all the contenders, parring the first five holes of the back nine before inching ahead with an up-and-down from the bunker for a birdie on 15 to reach six-under. Needing two pars for the title, he put himself in trouble with a weak drive to the right on 17, leaving a long, blind approach. Hoch struck it well, but airmailed the green and rolled down a hill, leaving an exceptionally difficult pitch. He handled it masterfully, the ball stopping four feet past the hole—but failed to convert the putt. A two-putt par at 18 left him with a 69 and tied with Faldo.

Hoch's companion, Crenshaw, fell to three-under with a bogey at 12, then fought back with birdies at 16 (eight feet) and 17 (30 feet, after a drive off a tree and a four-wood approach) and came to the home hole tied with Hoch and Faldo. Alas, his four-iron second shot went left—he blamed the lack of a dry towel, and a wet grip that caused his hand to slip—and he missed a 12-foot par putt. It was the third straight year Crenshaw played in the final twosome and came up empty; like Ballesteros, he followed a Masters title with a string of near-misses.

Faldo and Hoch headed to sudden death in near darkness as "sunset" approached under gloomy skies. Faldo's drive at the 10th was short and to the right, leaving a challenging long-iron approach that was also short and right, landing in a bunker. Hoch was on in two and ran his 30-footer two feet past. Faldo missed his 12-foot par putt, sank a three-footer for a bogey, and awaited his near-certain fate. With a two-foot putt to win the Masters, Hoch surveyed it longer than might have been necessary or prudent. Finally ready, he yanked the putt to the left of the hole—or aligned his putter too far left, as he later said—leaving a three-and-a-half-foot putt coming back. After tossing his putter high in the air in frustration, and catching it when it came down, Hoch settled his nerves and made that putt.

Enough light remained—barely—for one more hole. Hoch missed the green to the right, not as far right as the Larry Mize spot, and pitched six feet short on the green slowed by rain. Faldo had a 25-footer for birdie, and rolled it into the hole to end a crazy Masters. One of the game's premier ball-strikers won thanks primarily to his work on the greens, not to mention considerable help from his playoff rival. He did it with a final round 12 strokes better than his third round. And the Masters had its second straight champion from Great Britain.

1990

There was little reason to expect that 47-year-old Ray Floyd would be a factor in the 1990 Masters. It was looking as if his two-win season in 1986, including a U.S. Open title, was his last hurrah. His game declined sharply in 1987–88 and, in 1989, went in mothballs when he concentrated on his role as captain of the U.S. Ryder Cup team. A third-place finish at the Honda Classic in March of 1990 was a positive sign, but he followed that up by shooting 79–76 at the Players Championship.

Floyd's Masters preparation ended on a bright note when he won the Par-3 Contest on Wednesday. Of course, no winner of the Par-3 event, which began in 1960, had ever gone on to win the Masters in the same year—not that there's any reason a fun, nine-hole contest on a short course would be predictive of the tournament outcome. Still, it got Floyd feeling positive and reinforced his stated goal of having fun during the week.

The 1976 champion enjoyed a first-round 70, though he could have done without bogeys on 16 and 18 that kept him from joining the four players who shot in the 60s. Three were Masters rookies—Mike Donald with a 64, John Huston a 66, and Bill Britton a 68—joined by Peter Jacobsen at 67.

Defending champion Nick Faldo was in pretty good shape after a 71 with particularly sharp ball-striking. His five birdies were all from eight feet or less, and three of his four bogeys came on missed putts inside five feet. One of those that particularly upset him was on the 16th, where his downhill six-foot birdie putt went four feet past and he missed the comebacker.

"It really annoys me that you can hit great shots here and they don't come off," said Faldo of the difficulty of downhill putts on the slick greens.

The same kind of conditions prevailed in the second round, even a bit harder as the wind picked up, but the greens would become friendlier on the weekend after some rain on Friday evening. The fall of Thursday's unlikely 60s shooters was almost predictable, and all shot 74 or worse in the second round (Donald an 82), while Floyd took control with a 68 for 138. It was like 1976 all over again, as Floyd was five-under on the par fives for the day including an eagle on the eighth with a 12-foot putt. (Instead of a five-wood, the secret weapon for Floyd in his late 40s was a graphite-shafted three-wood from Japan.)

In second place at 139 was last year's heartbreaking runner-up Scott Hoch, also with a 68. The man who admirably won the Las Vegas Invitational weeks after his Masters debacle held a press conference on Tuesday to try to put to rest all questions about last year's missed two-footer, though of course he realized the blown Masters would never be completely put behind him. Masters redemption would ultimately be lacking; Hoch bogeying the 18th to let Floyd take the lead and finishing with rounds of 73–76 for a T14 result.

Not to be ignored at this point was 50-year-old Jack Nicklaus, who shot a 70 to stand at 142 and said, "I think I have a very good chance." Nicklaus missed his usual preparation in Augusta the week before the Masters for a good reason—he was winning the Tradition in Arizona, his first event on the senior tour.

Floyd's intent of having fun was tested when he played the first six holes of the third round in two-over. He didn't let the bad start get him down, going on to birdie the seventh hole and storm home with a 31 on the back nine when he was holing from seemingly everywhere. His birdies came from 12, 30, 25 (a chip-in), 15, and 35 feet, all from the 10th to 16th holes, to fashion a 68.

The long-range barrage was reminiscent of Faldo's final round in 1989. Meanwhile, Faldo was putting together a 66 built on brilliant approach shots. His three front-nine birdies all came from less than four feet, his three back-nine birdies on two eight-footers and a two-putt. The defending champion did hole a 12-footer for par on 18 to cement a 209 total, three behind Floyd. In between them was Huston at 208, who birdied Nos. 8–11 on the way to a 68. Nicklaus moved into fourth place at 211 with a 69, still feeling that he had a chance while admitting that it depended on what Floyd did in the final round.

Floyd restored his front-runner reputation in the eyes of many with his 1986 U.S. Open victory. Still, there were those third-round leads lost at Augusta in 1983 and 1985, and 47-year-old nerves that hadn't been tested in four years. He looked shaky early, hitting a number of errant shots. He snap-hooked an iron into the trees on his second shot on the par-five second, but made a par. He didn't get away with a wild drive on the fifth, which found an area in the trees to the right where few have ever strayed. It led to a punch-out and a bogey.

Floyd got back to even par on the eighth with his best drive of the day and a three-wood to the green for a two-putt birdie. Then he was back to scrambling, with one-putt pars on the ninth and 10th. Still, his lead remained safe through all of this. Only three players started within five strokes, and Huston quickly took himself out of it with bogeys on the first two holes. He would shoot a 75. Nicklaus missed four-foot putts to bogey the fifth and sixth, and, even when he holed a bunker shot to birdie the seventh, he was still four behind, which was the closest he would get.

Faldo, playing in the twosome with Nicklaus ahead of Floyd, also gave the leader some air with a double bogey on the first hole, where he drove into a fairway bunker and three-putted. The Englishman gritted his teeth and battled back with birdies at Nos. 2 and 7 from four feet and the ninth from eight feet. The front-nine 35 pulled him within two strokes, but he immediately gave one back when he bogeyed the 10th from the right bunker.

It looked dicey for Faldo when he flew the 12th green and his ball plugged in the back bunker. "When I stepped in, all I could see was water," said Faldo, referring to Rae's Creek looming on the other side of the shallow green on a shot that would be difficult to control. He extricated himself nicely with a shot that stopped 15 feet from the hole on the far fringe. Faldo thought he left the putt short, yelled "Go!" and the ball toppled in on its last roll.

Faldo was alive, but he fell four strokes behind when Floyd used a putter to hole out an 18-footer from the fringe on No. 12. At that point, Floyd later said, "I didn't think I could lose."

Faldo had other ideas. He took advantage of the par fives, two-putting from 20 feet for a birdie on 13 and pitching to five feet for a birdie on 15 after his two-iron second shot went over the green. Floyd settled for par on those holes. A drive to the right forced a lay-up on 13. He hooked his drive badly on 15 to the left of a stand of trees, yet still had a chance to go for the green. Leading by two, he elected to lay up, and missed a 15-foot birdie putt.

Soon the lead was one. Faldo continued to put the pressure on by holing a 20-foot putt on 16, reminiscent of his key birdie the year before, but from the opposite side of the hole. Floyd pushed his tee shot on 16, leaving a delicate 30-foot putt from the top shelf with such a sharp break he had to start the ball nearly sideways from the hole. He negotiated that beautifully for a tap-in. He promptly left himself yet another tough task when he pulled his approach to the 17th some 50 feet left of the pin. Floyd couldn't get away with a two-putt this time. The first putt slid eight feet past, and he was unable to convert. The four-stroke lead was gone.

Faldo parred the last two holes for 69—278, and Floyd almost missed even a playoff, finding bunkers with his tee shot and second shot on the 18th before saving himself with a blast to four feet and a good putt for a 72.

It was déjà vu time for Faldo as he went to the 10th tee for sudden death for the second straight year. Unfortunately, his first two shots were also déjà vu: a weak drive and a long iron into the bunker. This time, Faldo hit a much better bunker shot, to four feet. Getting a reprieve when Floyd's 15-foot birdie putt came up short. Faldo made his par putt to extend the playoff to the 11th hole. That's where it ended. Floyd pulled his seven-iron approach into the water, enabling Faldo to win with a solid par on a two-putt from 18 feet.

Floyd was stunned by letting the Masters slip through his fingers down the stretch. "This is the most devastating thing that has happened in my career. It would have meant so much to me."

Faldo, with a second title in his pocket, was leading a charmed existence. While Greg Norman's opponents were chipping in or shooting 30 on the back nine, Faldo's playoff foes were practically rolling

1990		
1	Nick Faldo	71–72–66–69—278*
2	Raymond Floyd	70–68–68–72—278
T3	John Huston	66–74–68–75—283
T3	Lanny Wadkins	72–73–70–68—283
5	Fred Couples	74–69–72–69—284
6	Jack Nicklaus	72–70–69–74—285
T7	Seve Ballesteros	74–73–68–71—286
T7	Bill Britton	68–74–71–73—286
T7	Bernhard Langer	70–73–69–74—286
T7	Scott Simpson	74–71–68–73—286
T7	Curtis Strange	70–73–71–72—286
T7	Tom Watson	77–71–67–71—286
*Faldo won on second playoff hole		

over. Let's not sell Faldo short, however. He did shoot a final-round 65 in 1989 and 66–69 over the weekend in 1990. The Englishman was becoming the comeback king, winning twice in a row when he never led outright in regulation. And he joined Jack Nicklaus (1965–66) as the only players to win back-to-back.

Even better, he did it with Nicklaus accompanying him in the final round. That was particularly special to Faldo, who was inspired to take up golf at age 13 when he watched Nicklaus in the telecast of the 1971 Masters (Charles Coody won, but it was runner-up Nicklaus who attracted the youngster's attention.) "That's what made it so emotional for me," said the man generally known for his icy cool.

1991

When Ian Woosnam won the USF&G Classic in New Orleans in late March, he declared that he was the No. 1 player in the world. This struck many as a hollow boast, considering that Nick Faldo had won two majors in 1990—the Masters and a runaway victory at the British Open.

The 33-year-old from Wales pointed out that he had won four European Tour events in 1990, compared to two for Faldo. And he added another European victory three weeks before New Orleans, giving him a case based on current form—Faldo had played very little in 1991 and not all that well. "I just don't get the recognition he does," said Woosnam. "I feel I've been underestimated."

Woosnam was well aware that the lack of a major championship on his career record was a strike against him and was very much looking forward to the Masters. "To be the best in the world, they say you have to win in America and you have to win a major. I won in America this week. Now let's see what we can do about the other in two weeks," he said.

The World Ranking had Woosnam just behind Faldo after New Orleans, but when the numbers were crunched the week before the Masters, Woosnam indeed came out No. 1. Rising Spanish star Jose Maria Olazabal slipped into the No. 2 spot ahead of Faldo, giving Europe the top three positions.

It was 25-year-old Olazabal who had the best first round of that trio in the Masters, a 68 to stand one behind three co-leaders. Woosnam and Faldo both had disappointing 72s on a day when 30 players broke par.

The leaders were Americans Lanny Wadkins, Mark McCumber, and Jim Gallagher with 67s. The 41-year-old Wadkins had been one of the top players in the game throughout most of the 1970s and '80s, but for whatever reason hadn't fared particularly well at the Masters. He never finished better than T7 in his first 18 appearances until things began looking up in 1990 with a T3 thanks to a 68 in the final round.

Another 41-year-old American stepped to the forefront in the second round— Tom Watson. The former world No. 1, who hadn't won since 1987, shot a second consecutive 68 to lead by two strokes. He did it in the company of 51-year-old Jack Nicklaus, the two old friendly rivals putting on quite a show. The highlight was Nicklaus holing a huge-breaking, 35-foot birdie putt on the 16th, and Watson—who had just eagled the 15th—following him by sinking a 30-footer.

It was the fourth straight birdie for Nicklaus, quite a turnaround since the streak immediately followed a quadruple bogey seven at the 12th, where he hit two balls into Rae's Creek.

That's the kind of day it was. With greens softened by rain on Tuesday evening and not firming up during humid, nearly windless days, red numbers were commonplace. Still, Augusta National was able to extract a toll on given occasions. Nicklaus wasn't the only player who went to extremes both ways in the same round.

Olazabal also made a quadruple bogey on a par-three, his coming on the sixth, the highest score ever recorded on that hole. His strokes included two pitch shots that rolled back to his feet in an effort to reach the top plateau of the green, another pitch, and three putts from 45 feet. He rallied with birdies on 13, 15, 16, and 17 to shoot 39–32 and finished the day just three shots out of the lead.

Wadkins also went 39–32, ending the front nine in embarrassing fashion with a four-putt double bogey on the ninth hole that included a backhanded miss from six inches. He said that fired him up, as he made two birdies and an eagle on the back nine to gain a tie for second at 138.

Woosnam avoided big-time trouble, making just one bogey along with five birdies and an eagle on the 13th for a 66 that got him into serious contention at 138. His rival for the No. 1 ranking, Faldo, played the last six holes three-over for a 73 and 145 total that wasn't far inside the cut line of 146. Not even a third-round 67 was enough to make him a threat to win a third straight Masters, Faldo ultimately settling for a T12.

Woosnam was playing in only his fourth Masters, his career not having kicked into high gear until 1987. Standing 5-foot-4½, the Welshman was nonetheless a powerful player who felt the course suited him if he could improve on his earlier efforts around and on Augusta's greens. It came together in the third round with birdies on 12, 13, 14, and 15 for a 67 and a 205 total, yielding him a one-stroke lead over Watson and two over Olazabal and Wadkins.

Olazabal went Woosnam one better with a streak of five straight birdies in the third round, his coming on Nos. 7–11 before he bogeyed two of the next four holes. Watson missed four putts inside five feet and admitted to being "antsy" on short ones. That was a major question heading into the final round as the once premier putter was now in the habit of losing tournaments on the greens instead of winning them.

Woosnam and Watson played together in the third round, and they would accompany each other again on Sunday. It was a meaningful pairing for Woosnam, who, as a teenager, studied Watson's swing and patterned his own after it. Watson, for his part, was an admirer of Woosnam's game, having tabbed the Welshman as one of his picks for the tournament early in the week.

Ahead of them on the course was another European/American pairing of Olazabal and Wadkins. While Steve Pate (65) and Ben Crenshaw (68) would come from behind to post nine-under totals, the tournament would essentially be decided by the last two pairs. Of those four, Wadkins was the only one never to grab a share of the lead, hurt by a double bogey on the fifth hole. He rallied to get to nine-under at the turn but could never get to double figures and finished nine-under.

Olazabal and Watson both had wild up-and-down rounds in their pursuit of the 54-hole leader. The Spaniard, seeking to follow in the footsteps of his mentor Seve Ballesteros as a Masters champion, played the first seven holes in three-under to briefly tie Woosnam. Olazabal proceeded to make consecutive bogeys on Nos. 8, 9, and 10, all due to errant tee shots. He didn't give up, though, and zoomed back ahead with birdies on 13 (a pitch and eight-foot putt), 14 (10 feet), and 15 (chip to one foot) to get to 11-under.

Watson's round was even more dizzying, at least on the back nine. After a disappointing 37 on the front that included a couple of three-putts, he birdied the 10th from 20 feet, quickly gave it back with a bogey on 11, and appeared to shoot himself out of it when his poorly struck seven-iron on the 12th finished in Rae's Creek, leading to a double bogey. Then he showed the determination and talent that had once made him the most feared player in the game and netted him two Masters titles. Watson hit a five-iron second shot to 15 feet on the 13th and made it for an eagle. He used the five-iron again for his second shot to the 15th, hitting an even better one to eight feet, and made that putt for what might be called a back-nine "double eagle." Suddenly, he was 11-under with a piece of the lead.

Woosnam wasn't setting the world on fire, but he was holding on to at least a share of the lead for almost the entire round. He made birdies on Nos. 2 and 5 and bogeys on Nos. 4 and 6 before a 15-foot birdie putt at the ninth gave him a 35 on the front and a three-stroke advantage. To convert that into a victory, he would need to battle not only his nerves but also an unfriendly element of the gallery. There was a nationalistic element to it, with many fans simply wanting to see an American win for a change. "This isn't a links course, it's Augusta," a heckler called out to Woosnam on the 14th tee, per-

1991		
1	Ian Woosnam	72–66–67–72—277
2	Jose Maria Olazabal	68–71–69–70—278
T3	Ben Crenshaw	70–73–68–68—279
T3	Steve Pate	72–73–69–65—279
T3	Lanny Wadkins	67–71–70–71—279
T3	Tom Watson	68–68–70–73—279
T7	Ian Baker–Finch	71–70–69–70—280
T7	Andrew Magee	70–72–68–70—280
T7	Jodie Mudd	70–70–71–69—280
T10	Hale Irwin	70–70–75–66—281
T10	Tommy Nakajima	74–71–67–69—281

haps forgetting that Europeans were handling Augusta like it was their home course these days.

When Woosnam's pulled approach landed on the fringe on the 10th, some in the crowd called for it to go down the hill to the left, which it did, resulting in a bogey. When he hooked his drive into the trees on the left on the 13th, some cheered. Another bogey ensued, dropping Woosnam to 10-under.

The Welshman hit a four-iron to the back fringe on the 15th and got down in two for a birdie, creating a three-way tie at 11-under heading to the last three holes. Olazabal, Watson, and Woosnam all parred 16 and 17, Woosnam holing a seven-foot par-saving putt on 16. It would come down to the 18th.

Olazabal went first, and his inaccurate driving caught up with him again. He tried to fade his drive, but it stayed straight and landed in the second fairway bunker. That one has a steeper face than the bunker Sandy Lyle escaped from in 1988, and Olazabal was unable to reach the green. His next shot from the front greenside bunker almost carried to the back tier, where the hole was located, before trickling back down the hill, leaving a 40-foot par putt, which was too much to ask. A 70 left him at 10-under.

Now it was down to Watson and Woosnam. Tom's three-wood tee shot drifted right into the trees, from where he had no real shot at the green. Woosnam powered his drive over the bunkers into the open area far to the left. His biggest problem from there was getting the large gallery out of the way, which he helped the marshals to do. An 8-iron came up a little short and left, in the fringe some 50 feet from the hole. Watson hit into the same bunker Olazabal had been in.

Watson's bunker shot nearly landed in the hole, but skipped 25 feet past. Woosnam used a putter from the fringe and watched the ball roll eight feet past. Sitting greenside in the scoring tent, Olazabal was still alive if both missed to turn it into a bogey trifecta. Watson's downhill putt drifted left and didn't have much of a chance. He would miss a six-foot comebacker to shoot a 73 and complete a back nine that included two eagles and two double bogeys in a failed bid for a third title. Woosnam's putt was true, and he punched the air in celebration of his first major victory—and validation of his self-proclaimed No. 1 status.

The Eagles Landed

This Masters reversed the recent high scoring trend and then some, with a record of 118 subpar rounds during the week, a mark that would be broken the next year with 145. Soft greens and a lack of gusting winds made approach shots more predictable and allowed players to shoot at flags. What winds there were blew from a direction that made the 13th and 15th holes play downwind every day and easily in reach in two shots. The field scored 37 eagles in the tournament, blowing past the old record of 26, Tom Watson leading the way with three.

....

1992

Very much like Ian Woosnam a year earlier, Fred Couples took over as No. 1 on the World Ranking two weeks before the Masters. His rise to the top was more dramatic, having finished first, second, second, and first in four straight PGA Tour events before a T13 at the Players in his last pre-Augusta start. What's more, he had 12 top-four finishes in his last 18 tournaments stretching back to the 1991 U.S. Open, including four victories.

Clearly, he was the best player in the game at the moment. Right, Fred? "I'm not even close," said Couples at Augusta when a writer made that suggestion.

The 32-year-old Couples was a reluctant superstar. Since joining the tour in 1981, people had marveled at his talent and questioned his drive and ambition. He won only four tournaments up until 1991, though one was the prestigious Players in 1984, and no majors, having come close only once at the 1990 PGA Championship. Now that he was winning with regularity, he wasn't comfortable with the attention he was getting outside the ropes. But once he got on the course, nothing seemed to bother him.

Couples was in reasonable position after the first round with a 69, one of a dozen players to shoot that number among 18 who broke 70. Lanny Wadkins and Jeff Sluman shot 65s, three better than a quartet at 68. It was a record-tying seventh straight subpar Masters round for Wadkins, who would come crashing down with 75–76–75. Sluman became the first player in tournament history to ace the fourth hole, sparking a surge to six-under through 10 holes before he slowed down. The 1988 PGA champion faltered with a 74 in the second round, recovering well enough to finish T4.

Ray Floyd also got off to a hot start, playing the first five holes in four-under, settling for a 69 that included double bogeys at Nos. 7 and 10. Despondent after his playoff loss in 1990 because he figured at age 47 it was his last chance, he was playing even better two years later—having won the Doral-Ryder Open in March. "I feel better about my game than ever before. It's a remarkable thing to say at 49," he said.

Woosnam was ranked No. 3 in the world despite a slow beginning to 1992. He felt better about his chances after an eight-birdie practice round on Wednesday, shot a 69 in the first round, and followed with a 66 to share the 36-hole lead with Australia's Craig Parry (also 69–66).

Right behind them was Couples, who could be a birdie machine when he was on. He churned out nine birdies on Friday, most of them from inside eight feet as he was dialed in with his irons. The problem with Couples was that he made more bogeys than most top players, whether because of lapses or wildness off the tee. He had two bogeys and a double bogey in this round, the latter in the "lapse" category as he failed to clear the hump on a chip shot on 14 and had it roll back to him. The bottom line was a 67 for 136.

Floyd had the same kind of day with seven birdies, a bogey, and a double bogey on 12 where he hit into the water. He was at 137 with three double bogeys in two rounds. With greens relatively soft and a bit slower because of denser growth and lack of wind, scoring was low for a second straight year. In fact, the cut came in at a record-tying-low 145.

Couples and Floyd played together in the third round, a comfortable pairing for both. The veteran Floyd, known for his mental toughness and course management, had taken Couples—not exactly known for either—under his wing at the 1991 Ryder Cup. With Floyd as a mentor/partner, the pair went 2–1 in foursome and four-ball matches against the Europeans.

Both shot 69s in a third round that extended into Sunday morning because of a one-hour, 50-minute delay in the late afternoon for lightning and rain that prevented play being finished before darkness. Couples had a steady round this time, with just one bogey and four birdies, two of them on the first holes he played on Sunday morning (15 and 16).

Woosnam was done in by the rain delay, making double bogeys on the first two holes he played after returning to the course, Nos. 4 and 5. He recovered to shoot a 73 and was four back entering the final round, but would fall to T19 with a closing 75.

The leader was Parry, a 26-year-old Aussie who at this point of his career was a regular on the European Tour, where he owned four victories. He overcame a double bogey on the fourth hole to shoot a 69 for 12-under 204 and a one-stroke lead over Couples, two over Floyd, and three over Australia's Ian Baker-Finch.

Parry birdied the second hole in the final round, while Couples got off to a shaky start with snap-hooked drives on the first two holes—he parred the first hole from the ninth fairway and bogeyed the second after his tee shot found the creek on the left. Parry was now three ahead of Couples and Floyd, who bogeyed the first, but the momentum made a sudden shift on the third hole.

Playing together in the last twosome, Couples hit a nine-iron inches from the hole for a birdie and Parry three-putted from 12 feet for a bogey. A flustered Parry followed by missing short putts on the fourth and fifth and added another bogey on the seventh. He was on his way out of the top 10 with a final-round 78.

Couples also bogeyed the fifth from a greenside bunker, and, for a moment, there was a four-way tie for first at 10-under among Couples, Parry, Floyd, and Ted Schulz, who eagled the eighth. Nick Faldo, Corey Pavin, and Baker-Finch were two behind. Instead of a multi-player shootout, this Masters evolved into a two-man game between Couples and Floyd, with only Pavin lurking.

Or, one might say it was a one-man game, with Couples staying ahead by two for nearly the entire back nine. He took control during a four-hole stretch of great putting and bunker play from the seventh through 10th. Couples saved par with a bunker shot to within a foot on the seventh, then matched a Floyd birdie on No. 8 with one of his own from 20 feet. They were tied at 11-under now, and Fred went in front by holing another 20-footer for birdie on the ninth.

The margin became two when Floyd three-putted the 10th for a bogey. Minutes later, Couples was in danger of making a bogey there, too, but walked off with a par thanks to a bunker shot to six feet and a good putt. A younger man's

1992		
1	Fred Couples	69–67–69–70—275
2	Raymond Floyd	69–68–69–71—277
3	Corey Pavin	72–71–68–67—278
T4	Mark O'Meara	74–67–69–70—280
T4	Jeff Sluman	65–74–70–71—280
T6	Ian Baker–Finch	70–69–68–74—281
T6	Nolan Henke	70–71–70–70—281
T6	Larry Mize	73–69–71–68—281
T6	Greg Norman	70–70–73–68—281
T6	Steve Pate	73–71–70–67—281
T6	Nick Price	70–71–67–73—281
T6	Ted Schulz	68–69–72–72—281

nerves on the greens might have been making the difference, as Floyd's putting touch abandoned him. His slip-up on the 10th was followed by a bogey on 12, where he left an eight-foot putt short and fell three behind. Floyd missed an opportunity to make up ground when he failed on a five-foot birdie putt on the 13th.

Perhaps the best recourse for Floyd at that point was to avoid putting, and that's what he did at the 14th, holing an extraordinarily difficult 50-foot chip over the hump of the green for a birdie. Two very good shots at the 15th gave him an eagle opportunity from 15 feet, but he left it dead-in short and settled for a birdie that proved to be his last gasp.

The birdie only momentarily brought Floyd within one of Couples, who soon holed a birdie putt from eight feet on the 14th to go back ahead by two, which is where he remained as he strung together pars to the finish.

A bogey-free back nine was the key to Couples maintaining his lead, as he didn't birdie either par five. Of course, he came very close to making a likely double bogey on the 12th hole, where his tee shot landed on the steep bank of Rae's Creek and didn't roll back into the water as most such shots do. He might have been lucky that his ball didn't hit higher on the bank. It most likely would have gathered more speed and made it through the slightly longer grass at the bottom and ultimately into the drink. Instead, it had settled just two feet from that fate. "It was the biggest break of my life," admitted Couples, who pitched to one foot from the hole and made par.

Consider, though, that it might have been a case of the breaks evening out. In the second round, Couples had his tee shot land in the cup on the fly on the sixth hole only to have it rattle out and end up six feet away. On Saturday, his approach shot to the par-four seventh did the same thing, the hole spitting it out to two feet away.

In any case, Couples was able to walk away with the major title that he seemed to be building toward for the last two months, if not his entire career. With a final-round 70 he just missed becoming the first player to shoot four rounds in the 60s, winning with a 13-under 275 total. He did become the first American to win since 1987, ending the four-year U.K. hold on the title. In fact, Americans took the top five places (Pavin third and Mark O'Meara tying Sluman for fifth), for the first time since 1984.

....

Breaking 30

Mark Calcavecchia's Masters was nothing special through 63 holes, with rounds of 73–72–75 leaving him in front of only three players, followed by an even-par 36 on the front nine of the final round. He then birdied the 10th hole, parred Nos. 11 and 12, and caught fire with birdies on the last six holes. The birdie streak tied the record for consecutive birdies, and the 29 on the back nine made him the first to break 30 on either nine at the Masters, though the 65 only moved him up to a T31 finish. It continued an unusual pattern for Calcavecchia, who averaged 74.83 in the third round in his first six Masters appearances and 68.83 in the final round.

....

1993

The great golfer Tommy Armour once said of the putting yips, "Once you've had 'em, you've got 'em."

Bernhard Langer had the yips early in his professional career, and in 1988 he had a relapse. It wasn't a full-fledged case, but his putting was bad enough to drop him to 111th on the PGA Tour money list that year. His solution was a new way of holding the putter, where he rested his left forearm on the grip and grabbed that arm with his right hand, restricting wrist movement.

It worked, if a bit slowly. He returned to respectability in 1989 and then by the next year to near the top of the European Tour, where he was now concentrating his efforts, ranking between second and fourth on the Order of Merit from 1990 to 1992. Limiting his appearances in the U.S. now, in his two pre-Masters starts in 1993 he finished sixth at Bay Hill and second at the Players Championship, demonstrating that he was ready for Augusta.

The 35-year-old German jumped to a quick start in the first round with birdies at the second, third, and fourth holes to set up a 68. That left him one stroke behind a quintet of leaders at 67, as pre-tournament rains softened the greens and led to an abundance of subpar scoring similar to the last two years.

None of those 67 shooters managed even to match par in the second round, all shooting between 73 and 75. Fifty-three-year old Jack Nicklaus turned out to be a one-day story, as did Larry Mize, Corey Pavin, and Lee Janzen. Masters rookie Tom Lehman disappeared from the main story line for two days, only to re-emerge in the final round.

The key number of the second round was also 67, four players shooting it to tie for lowest score. Two of them jumped to the forefront: Jeff Maggert taking the lead at 137 and Chip Beck settling in at 139, one stroke behind Langer and Dan Forsman. Maggert was a third-year tour pro running hot and cold in 1993, with three finishes in the top six and five missed cuts before the Masters. In this week, he stayed hot only for two days, sliding backward with 75–76 for a T21 finish.

Langer was able to keep his form well enough to shoot a 70 in a round that extended into Saturday for 10 players due to a suspension for rain late Friday. He played the last two holes on Saturday morning, missing both greens and saving pars. Forsman, who had missed the cut in both his previous Masters starts, was also steady with a pair of 69s. Ray Floyd, who came so close in 1990 and 1992, was hanging in there at age 50, shooting 68–71.

The weather turned unfriendly for the third round, and Langer was able to separate himself from the field by shooting a 69. With the other players in the top seven through 36 holes averaging 73.8, Langer emerged with a four-stroke 54-hole lead thanks to what he called "one of my top five rounds."

He overcame the wind, which in addition to its unpredictable gusting blew from the direction that makes Augusta National play its hardest—into the players' faces on the 13th and 15th holes, rendering them nearly unreachable in two. On top of that, the tournament committee located the holes in particularly tough spots close to green edges and slopes, according to veterans Nicklaus and Floyd.

Langer appeared unperturbed, going out in 33 with birdies on the second (12 feet), seventh (five feet), and eighth (15 feet). He missed the green to the right at the 11th and conjured memories of Larry Mize when he chipped in from not quite as far away. "I was yelling at it, 'Stop! Slow down!' I was hoping it would hit the flagstick, and it did." To that point, Langer had made only one bogey in the tournament, but he couldn't avoid trouble completely on this day, with bogeys at 13 and 18 against a birdie at 14 coming in.

If there were a question heading into the final round, it revolved around Langer's Sunday record at Augusta. Since winning the tournament in 1985, he had shot over par in all seven final rounds, averaging 74.1, and in most of those years he lingered somewhere near the lead through 54 holes.

He had a nice cushion, though, with Beck (72) and Forsman (double bogey on 16 and bogey on 18 for a 73) the closest to him four strokes away.

The cushion was a good thing to have as several players made their moves on Sunday from well behind. First-round co-leader Lehman, after scores of 75–73 left him eight back, birdied four of the first five holes and raced to a 31 on the front nine. Long-hitting John Daly, from seven behind, eagled the second hole and shot a 33 on the front. Lanny Wadkins, starting out five back, played the first 13 holes in two-under, good enough to pull within three as Langer shot a 36 on the front nine. That trio all stagnated on the back nine and ended up tied for third with Steve Elkington. Anyway, as it turned out, they wouldn't have had a chance. They needed help from Langer and didn't get it.

Forsman and Beck were making their moves, too, Forsman with a 33 on the front and Beck a 34 to pull within one and two, respectively. Langer's even-par front nine—a birdie at the first, bogey at the second, and seven pars—wasn't a case of playing safe. "I fired at every flag," said Langer, who said he didn't start out with that intention. "I felt so good about my swing and the way I was hitting the ball."

1993

1	Bernhard Langer	68–70–69–70—277
2	Chip Beck	72–67–72–70—281
T3	John Daly	70–71–73–69—283
T3	Steve Elkington	71–70–71–71—283
T3	Tom Lehman	67–75–73–68—283
T3	Lanny Wadkins	69–72–71–71—283
T7	Dan Forsman	69–69–73–73—284
T7	Jose Maria Olazabal	70–72–74–68—284
T9	Brad Faxon	71–70–72–72—285
T9	Payne Stewart	74–70–72–69—285

The putts weren't falling, though, as he missed from inside 15 feet four times on the front nine.

Langer's aggression almost got him in trouble once. With the pin at 11 on the left side, he pulled his shot slightly and watched in trepidation as it landed on the left edge of the green and rolled up the fringe. A foot or two farther left, and it would have been in the water. As it was, he made par.

Soon, he had even more reason to be relieved. Forsman, in the twosome ahead, hit his seven-iron tee shot so poorly on the 12th hole that it didn't even reach the far bank, plunging directly into the water. Things went from bad to worse when he dropped 100 yards from the green to leave himself a full shot, then hit that one in the water. The ensuing quadruple bogey knocked him out of it; now it was down to Langer and Beck in the last twosome.

Langer even went for the back right pin on the 12th hole, generally a no-no, but he was sure to hit plenty of club and went just over the green, making a par. On 13, he was in the same situation as Curtis Strange in 1985, with a two-stroke lead. Like Strange, he went for it. Unlike Strange, who hit into the water to help set up Langer's victory, he hit a crisp 3-iron to 20 feet—and made the putt for an eagle, only the second of the week on the hole. Beck two-putted for birdie, but found himself three behind.

Langer's tee shot on 15 wasn't long enough to consider going for it in two, so he laid up. Beck was about 10 yards ahead of him, with 235 yards to carry the water and 250 to the flag. In a much criticized move, he laid up. It was a defensible play, given the danger of going for it from that distance. A birdie was possible with a lay-up, and there were three more holes to try to make up ground. As it worked out, Langer was the one who made a birdie from short of the pond, with an eight-foot putt, while Beck hit his third shot over the green and made a par to fall four behind. In the end, with each making a bogey coming in (Beck on 16, Langer on 18), Langer won by four strokes with a back-nine 34 giving him a 70, the same score as runner-up Beck. Ultimately, it didn't really matter what Beck did at the 15th.

It's worth noting that Langer had only one three-putt in four rounds and ranked T2 in putts per round on Augusta's treacherous greens. "I'm not the best putter in the world," he said, "but I'm certainly not the worst."

1994

Jose Maria Olazabal came along a few years after the "Big Five" had brought European golf to prominence—Seve Ballesteros, Nick Faldo, Sandy Lyle, Bernhard

Langer, and Ian Woosnam. As a young prodigy, Jose Maria established himself as that group's co-equal in the late 1980s and formed a nearly unbeatable Ryder Cup partnership with his mentor and fellow Spaniard Ballesteros, nine years his senior.

By now, all five of those predecessors had won the Masters. Could Olazabal join them? He wasn't as long as Ballesteros, Lyle, or Woosnam or as precise as Faldo or Langer. His ball-striking certainly wasn't inadequate, as a 12-stroke victory at the 1990 World Series of Golf showed. But his strength was a marvelous short game, with a particularly fine touch on long putts—an important attribute on the greens of Augusta National.

Olazabal finished second to Woosnam in the 1991 Masters. Then came a bump in the road from March of 1992 through all of 1993 when Olazabal went without a victory. It wasn't as if he had completely lost his game—he finished 18th on the European Tour Order of Merit in 1993. Still, he was frustrated enough that he told his friend and business manager Sergio Gomez more than once that he was ready to quit.

Working with noted teacher John Jacobs in the offseason enabled Olazabal to fix a swing flaw, and he was on the upswing heading into the Masters. He ended his victory drought at the Open Mediterrania in March and was second in New Orleans the week before the Masters.

His Masters got off to a wobbly start, with a 74 in the first round. It wasn't an awful score on a windy day with firm greens and harsh pin positions. Still, T26 wasn't the best spot from which to mount a title bid.

For the second consecutive year, Larry Mize led after 18 holes, this time alone at the top of the leaderboard with a 68. Mize's 1987 Augusta win hadn't proved to be a breakthrough—he didn't win again on the PGA Tour until 1993, when he had two victories. He always seemed to feel at home at the Masters, anyway, with top-25 finishes the last four years.

At least Mize had a Masters title. Tom Kite was still in pursuit of his first at age 44 and was one of only three players to break 70, shooting a 69. He hadn't been a factor since coming close in 1986 and had missed qualifying for a Masters invitation in 1992 two months before winning his only major at the U.S. Open.

Kite temporarily jumped into the lead with birdies on the first two holes of the second round before making a double bogey on the 10th and settling for a 72 and a 141 total. He would linger on the fringe of contention through the weekend, finishing fourth as he was unable to summon enough birdies. Olazabal jumped into the picture on Friday with a no-bogey 67 that also put him at 141. That was two strokes behind Mize, who kept the lead with a relatively quiet 71.

In between at 140 were Dan Forsman, with a 66 in somewhat calmer conditions than Thursday, along with Greg Norman and Tom Lehman. Norman, on his own Masters quest, was the favorite despite his past Augusta letdowns. The 1993 British Open champion was in full flight, coming off a stunning 24-under performance in the Players Championship in March. He opened with a pair of 70s at Augusta, a wild one on Thursday with six birdies and an eagle, and a more conventional one with four birdies on Friday.

Norman didn't make a single birdie in the third round as he fell back with a 75; he would follow that with a 77. Instead of his usual slow start (he was over par in the first round in six of the last seven years), it was a poor finish that sunk him. Forsman's bid at redemption for his 12th-hole meltdown in 1993 also foundered with a third-round 76.

Saturday was a nasty day, with the wind whipping up again and drying out the greens even more. Lehman and Olazabal handled it better than anybody, posting the only rounds in the 60s with 69s to take over the top two spots on the leaderboard, Lehman at 209 and Olazabal at 210. Mize (72) and Kite (71) hung in there at 211 and 212, respectively.

At age 35, Lehman was a late bloomer who hadn't yet won on the PGA Tour. He toiled on various mini-tours after a fruitless first stint on the big tour in 1983–85, finally finding his way to success on the secondary Ben Hogan Tour in 1991, where he led the money list to earn his way back to the main circuit. A T6 at the 1992 U.S. Open earned him an invitation to the 1993 Masters, where he finished third. Lehman was 24th on the money list that year, but he was still looking to make that last step into the winner's circle.

He was certainly appreciative of his chance to take that step on perhaps the game's biggest stage. "Who would ever expect a kid from Minnesota to be leading the Masters? I know I sure wasn't, not three or four years ago," he told the assembled media Saturday evening.

Lehman was there partly thanks to "probably the greatest putt I've ever made," a 50-foot birdie on the 16th hole that broke about 20 feet, though he could have been more than one stroke ahead if he'd made a four-foot birdie putt on the 17th or not hit his nine-iron into a bunker to set up a bogey at the finishing hole.

Olazabal got to four-under on the day with a birdie at the second, an eagle at the eighth (three-iron to six feet), and a birdie at the tenth (six-iron to tap-in range). His lone bogey came at the 13th, where his five-iron caught the bank and fell into the creek. Even that wasn't all that bad a shot, he said. "My swing feels more comfortable now. I have to do what I did today—get out on the golf course, relax, and enjoy the round."

An encouraging note from Ballesteros in his locker Sunday morning may have helped Olazabal to relax. "Be patient. You know exactly how to play this course," it read in part.

Olazabal and Lehman both birdied the second and parred their way through No. 7, the Spaniard drawing on his Seve-like short-game resourcefulness to do so. Olazabal got up and down from a bunker on the fifth. On the seventh, his second shot caught a tree limb and fell well short of the green—no problem, he hit an exquisite pitch that nearly went in the hole and sank a four-footer for par.

Just ahead of them, Mize birdied the sixth, seventh, and eighth, the latter on a chip-in from 40 feet (an omen, perhaps?), to tie Lehman for the lead at eight-under. Olazabal joined them when he two-putted for a birdie on the eighth.

Olazabal found himself in the lead when Mize and Lehman both bogeyed the 12th, Mize chunking a chip from long and right of the green and Lehman three-putting from the fringe. Mize moved back into a tie with a two-putt birdie from 20 feet on 13 and promptly fell behind again when he missed a five-foot par putt on 14. A failed six-foot birdie putt on 15 effectively ended Mize's bid for a second Masters, considering what was to ensue on that hole behind him (he would bogey the 18th and finish third).

Neither Olazabal nor Lehman could birdie the 13th; Olazabal saved par on 14 by making a difficult chip from over the green look easy.

1994		
1	Jose Maria Olazabal	74–67–69–69—279
2	Tom Lehman	70–70–69–72—281
3	Larry Mize	68–71–72–71—282
4	Tom Kite	69–72–71–71—283
T5	Jay Haas	72–72–72–69—285
T5	Jim McGovern	72–70–71–72—285
T5	Loren Roberts	75–68–72–70—285
T8	Ernie Els	74–67–74–71—286
T8	Corey Pavin	71–72–73–70—296
T10	Ian Baker–Finch	71–71–71–74—287
T10	Raymond Floyd	70–74–71–72—287
T10	John Huston	72–72–74–69—287

The 15th was pivotal. Olazabal hit a five-iron second shot that carried about a foot past the spot where it would have rolled back down the bank into the pond; instead, it stuck and settled on the front fringe. It was akin to Fred Couples' ball staying dry on the 12th in 1992 and Bernhard Langer's close call on the 11th in 1993.

Lehman hit a beautiful six-iron that landed close to the hole and finished 15 feet past.

Olazabal maximized the good break by rolling his 30-foot putt from the fringe into the hole for an eagle. Lehman thought he matched it, only to see his putt barely miss the hole on the low side, causing him to fall to his knees and slap the ground with his hands three times. "I put my heart and soul in that putt. When it missed, it was like a stab to the heart," he said.

Lehman, now two behind, had another painful miss on the 16th, where he couldn't convert a four-foot birdie putt. His 15-foot birdie try on the 17th was nearly a carbon copy of the putt on 15. Still, he moved to the 18th tee just one shot behind when Olazabal bogeyed 17 from over the green.

Lehman hit a one-iron from the tee planning to stay short of the fairway bunkers, not confident in trying a fade with a driver since he was generally a right-to-left player. With adrenaline and a big bounce, his tee shot rolled into the first bunker and he was unable to reach the green from there. It still wasn't over. Olazabal pulled his approach into the swale left of the green, and needed all of his touch to cozy a pitch within seven feet. If Lehman made his 15-footer for par and Olazabal missed, there would be a playoff. Instead, the opposite occurred and Olazabal won by two with a 279 total while Lehman closed with a 72 for 281.

For the second straight day, Olazabal's 69 matched the low round. He negotiated the last 54 holes with only two bogeys and had only six for the week. Perhaps most impressively, he had only one three-putt. And Europe had yet another Masters champion, its sixth in seven years.

1995

Ben Crenshaw missed the cut at the Freeport McMoRan Classic in New Orleans the week before the Masters, his third missed cut in his last four tournaments. So, he was in Augusta on Sunday evening when he got a phone call telling him that his lifelong teacher, Harvey Penick, had died at the age of 90.

The call came from Tom Kite, who, along with Crenshaw, was taught by Penick (both men had grown up in Austin, Texas). Crenshaw, who was now 43 years old, got his first lesson from Penick at the age of six. His last came the previous Sunday when Ben visited the very ill Penick at his home. When Crenshaw said he was having putting problems, Penick told him to get a putter and hit some putts on the rug.

"Don't let the clubhead past your hands," was Penick's advice. It was an example of the great teacher's knack for simple, yet effective instruction, which made Penick's *Little Red Book* the biggest selling golf book of all time. Crenshaw and Kite would fly to Austin on Wednesday to be pallbearers at Penick's funeral, then fly right back to compete in the Masters. "Harvey will be with his pupils the rest of our lives," said Crenshaw.

Also on the Sunday before the Masters, Davis Love III won a playoff to earn a last-minute invitation to Augusta. Just short of his 31st birthday, Love now had nine career victories, but 1994 had been an off year and he came within a week of missing out on the Masters. Love's teaching professional father had been mentored by Penick, and Davis considered going to Texas for the funeral. Crenshaw convinced him that he should stay in Augusta and concentrate on his Masters preparation.

Love shot a 69 on Thursday, with an eagle on the 13th hole and 32 on the back nine, while Crenshaw had a 70 with three birdies and a bogey on the first nine and all pars coming home. Good scores, but not great on a day when there were 33 subpar rounds and 15 in the 60s. A course which had been playing firm and fast in practice rounds turned into a pussycat with greens softened by rain on Wednesday night and all day Thursday.

Defending champion Jose Maria Olazabal, 24-year-old Phil Mickelson, and South Africa's David Frost had 66s to share the lead. Olazabal chipped in twice in shooting a 31 on the back nine. Also noteworthy, he played with U.S. Amateur champion Tiger Woods. Already the center of attention at the age of 19, Woods wowed Greg Norman and Fred Couples in a practice round by driving 30 yards past them. "I needed binoculars to see how far his ball was going," said Olazabal after the first round. Woods still lacked some control of his irons, however. He made the cut with a pair of 72s, then went 77–72 on the weekend to finish T41.

Jack Nicklaus made news with a 67 at the age of 55, helped by an eagle at the fifth, where he holed out with a five-iron. Incredibly, he also eagled the fifth by holing a seven-iron on Saturday, though the feat was a footnote by that point, Nicklaus having fallen well back with a 78 in second round.

Nicklaus was an exception, as scoring was even lower on Friday than in the first round, and the lowest of them all was a 64 by Jay Haas to give him the lead at 135. Haas had gone low before at Augusta National, shooting 67s in the final round in 1985 and 1986 to earn backdoor finishes of fifth and T6 and a closing 69 in 1994 for a T5. The 41-year-old took advantage of the soft greens with dialed-in irons, making his first six birdies from eight feet or less before a 12-footer at 17 and a 15-footer at 18.

Scott Hoch was one stroke back at 136 after a 67. Of course, there was no escaping talk of his two-foot miss in the playoff of 1989. "That monkey on my back has a long life," he would say on Saturday.

Crenshaw joined the low-scoring brigade with a 67 in the second round. One of the best putters in the history of the game, Crenshaw had a four-putt at the Players Championship, but his lesson with Penick was beginning to take hold. So was a swing tip from his long-time Augusta caddie, Carl Jackson, in pre-tournament practice on the range—five of his seven birdies were from six feet or closer.

"I was beginning to get a feeling," Crenshaw wrote in his book *A Feel for the Game*, pointing in particular to a huge-breaking 45-foot putt on 14 ("the meanest putt I've ever seen," said Jackson) that he coaxed within 18 inches. "Everything felt seamless. I was playing smooth, steady golf.... I began to think I might be there at the end."

Love headed a group at 138 after another 69, hoping to put a dismal major championship history behind him, having never finished in the top 10 in 27 previous major starts despite a strong list of accomplishments in regular events. He now figured he might have been putting too much pressure on himself in majors. Perhaps his happy-to-be-here attitude after getting in at the last minute was the tonic he needed.

Saturday brought a logjam at the top that had never been seen at the Masters: seven players within a stroke of the lead. Crenshaw and Brian Henninger were on top at 206, closely followed by Haas, Hoch, Mickelson, Couples, and Steve Elkington at 207. Frost, John Huston, and Curtis Strange (with a 65) were at 208 and Norman and Love at 209.

Haas called a one-stroke penalty on himself after his ball moved at address on the third green, leading to a double bogey, playing the first six holes four-over before making a praiseworthy recovery to a 72. Henninger's bad start was in the first round when he played the first five holes in four-over. The 31-year-old Masters rookie recovered to shoot 70–68–68, though he would dip to a 76 on Sunday. Strange joined Hoch in seeking Masters redemption, saying of his four-wood into the water in 1985, "I still have nightmares about that shot."

In contrast to the up and down rounds of many of the contenders, Crenshaw was rock steady with three birdies and 15 pars for a 69. If Penick were alive, Ben said, "I would probably call him. He would say, 'Trust your swing, trust your judgment, play hard, and hope for the best.' I'm trying hard to win for him."

While Sunday provided the expected tension and excitement, there were fewer players involved in the fight for the title than expected. With the greens finally firming up, six of the 10 contenders who started within two of the lead shot over par in the final round. It came down to Crenshaw, Haas, and the twosome of Love and Norman, who were playing some 45 minutes ahead of the last group.

One other player briefly got into the mix, 1992 champion Couples, who eagled the eighth hole with a 250-yard shot to within two inches to pull within one. He took himself out of it with bogeys on 11 and 12 on a pair of misses from inside four feet as he went reeling to a 75. It ended an odd week for Couples, who had an eight-birdie 67 in the third round, but bogeyed the par-five 13th in every round, made a triple bogey on the 10th in the first round, and a double bogey on the fifth in the final round.

Crenshaw birdied the second hole from three feet, bogeyed the fifth, regained a one-stroke lead with a birdie from six feet at the sixth, and preserved it with a save from a back bunker at No. 7. Soon he was joined in a three-way tie at 11-under by Haas, who birdied the eighth to go two-under for the day, and Love, whose 12-foot birdie putt at the 10th followed birdies on Nos. 2, 5, and 8. Norman was just one stroke back after chipping in for a birdie on the 10th, previously his nemesis hole, to go three-under for the round.

When asked on Saturday evening whom to look for at the top on Sunday, Norman responded, "Me." Having just turned 40 two months before, could this finally be the Shark's time at Augusta? He did his best to make it so with his second shots to the two par fives on the second nine, giving him opportunities for eagles from 18 feet on the 13th and eight feet on the 15th. Both putts stayed out of the hole, leaving a pair of birdies. Norman played the par fives in an extraordinary 15-under for the week (one eagle, 13 birdies, two pars), but it could have been even better.

Norman finally gained a tie for the lead when he negotiated a difficult two-putt par on 16 while Love bogeyed. The ill-fated Aussie quickly made a bogey at 17, where he badly pulled a sand wedge approach and three-putted from 60 feet. In the big picture, Norman was hurt by an over-par first round, a 73 that was followed by three 68s.

Love let a birdie chance get away on the 13th, where he missed the green left with a seven-iron second shot. He made up for it with a beautiful approach to two feet on the 14th for a birdie that tied him for the lead. Love's drive on 15 was shot out of a cannon, leaving just a nine-iron to the green. He hit it to 12 feet and later lamented not making the eagle putt. "If either Greg or I had made our putts, there would have been an explosion of noise," he said. Still, the birdie put him ahead by one stroke.

Not for long. Love's tee shot on 16 was a little bit too far right and a little bit too long to take the slope down to the hole. Instead he had to deal with the slope on a huge-breaking 40-foot putt, which went six feet past, and he couldn't make that one.

At this point, Love, Norman, and Crenshaw were all 12-under. Haas was 11-under (he had bogeyed 11 and birdied 14) and about to hit a long-iron second shot to the 15th. He nearly reached the green with it, only to see it trickle back down the bank into the water. He saved a par, but his final-round 70 would fall short.

Crenshaw had reached 12-under with a sand wedge approach to a foot on the ninth hole, giving him the lead at that point. He made his second key sand save of the round from the front bunker on the 12th, making a five-foot par putt. His putting touch was back to prime Crenshaw, as evidenced by a 15-foot putt on the 13th that gave him a birdie despite a pulled five-iron well left of the green. That came right after Love and Norman finished the 16th, giving Ben a one-shot edge again.

Love wasn't finished. For the second time in four holes, he nearly holed his approach shot, his sand wedge second shot finishing two feet from the hole on 17 for a tying birdie. Davis left himself in a tough spot to the left of the 18th green, but he hit a marvelous shot out of the swale with a putter to tap-in range for a 66 and a 13-under total and settled in to watch the telecast.

1995		
1	Ben Crenshaw	70–67–69–68—274
2	Davis Love III	69–69–71–66—275
T3	Jay Haas	71–64–72–70—277
T3	Greg Norman	73–68–68–68—277
T5	Steve Elkington	73–67–67–72—279
T5	David Frost	66–71–71–71—279
T7	Scott Hoch	69–67–71–73—280
T7	Phil Mickelson	66–71–70–73—280
9	Curtis Strange	72–71–65–73—281
T10	Fred Couples	71–69–67–75—282
T10	Brian Henninger	70–68–68–76—282

"It's out of your control and you have to watch Crenshaw with 10-footers for birdie, and you know he's going to make them," Love would say.

When Love finished, Cren-shaw was also 13-under and over the green in two on the 15th with a difficult pitch that he didn't get up and down. He didn't exactly have 10-footers on the next two holes but made a pair of birdie putts of about that length. Crenshaw's six-iron on 16 was the perfect distance and ran down the slope to five feet below the hole for a birdie to take the lead. Next came a nine-iron to 13 feet on the 17th. "It was the prettiest putt I ever hit," said the man with the silky stroke.

Owning a two-stroke lead, Crenshaw came up short of the green at 18, pitched on, and missed a par putt. The moment his 18-inch bogey putt dropped into the hole for the win, he was overcome with emotion, immediately bending over and sobbing. "I said just get through this foot-and-a-half putt and then you can cry," he said afterward. "I just let it all go."

A final-round 68 gave Crenshaw a 14-under 274 total, matching the third best ever to that point, and his second Masters title in his 24th start. The meaningless bogey on the 72nd hole was his only bogey on the back nine all week and just his fifth of the tournament.

"It was like someone put his hand on my shoulder and was guiding me this week," Crenshaw said. "I believe in fate. Fate has decided another champion like it has so many times before."

A New Limit

With tickets to tournament days at the Masters unavailable to the general public, practice round attendance grew by leaps and bounds in the 1970s, '80s, and '90s. By 1994 the crowds had become so large that there were pedestrian traffic jams in parts of the course and waits as long as 45 minutes at restrooms and concession stands. Masters officials recognized that attendance needed to be cut down to provide a better patron experience, which meant that tickets would no longer be available at the gate. Practice round tickets for 1995 were sold the previous summer by mail, and, with demand far exceeding supply, a lottery was held to determine who got them. The lure of a pilgrimage to Augusta, just to roam the grounds and see the players up close, had become so strong that even tickets to practice had become precious.

....

1996

Greg Norman came into the Masters on a high note: He won three times in 1995, added a victory at Doral in March of 1996, was ranked No. 1 in the world, and was the favorite at Augusta according to Las Vegas oddsmakers. Or did he? In the short term, he had missed the cut in his last two tournaments. And, of course, there was his tortured Masters history, where he was always done in by *something*, whether it be one bad round, heroics by another player, or an ill-timed bad shot.

Following the missed cuts, Norman brought his teacher Butch Harmon to Florida to work with him for two days and came to Augusta feeling that he was back on track. On Thursday, the 41-year-old Australian proved it, tying the course record of 63 set by his good friend Nick Price in 1986.

It was a round where consistently solid ball-striking left him with birdie putts of between eight and 15 feet virtually all day. Norman started out missing them, parring the first six holes. He finished with a fantastic run of nine birdies and three pars over the last 12 holes, including birdies on six of the last seven. "When you get in that type of roll I was on today, hey, let it happen," he said.

The Shark birdied the seventh and eighth from 10 feet each and the ninth from 14 feet for a 33 on the front nine. He got up and down from a bunker for a par on the 10th (he also saved par from a bunker on the fourth, the only other green he missed). On 11, Norman's 18-foot birdie putt hung on the lip and refused to fall.

After that, it was almost nothing but birdies, starting with four in a row: An eight-iron to six feet on 12, two-putt birdies on 13 and 15, and a spectacular recovery on 14. His drive hit a tree on that par four, leaving him 220 yards from the hole, from where he hit a low four-iron that ran up onto the green and stopped three feet from the hole. A par on 16 was a blip, then he finished in style with a sand wedge to 10 feet on the 17th and his longest holed putt of the day, a 24-footer on 18.

The 63 put Norman only two strokes ahead of Phil Mickelson, a two-time winner in the year so far, who had a brilliant round of his own. The 25-year-old matched Norman's 30 on the back nine. He also birdied the ninth hole; the only difference was that Mickelson started making birdies two holes later than Norman. Ten players broke 70, including Nick Faldo, who earned a tie for sixth with a 69, where all four of his birdies were from eight feet or less.

Norman waited longer to make his move in the second round, going even par through 12 holes before birdies on 13, 15, and 18 gave him a 69—a record fifth straight round in the 60s over the course of two years. His first two bogeys of the tournament came at the third and fourth, offset by birdies on the second and eighth.

The most interesting holes of his round were the 11th and 12th, both pars. Norman had a downhill birdie putt from three feet on 11 that missed the hole and slowly trickled eight feet past. He made the comebacker. His tee shot on 12 came up short, but the ball did a Couples, stopping a foot short of rolling into the water, and Norman got up and down from there.

Norman's 132 total was one higher than Ray Floyd's 36-hole record of 1976. It gave him a four-stroke lead, albeit not an entirely comfortable one considering that second place was held by Faldo. The 38-year-old was coming off a year when he didn't have a top-20 finish in a major for the first time in nine campaigns and had fallen to ninth in the World Ranking, but he was still a formidable competitor and felt better about his work on the greens with a new putter and more upright stance. He fired a 67 on Friday with six birdies coming on putts of 20, 12, 12, 8, 8, and 6 feet.

Mickelson was plagued by wild driving in a second-round 73 for 138 and third place. That's where he would end up, as neither he nor anyone else was able to catch the two men who distanced themselves from the field.

The pairing of Norman and Faldo in the third round marked the first time they had played together since the 1990 British Open when they were tied for the 36-hole lead. That round was a disaster for Norman, who shot a 76 to a 67 for Faldo as the Englishman ran away with the title.

Norman got off to a poor start with bogeys on the third and fourth for the second straight day, with a lone front-nine birdie at the eighth for a 37. Just when he looked shaky with a tee shot in the water on the 12th—the ball didn't hold up on the bank this time—Norman rallied. After taking his penalty drop 88 yards from the hole, the Australian hit a wedge to 10 feet and made the putt for a bogey. He reprised his hot finish of Friday with birdies on 13, 15, and 16 down the stretch.

Noting the windy conditions, Norman said that his 71 was "the equivalent of a round in the 60s." Indeed, his score was bettered by only three players, two 69s and a 70. With Faldo shooting a 73, Norman again increased his lead by two strokes, heading into the final round ahead by six.

Saturday was a day when the two protagonists played against type, the normally steady Faldo making too many mistakes. His six birdies should have been enough to put the pressure on Norman, but Faldo offset them with five bogeys and a double bogey. He could only cling to a very small hope heading into the final round. "If I could shoot a 65 or 66, it might get me in the right direction," he said, not wanting to sound resigned to defeat.

Norman's record in major championships with the 54-hole lead was a red flag—he was just one-for-six. This should have been different because he was six strokes ahead. In a way, though, having such a big lead creates a perverse sort of pressure because losing would be such a black mark on your record.

Norman lost two shots to Faldo on the first four holes, making bogeys on the first (bad drive) and fourth (bunker) while both birdied the second with tap-ins. Faldo dropped to five back with a bogey at the fifth (bunker) and got back within four with a birdie at the sixth (seven-iron to four feet). On the eighth, Norman wildly hooked his second shot into the trees and had to scramble for a par while Faldo made a 20-footer for a birdie.

Hmmm, three back with 10 to play. Now it seemed like a deficit that could possibly be made up. Who knew it could happen so quickly? Norman's unraveling

1996

1	Nick Faldo	69–67–73–67—276
2	Greg Norman	63–69–71–78—281
3	Phil Mickelson	65–73–72–72—282
4	Frank Nobilo	71–71–72–69—283
T5	Scott Hoch	67–73–73–71—284
T5	Duffy Waldorf	72–71–69–72—284
T7	Davis Love III	72–71–74–68—285
T7	Jeff Maggert	71–73–72–69—285
T7	Corey Pavin	75–66–73–71—285
T10	David Frost	70–68–74–74—286
T10	Scott McCarron	70–70–72–74—286

began in earnest on the ninth hole. He had a 100-yard wedge shot to a front hole location, where the worst mistake was to come up short and roll back off the false front of the green. That's just what Norman did. Bogey for a 38 on the front nine.

On the 10th, Norman's approach missed on the side you're not supposed to miss on, the left. Bogey after a poor chip. He finally hit a green on the 11th, then three-putted, missing a par putt from three feet. Now it was tied, and it would get worse for Norman. His seven-iron on the 12th flew toward the traditional back right pin position—a longer carry—and came up short, finishing in the water. He said he wasn't aiming for the flag, but pushed the shot. He couldn't repeat his bogey save of Saturday, wedging nicely but missing from 12 feet. Double bogey. In the space of four holes, Faldo picked up five strokes while making two-putt pars on all of them, and suddenly the Englishman was ahead by two.

"It was a whole different game then. I thought to myself on the 13th tee, 'Now it's mine to lose,'" said Faldo. Or, more likely, to win.

A key moment came in the 13th fairway, where Faldo took a full three minutes choosing a club before hitting his second shot. He twice stood over a five-wood and stepped away, finally choosing a two-iron, he said, because he didn't like the way the five-wood set behind the ball on a sidehill lie. It was a bit of a risk because he knew he needed to hit the two-iron solidly to carry the creek, which he did, setting up a two-putt birdie from 30 feet. Norman laid up after a drive to the right, and temporarily ended his skid by making an 18-foot putt for a matching birdie.

Both parred the 14th and finished near the green with their second shots to 15, Faldo over the green and Norman short and right. When Norman's eagle chip lipped out, he fell to the ground in anguish; Faldo matched the birdie with a four-footer.

Still ahead by two, Faldo safely hit his tee shot to 30 feet on the 16th. Norman tried to draw his six-iron toward the pin; instead he hit a pull-hook that didn't even come close to dry land, splashing in the pond to set up his second double bogey on a par three on the back nine. It was essentially over. Faldo birdied the 18th for a 67 and a five-stroke victory at 276, while Norman made two pars for a 78.

"I honestly and genuinely feel sorry for Greg and what he's going through," said Faldo, who gave his vanquished foe a heartfelt hug on the 18th green.

"I played like shit. I don't know any other way to put it," was Norman's first comment in what turned into a lengthy, introspective press interview. "I must admit I got a good old ass-whipping."

Norman faltered in all aspects of his game, with his iron play the worst culprit. While one bogey resulted from a bad drive (the first hole) and one from a missed short putt (the 11th), three bogeys and both double bogeys were caused by poor iron shots.

Faldo, by contrast, was relentlessly consistent, hitting 17 greens in regulation to keep the pressure on. "I was in control, which is the big thrill. I hit all the shots where I intended to hit them on the day it had to be done," he said.

Faldo's third Masters victory fit the pattern of his first two, attributable in equal parts to his own heroics and others' miscues. He came from five behind with a 65 in 1989, from three behind with a 69 in 1990, and from six behind with a 67 in 1996. His sixth (and last) major title secured his position among the all-time greats of the game and enhanced his reputation as one who rose to the occasion in the biggest events.

Norman, with more overall wins than Faldo, nonetheless was stuck on two majors (and would add no more), with a litany of near misses. This one would sting more than any other because it was one he truly let get away.

1997–2005

Tiger's Time

Just as Jack Nicklaus and Arnold Palmer before him, Tiger Woods used the Masters more than any other major to build his superstar status. And he did it immediately, winning his first Masters as a professional in such a dominant fashion that it recalled—and even surpassed—the performance of a young Nicklaus in 1965. Woods' second green jacket in 2001 completed the "Tiger Slam" of four straight majors, his third in 2002 came against a chasing pack consisting of the best players of the time, and his fourth in 2005 was sparked by one of his most memorable shots ever.

Woods took the entire PGA Tour by storm, winning 46 tournaments and 10 major championships before turning 30 in December of 2005. He was particularly dangerous at Augusta with his prodigious length off the tee, enabling him to go at the par fives in two with mid- to short-irons and hit high approaches to the treacherous greens.

Shortly after Woods came on the scene, the course was lengthened slightly in 1999 and extensively in 2002. This was often referred to as "Tiger-proofing" and seen as a reaction to his record performance in 1997 and subsequent victory in 2001. While one aspect of the changes might have been to restore the integrity of the course by bringing troubles back into play that Woods was flying over, "Tiger-proofing" is overstating the case. In any case, the lengthening had as much to do with the overall increase of driving distance on the PGA Tour as with Woods in particular. Concurrently, the club sought to increase the cost of wild driving by planting trees on several holes and introducing a "second cut" of rough that, while short by most standards, was longer than the nearly fairway height that had previously been in place.

While Woods loomed large over this period with four titles in nine years, the other winners were pretty impressive, too. Mark O'Meara set himself up for a two-major year, Jose Maria Olazabal won a second Masters, and Vijay Singh and Phil Mickelson were the winningest non-Tiger players of the Tiger era. Only Mike Weir didn't win another major before or after his Masters victory.

1997

Jack Nicklaus and Arnold Palmer played a practice round with 20-year-old amateur Tiger Woods in 1996, after which Nicklaus told the assembled press at his pre-tournament interview, "You can probably take Arnold's four Masters and my six Masters, add them together, and this kid should win more than that."

It reads like a light-hearted exaggeration, but Nicklaus' demeanor and tone were serious. The greatest Masters champion of all time went on to say, "This kid is absolutely the most fundamentally sound golfer that I have seen at almost any age…. He will probably be the favorite over the next 20 years."

A year later, Woods was a professional already living up to the considerable hype that followed three straight wins in the U.S. Junior followed by three straight U.S. Amateur titles. Since making his pro debut at the end of the previous August, he had already won three PGA Tour events. He was the next big thing—in capital letters and boldface type, followed by exclamation points. And now he was playing in his first major championship as a pro.

Just to add to the buildup, Woods had shot a 59 the previous Friday in a friendly match with fellow pro Mark O'Meara at Isleworth Country Club, their home course in Orlando, in preparation for Augusta. And in the first round, Woods was paired with defending champion Nick Faldo. "It's going to be the full show, lights and action and everything," said Faldo. And the kid was ready.

Or was he? Tiger laid an egg on the front nine of the first round, shooting a four-over 40. Many in the throng of spectators who followed Woods around the front nine abandoned him (and Faldo, who had a 41) around the turn. That was a mistake.

The 21-year-old showed remarkable maturity in pulling himself together, physically and mentally, while he walked from the ninth green to the 10th tee. As he wrote in his book *The 1997 Masters: My Story*, while he was ticked off about his play on the front nine he focused on letting go of his anger as he made the turn. Then he started thinking about what he was doing wrong with his swing, and realized he was taking the club back too far on the backswing. The result was four badly hooked drives, leading to three of his bogeys (the other coming on an iron shot blocked way to the right on the par-three fourth).

Hitting a two-iron off the 10th tee, Woods concentrated on shortening his backswing—and made a swing that felt like the action he had when he shot his 59. He followed with an eight-iron to 15 feet and made the putt for a birdie. From there, it was lights out as he cruised around the back nine in 30 strokes.

Woods chipped in from 40 feet to birdie the 12th, two-putted for a birdie on 13, and made a 10-foot birdie putt on 14. He then took advantage of his prodigious length off the tee—shades of a young Nicklaus in 1963 or 1965—by reaching the par-five 15th with a pitching wedge second shot to four feet and making an eagle. He finished the assault with a 12-foot birdie at 17.

The nine of 30 was all the more impressive on a day when the average score was 76.105. The greens were as hard and fast as anyone could remember—"like putting down the hood of your car," said John Cook—and the committee, apparently expecting less wind than they got, set the pins in tough spots. Loren Roberts, one of the best putters on tour, was completely flustered as he had 40 putts and shot an 85. Woods' 70 put him in fourth place, behind John Huston (67 with a holed five-iron for an eagle on 18), Paul Stankowski (68), and Paul Azinger (69).

Woods was considerably better on the front nine on Friday, shooting a 34 with birdies on the two par fives and a sand wedge to two feet on the fourth against a bogey at the third. He again manhandled the back nine, shooting a 32 as for the second straight day he played the three-hole stretch of 13–15 in four-under. This time the eagle came on 13, where he made a 20-foot putt after an eight-iron second shot. He hit a sand wedge to tap-in range at 14 and again hit a pitching wedge second shot to 15, missing an eagle try from eight feet.

"If he plays well, the golf course becomes nothing [because of his length]," said Nicklaus. Azinger, who played with Woods and shot a 73, was just as impressed with Tiger's mental side. "I just got out-concentrated today," the veteran said. "He never had a mental lapse."

Last year's main protagonists, Faldo (75–81) and Greg Norman (77–74), both missed the cut. Huston, the 18-hole leader, shot a 77 with a 10 on the 13th hole. Woods' 136 total gave him a three-stroke lead over Colin Montgomerie, who shot a 67.

The 33-year-old Scotsman hadn't done much in five previous Masters appearances, but was in the midst of a seven-year run of leading the European Tour Order of Merit from 1993 to 1999. While mostly praising Woods in his post-round interview, Montgomerie also said, "I've got more experience, a lot more experience, than he does in major championships.... There's more to it than hitting the ball a long way. The pressure is mounting more and more."

Woods saw those quotes and used them as inspiration in his third-round matchup, outplaying Montgomerie to the tune of 65–74. When the dust settled, Tiger had a record 54-hole lead of nine strokes while tying Ray Floyd's record 201 total.

Woods wasted no time running away from Montgomerie and the rest of the field, shooting a 32 on the front nine. He birdied the second (chip to one foot after a nine-iron second shot), saved par on the third, and birdied the fifth (15 feet), seventh (12 feet), and eighth (two-putt). For a change, he only parred the 13th but still shot a 33 on the back with birdies at 11 (eight feet), 15 (hooked six-iron around trees, two-putted), and a capper at 18 (approach to one foot).

When brought to the press room, Montgomerie grabbed the microphone and before taking any questions said, "All I have to say is one brief comment today. There is no chance. We're all human beings here. There's no way Tiger Woods doesn't win tomorrow." Someone pointed out that Norman had lost a six-stroke lead to Faldo just a year ago. "This is different—very different. Faldo is not lying second, for a start, and Greg Norman is not Tiger Woods," Montgomerie replied.

For the record, Italy's Costantino Rocca was second at 210 after a wild 70, where he played the first 10 holes in four-over and the last eight six-under, earning the hot-seat position of playing with Woods on Sunday. Stankowski was next at 211, saying he might have a chance "if I can make five, six, seven birdies early...like on the first three holes."

1997		
1	Tiger Woods	70–66–65–69—270
2	Tom Kite	77–69–66–70—282
3	Tommy Tolles	72–72–72–67—283
4	Tom Watson	75–68–69–72—284
T5	Costantino Rocca	71–69–70–75—285
T5	Paul Stankowski	68–74–69–74—285
T7	Fred Couples	72–69–73–72—286
T7	Bernhard Langer	72–72–74–68—286
T7	Justin Leonard	76–69–71–70—286
T7	Davis Love III	72–71–72–71—286
T7	Jeff Sluman	74–67–72–73—286

A pair of 47-year-olds named Tom—Watson and Kite—were tied for fourth at 212. Watson said of Woods, "He's a boy among men, and he's showing the men how to play.... It looks like I'm playing for second place."

As an amateur, Woods had finished T51 and missed the cut in his two Masters appearances. He learned a lot, though. His focus this year was on controlling the distance with his irons and concentrating on leaving himself uphill putts, even if it meant intentionally coming up short of pin high. The smart, strategic golf, combined with overwhelming power and a swing that clicked into place midway through the first round, was producing a performance for the ages.

It was a performance that inspired Lee Elder, the first Black golfer to play in the Masters, to fly up from Florida and watch the final round as Woods, of African-American/Asian heritage, marched to victory.

Becoming the first Black man to win the Masters was just one of many thoughts that entered Woods' mind as he played the final round. He also thought about his father, Earl, who had undergone heart surgery a month-and-a-half before the Masters. Early in the round, he thought about how bad it would be to blow a huge lead at the Masters, later he thought about trying to break the 72-hole record of 271 and about joining legends like Nicklaus and Palmer as a Masters champion. Realizing that it would be impossible to block these thoughts out, he just let them drift through his mind.

His father, who had come to Augusta but wasn't able to make it to the course every day, warned Tiger that this would be the most difficult round he had ever played. In a sense, it was, despite his lead remaining at least eight strokes all day. One-over through seven holes, he picked up a welcome birdie at the eighth, where he recovered from an errant second shot to the edge of the woods on the left with a bump-and-run shot over a mound to within two feet. The back nine belonged to him again, with birdies on 11 (20 feet), 13 (two-putt), and 14 (eight feet), and no bogeys for a 33 that made him 16-under on the closing nine for the week, four strokes better than the record set by Palmer in 1962.

Needing a par on the 18th to set the 72-hole record, his approach left him a tricky 35-foot downhill putt which finished four feet from the hole. Of course, he knocked it into the heart of the hole for a 270 total that was all the more remarkable considering the 40 on his first nine holes. While the course softened up a bit for the last three rounds, nobody else found it as easy as Woods made it look. Kite finished second at 282, a distant 12 strokes behind as Tiger surpassed the record nine-stroke victory margin by Nicklaus in 1965.

Nicklaus' observation after the second round was even more appropriate on Sunday. "It's a shame Bob Jones isn't here," Jack said. "He could have saved the words he used for me in 1963 [actually, 1965] for this young man, because he's certainly playing a game we're not familiar with."

1998

A year after Tiger Woods dusted Mark O'Meara in a pre-Masters match, the Orlando friends staged a rematch at Isleworth Country Club. This time the cagey veteran shot a 65 to beat the young phenom. When O'Meara nonetheless complained about trying to play Woods without getting any strokes while being outdriven by 60 yards, Tiger replied, "You've got a putter."

O'Meara was indeed a fine putter, but that hadn't done him much good at Augusta National, where the 41-year-old had only one top-10 finish in 14 appearances, a T4 in 1992. On the bright side, he had made the cut in 12 of 13 Masters starts as a pro (missing one as an amateur). Also, O'Meara was playing as well or better than ever, having won two tournaments in each of the last three years.

That ran his career total to 14 PGA Tour victories. None of them, however, was a major championship, putting him in the conversation for being the best player never to win a major, a label which was either a backhanded compliment or sugar-coated insult.

Nobody had much reason to talk about O'Meara after the first round when he shot a 74, not a terrible score on a day the wind gusted to 40 mph but not particularly noteworthy as it put him in a T25 position. There was only one sub-70 round, a 69 by 38-year-old Fred Couples, who repeated his good fortune of 1992 when his tee shot on 12 stayed on the bank instead of rolling into the water. He didn't save par, but a bogey was better than a double.

"I don't think I'm quite the player I once was, but at any given time I'm capable of playing well," said Couples, who had seven birdies.

First-round starting times were delayed for recovery from a Wednesday rainstorm. Ten players didn't finish their rounds on Thursday due to the late start. One of them was David Duval, who got only four hours of sleep before getting up at 5 a.m. ("I have a bad habit of staying up late," he said) on Friday to par three holes and finish the first round with a 71. Following an hour-and-a-half nap he shot a 68 with birdies on 13, 14, 16, and 17 to tie with Couples for the 36-hole lead at 139.

The 27-year-old from Jacksonville, Florida, finished 11th and 10th on the money list in his first two full seasons on tour without a win. Duval finally broke through in a big way at the end of his third season, 1997, when he won his last three events including the Tour Championship, and he added a victory in Tucson in February of 1998.

The only other player better than one-under for 36 holes was 42-year-old Scott Hoch at 141, still pursuing Masters redemption (he would finish T16). Woods and Phil Mickelson headed a group at 143, while O'Meara moved into the picture with a 33 on the back nine for a 70 and a 144 total.

The top of the field bunched up in the third round when Couples shot a 71 and Duval a 74 on a day ripe for scoring. Couples managed to come away with a two-stroke lead thanks largely to an eagle on the 13th, where he hit a three-iron to within two feet. "I've yet to make too big of a blunder. I don't plan on making one tomorrow," said Couples after staying in front for the third straight day.

Tied for second at 212 were Paul Azinger and Mickelson with 69s and O'Meara with a 68. When it was noted that it was Azinger's first time in real contention at a major since he missed nearly all of the 1994 season due to cancer treatment, he replied, "In a major? How about period. I couldn't get in contention at my club championship."

Azinger did own a major title, the 1993 PGA Championship. Mickelson was perhaps the best player without a major among young players—he already had 11 victories at age 27—and O'Meara among veterans.

Mickelson would have had a share of the lead if not for bogeys on the last two holes. O'Meara didn't have a bogey in his 68, remarkable considering he hit only eight greens in regulation (he had 22 putts and chipped in on the first hole). A session with his teacher Hank Haney on the practice green after the first round, where they corrected a problem with alignment, was working wonders.

Duval and another 27-year-old, Jim Furyk, were next at 213. Furyk opened with a 76 and was six-over through 26 holes before playing the next 28 in nine-under, including a 67 on Saturday.

Woods wasn't firing on all cylinders, though he was still a factor five strokes back after 71–72–72. He didn't make enough of a move on Sunday, shooting a 70 to finish T8.

Another player at 215 through three rounds did create a lot of noise on Sunday in the form of full-throated roars from the gallery—58-year-old Jack Nicklaus. On Tuesday, Nicklaus was honored in a ceremony celebrating his 40th appearance in the Masters, with a plaque commemorating his accomplishments placed between the 16th green and 17th tee. Masters chairman Jackson Stephens noted that some space had been left at the bottom of the plaque, just in case.

The way Nicklaus started the final round made that look like a good idea. The six-time champion went three-under for the first seven holes, with four birdies, producing cheers that resounded around the Augusta National property and beyond. At four-under for the tournament, he was just two strokes off the lead.

A storybook seventh green jacket wasn't to be. Nicklaus' charge stalled as he missed some makeable birdie chances. The leaders took advantage of calm conditions to shoot some low scores of their own, so Jack's posted 68 didn't threaten them

1998

1	Mark O'Meara	74–70–68–67—279
T2	Fred Couples	69–70–71–70—280
T2	David Duval	71–68–74–67—280
4	Jim Furyk	76–70–67–68—281
5	Paul Azinger	71–72–69–70—282
T6	Jack Nicklaus	73–72–70–68—283
T6	David Toms	75–72–72–64—283
T8	Darren Clarke	76–73–67–69—285
T8	Justin Leonard	74–73–69–69—285
T8	Colin Montgomerie	71–75–69–70—285
T8	Tiger Woods	71–72–72–70—285

as they came down the back nine. It did earn him a creditable T6 finish, quite an accomplishment for a man in his ninth year of senior tour eligibility. Also in the tie for sixth was David Toms, a future PGA champion but then an unheralded 31-year-old, with a final-round 64 and a record-tying 29 on the back nine.

In the final twosome, O'Meara made some noise of his own with a birdie on the second from eight feet followed by long-range birdies on the third (25 feet) and fourth (40 feet). His playing partner, Couples, answered at the fourth with an 18-foot birdie to stay in a tie for the lead at seven-under, then burst ahead with birdies from inside two feet at both the seventh and eighth.

Couples immediately gave one back with the type of blunder he had hoped to avoid in the final round, coming up short on a 100-yard approach shot to the ninth after a big drive, resulting in a bogey.

Meanwhile, Duval was making a mid-round charge of near-epic proportions. After playing the first six holes in even par, he birdied the seventh (one foot), ninth (two feet), 10th (40-foot chip-in), 11th (12 feet), and 13th (two-putt). From out of nowhere, he was eight-under and tied for the lead with Couples and two ahead of O'Meara, who bogeyed the 10th.

Soon, Duval was ahead by two. Couples hooked his tee shot on the 13th so far left that it finished on a dirt maintenance road. He escaped jail by lofting a wedge over trees into the fairway but followed with his second blunder of the day. Choosing to hit an easy six-iron to the green instead of a hard seven-iron, he pushed the shot into the hazard to the right and made a double bogey. The lead that had been his all week was gone.

Duval birdied the 15th, nearly holing a 20-foot eagle putt, to lead by three over Couples and O'Meara. It was a misleading margin, as the final twosome still had the opportunity of the 15th. First, Duval, two twosomes ahead, played the 16th, where he bogeyed after a tee shot to the right side of the green left an exceptionally difficult 50-foot, downhill, big-breaking putt, and he missed a subsequent par try from 10 feet.

Couples made up for the double bogey on 13 by hitting a six-iron second shot to a foot from the hole on 15 for a spectacular eagle—in the space of three holes he had gone from tied for the lead to three behind to now tied for the lead again. O'Meara two-putted from 40 feet for a birdie to pull within one after his three-iron second shot cleared the pond with not much to spare.

Not to be completely forgotten, Furyk followed a bogey at 15 that dropped him four back with birdies on 16 and 17 to pull within one of playing partner Duval. A par on 18 gave Furyk a 68 and a 281 total that was one behind Duval, who narrowly missed birdie putts of 12 and 20 feet on the last two holes and finished with a 67 for an eight-under total.

In the next-to-last twosome, Mickelson was on the way to a 74 and out of the top 10, while Azinger got within two at six-under with a birdie at 15 and stayed there to claim fifth place behind Furyk.

Couples and O'Meara both gave themselves birdie chances at the 17th. Couples missed from 10 feet, and when O'Meara sank his from eight feet he made it a three-way tie at the top. All sorts of possibilities were in the air as Couples and O'Meara walked to the 18th tee deadlocked with Duval—everything from any of the three winning outright to a two- or three-way playoff.

Couples put himself in trouble with a tee shot into the second fairway bunker, leaving a tough shot which he hit into the right greenside bunker, from where he made a par. O'Meara faded his drive nicely into the center of the fairway and hit a seven-iron to 20 feet right of the hole. "When I was over the putt, I said to myself, 'This is what it's all about. This is what you come to play for,'" O'Meara said.

He played the right-to-left break perfectly, and when the putt dropped for a final-round 67, O'Meara was a "best player without a major" candidate no more (he would go on to win a second major at the British Open later in the year). He became the first to win the Masters with birdies on the last two holes since Arnold Palmer in 1960, and his 15 starts to win his first green jacket was a record (Billy Casper won in his 14th try in 1970).

Woods was right about O'Meara "having a putter." That club was the key for O'Meara, who led the field in putts per round with 26.25. The rest of his game came around on Sunday for his best ball-striking round, just enough for him to win with one of the great clutch putts in Masters lore.

....

Records for the Ages
With his T6 at the age of 58, Jack Nicklaus became the oldest player to finish in the top 10 in the Masters, surpassing Sam Snead and Ben Hogan, who were both 54 when they finished T10 in 1967. That wasn't the only age-related record. Gay Brewer shot a remarkable 72 in the wind on Thursday at age 66 to become the oldest player to shoot par or better. He missed the cut, but Gary Player qualified for the final 36 holes at age 62, a record for the oldest to make the cut. And Mark O'Meara at 41 was the oldest to score his first Masters victory. All of those records still stood through 2020, except the oldest to make the cut (Bernhard Langer, 63 in 2020).

....

1999
Jose Maria Olazabal watched the 1996 Masters on television from his home in Spain, sidelined by pain in his right foot that was so severe he couldn't even walk. He saw a 41-year-old Greg Norman endure a different kind of pain in that Masters,

throwing away a six-stroke lead in the final round. What were the odds that the two of them would end up as the final twosome on Sunday in 1999?

In 1998, Norman had his own physical problem, missing the last eight months of the year due to shoulder surgery. By then, Olazabal had thankfully recovered, his condition initially misdiagnosed as rheumatoid arthritis finally discovered to be a spinal hernia that affected his foot. He returned from an 18-month absence in the spring of 1997 and scored a European Tour victory that year and another in 1998. But the 33-year-old Spaniard had played only six 1999 events before the Masters with a modicum of success. Norman had played only three tournaments in 1999, and didn't figure to have shaken off the rust.

A far more likely duo for the final twosome was Tiger Woods and David Duval. Woods had slowed down only a little from his spectacular rookie season that featured his runaway 1997 Masters win, yet he had been surpassed by Duval, who was on an amazing run. Duval won the Players Championship and BellSouth Classic the two weeks before the Masters, giving him four wins on the year, the other two being a nine-stroke triumph at the Mercedes Championships and a final-round 59 to win the Bob Hope. After 1952, only Arnold Palmer (1960) and Johnny Miller (1974) owned four wins coming into Augusta. Duval had won 11 of 34 tournaments in the last 18 months and had taken over the No. 1 spot in the World Ranking from Woods. After a decade-and-a-half without a dominant American on the PGA Tour, now there were two.

The world Nos. 1 and 2 took a back seat to world No. 3 Davis Love III in the first round. Love had a 32 on the back nine for a 69 to take a share of the lead 35 years after his father Davis Love Jr. shared the first-round lead with the same score (Davis III was born the day after the tournament). The others at 69 were former world No. 1 Nick Price, Scott McCarron, and Brandel Chamblee.

While nobody shot a low number, 19 players broke par with Olazabal in a group of seven at 70 thanks to an eagle on the 13th. Duval lived up to the favorite role for nine holes with a 33 on the front nine, then succumbed to bogeys on 12, 13, and 14 as he shot a 71 along with Norman and six others. Woods had a 72, marred by a triple bogey at No. 8 set up by a wild drive to the left.

Olazabal jumped ahead with a 66 in the second round for 136, creating separation from most of the pack as there were only three others within three strokes and two more five behind. His six birdies came from 5, 6, 5, 18, 1, and 10 feet, and he didn't have a bogey as he saved par on the four greens he missed. He had 26 putts in a more solid effort than his 24-putt 70 in a scrambling first round.

McCarron was at 137 after a 68, with Norman (also a 68) and Lee Janzen at 139, and Love and Price at 141. The power duo of Woods and Duval were at 144 and 145, respectively; this time it was Duval making a triple bogey (third shot in the water on 15, then pitched long) while Woods double bogeyed 12 and was on the cut line until making three late birdies.

The leaderboard bunched up again in the third round when Olazabal shot a lackluster 73 for 209, making only one birdie as he failed to take advantage of the best scoring conditions of the week. He preserved a one-stroke lead thanks to an escape from the left trees on the 18th, conjuring up a low three-iron that scooted onto the green for a two-putt par.

Norman was one back after a 71 that featured an all-world bogey at the 12th hole. His tee shot landed in the bushes on the bank behind the green, and nobody could find his ball in the five minutes allowed for a search. Norman made the lonely walk back to the tee, hit a shot to 25 feet, and drained the putt. A bogey on 13 hurt his cause, but a birdie on 15 and another on 18 set up by an approach to three feet sent him into Sunday with a real chance.

Love and Steve Pate were two behind, Love (70) blowing a chance to tie for the lead by making a double bogey at the 15th, where he hit his second shot in the water and went over the green after a penalty stroke. Pate was the story of the day with a 65 that included a tournament record streak of seven consecutive birdies starting at the seventh hole. "I have no explanation for what happened out there," said Pate, who hit two iron shots within tap-in range during a run that also included two 20-foot putts and a 50-footer. The 37-year-old Californian fit right in to one of the week's themes, having missed virtually the entire 1996 season when he broke first his right wrist and then his left one. He was playing in his first Masters since 1993.

A total of 16 players were within five strokes, including Woods at 214, with Duval one more stroke back at 215, both gaining some ground on Olazabal with 70s.

Duval teed off an hour, 40 minutes ahead of the final twosome on Sunday, and turned himself into a contender with an eagle on the second hole, a 33 on the front nine, and a birdie on the 10th to pull within one of the lead. He fell back with a double bogey on 11, but hope was not lost. In the last twosome, Olazabal and Norman were having a hard time on the third, fourth, and fifth. Olazabal, who had only four bogeys in the first three rounds, bogeyed all three of those holes and Norman bogeyed Nos. 3 and 5.

For a while, it looked as if it were anybody's game with a cast of a dozen or so all having a chance. Over the span of about an hour as the contenders were strung along the latter part of the front nine to the early part of the back nine, players holding the lead at one point or another were Olazabal, Norman, Pate, Love, Lee Westwood, and Bob Estes, while Duval and Lee Janzen spent time one behind, and more players than it was possible to keep track of were within two at some juncture.

Duval pulled within one stroke twice more, after birdies on 13 and 15, until bogeys on 16 and 17 knocked him out. He finished with a 70—the best round of the day in gusty winds and on baked-out greens that were exceedingly hard to hold, but still somewhat disappointing with a back nine of four birdies, three bogeys, a double bogey, and one par. Duval finished T6, while co-favorite Woods was T18 after a 75, though he led the field in greens in regulation.

Westwood took himself out of it by playing the first three holes of the back nine in four-over after a 33 on the front, Janzen made two double bogeys on the back, and Estes stalled with mostly pars. Olazabal and Norman made strong recoveries from their shaky starts and were joined by Pate and Love in a four-way fight for the title on the back nine.

1999

1	Jose Maria Olazabal	70–66–73–71—280
2	Davis Love III	69–72–70–71—282
3	Greg Norman	71–68–71–73—283
T4	Bob Estes	71–72–69–72—284
T4	Steve Pate	71–75–65–73—284
T6	David Duval	71–74–70–70—285
T6	Carlos Franco	72–72–68–73—285
T6	Phil Mickelson	74–69–71–71—285
T6	Nick Price	69–72–72–72—285
T6	Lee Westwood	75–71–68–71—285

Olazabal and Norman had jumped ahead of the pack and into the lead at six-under, Ollie with birdies on Nos. 6 and 10 and the Shark with birdies on Nos. 8 and 11, the latter on a putt of 30 feet unleashing a deafening roar from the large gallery at Amen Corner. The fans were fired up to see if Norman could finally claim that elusive green jacket at a time in his career when it had seemed such a hope was lost.

Norman gave a stroke back with a bogey on the 12th, coming up short and left of the green. But he gained two strokes on par, and elicited another roar, by holing a 25-foot putt for an eagle on the 13th. In a moment that was to define the tournament, an undaunted and determined Olazabal responded by sinking a 20-foot putt for a birdie. The two friendly competitors pointed at each other in mutual admiration as they walked off the green.

Instead of leapfrogging into the lead, Norman had gained only a tie. He promptly backed up with bogeys on 14 (drive right, second long, missed 12-footer for par) and 15 (drive right, lay-up, missed the green with a wedge). When he missed an eight-foot birdie putt on 16, it was clear that he would come up short in Augusta again; Norman finished third with a closing 73. It was essentially his last chance. Norman played in four more Masters with no more top-10s, finishing his Augusta career with three seconds and three thirds in 23 starts.

Pate and Love were not to be forgotten. Pate parred the first 10 holes, in contrast to his fireworks of the day before, and bogeyed the 11th, then clawed back to six-under with birdies at 13 and 15 to pull within one of Olazabal. His bid ended with bogeys on 16 and 17 for a T4 with Estes.

Love followed birdies on Nos. 7 and 9 to get to five-under with a string of pars, including a 25-foot save on 13 after a drive in the creek and a disappointing one on 15 after going for the green in two and finding the bunker. His tee shot on 16 was long and left, from where he played his pitch shot up the slope well above and left of the hole and watched it trickle back down and into the cup for a birdie—the very same shot that Woods would make famous six years later. That got him to six-under and within one. Pars on the last two gave him a 71 and a 282 total that would be good if Olazabal faltered.

The 1994 champion absolutely didn't falter. Olazabal hit a brilliant tee shot on the 16th and holed a delicate downhill birdie putt from three feet that he said was anything but easy. His drive on 17 hit the Eisenhower tree and left him far back in the left rough, necessitating a low five-iron which he pulled off with aplomb. His 40-foot birdie putt ran seven feet past the hole, leaving an anxious moment. Olazabal hadn't three-putted all week, and this would be a decidedly bad time for a first. No problem, he rolled it in to maintain a comfortable two-stroke cushion over Love in the clubhouse and three over Norman.

A par on 18 gave Olazabal a 71, a 280 total, and a two-stroke victory. After his three-over start to the final round, he played the last 13 holes in four-under on a brutal day when nobody shot in the 60s. He answered the challenges of Norman's eagle and Love's astounding chip-in, denying them a first Masters title while claiming his second.

Olazabal was asked if he dreamed of winning a second green jacket while he watched that 1996 Masters. "This is not something I dreamed about," he said, sitting in the media interview room wearing his green jacket. "I honestly thought I would never play golf again."

....

Changes, Part I

This Masters marked the beginning of what would become major course changes over the next decade. The second hole was lengthened by 20 yards and the 17th by 25 yards and trees were planted between the 15th and 17th holes, particularly impacting 15, where a more accurate drive was now needed to go for the green in two. Also, the course grew the grass outside the fairways to 1⅜ inches instead of ⅝ of an inch—still shorter rough than found on virtually any other tournament course (Augusta National referred to it as the "second cut"), but enough to make approach shots harder to control. In 2000, the club would go further by narrowing the fairways on six holes.

....

2000

If David Duval was riding a wave coming into the 1999 Masters, Tiger Woods hung ten on a tsunami in 2000. The 24-year-old wunderkind had won 11 of 18 tournament starts since June of 1999, including six in a row spanning 1999–2000, and had finished first or second in 10 of his last 11. Not since the days of Byron Nelson and Ben Hogan in the 1940s had the tour seen such domination—and tournament fields were much deeper now.

Woods rolled into the tournament as a 2-to-1 favorite according to Las Vegas, odds unheard of in golf. He had more than double the World Ranking points than No. 2 Duval and nearly double the earnings of Hal Sutton (No. 2 on the money list), though "only" three wins in seven 2000 starts.

Imagine the surprise, then, when Woods shot a 75 in the first round. He was OK on the front nine at even par before running into big trouble with a double bogey on the 10th (greenside bunker, three-putt) and a triple bogey on the 12th (tee shot in the water, three-putt from 12 feet) and needed birdies on 13 and 16 just to shoot a three-over score.

Woods was surprisingly sanguine after the round, saying, "I think it's fine. It's not easy out there."

Indeed, it was one of those Augusta days when wind gusts that varied in direction and intensity created a stern test, with only nine players able to break par and many who challenged for the lead meeting with disaster. Craig Stadler was three-under through 14 before a quadruple bogey at the 15th; Steve Jones five-under through 10 before a bogey at 11 and a double bogey at 12; Ernie Els three-under through 14 before a double bogey at 15 and a bogey at 17; and Tom Lehman five-under through 17 before a double bogey at the 18th. Even the leader, Dennis Paulson, making a one-round cameo with a 68, had a double bogey on 11.

One of the steadier rounds was turned in by Vijay Singh, with one birdie, an eagle on 13, and three bogeys for a 72. Known for his solid ball-striking honed by countless hours on the practice range, Singh led the field by hitting 16 greens in regulation in the tough conditions. It was a round that could have been better without two three-putts or with less than 34 putts, but that was practically the norm for Singh at Augusta.

The 37-year-old native of Fiji had eight wins since joining the PGA Tour in 1993, including the 1998 PGA Championship, but in six Masters starts his best finish was T17. In 1998, he shot 76–80 at Augusta to end his streak of 53 straight made cuts, then the longest on tour. In 1999, he had nine three-putts while finishing T24.

It was a different Singh on the greens in the second round when he shot a 67, with four of his seven birdies coming on putts of more than 10 feet, the result, he said, of a conscious effort to change his attitude. After missing the cut in 1998, he talked about it with his wife, who told him, "You cannot come here thinking you will putt bad. You've got to come here very positive." So, said Singh, "I've tried to enjoy putting more than hating it," an ongoing attitude shift over the past year or so but especially important at Augusta National.

The 139 total tied Singh for second place with Els, who also had a 67, and Phil Mickelson, coming off a victory at the BellSouth Classic in Atlanta, with a 68 in the much calmer conditions. They all took a back seat to Duval, who fired a 65 to lead by one at 138.

Duval had gone exactly a year without a victory, his last win coming at the 1999 BellSouth, but he wasn't playing badly, as he ranked sixth on the money list. He was trim and fit, the result of a fitness regimen, and said he had been pointing to the Masters for six months. He surged into the lead with a 30 on the back nine, finishing with five straight threes—a six-foot birdie on 14, 10-foot eagle on 15, par on 16, four-foot birdie on 17, and 12-foot birdie on 18.

Woods, on the other hand, went the wrong direction on the back nine. Appearing on the way to getting back into it with a 34 on the front, he ran into trouble just after the turn for the second straight day with bogeys on 10 and 11. His birdies on the two back-nine par fives were canceled by bogeys on 16 and 18 for a 38 and a 72 that left him nine strokes back.

Tiger was miffed on Friday evening when he saw commentator Mark Lye on Golf Channel say he was "out of it." Determined to prove that a nine-stroke deficit through 36 holes wasn't too much to make up, he shot a 68 with four straight birdies on Nos. 7–10. The round was interrupted after the 10th hole by a two-hour rain delay. A little while after the restart, the weather made a sudden shift, the temperature dropping 16 degrees in 15 minutes to 53 while the wind whipped up to a steady 20–30 mph with gusts up to 40.

Davis Love III joined Woods as early starters shooting 68s played mostly before conditions worsened, both finishing at one-over 215. The leaders hadn't teed off before the delay, and got the worst of it, at least until play was halted by darkness with the final twosome in the 15th fairway.

Singh handled it better than anyone. An admirable even par through 11 holes, Singh somehow conjured up a couple of great iron shots as darkness began to set in and the wind chill plunged into the mid-30s. He birdied the dangerous 12th with a short putt and the 14th with a pitching wedge that knifed through the wind and finished within a foot of the hole.

He was able to do that even though, as he said, "It was freezing out there playing No. 14. I was hoping they'd call it off earlier." When play was suspended after he and Duval each played two shots on the 15th, Singh was seven-under, three ahead of Duval and four ahead of Els, both of whom were two-over on the day. Duval double bogeyed the 12th when a wind gust knocked his tee shot into Rae's Creek, though he did birdie the 13th. Els avoided too much trouble, with only two bogeys, but didn't manage a single birdie. The main victim was Mickelson, who had a 40 on the front nine on the way to a 76.

On Sunday morning, Singh and Duval both made all pars (as did Els), in very different fashion. With his new-found touch on the greens, Singh saved pars from six feet on 15 and 18 feet on 17 to wrap up a very fine 70, while Duval missed two birdie putts inside six feet to conclude a 74. At the end of the third round, Singh was at 209, and only Duval (212), Els (213), and Loren Roberts (213) were within five strokes, with Woods, Love, Mickelson, and Mike Weir at 215.

Nobody expected Woods to go quietly, and he birdied the second and fourth in the final round, pulling within three when Singh bogeyed the third. Woods stumbled with a bogey on the sixth and staged a too-short rally with birdies on Nos. 7 and 8 before a string of pars that failed to put any pressure on the leaders. His 69 left him in fifth place—his second worst finish in his last 12 events.

Duval mounted a challenge in the final twosome, with a birdie on the second hole and Singh's bogey on the third trimming the margin to one shot. Duval put up a strong fight with birdies on Nos. 6, 8, and 9—but couldn't tie for the lead as Singh answered with birdie putts from inside Duval on each of those holes, and also saved par at the seventh with a bunker shot to four feet.

Duval fell two behind with a bogey on 10, where his approach came up short, and pulled back within one when Singh bogeyed the 11th. It was a scrambling bogey for Vijay after his approach found the hazard. He was fortunate that with the back-left pin, his point of entry at the hazard line afforded him a drop near the front of the green instead of all the way back in the drop area, and he hit a nice pitch to three feet. Singh got another break when his tee shot on the 12th sailed too long but bounced off an azalea bush into the back bunker, from where he executed his second sand save of the day with a blast to three feet.

2000		
1	Vijay Singh	72–67–70–69—278
2	Ernie Els	72–67–74–68—281
T3	David Duval	73–65–74–70—282
T3	Loren Roberts	73–69–71–69—282
5	Tiger Woods	75–72–68–69—284
6	Tom Lehman	69–72–75–69—285
T7	Carlos Franco	79–68–70–69—286
T7	Davis Love III	75–72–68–71—286
T7	Phil Mickelson	71–68–76–71—286
10	Hal Sutton	72–75–71–69—287

The key moment in the last twosome came on the 13th hole. Singh found the green with a three-iron second shot. Duval had trouble deciding on a club, then hit a fat five-iron that went short and right, a double whammy that sent his ball into the creek. A birdie-bogey swing put Singh ahead by three.

Els was also three behind and cut it to two with a birdie at 15 to get to four-under on the day. Singh matched the birdie with a two-putt after a brilliant second shot from 210 yards in the left rough, hooking it around a tree to 18 feet from the hole. Duval kept pace with a birdie.

Singh's tee shot at 16 came up 60 feet short, and he three-putted from there (his first three-putt since two in the opening round) to lead Els and Duval by two. Els was locked in with his fluid swing on this day—he hit 16 greens—and gave himself birdie putts of eight, 15, and 12 feet on the last three holes, but didn't make any of them and finished with a 68 for 281.

Singh missed a 10-foot birdie try on 17, leaving Duval alive if he could pull off a two-shot swing on 18. Instead, there was a two-shot swing the other way, Singh making a birdie from 18 feet and Duval a bogey after his tee shot finished in a divot-hole in the fairway. Duval, with a 70, dropped into a tie for third with Roberts (69) at 282, while Singh polished off a 69 for 279 and his second major championship at what he would have considered his most unlikely venue.

"If you asked me two years ago, I don't think I could win this the way I was putting. Augusta's greens are so severe, if you're not a good putter you're not going to win," he said. "I think it helped when it rained [early in the week and again on Saturday] and slowed the greens a little bit."

While improved putting and three key short-game shots in the final round helped Singh get over the top, his typically sound ball-striking shouldn't be overlooked. He led the field by hitting 58 greens in regulation, four more than anyone else.

Singh could be thankful that Woods wasn't at his best in at Augusta. That was a rarity in 2000 when the undisputed world No. 1 went on to claim the other three majors, two of them in runaway fashion, and win nine tournaments, making it the Year of the Tiger everywhere but at the Masters, where Sunday was Vijay day.

Win and You're...Maybe Not In

The Masters added the top 50 in the World Ranking as a new invitation qualification in 1999 in recognition of the increasingly international nature of the game, a move that also ensured an invitation for PGA Tour players who might have slipped through the cracks.

It was announced at the 2000 Masters that PGA Tour winners wouldn't automatically receive an invitation, as they had since 1972, but that the invitation based on the previous year's money list was expanded from 30 to 40. Also, invitations from the previous year's Masters were reduced from 24 to 16, from the U.S. Open from 16 to eight, and the PGA Championship from eight to four (and the British Open up to four from only the winner). The reductions prevented the field from getting too large, while overall the thrust of the qualification criteria went more toward long-term performance rather than single events.

....

2001

The 2001 Masters was the most anticipated golf event since 1930, or perhaps ever. It was September of 1930 when Bobby Jones, who went on to found the Masters, headed to Merion Golf Club in Pennsylvania for the U.S. Amateur in an ultimately successful effort to complete the Grand Slam after already capturing the U.S. Open and the British Open and Amateur.

Now Tiger Woods was headed to Augusta National shooting for a fourth consecutive professional major championship after winning the last three—the 2000 U.S. Open by 15 strokes, the British Open by eight, and the PGA Championship in a thrilling playoff. Since it wouldn't occur in the same calendar year, it wouldn't be a pure Grand Slam as the term had always been used. No one was quite sure what kind of Slam to call it, but all agreed it would be an amazing feat.

Woods, who won nine times in 2000, endured a stretch of eight tournaments without a victory including the first five of 2001. Was something wrong? Not really. He won his last two starts before the Masters, the Bay Hill Invitational and Players Championship. Tiger was installed as a 3-to-2 favorite at the Masters, even more outrageously low odds than the 2-to-1 of the year before.

With Tuesday rains rendering the greens softer than they'd been in years, and little wind, conditions were ripe for scoring in the first round. Woods shot a 70 that was five strokes off the lead and tied for 15th place—not outstanding, but not cause for alarm with 54 holes remaining. His ball-striking was solid with 15 greens in regulation, and Woods seemed well enough satisfied. "Everyone knows it's awfully hard to go out there and shoot in the mid-60s every day in a major," he said.

Shooting in the mid-60s that day were Chris DiMarco with a 65 and Angel Cabrera and Steve Stricker at 66. Phil Mickelson, who said before the tournament that he had "a lot of confidence in the way I've been playing," was close behind with a 67 that included four straight birdies starting at the 12th and another at the 17th.

DiMarco was playing in his first Masters at age 32, a prospect that so excited him he had trouble concentrating at the BellSouth Classic the week before when he finished T6. The Long Island native, using the "claw" putting grip that had rescued his PGA Tour career, stayed in front through 36 holes with a 69 in the second round. Par saves on the last two holes preserved a two-stroke lead, but it wasn't a comfortable position considering that his two closest pursuers were Woods and Mickelson, the No. 1 and No. 2 players in the world.

Woods put together a 66 despite two bogeys, three-putting Nos. 9 and 16. He was in complete control of his ball-striking game, hitting 17 greens in regulation, two of them par fives in two shots. Tiger was making the course seem small with his prodigious driving, hitting sand wedge approaches into the 17th and 18th holes to four and eight feet for the last two of his eight birdies and a 33 on a back nine that had been giving him trouble in the last couple of years. Mickelson had a 69, overcoming a mistake on the 12th, where he hit his tee shot in the water for a double bogey with birdies on 13, 15, and 16.

Another stroke back at 137 were Cabrera, a long-hitting Argentinian making his second Masters appearance and demonstrating an affinity for the course, and David Duval, thrusting himself into strong Masters contention for the fourth straight year. Duval matched Woods, Mark Calcavecchia, and Japan's Toshi Izawa for the low round of the day with a 66, hitting his approach within a foot of the hole for a birdie on 18.

It was hard to know what to expect from Duval this year. He retreated from his No. 1 position with only one victory in 2000, missing some time with a bad back. His best finish in his last four starts before the Masters was a T51, followed by sitting out the last three weeks due to tendinitis in his right wrist. With the wrist holding up through two rounds, he said, "I'm excited about my prospects."

Woods moved to the front in the third round in a way that was so methodical it was almost scary. One-under through 12, where he made a bogey against two earlier birdies, Tiger strung together birdies on 13, 14, and 15 for a 68 on a day when he hit 16 greens in regulation.

"I didn't really do anything great. I just plodded my way along. That's how I've played all week," said Tiger, who was at 12-under 204 through three rounds. On a course that was playing relatively easy, at least compared to the way it usually played, Woods had taken the lead with a fairly conservative style combined with dominance of the back-nine par fives where he was reaching the greens in two with six-irons to eight-irons.

Mickelson, by contrast, made a double bogey for the second straight day, this time with an ill-advised flop shot from in front of the 14th green that rolled back toward him and led to a three-putt. He rallied with birdies on the last two holes from 15 and 12 feet for a 69 to pull within one of Woods and earn a spot with Tiger in a heavyweight Sunday final twosome. While Woods' 20–2 record with the 54-hole lead was daunting, Mickelson took encouragement from the fact that he was responsible for one of the "Ls" when he took down Tiger at the 2000 Tour Championship.

Two strokes back at 206 were 40-year-old Calcavecchia (68), back in the Masters after failing to earn an invitation in 2000, and DiMarco (72). Duval was at 207 after a 70 that he thought didn't reflect how well he played; he was tied with Ernie Els (68) and Cabrera (70), who had the lead until a double bogey at 15 and bogey at 18.

While Calcavecchia, Cabrera, and Jim Furyk hung in there for a while on Sunday, all of them two strokes back at various points in the middle of the round, the tournament settled into a tight battle among the headline trio of Woods, Mickelson, and Duval, all between 25 and 30 years old and highly accomplished. The main difference: Woods already owned five majors; Mickelson and Duval didn't have any. While Woods was going for a Slam, the other two were trying for major validation of their undeniable talents.

Woods showed a perhaps unexpected sign of nerves on his opening tee shot, hooking it into the trees to set up a bogey on the first hole to fall into a tie with Mickelson. Both birdied the second to get to 12-under. Mickelson hurt his cause by missing three-foot par putts on both the fourth and sixth holes, though he did make a birdie on the fifth from 12 feet. Woods saved par on the fifth with a deft shot from the back bunker.

Meanwhile, Duval was making a dynamic move. Two twosomes ahead of the final duo, the Georgia Tech alum didn't make a single par on the first eight holes. He bogeyed the first and fourth around birdies on the second and third, then reeled off four consecutive birdies. The last of those, a two-putt from 50 feet on the eighth, put him at 13-under and very briefly in the lead by himself.

Behind him, Woods hit a driver off the tee on the narrow, tree-lined seventh, which was then a 360-yard hole where the usual play was an iron to be sure to stay in the fairway. Tiger ripped a straight drive to within 45 yards of the hole, hit his second shot to eight feet, and made the putt to tie Duval. Mickelson made up for his short misses by holing a 25-foot birdie putt at the seventh to stay one behind. Woods and Mickelson matched birdies at the eighth, Tiger with a flop shot to 10 feet from well right of the green and Phil with an easier chip shot to three feet.

Now Woods was ahead of his two rivals by one shot—until Duval holed a 15-footer on No. 10 for his seventh birdie in 10 holes, building on his 32 on the front nine to go five-under for the round and again tied for the lead.

Woods faced a self-induced test on Nos. 9 and 10, emerging with two crucial par saves. He came up short with his approach on the ninth, pitched to six feet, and made it. He holed a 10-footer for par on the 10th after a weak effort with the putter from the left fringe.

The 11th hole was crucial in the Woods-Mickelson matchup. Woods hit an eight-iron to tap-in range for a birdie, while Mickelson bonked a tree on the right side with his drive, couldn't reach the green in two, and made a bogey. He fell three shots behind for the first time all day.

Woods couldn't save par on the 12th, missing from seven feet after chipping from behind the green. That dropped him back into a tie with Duval, who was finally making some pars, including a disappointing one on the 13th, where he hit the green in two but left a 45-foot putt 10 feet short and missed that one.

Woods made no such mistake there, two-putting from 30 feet for a birdie after lashing a three-wood around the corner (he would call it his best shot of the day) off the tee and hitting the green with an eight-iron.

It was the opposite on the next par five, the 15th. Duval made a birdie with a chip from behind the green to one foot for a tie for the lead. About 20 minutes later, Woods hit a seven-iron to 25 feet and had an uncharacteristic hiccup down the stretch of a major, three-putting with a miss from three feet.

2001

1	Tiger Woods	70–66–68–68—272
2	David Duval	71–66–70–67—274
3	Phil Mickelson	67–69–69–70—275
T4	Mark Calcavecchia	72–66–68–72—278
T4	Toshi Izawa	71–66–74–67—278
T6	Ernie Els	71–68–68–72—279
T6	Jim Furyk	69–71–70–69—279
T6	Bernhard Langer	68–70–70–71—279
T6	Kirk Triplett	68–70–70–71—279
T10	Angel Cabrera	66–71–70–73—280
T10	Chris DiMarco	65–69–72–74—280
T10	Brad Faxon	73–68–68–71—280
T10	Miguel Angel Jimenez	68–72–71–69—280
T10	Steve Stricker	66–71–72–71—280

By then, however, Duval had made a crucial error of his own. His tee shot on the 16th flew over the green—he said he couldn't believe he hit a seven-iron that far—and he missed a seven-foot par putt. He had now bogeyed the 16th in three of the four years he came down the stretch with a chance to win, following 1998 and 1999.

Mickelson birdied 13 and 15, so he joined Duval at one behind Woods as the last twosome stood on the 16th tee. Phil pulled his tee shot to the upper-right shelf, leaving a devilish 35-foot putt to the lower level. He unavoidably went seven feet past and missed that for a crushing bogey.

Duval narrowly failed to convert a 15-foot birdie putt at 17, then gave himself a golden opportunity to tie for the lead when his 101-yard approach shot to 18 settled five feet from the hole. He pulled the putt, though, settling for a 67 for 14-under 274, and could only hope for an unlikely Woods bogey.

Tiger did miss the green to the right on the 17th, saving par with a nice chip to one foot. He blasted a drive over the trees at the corner of the dogleg on 18 to within 75 yards of the hole, a shot which virtually nobody else could even dream of. He wrapped up his Slam in style with a sand wedge to 15 feet and a birdie putt for a final-round 68 and total of 16-under 272, just two strokes off his tournament record. It was the first time in the entire round that he led by more than one stroke.

Duval went on to win his first major later that year at the British Open. That was just in time, for the very next year he went into a tailspin, never winning another tournament and never finishing in the top 100 money winners after 2002. In the Masters, after finishing T2, T6, T3, and 2 in four consecutive years, he never made another cut in five more starts.

Mickelson had to wait four more years to claim his first major. As for his third-place finish at this Masters, he said after the round, "If I'm going to win with Tiger in the field, I can't afford to make the mistakes I made. I couldn't stay focused, I guess. Mentally, I'm not there for all the shots."

The opposite was true for Woods, especially since he was well aware during the final round he was making a run at history. "I was in such a zone today. Working so hard on every shot," he said.

It wasn't as easy a 68 as the one he shot on Saturday. He missed six greens in this round and needed some par saves to get the job done—and get the job done he did. His fellow players recognized the significance of the event, several of them waiting to greet Woods after he finished, Calcavecchia breaking off an interview to experience the finish in person.

As for what to call the four-in-a-row feat, the consensus settled on a suggestion made during the CBS telecast by Jim Nantz—the Tiger Slam.

2002

Changes to the Augusta National course were nothing new. Its design has been constantly tweaked since shortly after its 1933 opening. But never has the course been altered so much year over year than from 2001 to 2002.

New tees were built or existing ones extended on nine holes (Nos. 1, 7, 8, 9, 10, 11, 13, 14, and 18), adding 285 yards to make the total yardage 7,270. This was on top of Nos. 2 and 17 being lengthened in 1999, making a total of 11 of the 14 par-four and par-five holes (no par threes were lengthened).

There was perhaps an element of "Tiger-proofing," such as the 18th being lengthened after Woods drove over and around the corner in the final round in 2001, just as Jack Nicklaus bombing drives down a trouble-free left side was a factor in adding two fairway bunkers on 18 in the 1960s. Mostly, though, it was simply a reaction to an explosion of driving distance on the PGA Tour in the late 1990s. *Everyone* was hitting the ball farther, enabling most of the field to hit wedges or very short irons to even the longer par fours, while mid-iron second shots were common to par fives.

The idea was simply to get longer clubs back in players' hands on their approach shots to make the course play more like it used to. In fact, three-time champion Nick Faldo said that, in terms of distance, the course was playing much as it did when he first won the title in 1989.

The activist leadership of Masters chairman Hootie Johnson, who assumed that role in 1998, also contributed to the dramatic lengthening. Since taking over, he had also overseen changes that narrowed the course by planting trees and adding a "second cut" of rough. These modifications were lamented by purists, seeing them as diverting from the design philosophy of Alister MacKenzie and Bobby Jones, who favored wider corridors as a strategic element. In any case, though, the increased penalties for wild driving offset the perceived advantage for long hitters with a longer course.

Tiger Woods made two early-year trips to Augusta to acclimate himself to the newly tailored track, and Phil Mickelson, Ernie Els, and Vijay Singh were among those who made one visit before tournament time. Defending his championship, Woods was installed as a 2-to-1 favorite, while the next lowest odds were Els' at 12-to-1. Tiger had won only one of seven starts in 2002 but was still by far the most feared player in the game, especially in major championships.

Rain on Tuesday evening into Wednesday made the course play even longer, but that was more than balanced out by a softening of the greens that made them more receptive. With similar conditions as a year earlier, the longer course played almost a stroke harder in each round than in 2001.

Woods opened with a 70 on Thursday, the same score as the last year, but this time it put him in a tie for eighth instead of for 15th. The score was an omen, since he also shot a first-round 70 when he won in 1997 (he had never shot in the 60s in the first round, and wouldn't do so until 2010). "I didn't hit the best shots today, but I just hung in there," he said.

The first-round leader was a familiar name in Davis Love III with a 67, though it was a bit of a surprise since he had missed the cut in five of 10 starts in 2002. He reverted to that lackluster form with a second-round 75 and would finish T14.

Friday morning brought rain, but not quite enough to call off play—at least in the minds of the officials. Many players felt otherwise, saying that casual water was so pervasive they sometimes had to play out of it because there was no place to find relief. "It was borderline laughable," said Brad Faxon.

Warming up on the range before his 10:20 a.m. start, Singh was hoping the round would be delayed, because he didn't like playing in the rain. No such luck; nevertheless, he managed a 35 on the front nine with eight pars and a birdie on the eighth. The rain let up on the back nine, and the 2000 champion caught fire with birdies on 12, 13, 17, and 18 and an eagle on the 15th (seven-iron second shot to 25 feet) for a 30 and a 65—a score that left him "surprised but thrilled." Singh had gained confidence by winning the Shell Houston Open two weeks before; it was his first victory since the 2000 Masters.

Rain resumed at about 5 p.m., this time hard enough for play to be suspended with 38 players on the course who would finish their rounds Saturday morning. At nine-under, Singh was three ahead of Retief Goosen, who had completed 11 holes.

The morning players had to set their alarm clocks early (Woods got up at 4:30) for a scheduled 7:45 a.m. start and then wait around as the start was delayed to 9:00 to prepare the course. Based on the scoring, the early-morning guys got a pretty good deal. Goosen played his seven holes in two-under to pull within one at 136. Els played his first four holes (Nos. 13–16) in five-under with an eagle on 15 for a 31 on the back nine and a 67 for third place at 137. Woods, who had nine pars and one birdie before the second round was halted on Friday, added birdies on 13 and 15 for a bogey-free 69 and a share of fourth at 139.

Woods made his move in the third round with a 66. He kick-started a 32 on the back nine by hitting irons shots close to the hole on the tough 10th and 11th, hitting a nine-iron to the latter hole (now playing 490 yards). Tiger birdied the 15th and wrapped things up with a seven-iron to 12 feet for a birdie on the now-465-yard 18th. While he hit 15 greens in the third round, he was particularly pleased with the par-saving putts he made during the long day—from 10 feet on both the 11th and 17th in the morning and eight feet on the 14th in the third round.

The birdie at the 18th was a big deal, especially in combination with a bogey there by Goosen, who drove into the trees on the right to finish a somewhat disappointing 69 that started with birdies on the first three holes. Woods landed in a tie for first at 207. History weighed on his side: He had a 22–2 record when holding or sharing the 54-hole lead, including 6–0 in majors.

Singh bogeyed the 15th and 17th—blaming mud on the ball for his inaccurate iron shots (the Masters doesn't believe in lift, clean, and place)—to drop to third place, two behind. It was two more strokes back to Els (38 on the back nine for a 72), Sergio Garcia (70), and Mickelson (68).

The top six players in the standings all were in the top seven in the World Ranking, a likely unprecedented gathering of the world's best on a major championship leaderboard. Instead of final-round fireworks, however, Sunday just served to show that Woods was head and shoulders above the rest.

2002		
1	Tiger Woods	70–69–66–71—276
2	Retief Goosen	69–67–69–74—279
3	Phil Mickelson	69–72–68–71—280
4	Jose Maria Olazabal	70–69–71–71—281
T5	Ernie Els	70–67–72–73—282
T5	Padraig Harrington	69–70–72–71—282
7	Vijay Singh	70–65–72–76—283
8	Sergio Garcia	68–71–70–75—284
T9	Angel Cabrera	68–71–73–73—285
T9	Miguel Angel Jimenez	70–71–74–70—285
T9	Adam Scott	71–72–72–70—285

Goosen had won six of his last 24 tournaments worldwide, including the 2001 U.S. Open and the BellSouth Classic the week before the Masters. The South African just didn't have it on Sunday, falling back with three three-putt bogeys (one of them from the fringe) in a 39 on the front nine, blaming poor iron play that continually left him a long way from the hole. Birdies at 15 and 16 were far too little, too late in a final-round 74.

Singh was three behind through nine holes and went the wrong way with bogeys on 11 and 14 before the final indignity of a quadruple bogey nine on the 15th, where he hit two wedge shots into the water. Els had his own disaster, a triple bogey on the 13th set up by a wild drive to the left of the creek and an ill-advised risky escape attempt that hit a tree.

Garcia canceled two early birdies with three front-nine bogeys and shot a 75. Of the chasers, only Mickelson managed to break par, shooting a 71 on a day when there was only one round in the 60s; however, starting four strokes back, he needed something much better than that to catch Woods. "He's the only leader that you don't have hope that he'll falter," Mickelson admitted.

Woods clinically produced a final-round 71 that netted him a comfortable three-stroke victory over Goosen and four over Mickelson. Tiger quickly went three ahead with birdies on the second and third, momentarily dropped to two up with a bogey at the fifth, and dutifully restored the three-stroke margin with a birdie at the sixth. Woods never led by less than three the rest of the way, playing it safe on the back nine by laying up on both par fives. Again, he was pleased with a par-saving putt, this one on the 16th that preserved a comfortable four-stroke margin heading to the last two holes.

What the victory lacked in drama, it possessed in significance. Woods became the third player to successfully defend a Masters title, joining Jack Nicklaus (1965–66) and Nick Faldo (1989–90). It gave him a third green jacket at age 26, one year sooner than Nicklaus won his third, and a seventh major title. Most of all, it was perhaps the best evidence yet that this Tiger was the game's alpha dog.

....

Fast Start
Denmark's Thomas Bjorn opened the second round with birdies on the first five holes, a tournament record for consecutive birdies at the start of the round. Impressively, he did so on putts of merely 6, 4, 3, 10, and 7 feet. With a bogey at the seventh hole, Bjorn ended up with a 32 on the front nine and went on to shoot a 67, which tied for the second lowest score of the round. Bjorn was playing with Vijay Singh, who had the best score with a 65 including a 30 on the back nine. The two combined for a better-ball score of 59.

....

2003

Nobody had ever won the Masters three years in a row. Of course, only two players, Jack Nicklaus in 1967 and Nick Faldo in 1991, ever had the chance. Now Tiger Woods was trying for the feat, and there was no one who felt he *couldn't* do it.

Woods was his usual self in the run-up to the Masters, probably even better than the 2001–02 versions, with three victories in only five starts. He appeared to have some strong competition. Ernie Els won the first two events of the PGA Tour season and added two more wins worldwide. Davis Love III had two wins, including the Players Championship in his last start. Only a small blip on the pre-tournament radar screen, Mike Weir had also won two tournaments in 2003, rebounding from a lackluster 2002 campaign.

Much media attention was diverted even from Woods' three-peat quest by coverage focusing on Augusta National not having any women members. That moved to the forefront in the summer of 2002 when Martha Burk, chairperson of the National Council of Women's Organizations, wrote a letter to Masters chairman Hootie Johnson stating that Augusta's all-male membership would become an "issue," and Johnson publicly responded with a statement that the club wouldn't change its policy "at the point of a bayonet."

With media outlets pursuing the story, there was pressure on the Masters television sponsors to pull out. The club took matters into its own hands by saying the telecast would run without sponsorship. Burk scheduled a protest in Augusta during tournament week, but only 50 protesters showed up and the woman-member issue soon went on the back burner. Augusta National finally admitted its first women members in 2012.

There was no golf to write about on Thursday. Rain made it a washout before any players got onto the course, which had already been saturated with three inches from Sunday to Wednesday. With no one wanting a Monday finish, plans were made to play 36 holes—or however many could be gotten in—on Friday. Lights were installed on the practice range so players could warm up before the 7:30 a.m. start.

It didn't prove possible for the whole field to get in 36 holes, with 75 of the 93 players forced to come back on Saturday morning to finish Round 2. Only seven players broke par in the sloppy conditions of the first round, with two factors making it tough to control iron shots: longer fairway grass and mud on the ball. The average score was 76.2, making Darren Clarke's 66 an impressive feat as the next best scores were 69s by Sergio Garcia and U.S. Amateur champion Ricky Barnes.

Barnes was paired with Woods, and shockingly beat the tournament favorite by seven strokes as Tiger went without a birdie in his 76. Other high scores turned in by those expected to contend were Love with a 77 and Els with a 79.

By the end of the day, Clarke had fallen to four-under par through 10 holes of the second round and two strokes behind Weir, who had finished 12 holes. The Canadian shot a 70 in the first round—a 40-foot putt for a par on the first hole helped—and was four-under for 12 holes in Round 2 with consecutive birdies on 13, 14, and 15 (he started on the back nine in the split-tee setup) and on Nos. 2 and 3 just before darkness.

Weir finished off his second round on Saturday morning by playing six holes in even par for a 68 in a round where he hit only eight greens and needed just 22 putts. At 138, he had a four-stroke lead over Clarke, who shot a 76 (he would follow with a 78 and 74), with Barnes and Phil Mickelson the only two other players under par for 36 holes at 143. Mickelson had missed three weeks in March for the birth of his third child, and in his return missed the cut at the BellSouth Classic. Still, with three third-place finishes at Augusta, including the last two years, he couldn't be counted out. Nor could Els, who followed his 79 with a 66, where he was three-under for 11 holes on Friday and three-under for seven holes on Saturday.

The biggest story of Saturday morning was Woods, who instead of shooting for a third straight Masters title was fighting to keep alive his streak of 101 consecutive cuts made on the PGA Tour. Needing a par at the ninth hole to make the cut, he drove into the trees on the right, hit his second shot into the front left bunker, blasted out to three feet, and made the testy downhiller to make it on the number at 149 after a 73.

Woods was the story of Saturday afternoon, too, when he shot a 66 and was suddenly back in position where a three-peat was possible. The defender looked like himself again, hitting 15 greens in regulation, making routine up-and-down birdies from the fringe on three par fives, and tossing in birdie putts of 50 and 20 feet for good measure.

Tiger came from the cut line to within four strokes of the lead thanks in part to Weir falling back with a 75. Weir built a six-stroke lead by playing the first seven holes in one-under before it fell apart with five bogeys and one birdie after that. He hit only eight greens for the second straight round, and was unable to convert the par saves this time.

Jeff Maggert jumped into the breach with a 66 of his own to take a two-stroke lead over Weir. He did it with a wild back-nine 32 that included a double bogey on 11, six birdies, and only two pars—one of them thanks to a 15-foot putt on the 12th.

Maggert proceeded to birdie 13, 14, 16, 17, and 18, adding to his birdie on 10. He three-putted for a par on the 15th, an anomaly on a nine where he one-putted the other eight greens and in a round when he had only 21 putts.

Maggert wasn't a feared 54-hole leader. The 39-year-old was 1-for-8 in converting a 54-hole lead to victory on the PGA Tour and had only two career wins while finishing second 14 times. What's more, he had slumped in the last two years and fallen to 117th in the World Ranking, though he was coming off a T11 at the Players Championship.

If his Sunday fall from first place wasn't surprising, the way it happened was shocking. Maggert's shot from a fairway bunker on the third hole caught the lip, ricocheted straight back and hit him in the chest for a two-stroke penalty. He made a triple bogey there (needing a 15-foot putt to do it), then battled back within one of the lead with birdies on Nos. 5 and 10. It all came apart on the 12th with a horrid quintuple bogey eight: tee shot into a tough lie in the back bunker, second into the water, penalty drop, and another shot in the water. To his credit, Maggert birdied 13, 14, and 15; still, it was a final-round 75 and a fifth-place finish.

Much less predictably, Woods also shot a 75. He birdied the second hole, but it soon became apparent that he just didn't have it this week, the third-round 66 aside. With the tees moved up 35 yards on the third hole to tempt players to try to drive close to the green on the short par four, Tiger took the bait and sprayed his drive to the trees on the right. He successfully punched out left-handed from next to an azalea bush, but then knocked his pitch shot over the green and double bogeyed. That was followed by a three-putt bogey on the fourth, a bladed bunker shot for a bogey on the seventh, and a bad pitch for a bogey on the eighth. There would be no three-peat; Woods finished T15.

Instead of Woods, it was the least likely of players on the 54-hole leaderboard making a charge. Len Mattiace, who started five strokes back, was a 35-year-old whose only two PGA Tour victories came in 2002, his eighth year on the circuit and the first year he cracked the top 60 money winners. He had played in only one Masters, way back in 1988 as an amateur.

Mattiace birdied the second and third, then pitched in from 35 yards from behind a hump for an unlikely birdie on the eighth hole. His 33 on the front nine was followed by a 60-foot birdie putt on the 10th reminiscent of Ben Crenshaw's bomb in 1984. When his four-wood second shot on the 13th cleared the creek with about a foot to spare and finished 10 feet from the hole, it appeared that the Wake Forest grad was leading a charmed existence on this day. When he made the eagle putt, he got to six-under for the round and the tournament, jumping into the lead.

Vijay Singh got to four-under with birdies on 10 and 11 and just as quickly dropped from contention with bogeys on 12 (missed three-foot putt) and 13 (drive left leading to a punch-out). Mickelson and Jim Furyk made their moves too late in shooting 68s to finish third and fourth, respectively.

The tournament came down to Mattiace and Weir, both vying for their first major. Weir shot a 34 on the front nine with iron shots within four feet for birdies on

Nos. 2 and 6 and some serious scrambling on other holes—a 10-foot par putt on the fourth, superb pitch on the fifth, bunker shot to a foot on the seventh, and a pitch to five feet on the eighth.

Weir lost the lead to Mattiace's eagle and fell three behind when Mattiace birdied the 15th with a two-putt from the back fringe and the 16th from 10 feet. Weir still had both par fives to play, though, and he converted a 12-foot birdie putt on the 13th.

2003		
1	Mike Weir	70–68–75–68—281*
2	Len Mattiace	73–74–69–65—281
3	Phil Mickelson	73–70–72–68—283
4	Jim Furyk	73–72–71–68—284
5	Jeff Maggert	72–73–66–75—286
T6	Ernie Els	79–66–72–70—287
T6	Vijay Singh	73–71–70–73—287
T8	Jonathan Byrd	74–71–71–72—288
T8	Mark O'Meara	76–71–70–71—288
T8	Jose Maria Olazabal	73–71–71–73—288
T8	David Toms	71–73–70–74—288
T8	Scott Verplank	76–73–70–69—288
*Weir won on first playoff hole		

Mattiace came to the 18th needing only a par to match the final-round record of 64, not to mention preserving his lead. But his drive veered to the trees on the right, forcing a punch-out, and his nine-iron third shot finished 30 feet from the hole on the back fringe. He used a putter and came up seven feet short but avoided disaster by holing that one for a bogey.

Meanwhile, Weir was playing the 15th, where he drove to the left, laid up, and hit a wedge to four feet. He made that to tie for the lead at seven-under. Still seven-under on 18, Weir's approach didn't quite reach the top level and rolled back away from the hole, leaving a 45-foot putt, which he left six feet short. With a spot in a playoff on the line, Weir rolled that one in the middle.

Mattiace's magic, which ran out on the 18th hole, didn't return in the playoff. On the first extra hole, No. 10, he pulled his six-iron approach well left of the green, down a bank, and behind a tree. He managed to get his third shot within 30 feet, but his treacherous downhill putt just kept rolling until it ended up 18 feet past. When that putt missed the hole, Weir was able to win with a three-putt bogey.

That happened to be the only three-putt green Weir had all week. Fortunately, he didn't three-putt the 72nd hole. "I wouldn't wish that putt on anybody," he said of the six-foot second putt. "That was as nerve-wracking as it gets."

Weir's final-round 68 was without a bogey, and, after the scrambles of the front nine, he hit eight greens in regulation on the back and putted from the fringe on the other. His victory belied the notion that only a long hitter could win on the lengthened Augusta National course, which played even longer this year because of the wet conditions.

In addition to becoming the first Canadian to win a major championship, Weir was the second left-handed golfer to win a major, joining Bob Charles (1963 British Open). Mickelson, who had many chances to earn that honor, was still on the outside looking in.

Great Escape

Phil Mickelson drove into the creek to the left of the second fairway in the final round, and took a penalty drop amongst the trees. From the pine needles, he elected to play a risky shot with a driver, and somehow pulled it off, reaching the front of the green. For good measure, he holed a putt from some 90 feet for a birdie that would have made Arnold Palmer or Seve Ballesteros proud—but ended up as a footnote in a third-place finish.

2004

The talk about Tiger Woods this year was that he had gone six major championships without a victory, hadn't led the money list in 2003 after four straight years on top, hadn't won a stroke play event so far in 2004 (he did win the WGC-Match Play), and should reconnect with swing teacher Butch Harmon because going it on his own didn't seem to be working…yet Woods was still a 4-to-1 favorite.

Phil Mickelson had slipped even further in 2003, going winless and finishing 38th on the money list. In his case, though, things had turned around. He brought in teacher Rick Smith to work with him for five days in early January, won the Bob Hope, and had seven top-10s in eight 2004 starts.

The first round showed that the warning signs for Woods were real. He was four-over for 14 holes, with no birdies, when the round was suspended by darkness (now a nearly annual event, in this case caused by a two-hour rain and lightning delay at 4 p.m.), ultimately shooting a 75.

Mickelson fared better with a 72 in a round where there were only three scores in the 60s, saying that he was satisfied because tough pin positions made him play for par on most holes. That was a notable and welcome comment from a player whose aggressive tendencies seemed to work against him in major championships (where he was 0-for-46) compared to regular tour events, where he had racked up 22 victories at the age of 33.

The leader was 23-year-old Englishman Justin Rose with a round of 67 in which he was in virtually no trouble, hitting 17 greens in regulation. Chris DiMarco and 50-year-old Jay Haas were next with 69s, DiMarco scoring a hole-in-one on the sixth and parring all the other holes except for a birdie on the 15th. Ernie Els was the most prominent player at 70, while Korea's K.J. Choi birdied four straight holes starting at the 12th for a back-nine 33 and a 71.

Choi soared higher at the start of the second round with birdies on Nos. 2, 3, 5, 7, 8, and 9 for a 30 that tied the front-nine record and made him 10-under for his last 16 holes. The 33-year-old fell to earth with bogeys on 10, 11, and 12 and another on 16 for a 40 on the back nine. After the round, he preferred to look at the glass as half-full, saying, "I think two-under was a very good score for the day."

Rose held onto the lead at 138 with a two-birdie, one-bogey 71, hitting 15 greens. Two more Europeans were next at 140, Spain's Jose Maria Olazabal and Germany's Alex Cejka.

That trio plummeted off the leaderboard in the third round, Rose with six bogeys on the front nine for a 42 on the way to an 81, losing his tee-to-green accuracy as he hit only eight greens. Cejka and Olazabal weren't much better with 78 and 79, respectively.

Mickelson moved into a share of the 54-hole lead with 69s in the second and third rounds. His second round was notable for a good break on the 13th, where his second shot rolled most of the way down the bank of the hazard but stopped just short of the water, from where he nearly holed out and tapped in for a birdie. A 30-foot birdie putt on the 17th gave him a 33 on the back nine.

Phil added a 33 on the front nine on Saturday with three birdies and four par saves. He had all pars on the back nine, holing from 10 feet to get away with one on the 18th and run his streak to 32 holes without a bogey.

"I may not be making as many birdies, but I'm not nearly throwing as many [strokes] away," he said. Besides introducing an element of caution to his play, Mickelson had also worked with Smith on a more compact and efficient swing to improve his driving accuracy while also focusing on distance control with his wedges. He was on his way to leading the field in greens in regulation (ultimately hitting 53 of 72).

"Heading into the final round I feel much more at ease than I have in the past," he said, admitting that he'd gone into major Sundays wondering if his swing was going to be there. "I don't feel that anxiety. I haven't felt it all year."

While he had three seconds and five thirds in major championships, Mickelson had never held a 54-hole lead. Here he had to share it with DiMarco, who recovered from a 73 in the second round (40 on the back nine) with a 68 on Saturday. Like Mickelson, DiMarco preserved a bogey-free round with an escape on 18, finding the green with a sliced two-iron from the trees.

DiMarco held the 18- and 36-hole leads in his first Masters in 2001, finishing T10, and added a T12 the next year. In 2003, however, he was 16-over par for 35 holes when play was suspended by darkness and withdrew rather than show up to play one hole the next day—then wrote a letter of apology to Masters chairman Hootie Johnson.

Woods would not be a factor on Sunday. He climbed back into contention with a second-round 69, then dropped right back out of it with a 75 in Round 3. He said he was "a little off" in a front-nine 38; when he slid to four-over on the day with a double bogey on the 13th, that was the end of his title hopes. He finished T22 with a closing 71.

The final round would turn into one of the greatest shootouts ever, but it didn't start out that way. Mickelson was very shaky over the first six holes. He drove into the left rough on the first hole and punched a low shot onto the green for a two-putt par. His second shot was well left of the second green, his flop shot went 20 feet past, and he made that from the fringe for a birdie. Mickelson's approach went over the green on No. 3, and he missed a par putt from three-and-a-half feet.

He got up and down from a bunker to par the fourth, blasting to three feet. Phil found another bunker on the fifth and failed to escape with his first try, emerging

2004

1	Phil Mickelson	72–69–69–69—279
2	Ernie Els	70–72–71–67—280
3	K.J. Choi	71–70–72–69—282
T4	Sergio Garcia	72–72–75–66—285
T4	Bernhard Langer	71–73–69–72—285
T6	Paul Casey	75–69–68–74—286
T6	Fred Couples	73–69–74–70—286
T6	Chris DiMarco	69–73–68–76—286
T6	Davis Love III	75–67–74–70—286
T6	Nick Price	72–73–71–70—286
T6	Vijay Singh	75–73–69–69—286
T6	Kirk Triplett	71–74–69–72—286

with a bogey after coming out to five feet. He made another bogey at the sixth when he came up short, pitched to 12 feet, and missed. After three over-par holes in the first three rounds (two bogeys and a double bogey), he had three in the space of four holes.

DiMarco was faring even worse. After a birdie at the second, he played the next five holes in five-over. At that point, Mickelson was tied for the lead at four-under with 46-year-old Bernhard Langer, who was three strokes back through 54 holes after a third-round 69. A host of other players were in the mix, within three strokes at that point or shortly thereafter: Els, DiMarco, Paul Casey, Vijay Singh, Choi, Fred Couples, Davis Love III, and Sergio Garcia, who was on his way to a 66 and a tie for fourth. Singh, who supplanted Woods at the top of the 2003 money list and would repeat in 2004, shot a 32 on the front nine to get to three-under but bogeyed the 10th and parred the last eight holes.

All the rest would become bit players as Els, Mickelson, and Choi burned up the back nine. Or, in the case of Els, the final 11 holes. The 34-year-old South African sent a signal with a booming drive and a five-iron that bounced and rolled to within five feet on the eighth; he jumped from one behind to one ahead when he made the eagle putt. He stayed at five-under with par saves at the ninth with a clever pitch and 11th with a nine-foot putt.

Mickelson managed to collect himself, maintain a positive attitude, and piece together his swing despite the poor start. Starting at the seventh, he parred the next five holes, hitting four of the greens. He was still two-over on the day but back on track and feeling confident enough to take a fairly aggressive line on the 12th hole, hitting his tee shot 12 feet left of the pin.

Meanwhile, Els had hit a six-iron second shot to 10 feet on the 13th. While Mickelson was walking to the 12th green, he heard the roar from Els making his second eagle of the round to go ahead by three. That's OK, thought Mickelson, I can make this putt and birdie 13 and I'll be within one.

"I kept saying to myself, 'This is my day,'" he said. Mickelson did make that putt and he birdied 13 with a seven-iron to 20 feet and two putts.

Choi was producing some fireworks of his own. He eagled the tough par-four 11th—made even tougher this year with the addition of 35 trees to the right of the fairway—by holing a five-iron from 210 yards, birdied the 13th with a downhill 40-foot putt, and birdied the 14th from six feet. Els maintained his lead at seven-under thanks to a seven-foot par putt at 14, with Mickelson at six-under, and Choi five-under.

The eagle party wasn't limited to Els and Choi, who were playing together. Not long after Els' second eagle, Padraig Harrington and Kirk Triplett made aces on the 16th in consecutive twosomes.

The gallery roars kept coming as Mickelson came within an inch of an eagle of his own on the 14th, when his pitching wedge approach slid past the lip and stopped six inches from the cup. The brilliant shot came after Mickelson heard the cheering for a tap-in birdie by Els after a deft chip from behind the green on 15. Phil's birdie brought him back within one stroke.

Els made a 10-foot par putt on the 16th, while Choi birdied to get back within two. Mickelson had to lay up on 15 after driving behind the trees on the left and settled for a par. On the 16th, where he made a crushing bogey in 2001 after a tee shot to the right side of the green, the lefty found the proper level of the putting surface, 15 feet from the hole. He canned the putt to tie for the lead.

Mickelson's caddie Jim "Bones" Mackay later recalled, "After Phil made that putt, he came over to me and gave me a nudge. 'Let's get one more, Bones,' he said. He had this unbelievable look in his eye. I just knew he was going to do it."

Up ahead, Els was missing 20-foot birdie putts on the last two holes, signing for a 67, and waiting to see what Mickelson would do. Choi also made two pars to complete a 31 on the back nine and a 69 to finish third, the best showing ever by an Asian.

A month before the Masters, Mickelson's short-game teacher, Dave Pelz, told him that he looked too serious on Sundays. "When you are at the top of your game, you are laughing, smiling," Pelz said.

Mickelson left himself a dangerous downhill putt of 40 feet on the 17th hole, but, true to Pelz's advice, he was smiling as he looked it over. He had even more reason to smile when he coaxed it within a foot for a tap-in par.

Mickelson showed control, distance, and course management on his three-wood tee shot on the now lengthy 18th, leaving an eight-iron approach from the middle of the fairway which he hit to 18 feet behind the hole.

In a bit of serendipity, DiMarco's shot from the front left bunker settled three inches behind the coin marking Mickelson's ball, giving Phil a read on his putt. DiMarco's ball broke just a little too much to the left, leaving him with a 76. The stage was set for Mickelson, who tapped his downhill putt, watched it veer toward the left lip, catch that lip, do a half-circle around the cup, and drop for a 31 on the back nine, a 69, and a one-stroke victory.

What a way to finally win a first major! As he held his two-year-old daughter Sophia behind the 18th green, the new champion said, "Daddy won, can you believe it?" To the assembled media shortly afterward, he said, "It's almost make-believe. Having come so close so many times makes it much more special."

Els was disconsolate. "I had this image in my mind that I'd finally be wearing that green jacket," he said.

It could be fairly said that he played well enough to earn one. But they only give out one per year, and Mickelson—who had a premonition of his own—was even better.

Vijay's Waterloo

Vijay Singh finished T6, seven strokes back, and it's easy to pinpoint where he lost—he hit six balls in the water. Four of those came on the 15th hole, two on Thursday when he made a triple bogey, one on Friday in a double bogey, and one on Sunday though he saved par after his second shot was wet. This was the same hole where the 2000 champion made a quadruple bogey in 2002 to end his title bid.

2005

Tiger Woods was once The Man, but coming into the 2005 Masters he was merely one of the Big Four, along with Vijay Singh (winner of nine tournaments in 2004), Phil Mickelson, and Ernie Els. While reworking his swing with new instructor Hank Haney, Woods had a down year in 2004 with only one victory and a ranking of fourth on the money list.

Things were looking up in 2005, with victories at the Buick Invitational and Doral. But he wasn't all the way back, as evidenced by finishes of T23 and T53 in his last two pre-Masters starts.

Mickelson, by contrast, arrived in Augusta on a high note off a victory at the BellSouth Classic up I–20 in Atlanta, though with that tournament ending Monday his prep was abbreviated. The start of the BellSouth had been delayed two days by rain, with Chris DiMarco withdrawing from that tournament to preserve what he considered his all-important practice rounds for the Masters.

It proved to be a wise move for DiMarco. The 54-hole co-leader of the year before became the 18-hole leader in 2005 with a 67. It took more than one day to do it, as weather wreaked havoc on the Masters schedule again.

The start of the first round was delayed five-and-a-half hours, with a change made to send players off both the first and 10th tees. DiMarco started on the 10th, where he made his only bogey. A back-nine 35 and consecutive birdies on Nos. 1–3 brought him to four-under through 14 holes when play was suspended by darkness. The next morning, he hit his tee shot to inches from the hole on the sixth—the same hole he aced in the first round the year before.

Woods was two-over through 12 holes when play was suspended and ultimately shot a 74. It was a wild round, full of unlikely misadventures. Starting on the back nine, Tiger had a downhill eagle putt from 40 feet on the 13th, hit it too hard, and watched it trickle into the water hazard beyond the hole. He took a stroke-and-distance penalty and two-putted from the same spot for a bogey. That was only the beginning.

Even a tap-in on the 14th led to an adventure. A viewer thought Woods had violated the rules by straddling the line of his putt; the rules committee looked at the video and judged it inconclusive, so there was no penalty. Tiger hit a beautiful approach shot on the first hole that clanged off the flagstick and ended up in a bunker, from where he made a bogey. Then, on No. 2, he snap-hooked a drive that hit a tree and kicked into the fairway only 100 yards from the tee. His second sailed into trees on the right, but he ultimately escaped with a 25-foot putt for a par five.

The strangeness didn't stop Friday morning when the round concluded. Woods' tee shot on the sixth landed six feet from the hole on the top shelf, but drew back and rolled down the slope and off the green. Using a putter from the fringe, his first try failed to clear the hill and rolled back to him; he ended up making a 15-foot bogey putt. On the eighth hole, he hit another tree and made a bogey six.

Woods got out of the Twilight Zone and into contention with a 66 in the second round. Seventeen holes of that occurred on Saturday (the second round had been halted at 12:40 p.m. on Friday). Tiger birdied the first two holes he played on Saturday, Nos. 2 and 3, and went on to collect a total of seven birdies in the second round while shooting 33s on each nine and hitting 16 greens in regulation. Referring to the first round, he said, "I kept telling myself I was hitting good golf shots, and then I'd mess it up. Or I'd get a bad break. So if I kept hanging in there, kept hitting quality golf shots, it will turn. And luckily, it turned."

DiMarco, also playing 17 holes of his second round on Saturday, was hitting his share quality golf shots, posting a second consecutive 67 to lead by four strokes over Thomas Bjorn and six over third-place Woods. Two of Woods' fellow members of the Big Four were hanging in there, Singh at 141 and Mickelson at 142. By the time the third round was suspended by darkness with the last group just making the turn to the back nine, they were practically out of it. Singh, who would end up leading the field in greens in regulation, couldn't make enough putts. Mickelson, unlike last year, carded too many bogeys. But it was less their own troubles that knocked them out; it was rather the outstanding play of DiMarco and Woods.

DiMarco birdied the second, seventh, and eighth holes for a 33 on the front nine. Woods matched those birdies and trumped DiMarco with additional birdies on the third and ninth, where he hit his approach shot to two feet, for a 31. Play was suspended at that point, with DiMarco 13-under, Woods nine-under, Bjorn eight-under, and nobody else better than four-under. Woods was 11-under for the 26 holes he played on Saturday, DiMarco eight-under for his 26.

The DiMarco-Woods duel took a quick and dramatic turn when the third round resumed at 8 a.m. on Sunday. It took only 33 minutes for Tiger to make up the four-stroke deficit and another 10 minutes to assume the lead. The first blow was a 15-foot birdie putt by Woods at the 10th.

DiMarco, in the next twosome, sprayed his second shot to the right and it ended up unplayable under a bush, leading to a double bogey. It ended a streak of 44 holes without a bogey, the second longest in Masters history (Stuart Appleby went 50 in 2001).

Woods added another 15-foot birdie putt on the 11th and a birdie from seven feet on the 12th. He got a good break when his poor second shot on 13 stopped just short of the creek thanks to a soft bounce; he pitched to 10 feet and made it. That was his seventh straight birdie, including the three at the end of the day on Saturday, tying the Masters record set by Steve Pate in 1999 on the same stretch of holes.

At eight-under for the round through 13 holes, Woods had the course record of 63 in his sights but was sidetracked by a three-putt bogey on 14 and a bogey on 15 where his second shot plugged in the bank inside the hazard line. Anyway, a 65 gave him a 131 total for the middle rounds and 205 for 54 holes. That was good for a three-stroke lead over DiMarco, who bogeyed 14, 15, and 17 for a 41 on the back nine and a 74. Bjorn at 209 was the only other player within five strokes, but he was destined for an 81 in the final round, leaving it strictly a two-man battle on Sunday afternoon.

DiMarco tried to put his dreadful morning behind him by coming out in a complete change of clothes, including different shoes, for the final round. He played like a different man in the afternoon, striking the ball beautifully on the front nine. The ex-Florida Gator birdied the second and ninth holes from four feet and two feet to shoot a 34 that could have been much better if he hadn't missed four birdie putts of between six and 12 feet.

Woods equaled the 34 with birdies on the first two holes from seven and 14 feet, a three-putt bogey on the fifth, and an eight-foot putt on the eighth to match DiMarco's birdie and retain a three-stroke lead.

The margin shrank to two on the 10th hole, where Woods hooked his three-wood tee shot toward the forest left of the 10th fairway. He got a break when the ball hit a tree and kicked to the right instead of deep into the woods, but still ended up with a bogey to cut the lead to two as DiMarco got up and down for a par. Now it was getting interesting, and it would stay that way as Woods' advantage went back and forth between one and two strokes all the way to the 18th hole.

DiMarco birdied the 11th from 35 feet and gave it back when he bogeyed the 12th, missing the green to the left. Both settled for par fives on the 13th and DiMarco clawed back within one thanks to an approach shot within a foot for a birdie on 14. Both birdied the 15th, DiMarco laying up and hitting a wedge to four feet and Woods hitting the green in two with an eight-iron.

Tiger tugged his tee shot to the left on the 16th and DiMarco hit a nice one to 15 feet, giving him a reasonable chance to tie or move in front. Woods would have to play his 35-foot chip shot well beyond the hole and to the left before letting the slope of the green take it down toward the hole. Complicating matters, his ball came to rest on the edge of the second cut, not an easy lie.

Woods remembered that Davis Love III had chipped in from a similar spot in 1999, but didn't expect to repeat the feat. "I was just aiming at a spot. It was a little spot in the [shadows of the] trees that had a little light coming through, and I was just trying to hit the ball somewhere in that area, which should leave me somewhere in the range of the hole," he said.

He found the spot. Chipping about 25 feet above the hole, the ball trickled down slowly, first breaking to the right and then just slightly left as it neared the cup. It rested on the cusp for a couple of seconds, as if to milk the drama, and then dropped. The gallery roar reached a thunderous crescendo. Tiger responded with signature fist pumps and a high-five with his caddie, Steve Williams. Woods called it one of his greatest shots ever, not so much because of the difficulty as the timing.

Facing a possible two-stroke swing against him, he instead *gained* a stroke when DiMarco's birdie putt just missed.

If this were the 2000–02 version of Tiger Woods, the door would have slammed shut right there. But his game wasn't quite as airtight now, and Woods proceeded to block his drive 30 yards to the right of the fairway on the 17th, setting up a chip-and-putt bogey. He pushed an eight-iron approach on 18 into

2005		
1	Tiger Woods	74–66–65–71—276*
2	Chris DiMarco	67–67–74–68—276
T3	Luke Donald	68–77–69–69—283
T3	Retief Goosen	71–75–70–67—283
T5	Mark Hensby	69–73–70–72—284
T5	Trevor Immelman	73–73–65–73—284
T5	Rod Pampling	73–71–70–70—284
T5	Vijay Singh	68–73–71–72—284
T5	Mike Weir	74–71–68–71—284
10	Phil Mickelson	70–72–69–74—285
*Woods won on first playoff hole		

the right greenside bunker and made another bogey. DiMarco's chip from short of the green on the 72nd hole caught the lip but stayed out, and he made a clutch five-foot putt to force a playoff.

Under a policy first announced in 2004, the playoff started on the 18th hole. Woods got it back together with a three-wood to the fairway and an eight-iron to 15 feet behind the hole. DiMarco reprised his short approach from regulation, and had another near chip-in, this one settling inches from the hole. His par save became moot when Woods holed his birdie putt for his first major championship victory in 34 months and his fourth green jacket at the age of 29.

"It was one fun victory, but also a lot of work," said Woods after winning with a closing 71. "The guy I played against is one heck of a competitor."

DiMarco indeed gave Woods all he could handle with a 68 in the final round before losing a playoff in the second consecutive major, having fallen to Singh in the 2004 PGA Championship. Even more than Els in 2004, DiMarco could say he played well enough to win. It all turned on two chip shots—if Woods' ball had stayed on the lip on 16 or DiMarco's had fallen on 18, Chris would have won. DiMarco's 12-under 276 total was a whopping seven strokes ahead of third-place Luke Donald and Retief Goosen. His only misfortune was happening to run into Tiger Woods on the week when things clicked back into place.

While Woods was more erratic than he was in his most dominant phase, when he was winning majors by double-digit margins, his good was plenty good enough. His new swing and an equipment change restored his long-distance advantage, enabling him to hit as little as a nine-iron for a second shot to the par-five 15th and uncork a drive of 344 yards on the first hole of the final round that was 62 yards past DiMarco. When his iron play and putting were dialed in, he was able to go on a tear that saw him play a stretch of 30 holes in 15-under. Tiger was back.

2006–2014

A Couple of Lefties and a New Course

Until Mike Weir won the Masters in 2003, only one left-handed player had won a major championship: Bob Charles at the 1963 British Open. Weir started a run of six lefty winners in 12 years at Augusta, including three by Phil Mickelson (2004, 06, 10) and two by Bubba Watson (2012 and 14).

The left-leaning trend had a lot to do with the quality of the left-handers, of course. Mickelson is by far the winningest lefty of all time with 44 PGA Tour victories through 2020; Watson has 12, and Weir eight. It could be argued that the course favors left-handers, at least slightly. Working the ball right-to-left is an advantage on a number of holes at Augusta National, perhaps even more so for a long-hitting power fader like Mickelson or Watson. (Mickelson worked the ball primarily left to right early in his career, but started winning Masters after perfecting a "go-to" fade.) Also, high, soft-landing irons are beneficial at Augusta, requiring no adjustment for a left-handed fader, whereas a right-hander utilizing his right-to-left draw game on tee shots needs to switch swing modes to hit a softer fade into the green.

It also happens that Mickelson and Watson are two of the most creative players in the game, a greater edge than their handedness. Mickelson is a wizard around the greens, where a deft touch is required on shots to the fast, sloping surfaces at Augusta. Watson can work the ball either way better than anyone—he rarely hits a straight shot. This comes in handy not only off the tee but also out of the trees lining Augusta National's fairways. This was most famously demonstrated with his hook from the forest in the playoff to win his first title in 2012. The duo's Augusta affinity is shown by the fact that through 2020 they had accounted for only two career titles in the other three majors, both by Mickelson.

The advantages of creativity and aggressive play were thought to be on the wane at the beginning of this period. The course underwent its final stage of lengthening and narrowing before the 2006 tournament, and many critics and players complained that it had been made too tough and therefore less exciting. That chorus grew louder in 2007 and 2008 when an over-par score won in the former year and the final round was dull in the latter. In truth, weather conditions were the largest factor.

That said, the transition from Masters chairman Hootie Johnson (the mover behind the course changes) to Billy Payne made a difference. A number of tweaks back in the other direction were made under Payne's leadership, including the removal of some recently planted trees and the introduction of more flexibility in moving various tees forward on given days. By most accounts—nothing said officially, of course—the severity of the pin positions was softened a bit. Particularly on Sundays, flags were regularly placed near slopes which could be used to feed the ball to them. Also, players continued to get longer and longer off the tee. Angel Cabrera, the 2009 champion and 2011 runner-up, was hitting nine-irons to even the longest par fours, and Watson was hitting short irons for his second shot to par fives.

Starting in 2009, the number of subpar rounds began to hit levels not seen since the early 1990s, and, for the most part, stayed there over ensuing years. Mickelson won with a 272 total in 2010, two off the record, and Charl Schwartzel with a 274 in 2011 when he birdied the last four holes. The roars were back in Augusta, after a brief absence.

2006

For the second consecutive year, Phil Mickelson came to the Masters fresh off a victory in the BellSouth Classic, and this time he had even more momentum. He posted a 28-under total to win the Atlanta event by 13 strokes, the second largest victory margin in the modern era on the PGA Tour.

The only question was whether he peaked too early, but Mickelson said he wasn't concerned and pointed out that twice in his career he had won in back-to-back weeks. The 2004 champion was thinking about the Masters even as he was playing the BellSouth, unveiling a new strategy designed for Augusta by putting two drivers in the bag. One he used when he wanted to fade the ball. The other was designed for a draw and added 20 yards.

The extra distance would be especially useful this year, as another stage of course expansion had taken place with six holes lengthened by a total of 155 yards bringing the course yardage to 7,445. The affected holes were No. 1 (now 455 yards and trees added to the left), No. 4 (a dramatic addition of 35 yards to make it a killer par-three at 240), No. 7 (now 450 yards through a narrow corridor), No. 11 (now 505 yards with trees added to the right), No. 15 (now 540), and No. 17 (now 440 with trees added to the right).

Even Mickelson's Atlanta performance didn't make him the oddsmakers' favorite. That role still perennially belonged to Tiger Woods (twice a winner on the year so far), who was 3-to-1 on an online betting service while Mickelson was 13-to-2.

For the first time in several years, the course was dry and fast—at least for the first two rounds. The players handled the conditions and the toughened course pretty well, with scores similar to the year before. Only three players broke 70 in the first round, but 18 were under par. Leading the way was 2000 champion Vijay Singh at 67 with five birdies and no bogeys, followed by Rocco Mediate at 68 also without a bogey.

Mickelson was tied for fourth with a 70, getting it together to hit the last seven greens in regulation and play those holes in two-under. Woods had a 72 that featured an eight-iron holed for an eagle on the 14th, only to be followed by a double bogey at 15 where his lay-up second settled in a divot hole and he hit his third in the water.

Chad Campbell, a 31-year-old with three tour wins and a runner-up finish in the 2003 PGA Championship, took a three-stroke 36-hole lead with a 67 on Friday for a 138 total. Singh had a 74 that was marred by three double bogeys. He went over the green on the fourth and fifth and continued his recent-year trend of water trouble on the back-nine par fives, making a double bogey at the 13th. He was tied for second at 141 with Mediate and Fred Couples. "I'm a guy who can win, but I'm not the guy to beat," said Couples, a reasonable level of confidence for a 46-year-old.

Mickelson, playing in the afternoon when the wind picked up, birdied all four par fives to make up for four bogeys elsewhere for a 72 and 142, and said he was excited to be within striking distance heading to the weekend. Woods was within striking distance, too, with a 71 for 143.

The dry conditions were too good to be true. The rain came on Saturday, with a delay of more than four hours causing the last twosome to tee off at 6:52 and play only four holes. Campbell played them birdie, birdie, bogey, bogey and, at six-under, his lead was down to one over Tim Clark and Mediate. Those were the only players ahead of Mickelson and Woods at three-under. Mickelson had an up-and-down start with birdies at the first (eight feet), second (five feet), and third (15 feet) followed by bogeys at the fourth (bunker, missed from four feet) and fifth (bad drive) before darkness set in. Woods played nine holes two-under with two birdies and four par saves along the way.

When play resumed at 7:45 Saturday morning, Clark holed a six-foot birdie putt on the sixth, his first stroke of the day, to tie for the lead. The 30-year-old South African and North Carolina State alumnus, one of the shortest hitters on tour, was handling the longer course without a worry so far. A birdie at the eighth hole put him five-under for the round and he held the lead through bogeys at Nos. 9 and 14—but not after a double bogey at 17 and bogey at 18 gave him a 40 on the back nine and a 72.

Woods picked up the suspended round on the 10th hole, just like last year (except from the tee instead of the fairway) when he birdied the first four holes he played. He birdied the 10th again this time, but that was the only similarity. He hit his approach into the water on 11 and saved a bogey, then followed a birdie at 13 with three straight bogeys—three-putts on 14 and 16 and a second shot into the water on 15. It was the first time he ever made three straight bogeys in the Masters as a pro. A birdie on 18 gave him a 71.

Campbell bogeyed two of the first five holes he played on Sunday morning and finished the third round with a 75. Campbell's troubles, along with Clark's stumble at the end, enabled Mickelson to slip into the lead at 212 without having to do anything spectacular—he played the last 13 holes of his third round in one-under for a 70. Couples, with a quiet 72, was tied for second with Campbell at 213, while six players lurked at 214, including Woods and Singh, so Mickelson couldn't feel too comfortable.

Mickelson parred the first six holes of the final round and found himself in a five-way tie for the lead at four-under with Couples, Campbell, Mediate, and Miguel Angel Jimenez. That's when Phil took command, making a birdie from seven feet on the seventh and pitching within two feet for a birdie at the eighth. He didn't go backward from there, and none of his challengers went forward.

2006		
1	Phil Mickelson	70–72–70–69—281
2	Tim Clark	70–72–72–69—283
T3	Chad Campbell	71–67–75–71—284
T3	Fred Couples	71–70–72–71—284
T3	Retief Goosen	70–73–72–69—284
T3	Jose Maria Olazabal	76–71–71–66—284
T3	Tiger Woods	72–71–71–70—284
T8	Angel Cabrera	73–74–70–68—285
T8	Vijay Singh	67–74–73–71—285
10	Stewart Cink	72–73–71–70—286

The 43-year-old Mediate had a 34 on the front nine, but had two bad breaks on his second shot to the ninth hole. The ball hit the flagstick and caromed off the green; but, even worse for his fortunes, Mediate hurt his back when he hit the shot. In pain, he bogeyed the 11th and made a 10 on the 12th, hitting three balls in the water. Campbell made five birdies in his round but also four bogeys and never advanced past four-under; Jimenez dropped from sight with a 39 on the back nine.

There were other contenders. Singh birdied the ninth for a 34 on the front to get to four-under just after Mickelson moved to five-under; Vijay didn't make a birdie in a back-nine 37. Jose Maria Olazabal charged out of the pack with a 32 on the front and went to five-under with a three-wood to three feet for an eagle on the 15th. Not quite good enough, especially after a bogey on 16. Clark shot a 69 but didn't get to five-under until he holed a bunker shot for a birdie at the 18th to claim second place.

Woods was the first player on the practice green under the lights at 6:45 a.m. It didn't help. In fact, Tiger's putting had been pretty good in the first two-and-a-half rounds, but it was awful on Sunday, costing him a chance to become the first player to win back-to-back titles twice. While he did make a couple of nice par saves, Woods had three three-putt bogeys in the final round and missed eagle putts from six and nine feet on the 13th and 15th holes after brilliant second shots. He needed those eagles to threaten Mickelson; instead, he settled for a 70 to finish four-under.

Couples had perhaps even more reason to lament his putting. Trying to repeat Jack Nicklaus' feat of winning the Masters at age 46, Couples outplayed Mickelson from tee to green in the final twosome, hitting 16 greens in regulation, many of them within 10 feet of the hole, and putting from the fringe on the other two. He even outdrove his younger playing partner on many holes.

The 1992 champion missed five-foot birdie putts on the second and third holes, or a front-nine 34 would have been even better. He three-putted the 11th, missing from three feet. A birdie on 13 kept Couples within two, making him the only real threat at that point. He hit yet another excellent approach to three feet at the 14th—and proceeded to three-putt from there, knocking the downhiller three feet past and missing the comebacker. Instead of pulling within one, he fell three behind and finished with a 71 to tie for third with Campbell, Olazabal, Woods, and Retief Goosen (three late birdies for a 69).

"If he knocks that first putt in [on 14], we would've had a heck of a time on the last four holes," said Mickelson of a final pairing with Couples.

Instead, Mickelson had a stress-free stroll to the clubhouse, thanks in no small part to his birdies on 13 (two-putt from 20 feet) and 15 (eight feet after a near chip-in). His only bogey of the round was a meaningless one on the 18th that cut his final margin from three to two after a 69 for a 281 total.

"What I'm most proud of is that I didn't let other people back into it," he said.

It wasn't a runaway like the BellSouth the week before, but against a major championship field it was quite a convincing victory. In addition to a second straight tour win in as many weeks, it marked a second consecutive major for Mickelson, who had captured the 2005 PGA. Not bad for a player who once couldn't buy a major.

More Than Tough

The 11th hole played as the hardest on the course in 2005 and was even harder in 2006 with 15 yards added to make it 505. Just as significantly, more trees were added to the right and the fairway shifted to the left, making a narrower landing area and tougher second shot. The scoring average went from 4.358 to 4.474 and, most notably, it became much harder to birdie. There were only six birdies and one eagle (by Rory Sabbatini) all week compared to 18 birdies in 2005. The seven birdies or eagles on one hole were the fewest since 1973, when a smaller field made seven birdies on the 11th and fifth holes.

2007

A headline for an item in the notes section in the *Atlanta Constitution* on Tuesday read, "Run Of Bad Weather May Well End This Week."

Be careful what you wish for. The rainy weather that plagued the tournament in recent years did end, and there were no suspensions of play. But the dry weather that replaced it made conditions even tougher for scoring, especially combined with wind that dried out the greens even further and played havoc with balls in the air. Add in the frigid weather of Saturday and you had the perfect storm (not of the rainy variety) for course difficulty—especially on a layout that had recently been toughened.

The wind wasn't all that severe on Thursday, yet only nine players broke par and the best scores were 69s by Justin Rose and Brett Wetterich. The greens were firm and hard to hold with approach shots, as Rose could attest. He hit only five greens in regulation yet didn't make a bogey and was three-under. The 26-year-old from England pointed out that he avoided missing greens in impossible spots, while conceding "my short game was unbelievable" in a round of 20 putts and two hole-outs from off the green.

All eyes were on Tiger Woods, who was looking like the dominant 2000–01 version. He won the last two majors of 2006, propelling him to a streak of seven straight victories that extended to the first tournament of 2007. For good measure, he won at Doral in his last start before the Masters. Woods was in good shape at one-under through 16 holes before wild drives to the right led to bogeys on 17 and 18. After a quick interview, he stalked off to the practice range.

With the last three Masters going to Phil Mickelson, Woods, and then Mickelson again, there was talk of that duo trading titles like Arnold Palmer and Jack Nicklaus did in the 1960s. If so, Mickelson wasn't due, and he didn't look like it in the first round, playing the first seven holes five-over though he recovered for a 76. He would climb back into the fringe of contention before a closing 77 dropped him to T24.

Woods shot a 74 in the second round, still good enough to maintain his T15 position of the day before and feeling fortunate to be there after various misadventures. He hit into the water on the 12th and 13th, emerging with a bogey (40-foot putt on 12) and a par (up-and-down on 13 after second shot in the water). He hit three drives into the trees and played those holes even par with a birdie on No. 8. "I turned a 90 into a 74," he said.

Last year's runner-up, Tim Clark, was on the leaderboard again, reaching the top of it with a second consecutive 71 to tie for the lead with Wetterich at 142. The 33-year-old Wetterich was playing in just his third major championship, having missed the cut in his first two. Augusta native Vaughn Taylor, playing in his fifth major, was at 143. He *attended* his first major in 1987, an inspirational event as he watched native Augustan Larry Mize earn a green jacket.

Zach Johnson, who came in at 4-for-11 at making cuts in majors, was at 144 after a 73. A short hitter, Johnson decided before the tournament that he would lay up on all of the par fives. His strategy was working, thanks to a brilliant wedge game, as he birdied the first seven par fives he played in the first two rounds until a par on the 15th on Friday. Unfortunately, that was followed by bogeys on 16 (three-putt from three feet), 17, and 18, or he would have been in better position.

The temperature never got out of the 50s on Saturday, made more miserable by an unrelenting, bone-chilling wind gusting up to 23 mph, which dried out the already hard greens. "The last five or six holes I could barely feel my hands," said Johnson, who shot a 76. Freezing hands took away feel for chipping and putting on Augusta's treacherous greens, while the wind had its way with full shots. The scoring average of 77.35 was the highest since the third and fourth rounds of 1956.

There was only one subpar round, a 70 by Retief Goosen. The two-time U.S. Open champion, ranked ninth in the world, shot a pair of 76s in the first two rounds and made the cut only by dint of the 10-shot rule. He started the third round early, when the greens hadn't quite reached billiard-table firmness, and at the end of the day was tied for eighth, within four strokes of the lead.

Woods was one of only two players to match par of 72. When he finished his round, he was four strokes off the lead in eighth place. When the field finished its slog around the course—while Woods was on the practice range after another bogey-bogey finish on the last two holes—he was one stroke behind and had a spot in the final twosome.

Neither of the 36-hole leaders broke 80, with Wetterich sinking to an 83 and Clark struggling to an 80 that still left him within four of the lead. That lead was held by Australia's Stuart Appleby, who nonetheless had his own tale of woe. Two-under on the day through 16 holes, he hit his drive on the 17th into a greenside bunker on the seventh hole and made a triple bogey. The 35-year-old, who owned eight tour victories and was runner-up in the 2002 British Open, had a 73 for a 218 total that was the highest to ever lead the Masters through 54 holes.

Rose had a 75 that actually moved him closer to the lead, tied for second with Woods at 219. Johnson was at 220, along with Taylor and Padraig Harrington, the rare player who said, "I like the cold."

The first three rounds were decidedly lacking in gallery roars. They would return on Sunday when the temperature reached the low 60s, the wind subsided to a gentle breeze, the greens had been watered Saturday evening, and the pin positions were relatively generous. After three days of survival, it turned into an exciting final round with a large cast of characters producing something like the usual share of birdies and eagles down the stretch, even on a leaderboard showing only green numbers.

In fact, there was nothing better than a green "4" on the leaderboard after the first hole, where Rose double bogeyed and, in the last twosome, Appleby double bogeyed after a drive under a bush and Woods made a bogey. Johnson also bogeyed the first, but he birdied the second (five feet) and third (20 feet) to get to three-over. Woods got to three-over with a birdie at No. 2 and stood on the fourth tee with the lead by himself when Johnson bogeyed the fifth.

For the 16 previous years, the winner had emerged from the final twosome. With Woods in that position this year, the streak seemed likely to continue. Tiger was 12-for-12 when leading going into the final round; he didn't have the 54-hole lead this time, but now he was ahead with 15 holes remaining.

There were plenty of challengers, as 15 players were within four of the lead when the day began. A pair of South Africans who started four back at six-over made big moves on the front nine. Retief Goosen shot a 32, including a birdie with a spectacular shot from the trees on the seventh, to take the lead at two-over. Rory Sabbatini had a 33 that featured an eagle at the eighth on a big-breaking 60-foot putt.

Meanwhile, Johnson chipped in for a birdie on the eighth to pull within one. Out of character, Woods was going in the wrong direction with a three-putt bogey on the sixth and a missed three-foot par putt on the 10th to go to five-over and three behind. For a second consecutive Masters Sunday, his putter was letting him down.

Sabbatini took the lead from Goosen when he birdied the 13th while Retief three-putted for a bogey at 12. When Sabbatini bogeyed 14 after a drive into the trees on the left, it created a four-way tie for first at three-over with Goosen, Johnson, and Appleby.

Appleby promptly dropped out by becoming this year's victim of a water ball at the 12th, making a double bogey. Goosen stalled at three-over, hitting every green on the back nine but not recording a single birdie in a 37 for a 69. Sabbatini bogeyed 16 and birdied 18 for a 36 on the back nine and 69 to also finish three-over.

Johnson was a 31-year-old with one PGA Tour victory, the 2004 BellSouth Classic in Atlanta as a rookie, and a World Ranking

2007		
1	Zach Johnson	71–73–76–69—289
T2	Retief Goosen	76–76–70–69—291
T2	Rory Sabbatini	73–76–73–69—291
T2	Tiger Woods	73–74–72–72—291
T5	Jerry Kelly	75–69–78–70—292
T5	Justin Rose	69–75–75–73—292
T7	Stuart Appleby	75–70–73–75—293
T7	Padraig Harrington	77–68–75–73—293
9	David Toms	70–78–74–72—294
T10	Paul Casey	79–68–77–71—295
T10	Luke Donald	73–74–75–73—295
T10	Vaughn Taylor	71–72–77–75—295

of 56th. He was playing the final round in the company of Taylor, a former room-mate in their days on the mini-tours. Johnson was a soft-spoken Iowan, but Taylor (who shot a 75 in the final round) said, "He's one of the toughest guys I've ever competed against."

Johnson dug deep into that hidden well of competitiveness to take control of the Masters with three birdies in a four-hole stretch. The first came at the 13th, where he stayed true to his game plan by laying up despite being only 213 yards from the hole and ended up with a birdie after a wedge to eight feet. He went ahead by two with an approach to six feet and a birdie on 14.

As Johnson was playing the 15th, a roar arose from the 13th, where the gallery was watching Woods' second shot gather down a slope and roll to within three feet of the hole. The resulting eagle pulled Tiger within two, which should have left Johnson quaking.

Instead, after a par on 15, Johnson stuck his tee shot to eight feet at the 16th. He rolled in the birdie putt to get to even par just as Woods was missing a 12-foot birdie try at 14. The lead was three. Johnson used up some of that cushion when he missed a four-foot par putt on 17 to slip to one-over, and suddenly he had another challenger.

Rose appeared out of contention with double bogeys on two of the first three holes, but he rallied by playing a nine-hole stretch in five-under, culminating with birdies on 15 and 16 to get to two-over. Never mind—Rose's drive hit a tree on the 17th and he made his third double bogey of the day.

Johnson saved a par on the 18th with a near chip-in for a 69 and a posted 289 total that only Woods had a chance to catch.

Tiger had boldly tried to fade a five-iron around a tree and over the water on the 15th, only to make poor contact and bounce the shot into the pond. He salvaged a par with an up-and-down, and a par on 16 left him two behind Johnson. Woods thought he hit a good approach to 17, and blurted out to his caddie, "What the hell just happened?" when the ball plummeted into the bunker short of the green. He saved par there, but now needed a miracle hole-out on 18. Instead, a par gave him a 72 and a share of second with Sabbatini and Goosen, who had now gone 3–3–2 in the last three Masters in addition to a second in 2002.

The victory by the self-described "normal guy" was the first by a player from outside the top 10 in the World Ranking in eight years. The 289 winning total matched the highest in Masters history, alongside Sam Snead in 1954 and Jack Burke Jr. in 1956. Yet somehow Johnson, while laying up on every par five, managed to play them in 11-under for the week—better than anybody in the field (Woods was nine-under, Goosen just two-under, and Sabbatini three-under) and the key to an unexpected victory.

Winners Back In

Billy Payne took over as Masters chairman before the 2007 tournament, and one of his first moves was to restore the invitation for winning a PGA Tour event, which had been rescinded after the 1999 tournament. Payne said he recalled many times when the winner of a tournament was more excited about qualifying for the Masters than anything else, and he wanted to restore that excitement. Fall tournaments were not included (they were added for the 2015 Masters), nor were events held the same week as a bigger tournament.

2008

Like Jack Nicklaus in the 1970s, Tiger Woods openly spoke of shooting for the Grand Slam, saying early in the year that it was "easily within reach." Woods was talking about the true Grand Slam of winning all four majors in one year—which, if he did it in 2008, would mean *five* straight majors, since he won the last one of 2007.

Woods was doing nicely in non-majors, too, winning five tournaments in a row, his last two in 2007 and first three in 2008. He'd only played four events on the year, with a fifth-place finish at Doral ending his victory streak. The Masters was shaping up as Tiger against the field. The course itself was also a formidable foe, considering the carnage its toughened layout had inflicted in 2007, even if weather-related.

In Round 1, the course and field battled to something like a draw, while the field beat Tiger. That continued an opening-round theme for Woods, who never could seem to get untracked in Augusta until Friday. His 72 marked the sixth straight year he failed to break par in the first round, and at least was better than four of those years when he was over par. Woods didn't make a birdie, a factoid that comes with an asterisk since he did make an eagle, chipping in from behind the green on the 15th. That came on the heels of bogeys on the 13th, where he was next to the green in two but hit a bad pitch, and 14th. Other than that, it was all pars.

Justin Rose, on the other hand, always came out of the gate fast. He took at least a share of the first-round lead for his third straight Masters (2004, 2007, and 2008) with a 68. Unlike a year earlier, when he hit only five greens while breaking 70 in the first round, this time he hit 15 greens. It didn't promise greater things; in fact, he shot a 78 in the second round, a bigger fall than his 75 of a year ago (in 2004, his big number was a third-round 81).

The first-round co-leader was Trevor Immelman, the only player to go without a bogey on the Augusta National minefield, recording three of his birdies from between two and six feet in addition to sinking a 35-footer on the ninth hole. Immelman, Rose, and Ian Poulter had made a road trip from their homes in Orlando to practice at Augusta National two weeks before the tournament. The preparation was paying off for Poulter, too, who shot a 70 that featured a hole-in-one at the 16th.

Immelman shot another 68 in the second round to take the lead by himself. He had one bogey, a three-putt on the sixth, while making all five of his birdies on par fours, none with a putt longer than 15 feet. For the second straight day, he birdied the fifth and 11th, two of the toughest holes on the course.

Less than four months earlier, the 28-year-old was in a hospital in his native South Africa having a large tumor removed from his diaphragm. It thankfully turned out to be benign, but Immelman was in the hospital for six days and didn't pick up a golf club for several weeks. Since returning to the PGA Tour in February, he had made four of eight cuts and ranked 129th on the money list.

Immelman birdied the 17th and 18th, as did Brandt Snedeker in a 68 of his own to claim second place at 137. Woods was in a tie for 13th at 143 after a 71 that he preserved with a par from the right trees on the 18th, where he punched his second shot to the 10th fairway and hit a wedge to six feet.

Left-hander Steve Flesch had what would be the week's best round, a 67 in which he played the par fives in five-under (eagle on 13) and didn't have a bogey. He was tied for third at 139 with Phil Mickelson (bogeyless 68) and Poulter.

Immelman and Snedeker stayed in front in the third round with a 69 and 70, leaving the South African ahead by two at 11-under 205. Immelman continued his nearly mistake-free play, missing only one fairway and three greens while making just one bogey. Snedeker bogeyed his way through Amen Corner, then recovered with birdies on 14, 15, and 18, the latter getting the 27-year-old 2007 PGA Tour Rookie of the Year into the final twosome on Sunday.

Flesch and Paul Casey were at 208 and 209, respectively, the only other players within five strokes. Woods moved into fifth place by matching the day's best round with a 68 but trailed by six strokes and needed something special on Sunday. Mickelson was three shots behind through eight holes, but out of contention by the end of the round with a 75.

Through 54 holes, the course was somewhat yielding to outstanding play, as Immelman's three rounds in the 60s attested, but still a stern test with only six players better than two-under. It would turn into a monster in the final round in a swirling wind with gusts up to 23 mph. Only four players broke par, and the conditions took a particular toll on the late starters with nobody in the last 10 pairings breaking par. That played right into Immelman's hands, especially with the three players who started within five strokes of him shooting a combined 18-over (Snedeker 77, Flesch 78, Casey 79).

2008

1	Trevor Immelman	68–68–69–75—280
2	Tiger Woods	72–71–68–72—283
T3	Stewart Cink	72–69–71–72—284
T3	Brandt Snedeker	69–68–70–77—284
T5	Steve Flesch	72–67–69–78—286
T5	Padraig Harrington	74–71–69–72—286
T5	Phil Mickelson	71–68–75–72—286
T8	Miguel Angel Jimenez	77–70–72–68—287
T8	Robert Karlsson	70–73–71–73—287
T8	Andres Romero	72–72–70–73—287

Woods managed to match par 72, a reasonably good score in the wind but not what he needed. He bounced between four-under and five-under for the entire round, never getting closer than four strokes to Immelman until a birdie on 18 brought him within three and gave him a runner-up finish for the second consecutive year. "I didn't make the putts I needed to make this week," said Woods in what was now a recurring Masters theme. He missed four putts inside six feet on Sunday. There would be no Slam, either of the Grand or Tiger variety. In fact, Woods would undergo arthroscopic knee surgery two days after the Masters, return to limp to victory in the U.S. Open, and miss the rest of the year after more extensive surgery.

Immelman found himself tied for the lead when Snedeker eagled the second hole after both had bogeyed the first. Trevor quickly went back up when Snedeker bogeyed the third, the first of five bogeys in a nine-hole stretch. Immelman made a nervy par putt from eight feet on the fourth and birdied the fifth with an eight-iron to three feet to go ahead by two. He three-putted the eighth for a bogey before saving par with a 10-footer on the ninth.

At that point, Flesch, even par for the day, was closest at two strokes behind. His round took a decided turn for the worse when he hit an eight-iron into the water on 12 and double bogeyed. Meanwhile, Immelman was saving par at 11 with a 15-foot putt from the fringe to go ahead by four.

The margin went back down to three over Flesch and Snedeker when Immelman bogeyed the 12th, needing a one-putt from four feet to do that, while Snedeker birdied. There was a two-stroke swing the other way in the final twosome on the 13th when Immelman birdied with a lay-up and a wedge to three feet while Snedeker hit his second shot in the water for the second straight day and bogeyed. With Flesch making the first of four straight bogeys on the 14th, Immelman was up by five.

That gave the South African the luxury of a mistake, which he made on the 16th, where he pulled a seven-iron into the water and made a double bogey. Immelman's approach into the bunker on 17 created a bit of tension, but he got up and down from there and made a routine par on 18. His final-round 75 matched the highest for a Masters champion (Arnold Palmer, 1962). Nonetheless, his eight-under 280 total was good enough to win by three.

While aided by the travails of his would-be challengers, Immelman's victory was well deserved as he led the field in fairways hit, was T2 in greens in regulation, and T4 in putts per round. His play on the par fours was stellar; his 10-under total for four rounds still stands as the tournament record for par-four scoring.

After a total of six runner-up finishes by South Africans since 2000 (two each by Ernie Els and Retief Goosen, one each by Tim Clark and Rory Sabbatini), Immelman became the second South African to win the Masters, joining three-time champion Gary Player, from whom he received an encouraging voicemail on Saturday evening.

The Masters victory seemed to fulfill the promise Immelman had shown as an up-and-comer in his early 20s on the South African and European tours and as the 2006 PGA Tour Rookie of the Year. Instead, tendinitis sidetracked him for a couple of years and he never regained his form. At least he had his one shining moment.

A Great "Putt"

Brandt Snedeker faced an impossible putt on the sixth hole of the second round from the top right shelf to a back-left hole location—the required path would take him far into the fringe. So, he pulled out his lob wedge to take a more direct line in the air. Carefully clipping it so as not to take a divot in the putting surface, the shot came out better than even Snedeker could have hoped, bouncing and rolling into the hole for an unlikely birdie two.

2009

In the three years since the final stage of course lengthening and narrowing, there had been many complaints and criticisms from players and media that the course now forced defensive play and that the decline in birdies and eagles led to less excitement, as indicated by the diminished frequency of gallery roars.

Third-year chairman Billy Payne acknowledged that the roars were less frequent in the last couple of years. While rightfully pointing out that this was to a large degree due to the weather, his administration did set about making some tweaks to soften some of the changes. About 10 yards were added to the front of the tees on Nos. 1, 17, and 18, with the scorecard yardage reduced on the first hole and the others simply adding flexibility (the same was done to Nos. 5 and 13 the next year). Some of the recently planted trees were removed from the right side of the 15th this year after the same was done on the 11th in 2008.

During the tournament, tees were moved up on different days on various holes and the hole locations were generally more accessible, particularly in the final round. Add in the absence of a stiff wind and greens that were softer than the last couple of years—not necessarily by design—and the recipe for better scoring was in place.

Drastically better scoring, in fact. There were 19 scores in the 60s in the first round, the second most in any round in Masters history, and 38 subpar scores, the most in any first round. Chad Campbell had a great chance to tie or beat the course record of 63, playing the first 15 holes in nine-under before bogeys on 17 (bad drive) and 18 (three-putt) left him with a 65, still good for the 18-hole lead.

Campbell birdied the first five holes—the most ever at the start of the tournament—and birdied four straight on the back nine, Nos. 12–15. Both players who shot 66 also had streaks of four straight birdies, Jim Furyk on holes 14–17 and Hunter Mahan on 13–16. Only one player—Furyk—went without a bogey, a sign that the course still had enough teeth to extract a toll on virtually everyone even while vulnerable to good play.

Mahan and Campbell each had nine birdies on Thursday, and that total would be eclipsed on Friday by Anthony Kim with a tournament record of 11. It was a particularly impressive feat because this was a day with enough wind to make the scoring average about a stroke higher, with only nine rounds in the 60s. Kim's achievement was tempered by the fact that he made a double bogey on the 10th and two bogeys, resulting in a 65, which—after an opening 75—put him at 140 and five strokes off the lead. Kim had two streaks of four straight birdies, on Nos. 5–8 and 12–15.

Campbell opened up a five-stroke lead at one point on Friday, playing the first 10 holes in four-under before coming down to earth with three back-nine bogeys. A birdie on 18 gave him a 70 and a tie for the 36-hole lead with Kenny Perry, who converted solid ball-striking into a bogey-free 67.

Perry was staging a career revival at 48 years old, having won three times in the summer of 2008, starring in the Ryder Cup Matches in his native Kentucky, and adding another victory in February of 2009 at Phoenix. This was the first time he'd qualified for the Masters since 2005, and his record in Augusta wasn't encouraging—five missed cuts in eight starts and only one top-25 finish (T12 way back in 1995). The 34-year-old Campbell had missed three cuts in five tries at the Masters, but at least could point to a T3 finish in 2006 when he also led at the halfway point.

Players with thicker Masters resumes lurked, but not too closely. Two-time champion Phil Mickelson, a winner twice so far in the year, was in danger of missing the cut—which came at a record-tying low 145—until playing the last seven holes in five-under for a 68 and a 141 total to stand T11. Four-time champion Tiger Woods had a 72 for 142 with a bogey on the 18th for the second straight day. He had played only three tournaments since returning from knee surgery, but the last one was a victory at the Arnold Palmer Invitational, so he had high hopes coming to Augusta.

Those hopes were fainter after a third round where he had to rally to salvage a 70. Woods hit his drive into the trees on the first hole and made a double bogey. He drove into the woods again on the second, and had to play his second shot from his knees, salvaging a par. He visited the trees twice more during the round, yet birdied 13, 15, and 17 and saved par at 18 for a two-under round. He was tied at 212, seven strokes off the lead and in a nine-way tie for 10th. Mickelson was also in that tie after a 71 where he birdied all four par fives but no other holes. The big news at the end of the day was that Woods and Mickelson would be paired on Sunday, adding intrigue to the final round.

They were seven strokes behind two men at 205, Perry and Angel Cabrera. Perry shot a 70 with bogeys on 11 and 12 partly offsetting four birdies. "This might be the last time I have this kind of opportunity," admitted Perry, who was four months older than the oldest player ever to win a major championship, Julius Boros at the 1968 PGA.

Argentina's Cabrera owned one major at age 39, the 2007 U.S. Open, but hadn't been a big winner in his career, with three wins in Europe and only that U.S. Open in part-time play on the PGA Tour. Being one of the longest hitters in the game served him well at Augusta where he had a T8, T9, T10, and T15 in nine appearances. His opening rounds of 68–68–69 were just the same as the previous year's 54-hole leader, Trevor Immelman.

Campbell would have shared the lead if he hadn't double bogeyed the 16th hole, hitting too much club on his tee shot and leaving a very difficult bunker shot. His 72 shuffled the order of the Perry-Cabrera-Campbell trio, which remained the top three for the second straight day.

The Woods-Mickelson pairing proved to be much more than a sideshow on Sunday—each had a real chance to win the tournament. Mickelson made his move first with a record-tying 30 on the front nine. He birdied the second (12 feet), third (five feet), and fifth (14 feet), and that was just the start. The left-hander planted his tee shot three feet from the hole on the sixth, then hooked his approach shot around trees to within two feet of the hole on the seventh, turning a likely bogey into a birdie. A more normal birdie with a pitch to five feet on the eighth was followed by a par save from the bunker on No. 9.

Mickelson was within one of the lead on the 12th tee when he made a blunder by pulling a nine-iron ("a terrible swing," he called it) into Rae's Creek and making a double bogey. Birdies on 13 and 15 brought him back within one, but the latter was a four-foot miss of an eagle putt. His last chance slipped by when he missed a four-footer for birdie on 17, and a bogey on the 18th gave him a 37 on the back nine for a 67.

Woods seemed to be fighting his swing all week and arrived on the first tee following "one of the worst warmup sessions I've ever had." He proceeded to pull-hook his first drive not only over a row of trees but also to the far side of the adjacent ninth fairway. He made a par from there, and also holed putts for par from eight to 12 feet on Nos. 4, 5, 9, and 10. A birdie on the second and eagle on the eighth after a three-wood to 25 feet gave him a 33 on the front nine. His swing came together for two-putt birdies on 13 and 15 and a tee shot to four feet for a birdie on 16 that brought him to within one of the lead (at that point, Perry was 11-under, Woods and Mickelson 10-under, and Cabrera and Campbell nine-under). Woods' swing fell apart again on the last two holes, with drives into the trees left on 17 and right on 18 leading to a pair of finishing bogeys and a 68.

As it turned out, Woods and Mickelson would have needed 64s to reach a playoff. That number was decidedly within both their reaches. But, after electrifying the galleries and putting a scare into the leaders playing several holes behind them, they came up wanting in the end.

Perry parred the first 11 holes, missing a couple of short birdie putts along the way but also making a couple of nice par saves. He held at least a share of the lead all the way, except when Cabrera birdied the third hole. The Argentinian fell back with bogeys on Nos. 4, 5, and 10. Campbell chipped in for a birdie on the third and birdied the eighth to briefly tie Perry before poor drives on Nos. 9 and 10 led to bogeys.

2009

1	Angel Cabrera	68–68–69–71—276*
T2	Chad Campbell	65–70–72–69—276
T2	Kenny Perry	68–67–70–71—276
4	Shingo Katayama	67–73–70–68—278
5	Phil Mickelson	73–68–71–67—279
T6	Steve Flesch	71–74–68–67—280
T6	John Merrick	68–74–72–66—280
T6	Steve Stricker	72–69–68–71—280
T6	Tiger Woods	70–72–70–68—280
T10	Jim Furyk	66–74–68–73—281
T10	Hunter Mahan	66–75–71–69—281
T10	Sean O'Hair	68–76–68–69—281

*Cabrera won on second playoff hole

The leading trio finally got it going on the back nine. Perry birdied the 12th with a 25-foot putt from the fringe and, after a disappointing three-putt par on 13, he two-putted for a birdie on 15 and fired an eight-iron at the flag on 16 to within a foot for another birdie. Campbell birdied the 12th from 12 feet, two-putted for birdies on 13 and 15, and missed a birdie chance from six feet on 16. Cabrera found himself three behind through 12 holes, then two-putted for a birdie on 13, chipped to two feet for a birdie on 15, and matched Perry's birdie on 16 with one of his own from 14 feet.

At that point, Perry had a two-stroke lead over Cabrera and Campbell. His rivals parred 17 and 18, needing two saves from off the green by Cabrera and one by Campbell, clearing the way for Perry to become the oldest player to win a major. It would have been the crowning achievement of a career that featured 13 victories to that point (ultimately 14), with a playoff loss in the 1996 PGA Championship in his only previous brush with major glory, and a popular win for one of the tour's nicest guys.

It didn't happen. Perry hit his approach over the green on the 17th. It wasn't a particularly difficult chip shot to a hole location that was more generous than usual, but Perry skulled it across the green to the front fringe and made a bogey. His tee shot on the 18th found the first bunker on the left and his approach went left, leaving a very difficult pitch that he hit 20 feet past, and two-putted for a 71 and a 276 total. Cabrera (71) and Campbell (69) were given new life as they headed to a three-way playoff.

Cabrera got a break on the first playoff hole when his shot from the forest right of the 18th smacked a tree and caromed into the fairway instead of into deeper trouble. The other two missed the green with their approach shots, and Cabrera hit his third shot from 114 yards to eight feet to give himself a fighting chance. He calmly holed that one for par. Perry tapped in for a par after a nice chip, and Campbell eliminated himself by missing from four feet after a fine bunker shot.

Perry played the first 70 holes of regulation with only four bogeys. On the second playoff hole, the 10th, he hit his approach way left, pitched to 20 feet, and two-putted for his third bogey in four holes. Cabrera hit two solid shots and two-putted for a par from 18 feet to become the first Argentinian to win the Masters—41 years after Roberto de Vicenzo lost a chance to make a playoff as a result of his scorecard blunder.

Cabrera hadn't done much since his U.S. Open victory and was 69th in the World Ranking, the highest of any winner in Augusta since the ranking started in 1986. This Masters didn't produce an expected champion, but it did deliver plenty of drama and restore the roars. It wasn't a wholesale retreat from the Hootie Johnson era. The toughened course was left mostly intact to challenge a new generation of players wielding 21st-century golf equipment, with just enough massaging around the edges to make sure that what Cabrera called Masters "magic" wasn't lost.

2010

Golf wasn't exactly at the forefront on the Monday of Masters week when a highly anticipated media interview session with Tiger Woods took place. Woods chose the Masters for his return from five months of tournament inactivity following a scandal that erupted in November. The tawdry details included tabloid reports of extra-marital affairs and a late-night incident when he drove his car into a row of hedges and a fire hydrant close to his driveway.

The world's No. 1 golfer had gone out of public view and spent time at a rehab center, emerging in February to issue a public statement apologizing for his actions and intimating his return to golf some time during the year. Apparently, a major championship was something Woods didn't want to pass up, especially not one he had won four times.

It led to a circus of media attention, but, after other matters were dealt with— more apologies from Woods and little new information—golf was addressed. Asked about his expectations of how he might fare after such a long layoff, Woods said, "I'm going to go out there and try to win this thing."

An unlikely aspiration, it seemed. Then again this was the kind of attitude that helped fuel Woods to 14 major championship titles so far, including a 2008 U.S. Open where he limped on a leg that was due for major surgery. Tiger's return to competition was such a big deal that ESPN broke away from SportsCenter just to show his opening tee shot live.

Woods hit that tee shot down the middle and went on to shoot a 68—all the more surprising since it was the first time he had ever broken 70 in the first round at Augusta. It was also his first Masters round with two eagles, which he made on the eighth and 15th. The round could have been even better, if not for three bogeys and several makeable birdie putts missed.

There was a bit of an asterisk to the low number, as the course was vulnerable on this day with 16 rounds in the 60s and 31 below par. While there was a blustery wind, the course's teeth had been blunted. A number of tees were moved up and there was universal agreement that pin positions were accessible, leading to the abundance of red numbers.

This was one of the most intriguing first rounds ever at Augusta, and not just because of Woods. Fred Couples took the lead with a 66 at the age of 50, fresh off three straight victories in his rookie year on the senior tour. While saying that winning was "a pipe dream," the 1992 champion also said, "Can I still win? Of course." Couples tied the record for low Masters round by a player over 50 set by Ben Hogan in 1967.

Even more remarkably, 60-year-old Tom Watson birdied three of the last four holes to shoot a 67, matching his best score ever at Augusta, nine months after his spirited run at the British Open where he lost in a playoff. Watson couldn't mount that kind of sustained challenge here; still, his finish of T18 was the best ever for a player in his 60s. Couples hung in there well enough to pull within two strokes of the lead at one point in the final round before finishing sixth.

Among four others tied with Watson at 67 was Phil Mickelson, who, for the first time since 2003, didn't have a tour win before the Masters and had only one top-10 finish. The two-time champion felt that Augusta National brought out the best in him. "There's just something about this place that when I get on the golf course I don't feel like I have to be perfect. It relaxes me," said Mickelson, explaining that he could freewheel it off the tee on the relatively open course where the rough was not as penal as other majors. He felt that even if his drives ended up in the trees, he could usually get close enough to the green to rely on his short game to save pars.

The pin-setters were not as generous on Friday when in relatively similar weather conditions there were only three rounds in the 60s. Two of them were by a pair of Englishmen who shared the 36-hole lead at 136, Lee Westwood after a 69 and Ian Poulter a 68.

Westwood had finished third in the last two majors, missing a British Open playoff by one stroke with a bogey on the 72nd hole. His Masters record wasn't inspiring, with only two finishes better than 30th in 10 tries. "Over the past few years, I've found a way to plod my way around the course and feel more comfortable," he said. Certainly not as comfortable as Mickelson, but perhaps comfortable enough.

Westwood was fourth in the World Ranking and Poulter, winner of the WGC-Match Play in February, was seventh. In the group of five players next at 138 were No. 1 Woods and No. 3 Mickelson. Woods shot a three-birdie, one-bogey 70 and felt that he played as well or better than the first round, the difference being the difficulty in the course setup. Mickelson also had a relatively quiet round with three birdies in a 71, but felt better things were coming. "As soon as a couple of the 12- to 15 footers start to go in rather than catching the lips, I think I'm going to have a really low round," he said.

Mickelson had a low round on Saturday (a 67), and he did it in a more electric fashion than holing a bunch of 12-foot putts. He became the third player ever to eagle consecutive holes in the Masters, doing it on 13 and 14, the same piece of ground where Dan Pohl (1982) and Dustin Johnson (2009) accomplished it, and nearly went one better as he missed an eagle by inches on 15. A seven-iron to eight feet set up the eagle on 13 and a wedge shot from 141 yards found the hole on 14. Mickelson drove behind trees on 15, laid up, and watched his shot from 87 yards graze the cup and finish eight inches behind it for a birdie.

The three-hole burst shot Mickelson from four behind to one ahead, though he finished the day one back after a bogey on 17 and a Westwood birdie on 15.

Westwood persevered through the eagle roars ahead of him to shoot his third round in the 60s, a 69 for the 54-hole lead at 205. Poulter dropped back with a 74, leaving Woods and K.J. Choi at 208 as the only others besides Mickelson within four strokes.

Woods showed signs of both brilliance and of rust on a day that included seven birdies and five bogeys. He grabbed everyone's attention with birdies on the first and third holes to pull within one of the lead, then bogeyed three of the next four. The back nine featured three straight birdies on 13–15, a bogey at 17, and an approach to three feet for a birdie at 18.

Tiger's final round was just as erratic. He shot himself out of it by playing the first five holes three-over, hitting none of the greens in regulation, hooking his opening drive into the ninth fairway, popping up another tee shot, leaving a shot in a bunker, blading a pitch, and hitting a fat four-iron along the way. Then he summoned some of his best stuff, if only for entertainment value as he never got closer than three strokes off the lead. Woods played the last 12 holes in six-under, despite two bogeys in that stretch, with eagles on the seventh (holed eight-iron) and 15th and four birdies. A 69 gave him a tie for fourth that was better than many expected after the layoff. Perhaps even more surprising, it would be his best finish of the year.

Choi played in the charged atmosphere of Woods' group for all four days, the first two days because he was perhaps a man the pairing committee felt could handle the hubbub, and the last two by scores. The 39-year-old Korean with seven tour victories (he would finish with eight) made a strong bid for what would have been his only major title, playing the first 10 holes four-under and tying for the lead with a birdie on the 10th. Bogeys on 13 and 14 took him out of it, a 69 giving him a tie for fourth with Woods.

One more player made a run at the final twosome. Anthony Kim was a precocious 24-year-old with three tour victories, including a week earlier at Houston, not to mention his 11-birdie round in the 2009 Masters. He got on another of his runs with birdies on 13 and 14, an eagle on 15, and a birdie on 16 to get to 12-under and briefly within one stroke after starting the day seven back. He stayed 12-under for a 31 on the back nine and a 65 that turned out to be good only for third place.

Neither Westwood nor Mickelson burned it up on the front nine. Westwood went bogey-birdie on Nos. 1 and 2 and again on 4 and 5, then three-putted for a bogey on the ninth for a 37. Mickelson parred the first seven holes and took advantage of a break on the eighth when his second shot hit a tree and came back into the fairway. He hit an 84-yard shot to three feet for a birdie and moved into the lead when he parred the ninth while Westwood bogeyed.

That was the first of three straight holes where Mickelson recovered for pars after errant drives, a stretch that was just as important as the birdies that were to come later. He was in the trees on the ninth, got his second close to the green, pitched to five feet, and made the putt. The 10th was the same, except he chipped within tap-in range. He was fortunate on the 11th where his drive hit a spectator and finished in the right rough instead of deeper in the stand of trees, and he was able to hit the green and two-putt from there.

2010

1	Phil Mickelson	67–71–67–67—272
2	Lee Westwood	67–69–68–71—275
3	Anthony Kim	68–70–73–65—276
T4	K.J. Choi	67–71–70–69—277
T4	Tiger Woods	68–70–70–69—277
6	Fred Couples	66–75–68–70—279
7	Nick Watney	68–76–71–65—280
T8	Hunter Mahan	71–71–68–71—281
T8	Y.E. Yang	67–72–72–70—281
T10	Ricky Barnes	68–70–72–73—283
T10	Ian Poulter	68–68–74–73—283

The 12th hole was where Mickelson let his chances slip away with a double bogey in 2009. This time it was where he turned things in a positive direction with a tee shot to 20 feet and a birdie that put him one ahead of Choi and Kim and two clear of Westwood. An even more telling blow would come on the next hole.

Mickelson's tee shot drifted too far to the right on the 13th and came to rest on the pine needles among the trees on that side. His caddie, Jim Mackay, suggested laying up, but Mickelson was having none of that. Grabbing a six-iron, he aimed through a gap in the trees and fired at the flag, clearing the water in front and avoiding the water on the right to finish four feet from the hole. "It was one of those shots that probably only Phil could pull off," said Westwood.

Some of the bloom was taken off the rose when Mickelson missed the putt and Westwood birdied to stay within two. Still, Mickelson was now two ahead of Kim, three ahead of Choi, and had shown his mettle with the superb shot.

Mickelson birdied the 15th with a massive drive and an eight-iron to 15 feet while Westwood went over with a six-iron and couldn't get up and down. The Englishman managed to get back within two when he birdied the 17th, but the necessary birdie-bogey swing didn't materialize on the finishing hole. Westwood led the field in greens in regulation for the week and hit 15 of them in the final round but could only convert that into a 71.

As he did in his first Masters victory in 2004, Mickelson birdied the 72nd hole, on this occasion just icing on the cake when he holed his 10-footer to win by three. He almost matched his back-nine 31 of 2004 with a 32 for his third 67 of the week and a 16-under 272 total just two off the 72-hole record, further putting to rest the worries about Augusta National now being too difficult, while lifting 39-year-old Mickelson to a third Masters title, trailing only Jack Nicklaus, Arnold Palmer, and Woods.

2011

The assault on par continued in 2011 with 30 subpar rounds on Thursday and a near record 41 on Friday (behind only 47 in 1992). Rory McIlroy led the way with rounds of 65 and 69 for a two-stroke lead at the midway point.

Northern Ireland's McIlroy was already an accomplished player at the age of 21. He won the Wells Fargo Championship in North Carolina with a final-round 62 in May of 2010 just after his 21st birthday and already had three third-place finishes in major championships, including the last two. The 65 on Thursday was his sixth round of 68 or better in a major. One of those was a 63 in the 2010 British Open at St. Andrews, which he followed with a second-round 80.

His first round had the potential to be a 63, as he missed five birdie putts from inside 10 feet while making only one long putt among his seven birdies. The pairing committee had McIlroy playing with 23-year-old Jason Day and 22-year-old Rickie Fowler in the first two rounds. On Friday, Day went one better than McIlroy's opening round with a 64. Playing in his first Masters after posting his first PGA Tour victory in 2010, Day needed only 10 putts in posting a 31 on the back nine, capped by an approach to one foot on the 18th. He took over second place at the halfway point at 136, while the third young gun, Fowler, was tied for seventh at 139.

McIlroy threatened to run away and hide when he shot a 33 on the front nine of the second round, all three birdies from short range. He stalled on the back nine with his first bogey of the week at the 12th and only one birdie; still, he was ahead by two.

The trend toward relatively accessible hole locations and another year of favorable weather contributed to the low scoring, but Augusta National wasn't a pushover—it was still able to inflict pain. Day was three-over through 11 holes of the first round after a double bogey on the 11th before reeling off four straight birdies on 13–16. Retief Goosen went the other way with a 31–39 first round. Martin Kaymer, the 2010 PGA champion and newly No. 1 ranked player in the world, missed the cut with rounds of 78 and 72.

The world's former No. 1, Tiger Woods, came to Augusta still looking for answers, without a victory since 2009. His pre-tournament goal for the week was a bit more humble than the year before: "My goal is to get to the back nine on Sunday. I just want to be part of the action and let the chips fall where they may."

Woods didn't get much going in a first-round 71 and was one-over through seven holes of Round 2. Suddenly, he came alive to play the last 11 holes in seven-under for a 66 with consecutive birdies at 8–10, three more at 13–15, and a final one at the 18th. He was tied for third at 137 with K.J. Choi, who was playing well at Augusta yet again.

Largely unnoticed at 140 was 26-year-old South African Charl Schwartzel with rounds of 69, featuring a chip-in eagle at the eighth, and a scrambling 71 despite hitting only nine greens in regulation.

McIlroy expanded his lead to four strokes with a 70 in the third round. Of the top 11 players through two rounds, seven shot over par on Saturday and McIlroy's was the best score—this on a day when nine players shot in the 60s. Woods was one of the over-par scorers with a 74 in a round where he said he hit "a lot of beautiful putts that didn't go in." Not so beautiful was a miss from two feet on 11. Tiger was seven strokes behind, marking the fourth straight year he was between four and seven back heading into the final round.

McIlroy was one-over through 12 holes before finishing strong with two-putt birdies on 13 and 15 and a 33-foot birdie putt on 17 to give himself some separation. Not that he felt totally comfortable. "I know how leads can dwindle away very quickly," he said.

Four players were tied for second at 208. Day briefly had the lead when he birdied three of the first five holes before sliding back to a 72. Angel Cabrera, who hadn't done much since his 2009 Masters victory, rode his good Augusta vibes to a 67, while Choi stayed in contention with a 71. Schwartzel moved into position with a 68 that featured back-to-back birdies on 2–3 and 7–8 and two coming home on 12 and 15.

Australia's Adam Scott eagled the 13th for the second straight day, shooting a 67 to tie England's Luke Donald at 209, giving the top seven places to international players. In fact, 52 of the 99 players in the field that started the tournament were from outside the U.S., a reflection of more players from around the world playing the PGA Tour and the top 50 on the World Ranking getting in.

By the time McIlroy was standing on the second green on Sunday, he had already lost all four shots of his lead. Schwartzel started with a bang—two, actually. After missing the first green well to the right, he holed a bump-and-run six-iron—choosing that shot because he couldn't play a high lob wedge from trampled ground—for a stunning birdie. He topped himself on No. 3 by holing a 114-yard shot with a sand wedge for an eagle. McIlroy bogeyed the first hole, so both were 11-under.

That started the craziness in a final round where eight players held at least a share of the lead. One of them was Woods, who put an electric charge into the proceedings by playing the first eight holes in five-under, following birdies on Nos. 6 and 7 with a three-wood to 10 feet on the eighth and an eagle putt, setting off a roar that reverberated around the course. He holed a 20-foot putt for a par on the ninth for a 31 and was tied for first at 10-under with Schwartzel, who bogeyed the fourth, and McIlroy, who bogeyed the fifth.

Woods had gotten what he wished for, to be in it on the back nine Sunday. Then, unlike the younger Tiger, this 35-year-old version did nothing with the opportunity. He went flat on the back nine with seven pars, a three-putt bogey on the 12th with a miss from two-and-a-half feet, and a birdie on the 15th, where he missed a four-foot eagle putt. One stroke out of the lead when he finished at 10-under, he could only wait.

McIlroy birdied the seventh hole and escaped the front nine with a 37 and a one-stroke lead despite a lack of sharpness. The end would come with shocking swiftness. His drive on the 10th was hooked far to the left and was propelled even farther left when it hit a tree. The ball came to rest between two of the member cabins that line the 10th hole, far enough from the fairway that they are almost never in play. McIlroy punched out sideways to the fairway, pulled a three-wood well left of the green, hit a branch with his pitch, and walked off with a triple bogey.

A stunned McIlroy made things even worse by missing a two-foot par putt on the 11th and four-putting the 12th from 15 feet for a double bogey. "I just unraveled," he admitted. McIlroy was on the way to a 43 on the back nine, an 80, and a T15 finish—the first player to lead or share the lead after each of the first three rounds (he was tied with Alvaro Quiros after Round 1) and not finish in the top three.

McIlroy's triple bogey created a four-way tie for the lead at 10-under among Cabrera and Choi, who both made two late birdies on the front nine, along with

Schwartzel, riding a string of pars after playing the first four holes two-under, and Scott, who had a 33 on the front. Woods soon joined them to make it five at the top with his birdie that could have been an eagle on 15.

Choi and Cabrera fell out of the lead for good with bogeys on the 12th hole. Soon it was a five-way tie again with two new faces. Day followed an even-par front nine with birdies on 12

2011		
1	Charl Schwartzel	69–71–68–66—274
T2	Jason Day	72–64–72–68—276
T2	Adam Scott	72–70–67–67—276
T4	Luke Donald	72–68–69–69—278
T4	Geoff Ogilvy	69–69–73–67—278
T4	Tiger Woods	71–66–74–67—278
7	Angel Cabrera	71–70–67–71—279
T8	K.J. Choi	67–70–71–72—280
T8	Bo Van Pelt	73–69–68–70—280
10	Ryan Palmer	71–72–69–70—282

and 13 to get to 10-under, and Geoff Ogilvy came from nowhere with five straight birdies from the 12th to 16th. That made it three Australians in the leading quintet, all with a chance to become the first from their country to win the Masters.

The other two, Day and Scott, were playing together, and both had a chance to get to 11-under on the 14th. Only Scott took advantage, sinking a seven-foot putt for a birdie while Day missed a birdie putt from five feet.

Soon yet another player thrust himself into the thick of it in dramatic fashion. Bo Van Pelt eagled the 13th and the 15th, both on putts of less than 10 feet, to get to 10-under. He just as quickly dropped out of it with bogeys on 16 and 17. One more player deserves mention. Donald, who had fallen to seven-under with a double bogey at 12, birdied the 16th to get to 10-under, bogeyed 17, and then birdied the 18th in wild fashion, his approach hitting the flagstick and coming back off the front of the green, followed by a chip-in. That got him in the clubhouse with Woods and Ogilvy at 10-under.

By then, their hopes were diminishing. Scott had followed a disappointing par at 15, where his five-iron second shot went well to the right, with a tee shot to two feet at the 16th to become the first player to reach 12-under since McIlroy started the round at that figure. While Scott parred the last two holes for his second straight 67, Day got to 12-under himself with birdies on 17 and 18 from 35 and eight feet for a 68. That was great stuff from the Aussies, but behind them Schwartzel soon made it academic with an even better finish.

When the South African came to the 15th hole following a string of 10 straight pars, "I knew it was now or never," he said. He hit a six-iron over the green and chipped to eight feet. "I had so much confidence in my putting at that stage, I knew if I could relax my hands I would be able to make a proper stroke." Amid the tension and the gallery roars—Scott was about to birdie the nearby 16th—Schwartzel calmed himself and made the putt.

At this point in his career, Schwartzel had five victories on the European Tour, three of them in his native South Africa, a best finish of T14 in a major, and was playing in his second Masters. He was cool as a cucumber, though, sinking another putt on the 16th, this one from 15 feet, to tie at 12-under.

Schwartzel's tee shot at 17 drifted just far enough right that he had a tree in his line. No problem. He faded a nine-iron to 12 feet and made the putt to take the solo lead. Needing a par on the 18th, he got a birdie instead with a perfect drive, a pitching wedge to 14 feet, and yet another good putt.

In a Masters where it seemed everybody had a chance, the soft-spoken Schwartzel was the one who took charge in the end, becoming the first Masters winner to birdie the last four holes. The victory came 50 years after countryman Gary Player became the first international player to win the Masters—and in a year when there was only one U.S. player in the top seven.

2012

Bubba Watson matched the low score of the third round at the 2011 Masters with a 67 and was seven strokes off the lead, poised to perhaps make a run if Rory McIlroy faltered. Instead, Watson shot a 78 in the final round.

There was reason to think the 33-year-old lefthander had a chance in 2012. He was playing the most consistent golf of his career, with three top fives and nothing worse than T18 in seven starts leading into the Masters—on top of scoring his first three career victories in 2010–11.

The big story, though, was Tiger Woods. The once-dominant figure in the game had sat out a large part of 2011 after injuring his left Achilles tendon in the final round of the Masters when he took an awkward stance to play a shot from underneath a tree on the 17th hole. Now he had finally scored his first victory since 2009 at the Arnold Palmer Invitational two weeks before the Masters.

Then there was McIlroy, who had made a quick recovery from his Masters disaster with a victory at the 2011 U.S. Open and appeared ready to take his place as the next big thing, having won the Honda Classic in March. "Tiger Woods versus Rory McIlroy is the only story in golf today," declared *Sports Illustrated* in its Masters preview.

"I'm cool with it," said three-time champion Phil Mickelson of being overlooked even though he had won at Pebble Beach earlier in the year.

Another player not to be forgotten was England's Lee Westwood, ranked No. 3 in the world after four worldwide victories in 2011. For the second time in three years, he shot a 67 in the first round, this time giving him the lead. All seven of his birdies, including four in a row from Nos. 5–8 were from 10 feet or less.

One stroke behind were Sweden's Peter Hanson and South Africa's Louis Oosthuizen, a good friend and frequent practice round partner of last year's champion Charl Schwartzel. The 29-year-old Oosthuizen, who had missed the cut in his three previous Masters appearances, almost matched Schwartzel's 2011 Sunday feat of birdies on the last four holes, settling for a par on 17. Watson headed a group at 69.

Woods shot a 71 and admitted he had to grind because he didn't hit the ball well. His ball-striking was even worse in the second round when he hit only seven greens in regulation while shooting a 74. Recent victory notwithstanding, he wasn't all the way back, with a 72–74 weekend leaving him T40.

McIlroy also had a 71 in the first round and followed it with a nice 69 to move within one stroke of the lead. In an unlikely turn of events, the game's top young gun had a nine-hole score in the 40s for the second straight year at Augusta, a 42 on the front nine of the third round. His 77–76 scores on the weekend dropped him to a T40 with Woods.

The lead at 139 was shared by Jason Dufner and ageless wonder (at least at Augusta) Fred Couples, whose 67 nearly matched the 66 he shot as a 50-year-old in 2010. Neither would stay on the leaderboard for long on the weekend.

Westwood fell out of first with a three-putt double bogey on the 18th for a 73—140. Also at 140 were Oosthuizen, with a double bogey of his own at the second hole in a 72, and Watson, who played the last six holes in three-under for a 71.

Mickelson had an even faster finish, playing the last seven holes in four-under for a 68. He was happy to be three strokes off the midway lead after a 74 in the first round, which included a triple bogey on the 10th hole, where he suffered a lost ball after a wild tee shot into foliage on the left. "I'm putting well," Mickelson warned, having taken just 25 putts in a scrambling first round and 26 in the second.

The 41-year-old lefty put on a show on the back nine on Saturday with a 30, highlighted by a 30-foot eagle putt on the 13th, which rolled in slow motion downhill before falling into the cup. He also dazzled with a daring flop shot from behind the green on 15 to five feet for a birdie and a seven-iron from the rough to 15 feet on 18 for a closing birdie. Along with birdies on 10 and 12, following a nine-par front nine, the result was a 66.

That didn't quite get him the lead. Hanson, saying he was inspired by the cheers for Mickelson in the twosome behind him, fired a 31 on the back nine, including approaches to two feet on the 14th and three feet on the 18th. The Swede was at 207 for 54 holes, with Mickelson at 208, Oosthuizen (69) 209, Watson (70) 210, and Matt Kuchar (70) 211.

Oosthuizen hit 15 greens and felt he missed a lot of birdie chances, while Watson recovered from a slow start with birdies on 13, 15, and 18. Westwood was barely hanging in there among four players at 212 after a disappointing 72 that included a missed one-foot putt on the ninth hole.

The final round featured not one, but two shots that will forever have prominent places in Masters lore. The first was struck by Oosthuizen, a four-iron second shot to the second hole that carried 210 yards to the front of the green and rolled some 100 feet, taking a left-to-right break like a putt and toppling into the hole for a double eagle. It was just the fourth double eagle in Masters history, and the second that vaulted a player into the lead during the final round.

Gene Sarazen said after his 1935 double eagle on the 15th hole that he felt more pressure while playing the last three holes than he ever had. Oosthuizen, whose bolt from the blue came earlier in the round, said it was tough to regain his concentration over the next few holes. He scrambled for a par on the third and bogeyed the fourth.

2012

1	Bubba Watson	69–71–70–68—278*
2	Louis Oosthuizen	68–72–69–69—278
T3	Peter Hanson	68–74–65–73—280
T3	Matt Kuchar	71–70–70–69—280
T3	Phil Mickelson	74–68–66–72—280
T3	Lee Westwood	67–73–72–68—280
7	Ian Poulter	72–72–70–69—283
T8	Padraig Harrington	71–73–68–72—284
T8	Justin Rose	72–72–72–68—284
T8	Adam Scott	75–70–73–66—284

*Watson won on second playoff hole

The double eagle shot Oosthuizen into the solo lead at 10-under, Hanson having already dropped to eight-under with a bogey on the first. The Swede also bogeyed the third as he drifted backward to become a non-factor, though he made two late birdies for a 73 and a tie for third place.

A terrible shot also featured prominently in the developments of this day. Mickelson, saying he was intentionally aiming left because he didn't want to be putting from above the hole, hit his tee shot on the third even farther left where it bounced off a grandstand and finished in a bamboo stand. He needed two right-handed swipes to barely escape the jungle, dumped his next into a greenside bunker, and got up and down for a triple bogey. It was Phil's only over-par hole in the round, but enough to leave him fighting an uphill battle. Three birdies enabled him to get back to even par for the day, but the 72 only got him a tie for third, two shots back with a pair of triple bogeys on the week.

Even with bogeys on the fourth and 10th dropping him to eight-under, Oosthuizen was tied only twice after his double eagle. Matt Kuchar forged the first tie with a shot that was nearly epic, though ultimately overshadowed. He hit a three-wood from 268 yards to three feet on the 15th hole for an eagle that put him nine-under and tied with Oosthuizen, who had birdied 13.

Kuchar promptly fell back to eight-under with a bogey on 16, pushing his tee shot to the right and ultimately missing a 10-foot par putt. In the big picture, his biggest mistake came at the ninth hole, where he three-putted from seven feet for a double bogey. He had four birdies and the eagle in a 69 that put him in the tie for third.

Westwood could commiserate with Kuchar about putting; in fact, for the whole of four days his was worse as he missed five putts from inside three feet. Those gaffes were costly in the end. The Englishman played the last six holes in four-under for a 68 to finish two strokes back in the four-way tie for third.

Watson, who got a closeup view of Oosthuizen's double eagle as his fellow competitor in the next-to-last twosome, trailed by four after two holes with a bogey-birdie start. Dressed all in white, he pulled within one shot through 10 holes thanks to a 35-foot birdie putt on the fifth and the South African's two bogeys, and fell two behind with a bogey at the 12th, where he went over the green and missed a 12-foot par putt.

Bubba launched a huge drive on the 13th, hitting the green with a nine-iron second shot to match Oosthuizen's birdie and got back within a stroke with a birdie from six feet on the 14th. Both birdied the 15th, Oosthuizen with a seven-foot putt and Watson a two-putt from 20 feet after a seven-iron second shot. When Watson rolled in an eight-foot putt on the 16th for a fourth straight birdie, the two were tied.

They both made the 17th hole interesting, Watson with an escape from the trees to hit the green with his second shot and Oosthuizen an up-and-down from the bunker with a four-foot putt. Pars on 18 sent them back to the tee for a playoff at 10-under 278, Watson with a 68 and Oosthuizen a 69. In the last three days, Bubba played the final six holes a total of 10-under, toying with the par-five 13th and 15th by hitting short-iron second shots and making a pair of birdies each day.

Watson had lost the PGA Championship in a playoff in 2010, the same year Oosthuizen won the British Open. Both had good birdie chances on the first extra hole, No. 18, Oosthuizen barely missing from 14 feet and Watson not quite as close from 10 feet.

Bubba hit a huge hook off the 10th tee deep into the trees. Fortunately, he had an arsenal of creative shots to escape trouble. The first time his caddie, Ted Scott, worked for him, Watson told him, "If I've got a swing, I've got a shot." Scott reminded his player of that as they walked toward the ball in the woods.

Watson indeed had an unrestricted swing and an opening through the trees—but one that required a 40-yard hook with a gap wedge on a shot of about 160 yards. Too much to ask from most players, but not Bubba, who controlled the trajectory and the flight pattern so well that it hooked not only at the green but at the flagstick, finishing 12 feet away.

Oosthuizen's tee shot caught a break when it hit a tree and dropped into the rough, leaving a clear shot. His five-iron came up short of the green, though, and his pitch ran 15 feet too far. He narrowly missed the par putt, enabling Watson to two-putt for a victory. "I hit a crazy shot that I saw in my head, and somehow I'm in a green jacket," said Watson in a post-round daze—perhaps even more emotional in victory because he and his wife had just completed adoption of a baby boy the week before.

Eight Is More Than Enough

Henrik Stenson had a great first round going—until the 18th hole. The Swede shot a 31 on the front nine with two eagles and birdied the 10th to get to six-under. He was five-under going to the finishing hole, where a par would have given him a share of the lead. Instead, he made a quadruple bogey eight that matched the highest score ever on the 18th. His drive was way left, he hit a tree with his first escape attempt, punched out sideways, knocked a wedge over the green, chunked a pitch, chipped to three feet, and missed. His tournament followed a similar pattern. Despite the crazy eight, his first three rounds of 71–71–70 had him within five strokes of the lead, only to shoot an 81 on Sunday.

2013

Finally, Tiger Woods was back in form. He had won six tournaments since the last Masters, three in 2013, and the last two in a row—the WGC-Cadillac Championship at Doral and the Arnold Palmer Invitational. His putting had come around thanks to an hour-long session with Steve Stricker before the Doral event, where Stricker ended up finishing second to Woods.

Tiger was a 7-to-2 favorite and opened with a 70—not great, but not altogether bad news, since he had shot a first-round 70 in three of his four victories and had only broken 70 in the first round once. With calm conditions, the low-scoring trend of recent years continued as Sergio Garcia and Marc Leishman led with 66s.

Only last year after a T12 finish, a dejected Garcia told reporters, "I'm not good enough. I don't have the thing I need to have." When asked if he meant at the Masters, he said, "In any major." But over the years he seemed more negative about the Masters than other majors, and he didn't even seem all that confident after his 66. "Obviously, it's not my most favorite place, but we'll try to enjoy it as much as we can," he said.

Leishman was one of three Australians who would have a chance this year to become the first from their golf-rich country to win the Masters—the only major no Aussie had ever won. He hung around all week, ultimately finishing T4. Two other Aussies would come down the stretch with an even better chance to win, Adam Scott and Jason Day.

Scott opened with a 69, an encouraging sign compared to the last couple of years. He had a first-round 72 in 2011 when he went 67–67 on the weekend to finish T2 and a 75 in 2012 when he closed with a 66 for T8. "I think I've certainly developed a real level of comfort with the golf course in the last three years, so I'm quietly confident that I can make it happen one of these years," he said before the tournament began.

Day surged to the 36-hole lead with a second-round 68 that was the best of the day in gusty winds that produced a scoring average of 74.183, about a stroke higher than the first round. He had six birdies and two bogeys, including a save on the 12th hole, where his tee shot found the water.

The 25-year-old was playing in only his third Masters, having tied for second with Scott in his 2011 debut and been forced to withdraw during the second round due to an injury in 2012. Day had already decided it was his favorite tournament and arrived on the previous Friday to fully prepare.

The second round was most notable for a controversy involving Woods. He came to the 15th hole three-under for the day, laid up after a drive to the right, and hit a deadly accurate third shot that struck the flagstick on the fly and caromed straight back into the pond in front of the green, a horrible break. Woods took a penalty drop, hit it close, and made the putt for a six on the scorecard. With a three-putt bogey on the 18th, he signed for a score of 71.

The next morning, his score turned into a 73. During a post-round television interview, Woods stated that he dropped the ball two yards behind the spot of his previous stroke in order to avoid flying long again. This was a problem, because the Rules of Golf required dropping as nearly as possible to the point last played from. At 11 p.m., competition chairman Fred Ridley was informed of the interview by CBS, and he contacted Woods' agent to set up a meeting Saturday morning.

At that meeting, Woods admitted he didn't drop at the required spot, saying he hadn't thought about the specifics of the rule because he was "a little ticked" at what happened with the flagstick. Normally, Woods would have been disqualified for signing an incorrect scorecard that didn't include a penalty for playing from the wrong place. But Ridley invoked a clause whereby Woods could retroactively be charged the two-stroke penalty while the disqualification was waived under extraordinary circumstances. The reasoning: A television viewer had called in during the round to say that Woods hadn't dropped at the proper spot, the committee had reviewed the video (on which the proper spot wasn't clearly obvious), determined there was no penalty, and allowed Woods to sign his scorecard. Some called for Woods to withdraw, but he reasoned that if the committee had ruled he could play, he would play. He started the third round T19 at 143 instead of T7 at 141.

Garcia had a joyless and birdie-less 76 in the second round; he would make only a slight recovery for a T8 finish. Dustin Johnson had a quicker collapse. After a first-round 67, he was six-under for the tournament through 13 holes on Friday before playing the last five holes in six-over.

On Saturday, Woods was able to put the turmoil of the morning out of his mind to shoot a scrambling 70 with birdies on 12, 13, and 15 and a 12-foot par putt on 18 keeping him in the hunt, four strokes behind—similar to his position in every year from 2008 to 2011.

Day chugged along with pars on each of the first 16 holes except for a birdie at the 13th, and clung to the lead as greens that were firming up forced defensive play. A three-putt bogey at the 17th and three from the fringe for a bogey at the 18th saddled him with a 73 to trail by two.

Angel Cabrera and Brandt Snedeker moved into the lead with 69s for 209 totals. The 43-year-old Cabrera was now the 269th-ranked player in the world, but Augusta brought out the best in him. Snedeker was looking to better his showing in 2008 when as a Masters rookie he had entered the final round one stroke behind only to shoot a 77. "I had no clue what I was doing in 2008," he said. "I had no game plan."

Scott proceeded around the course cautiously with only one bogey and finished strong with birdies on 13, 15, and 17 for a 69 to stand one stroke off the lead. The 32-year-old had decided in 2011 to focus more on the majors, building his schedule around them and learning to rein in his aggression when necessary. He still hadn't won a major, but the plan worked well enough to get him into contention, finishing T2 in Augusta two years ago and suffering a dispiriting loss in 2012 at the British Open, where he blew a four-stroke lead with bogeys on the last four holes.

Then there was the matter of bearing the weight of a country on his shoulders—a burden shared with Day and Leishman. The pressure of trying to become the first Australian to win the Masters "is just a fact; you can't not deal with that," Scott said.

Snedeker birdied the first hole on Sunday to briefly take the lead, was two strokes back after an even-par front nine, then dropped out of the race with bogeys on 10 (miss from three feet) and 11 on the way to a back-nine 38 and 74.

Up ahead, the attention was on Woods, but he waited way too late to get anything going. Two over through seven, he birdied Nos. 9, 10, 13, and 15, never getting closer than three strokes from the lead and finishing with a 70. He ended

2013

1	Adam Scott	69–72–69–69—279*
2	Angel Cabrera	71–69–69–70—279
3	Jason Day	70–68–73–70—281
T4	Marc Leishman	66–73–72–72—283
T4	Tiger Woods	70–73–70–70—283
T6	Thorbjorn Olesen	78–70–68–68—284
T6	Brandt Snedeker	70–70–69–75—284
T8	Sergio Garcia	66–76–73–70—285
T8	Matt Kuchar	68–75–69–73—285
T8	Lee Westwood	70–71–73–71—285

*Scott won on second playoff hole

up four strokes behind, so the penalty for the bad drop didn't cost him the title. But what about the bad break of the flagstick-to-water bounce? Including the ensuing penalty, that cost him three or four strokes, depending on whether or not he would have made a birdie if the flagstick hadn't gotten in the way. So, we'll never know. In any case, he had now gone eight years without a Masters victory, with seven top-six finishes in that span.

Cabrera assumed a two-stroke lead at the turn with a 34 on the front, making birdies on the second and seventh. Day started birdie-eagle, holing out from a bunker to take the lead on the second hole in nearly as dramatic fashion as Louis Oosthuizen a year earlier. Bogeys on the seventh and ninth, however, dropped him three off Cabrera's pace.

Scott bogeyed the first hole after a drive to the left and birdied the third with a 20-foot putt and otherwise made pars on the front nine. A three-putt par at the eighth was a disappointment, and he trailed by three at the turn. "I just kept plugging away, and I didn't know if it was going to happen through nine," Scott said.

He was piecing together a solid, if unspectacular, ball-striking round, hitting 15 greens in regulation (he led that stat for the week) and all nine on the back nine without getting any full shots inside 10 feet but most of them within 25. Scott made his move on the par fives on the back nine. He took advantage of a break on the 13th, where his seven-iron second shot came back off the green and started rolling down the bank of the hazard but stopped before reaching the water. He pitched to two feet and birdied, then birdied the 15th with a two-putt from 25 feet.

Cabrera slipped to seven-under with bogeys on 10 and 13, the latter where he tried a second shot from the pine needles. He came oh-so-close to pulling off a "Mickelson," the ball landing high on the bank of the creek before rolling back in. Day took up the mantle with consecutive birdies on 13 (bunker shot to three feet), 14 (12 feet), and 15 (two-putt) to get to nine-under.

Day's lead was short-lived. He hit his tee shot over the green on the 16th, used a putter from the fringe to five feet, and missed the par putt. Scott birded 15 at about the same time, creating a two-way tie at eight-under before Day made a second straight bogey, hitting an eight-iron into the bunker on 17 and missing from 15 feet. Cabrera took Day's place in the tie with Scott, making a birdie from 15 feet on the 16th just as he had done in his 2009 victory.

The rain that started falling when the leaders were early on the back nine was coming down harder now as Scott looked over a 25-foot birdie putt on the 18th. "I felt I had to seize it right there, put all the pressure on the guy in the fairway

[Cabrera, in the twosome behind had hit his tee shot on 18]," said Scott. The ball caught the left lip and dropped. Showing clearly what was on his mind, Scott yelled, "C'mon Aussie!" so loud that it could be heard above the din of the gallery.

Cabrera wasn't rattled. He rifled his approach shot to two feet from the hole to match Scott's birdie, sending him to a Masters playoff for the second time.

Both came up short of the green on the first playoff hole, the 18th. Cabrera nearly ended it, his chip rolling over the right edge. Scott matched the par with a three-foot putt. With dark clouds promising an imminent onset of darkness, both played the 10th in textbook fashion, driving in the fairway and hitting approaches into makeable birdie range. Cabrera's 15-foot putt curled around the edge of the hole, stopping perched on the back lip—another narrow miss. Scott got a read on his 12-footer from caddie Steve Williams, who toted for Woods in three of his Augusta victories, and knocked it in the center of the hole.

Afterward, Scott saluted Greg Norman, the Australian who had come so close in so many Masters and served as a mentor to him early in his career. "Part of this belongs to him," said Scott. "He inspired a nation of golfers."

Youth Is Served (With a Penalty)

The two-stroke penalty added to Tiger Woods' score wasn't the only controversial second-round ruling. China's Tianlang Guan, the youngest Masters competitor ever at 14 years old, was given a one-stroke slow-play penalty for taking too long to play a shot on the 17th hole after his group was on the clock. Fortunately, the Asia-Pacific Amateur champion made the cut on the number at 148 even with the penalty, ultimately finishing 58th.

2014

It had been 35 years since a first-time participant won the Masters (Fuzzy Zoeller in 1979), but an exceptional crop of Augusta rookies made it a more realistic possibility than usual this year. There was Jordan Spieth, the 20-year-old who won as a teenager on the PGA Tour in 2013; Patrick Reed and Jimmy Walker, multiple winners on tour over the last eight months; seven other players in the top 50 of the World Ranking; and Jonas Blixt, 54th in the ranking but fourth in the 2013 PGA Championship.

They didn't have to worry about beating Tiger Woods, who underwent back surgery 10 days before the tournament and was absent from the field for the first time since 1994.

Blixt had a chance for the first-round lead before bogeys on 15 and 18 dropped him to a 70, two strokes behind first-place Bill Haas (who would soon drop out of sight with a 78 in the second round). The greens were firmer and faster than they'd been in years, yet the pin-setting committee turned away from its recently lenient stance, presenting the field with hole locations that players labeled anywhere from "brutal" to "on the tougher side."

The scoring average was 74.47 on a day when playing for the center of greens was a better bet than firing at flags close to the edges. Surprisingly, one of the players opting for the safer strategy was Bubba Watson, who hit 16 greens in regulation and missed by less than three feet on the other two. "Just trying to make par and throw in a birdie here and there," said Watson, putting Bubba Golf on the shelf, at least temporarily. It worked, as he shot a bogey-free 69. Spieth played similarly, hitting 15 greens, except that two three-putt bogeys left him with a 71.

Watson grabbed a three-stroke lead with a 68 in similar conditions in the second round, playing a bit more boldly. When Bubba won in 2012, he had birdied four straight holes starting at the 13th. He went one better in this round, starting a five-birdie run at the 12th with a tee shot to three feet and ending it at the 16th with a near ace. In between, he had a two-putt birdie and an up-and-down on the two par fives and holed a 40-foot bomb on the 14th. Bogeys on Nos. 9 and 18 were his first two of the tournament.

Spieth (70) and Blixt (71) reversed their scores of the first round and were in a tie for third at 141, Spieth benefiting from an eagle at the 15th. Defending champion Adam Scott was also at that number, but chances for a repeat went out the window with a 40 on the front nine of a third-round 76. Fellow Australian Marc Leishman's fall from grace came on Friday. He birdied the first three holes of the second round to take the lead at five-under, then went 10-over the rest of the way for a 79 and missed the cut.

Watson went ahead by five strokes with a bogey-eagle start on Saturday only to see it vanish by the time he finished the eighth hole after bogeys on Nos. 4, 6, and 7 to drop to five-under. He got to six-under with a birdie at the 10th, and was frustrated by not going lower considering that he had nine-iron second shots to both par fives on the back nine (a three-putt par and a failure to get up and down). Then he slipped back to five-under with a bogey on the 16th and a third-round 74.

Several others got to five-under, but Spieth was the only one to stay there, ending the day tied for the lead with Watson. Birdies on 14 and 15 delivered a 70 for Spieth, the best score among the last seven twosomes as the greens became dangerously slick late in the day. "You just have to accept par and accept the fact that you're going to have some wicked fast putts," Spieth said with a maturity that belied his youth.

Playing ahead of the other leaders, Matt Kuchar birdied 13, 14, and 15 to reach five-under before a bogey at 18 left him with a 68. Blixt bogeyed 17 to also enter the final round one out of the lead. Denmark's Thomas Bjorn was five-under at the turn, then hit into the water on both 13 and 15 for bogeys and finished two-under.

Spain's 50-year-old Miguel Angel Jimenez made the biggest splash in the third round with a 66 to match the record of Ben Hogan and Fred Couples for the best score by a senior player and pull within two of the lead at three-under, along with a player literally half his age, Rickie Fowler (67). In all, there were 13 players trailing by between one and five strokes.

Threats from that corps of contenders, which also included such stalwarts as Couples, Lee Westwood, Jim Furyk, and Justin Rose, never materialized except for a very early one from Kuchar that flamed out quickly. The Georgia Tech alum birdied the second and third holes to tie for the lead at six-under, and promptly four-putted the fourth hole, a slick and dangerous surface (Brandt Snedeker, one of the tour's best putters, five-putted from six feet there on Saturday). He went on to shoot a 74, as the tournament settled into a duel between Watson and Spieth in the final twosome.

It was quite a duel on the front nine. Spieth jumped ahead by two early with a birdie on the second from 15 feet and a Watson bogey on the third from over the green. Spieth answered Watson's great tee shot to seven feet on the long par-three fourth with a hole-out from the front bunker for a birdie; Watson made the putt to stay within two. Bubba pulled within one with a four-foot par save on the fifth, while Spieth visited another bunker and came away with a bogey this time.

The pair traded birdies on the sixth, giving them four twos on the front-nine par threes, Watson from 12 feet and Spieth from three. Jordan went back ahead by two with a 12-foot birdie putt on the seventh, where Watson avoided a larger deficit with a brilliant bunker shot that came back down the slope to within a foot.

The tournament took a dramatic, and permanent, shift in Watson's direction on the eighth and ninth holes, where a pair of two-stroke swings in his favor put him ahead by two. Spieth, after playing the first seven holes three-under, three-putted for a bogey on the eighth, missing a four-footer. He committed the cardinal sin on the ninth: hitting his approach shot short of the front pin and having it roll back down the green's false front into the fairway. A missed five-foot putt saddled him with a second consecutive bogey.

Watson blasted a huge drive on the eighth, hit a five-iron second shot over the green on the uphill par five, and chipped to two feet for a birdie. Another big drive on the ninth left a wedge. He hit it to 15 feet and deftly sank a big-breaking putt for a 33 on the front nine and a two-stroke lead.

Intrigue was maintained through the first part of the back nine. Watson lost a stroke on the 10th when he left himself a tough pitch and bogeyed, while Spieth saved par from a bunker. The youngster missed a chance to tie when he couldn't convert a 12-foot birdie putt on the 11th. Spieth committed his second cardinal sin— or rookie mistake—on the 12th when he decided while standing over the ball to try to fade his tee shot to the back right pin instead of just hitting to the center of the green. The ball landed a foot short of the green and rolled back down the bank into the water. Spieth kept himself in the game by making a bogey putt from 12 feet.

Watson delivered a crushing blow on the 13th—literally and figuratively. His tee shot flew the tall trees on the corner, cutting off more of the dogleg than anyone had ever seen, leaving him a 144-yard second shot with a sand wedge. "That's not the line I really wanted to go on," said Watson. "I knew I hit it really hard. I could start breathing again once I heard them clapping and roaring." Watson two-putted for a birdie to go three ahead of Spieth, who drove to the right, laid up not far past Watson's tee shot, and missed a 10-foot birdie putt.

Both parred in from there, maintaining the three-stroke margin. The 15th delivered one moment of Bubba Golf when he cut a six-iron through a gap in the trees instead of laying up on his second shot. He settled for a par from behind the green,

2014		
1	Bubba Watson	69–68–74–69—280
T2	Jonas Blixt	70–71–71–71—283
T2	Jordan Spieth	71–70–70–72—283
4	Miguel Angel Jimenez	71–76–66–71—284
T5	Rickie Fowler	71–75–67–73—286
T5	Matt Kuchar	73–71–68–74—286
7	Lee Westwood	73–71–70–73—287
T8	Thomas Bjorn	73–68–73–74—288
T8	Bernhard Langer	72–74–73–69—288
T8	Rory McIlroy	71–77–71–69—288
T8	John Senden	72–68–75–73—288
T8	Kevin Stadler	70–73–72–73—288
T8	Jimmy Walker	70–72–76–70—288

while Spieth missed a birdie chance from seven feet. The final bit of suspense came on the 17th green, where Watson holed a six-foot par putt and vigorously punched the air with his fist in celebration of being ahead by three instead of two heading to the last hole.

Blixt tied Spieth for second with a two-birdie, one-bogey 71 for a 283 total, the birdies coming late in the round. Spieth played the last 11 holes in three-over for a disappointing 72. Zoeller's status as the last first-timer to win was intact. So was the record for the youngest to win the Masters, Woods at 21 in 1997.

Watson's 69 was the only sub-70 round in the last 11 twosomes, and his eight-under 280 total a strong showing in a year when only seven players were under par for 72 holes. He did a bit more scrambling on Sunday than the early rounds, but either way he was able to avoid bogeys—his nine bogeys for the week were the least over-par holes of anyone. And he kept his prodigious drives in play, ranking a solid T13 in fairways hit.

"The shot from the woods [in the 2012 playoff] made me famous, but this one was a lot better for my nerves," he said.

Rory's 40s

From 2011 to 2014, Rory McIlroy won 12 tournaments worldwide, four of them majors. He had his problems at the Masters, though, shooting in the 40s for nine holes in each of the four years. It started with the back-nine 43 to blow the lead on Sunday in 2011, continued with a 42 on the front nine of the third round in 2012 after being one stroke out of the lead through 36 holes, a 42 on the back nine of the third round in 2013, and a 40 on the back nine of the second round in 2014 that gave him a 77. This time he recovered with 71–69 on the weekend for his best Masters finish to date, a T8.

2015–2020

A Precocious Youth, a Comeback, and a November Masters

Never has a young player made such an immediate impact on the Masters as did Jordan Spieth over his first half decade as a competitor—not Jack Nicklaus, Seve Ballesteros, nor even Tiger Woods. Spieth was a fixture at the top of the leaderboard. After sharing the 54-hole lead in his Masters debut as a 20-year-old in 2014, Spieth sat atop the field at the end of a record seven straight rounds in 2015-16 and added an 18-hole lead in 2018. His first five Masters finishes: T2-1-T2-T11-T3, all before reaching the age of 25.

Spieth posted five rounds of 66 or better in those five years (two 64s and three 66s) and tied the 72-hole scoring record of 270 in his 2015 victory. He didn't overwhelm the course with power in the mold of a young Nicklaus or Woods; instead, he found ways to cut strokes with all aspects of his game. As successful as he was, there were still chinks in the armor, as revealed in a back-nine meltdown to lose the lead in 2016 among a number of other over-par rounds.

Another young talent hurt by inconsistency at Augusta was Rory McIlroy, who completed the other three legs of the Grand Slam but found frustration in his annual Masters quest. The Northern Irishman finished in the top 10 every year from 2014 to 2018, but never better than fourth as he was unable to string together four good rounds. Perhaps he could take solace in the story of Sergio Garcia, a former young phenom who finally broke through at the age of 37 after years of frustration to win the Masters in 2017.

A different kind of perseverance paid off for Woods in a dramatic 2019 victory. The event in some ways evoked the iconic 1986 triumph of a 46-year-old Nicklaus in that the 43-year-old Woods was a great past champion who seemed unlikely to win again, and had to fight off a host of contenders in a thrilling back nine. But while Nicklaus was merely considered to be past his prime, Woods' victory was a comeback from a debilitating back condition that required four surgeries and side-lined him for two entire years. There was no better setting for a return to glory than Augusta National and the Masters.

Through this period, the course continued to shine as a major venue. It yielded low scores to great play under the right conditions, such as Spieth's performance in 2015, or Johnson's record-breaking 268 total for 72 holes in 2020, while retaining enough danger and treachery to demolish the hopes of a player not on his game, such as Spieth in the final round of 2016. Entering the back nine, a score of 30 and a score of 40 are both realistic possibilities for any contender, making for drama unsurpassed by any other venue.   .

2015

After losing a lead during the final round and finishing second the year before, Jordan Spieth lamented, "It stings right now. The only thing I'm thinking about is when am I getting back next year."

Next year was here, and Spieth was entering the Masters in top form with a win and two runner-up finishes in his last three starts. Even so, he was not the prime story in tournament previews.

Rory McIlroy had won the last two majors of 2014, the British Open and the PGA Championship. A victory at the Masters would give the 25-year-old Northern Irishman a third straight major and a career Grand Slam at the same time.

Then there was Tiger Woods. His return from 2014 back surgery had thus far been disastrous. He'd played only six events since returning the previous summer, finishing in the money in just one. In his two 2015 starts, he went 73-82 at Phoenix and withdrew after 11 holes in San Diego, saying that he needed to work on his game and wouldn't come back until he was ready to play at the highest level. Two months later, he was finally returning to the tour at the Masters. The circumstances were different, but the questions surrounding how well he could play after a long absence echoed those of 2010.

Spieth grabbed the spotlight in the first round with a 64 for a three-stroke lead. Two-under through seven, he collected six birdies on the next seven holes, at Nos. 8-10 and 12-14. The last of those came on a seven-iron from the rough that was still rolling fast when it hit the flagstick and stopped three feet away.

At eight-under through 14, the course record of 63 was in sight, but he made his only bogey of the day at the 15th, where his hybrid second shot finished way over the green and he failed to reach the putting surface with his first pitch. A 20-foot birdie putt on the 18th got him back to eight-under at the finish. "I wasn't aware what the course record was here," said Spieth, who had 10-under on his mind mainly because it would have been the lowest he shot anywhere.

The course was ripe for scoring, with greens that were commonly described as "receptive" and would stay that way all week with a little bit of overnight rain. Four players shot 67s, including Justin Rose in yet another of his fast starts at Augusta. McIlroy had a disappointing 71 and Woods was at 73. The good news for Tiger was that there was no sign of the chipping yips that plagued him in his earlier 2015 starts. The bad news was that he was spraying the ball around the course, with four drives into the trees or adjacent fairways.

Spieth hardly slowed down on Friday, shooting a 66 for a record 36-hole total of 130. He didn't have a bogey, with his birdies coming on two tough par fours—the fifth and 10th—and all four par fives. A chip and short putt for a birdie on the second was fairly routine, but the eighth hole was anything but. Spieth's drive plugged in the lip of a fairway bunker, and all he could do was blast out with a sand wedge. Still 228 yards from the hole, he pulled out a hybrid and hit it to three feet. He laid up on both back-nine par fives, after a drive into the trees on 13 and into the wind on 15, wedging to eight feet each time.

When questioned about his ability to play so well at such a young age on a course where experience was considered to be a major factor, Spieth pointed to Seve Ballesteros winning at 23 and Woods at 21. "It means it can be done," he said.

The young Texan wasn't overpowering the course in the manner of Seve or Tiger, yet his scoring ability was no less impressive. His strength essentially was that his game had no weaknesses—and there was also his preternatural maturity, which made him seem like a wise old head instead of a callow youngster.

Charley Hoffman was second at 135 after a 68, and it was two more strokes back to Rose, Dustin Johnson (who set a Masters record of three eagles in a round), and Paul Casey. Rose, with his history of falling back after strong early rounds, could have thought "here we go again" after playing the first four holes three-over, but recovered for a 70. Phil Mickelson, age 44 and coming off a winless season, showed signs of life with a 32 on the back nine for a 68 and sixth place at 138.

McIlroy and Woods were in a group T19 at 142. McIlroy's unfathomable nine-hole blowups continued at Augusta as he shot a 40 on the front nine—his fifth straight year with a nine in the 40s—but he rallied for a 31 on the back. Woods rediscovered his long game, hitting 14 greens while shooting a 69.

Spieth didn't exactly sit on the lead Saturday, as he played aggressively enough to make seven birdies. He also had three bogeys through 16 holes; still, he had built a seven-stroke lead at that point. Then he made what he later called a mistake, hitting a driver on the downwind 17th. He found the trees and ended up with a double bogey. He almost gave a stroke away on the 18th, too, hitting his second shot right of the green in a very tough position. Demonstrating in equal parts his short-game touch and his coolness under pressure, Spieth lofted a risky flop shot and got it to stop nine feet from the hole. He sank the putt for a 70 and a 54-hole record 200, preserving a four-stroke lead over Rose, who clawed back from near oblivion with birdies on five of the last six holes for a 67.

The 34-year-old Englishman birdied Nos. 13-16, capping that four-hole stretch with a hole-out from a bunker, and added a 20-foot birdie putt on the 18th. Mickelson followed his 32 on the back nine Friday with a 32 on the front nine in the third round, slowing down a bit for a 67 to claim third at 205. Hoffman (71) was at 206, so with three pursuers inside six strokes the final round wouldn't necessarily be a cakewalk for Spieth. Nobody else was closer than 10 strokes, though. Woods,

McIlroy, and Johnson would have been a formidable trio in a tie for fifth if they hadn't been so far behind.

Woods, who moved up with a 68, invoked the precedents of collapses by Greg Norman and McIlroy, saying, "Anything can happen." McIlroy also had a 68, but could have been a little closer if not for bogeys on 16 and 18. Tiger and Rory were paired on Sunday, reminiscent of the marquee Woods-Mickelson pairing that went out ahead of the leaders in 2009.

Unlike 2009, the early-starting duo didn't put any pressure on the leaders. Woods hit only two fairways all day—none until the 13th—and seven greens in regulation, scrambling to a 73. McIlroy parred the first six holes before playing the last 12 in six-under to match Hideki Matsuyama for the best score of the day, a 66. Rory finished fourth at 276 by playing the last 45 holes in 15-under, yet was simply too far off Spieth's hot pace to be a factor.

A combination of soft greens, little wind, and a number of birdie-favoring pin positions made it the lowest scoring round in Masters history to date, with the field averaging 70.91. None of the trio within realistic striking distance of Spieth was able to take advantage to shoot a mid-60s round, but the last round wasn't completely without suspense.

Rose birdied Nos. 1 and 2 to make it seven birdies in his last eight holes, dating back to the third round. That brought him within three, Spieth having birdied the first hole from 11 feet but taken three from the fringe to par the second. The margin bounced back and forth from three to four strokes on the next few holes in the final twosome—a Spieth birdie at the third (big-breaking 15-footer), a Spieth bogey at the fifth (poor drive, eventually made a six-foot bogey putt), a Rose bogey at the sixth, and a Spieth bogey at the seventh (missed a five-foot putt after Rose made an unlikely up-and-down for a par). For the second year in a row, the eighth and ninth holes were a turning point, this time in Spieth's favor.

Jordan birdied the eighth with a chip to three feet to go ahead by four, and went up by five for the first time in the round when Rose three-putted the ninth for a bogey while Spieth's second shot stayed up inches clear of rolling back down the false front—what a difference a year makes. A 23-foot birdie putt at the 10th gave Spieth a six-stroke advantage over Rose and Mickelson.

Phil got within four twice, first with a birdie at 13 while Spieth three-putted for a bogey at the 12th and then when he followed a bogey at 14 with a hole-out from the bunker to eagle 15. Three pars followed, giving Mickelson a 69 and a 14-under 274 total.

The game of inches worked in Spieth's favor again at the 13th, where he aimed left of the pin and pushed his five-iron second shot right at the flag, barely clearing the hazard for a two-putt birdie. Rose made one last move with birdies on 13, 14, and 15, Spieth getting up and down for a birdie on 15 to lead by four and become the first player ever to reach 19-under at the Masters.

One last moment of mini-drama occurred on the 16th where Spieth missed the green to the left and Rose had a 15-foot putt for a birdie. A two-stroke swing would close the margin to two. Instead, Rose missed his putt and Spieth holed a downhill eight-footer for a par.

The only remaining question was whether Spieth would break Woods' 72-hole scoring record. He let that slip away with a bogey on 18, coming up short with his approach, chipping on, and missing from five feet to post a 70 and a record-tying 270 total. (Rose also bogeyed 18 for a 70 to end up in a tie for second

2015		
1	Jordan Spieth	64-66-70-70—270
T2	Phil Mickelson	70-68-67-69—274
T2	Justin Rose	67-70-67-70—274
4	Rory McIlroy	71-71-68-66—276
5	Hideki Matsuyama	71-70-70-66—277
T6	Paul Casey	69-68-74-68—279
T6	Dustin Johnson	70-67-73-69—279
T6	Ian Poulter	73-72-67-67—279
T9	Charley Hoffman	67-68-71-74—280
T9	Zach Johnson	72-72-68-68—280
T9	Hunter Mahan	75-70-68-67—280

with Mickelson. At least he'd held it together for four rounds this time.)

Spieth also came up just short of another Woods record from 1997, the youngest ever to win. Woods was 21 years, three months; Spieth 21 years, eight months in 2015. Spieth missed his opportunity for *that* record when he finished second a year earlier. By historical pattern, he *should* have won then. Jack Nicklaus became the youngest winner in 1963, Ballesteros 17 years later in 1980, and Woods 17 years after that. Spieth was a year off schedule, but no less a phenom.

2016

Jordan Spieth followed his 2015 Masters title with a victory at the U.S. Open and made a real bid for a Grand Slam, finishing T4 at the British Open and second at the PGA Championship. He won five times on the year, including the Tour Championship, to capture the season-long FedExCup, and started 2016 by winning the Tournament of Champions with a 30-under-par total.

Despite all of that, Spieth wasn't even ranked No. 1 in the world by the time the Masters rolled around in April. Jason Day had won six times since last July, including the 2015 PGA Championship and his last two events before the Masters, the Arnold Palmer Invitational and WGC-Match Play, taking over the top spot in the World Ranking. Not to be forgotten was world No. 3 Rory McIlroy, giving the game a trio of 20-somethings (Spieth 22, McIlroy 26, Day 28) playing great golf and filling the void left by Tiger Woods, absent from this Masters—and the entire 2016 season—due to a pair of back surgeries in the fall of 2015.

Spieth picked up where he left off after his wire-to-wire 2015 Masters victory by shooting a 66 on Thursday to lead for the fifth consecutive round in Augusta. "I'm still trying to figure out why people think I'm struggling," said the Texan, who had finished between T9 and T21 in five of his six starts since the season-opening win.

It came on a day when winds ranged from 12 to 26 mph and Spieth said he would have taken a 70 before he teed off. He called it "one of the best rounds I've played," right up there with the 64 in last year's first round. The defending champion had six birdies and, just as importantly, no bogeys. His short game was a big factor, with great pitch shots to save par from tough spots on the first and fourth holes and a 15-foot par putt on the 16th. He also got away with what he called a "dumb" risky shot from the trees to par the 11th.

Day appeared headed for a spot aside Spieth on top of the leaderboard with a 31 on the front nine and was still five-under through 14 holes before going bogey-triple bogey-bogey on 15-17 for a 72. McIlroy bogeyed the 16th and 18th to let a round in the 60s get away as he shot 70. There were eight rounds in the 60s, a 68 by Danny Lee and six 69s.

The wind was a bit gustier on Friday and the greens harder, especially late in the day, and nobody shot better than 71—there were four of those. Spieth got around in 74 and was able to stay in the lead at 140 with only seven players posting subpar totals for 36 holes.

Spieth birdied two of the first three holes and had as much as a five-stroke lead. He couldn't maintain it, as he played the last 10 holes in three-over and ended up leading by one after bogeys on 16 and 17. It could have been worse, as he holed a 14-foot par putt on the 18th.

"I can't rely on the putter the way I did today. I've got to strike the ball better," he said. "That's what leaves me a little uneasy compared to last year."

McIlroy had one of the 71s and moved into second place at 141 thanks to birdies at 13, 15, and 16 and a scrambling par from the woods on 18. Day again had trouble on the back nine, shooting 34-39—73 for a 145 total.

Not gaining much attention was England's Danny Willett with rounds of 70 and 74. The 28-year-old was a player on the rise, ranked 12th in the world after finishing No. 2 on the 2015 European Tour and winning the Dubai Desert Classic in February. He was playing in his second Masters, though it had been uncertain whether he would even be there. His wife was expecting their first child, with a due date of the Sunday of the Masters, and he announced he wouldn't play if the baby hadn't yet arrived. Fortunately, the boy was born on the Tuesday before Masters week, and, after helping his wife through the first few days, Willett arrived in Augusta on Monday evening—the very last of the 89 players to register.

Saturday was the toughest day yet, with a 75.72 scoring average compared to 75.02 for the second round, the wind playing havoc with putts on the slick greens as well as full shots. Smylie Kaufman did produce a round in the 60s, a 69 to gain a spot in Sunday's final twosome where he would shoot an 81.

The third round followed a similar pattern for Spieth as the second, building a four-stroke lead and finishing ahead by only one at 213 with a 73. In an up-and-down back nine, he answered a double bogey on 11 (second shot to the right, three putts) with birdies on 12, 14, and 15 only to finish with a bogey on 17 and double bogey on 18 after pushing a drive into the trees. He lamented being five-over on the last three holes in Rounds 2 and 3. "They are not the hard holes out here," he said. "You should be able to hit those greens in regulation."

While not having the cushion he wanted—and that he had one year before—Spieth set a record by leading for the seventh straight round, breaking Arnold Palmer's mark of six in 1960-61. He also became the third player to hold at least a share of the 54-hole lead in three straight years, joining Ben Hogan (1952-54) and Palmer (1958-60).

Kaufman was one stroke behind at 214, followed by 58-year-old Bernhard Langer, with an impressive 70, and Japan's Hideki Matsuyama at 215. None would be a factor on Sunday. Nor would Day, who had one of five subpar rounds with a 71 to join Willett and Dustin Johnson (73-71-72) at 216.

"I'm going to have a reasonable chance, but I'll have to do something special," said Willett after a four-birdie, four-bogey round of 72. That comment was made with the assumption he'd be trailing by five or six entering the last round, but, ultimately, he ended up only three back going into Sunday. The "something special" thought still applied.

Fellow Englishman Lee Westwood, just short of his 43rd birthday, had dropped to 67th in the world, but his late-career surge at the Masters continued. On a day when many contenders lost shots down the stretch, Westwood played the last seven holes four-under for a 71 and made a 34-foot birdie putt at the 18th for a 217 total.

McIlroy, on the other hand, shot himself out of it. He avoided the embarrassment of what would have been a sixth straight year with a nine in the 40s, which was little consolation after a 38-39—77.

The wind calmed on Sunday, leaving the door open for someone to make a run from behind. It was a strange final round for Spieth as it played out in four distinct stages. He was just OK over the first five holes, with a two-putt birdie at the second, a great break at the fourth, where his tee shot rattled out of some dense bushes to the right and he ended up making a 14-foot putt for par, and a bogey after a drive to the left on the fifth.

Then Spieth caught fire with four straight birdies and appeared to be on his way to becoming the fourth defending champion to win and the first to do so wire-to-wire. He holed 20-foot putts at the sixth and ninth, a four-footer at the seventh, and chipped to two feet on the eighth. Willett had become the main contender with birdies on the sixth and eighth to get to two-under and within one at that point, but Spieth's burst gave him a five-stroke lead at the turn.

It didn't take long for the margin to go back from five strokes to one. Spieth bogeyed the 10th hole from the greenside bunker and the 11th with a drive into the trees and an eventual miss from seven feet. At the same time, Willett was making birdies at the 13th and 14th. He went with a driver instead of a three-wood for the first time all week at 13, reached the green with a five-iron, and two-putted. On 14, he staked a nine-iron approach to three feet.

Now it was up to Spieth to try to right the ship. Instead, it sank. All week long, he'd been plagued by pushed iron shots to the right. It happened again, at the worst time, on the 12th where his nine-iron tee shot didn't have a chance and finished in Rae's Creek. After a penalty drop 80 yards from the hole, he compounded the

2016

1	Danny Willett	70–74–72–67—283
T2	Jordan Spieth	66–74–73–73—286
T2	Lee Westwood	71–75–71–69—286
T4	Paul Casey	69–77–74–67—287
T4	J.B. Holmes	72–73–74–68—287
T4	Dustin Johnson	73–71–72–71—287
T7	Matthew Fitzpatrick	71–76–74–67—288
T7	Soren Kjeldsen	69–74–74–71—288
T7	Hideki Matsuyama	71–72–72–73—288
T10	Daniel Berger	73–71–74–71—289
T10	Jason Day	72–73–71–73—289
T10	Rory McIlroy	70–71–77–71—289
T10	Justin Rose	69–77–73–70—289
T10	Brandt Snedeker	71–72–74–72—289

error by hitting his next shot so fat that it bounced into the creek. Re-dropping, he hit into the back bunker, and got up and down from there for a quadruple bogey.

Somehow, in the space of just three holes, Spieth had gone from five strokes ahead to three behind. It was reminiscent of McIlroy's self-destruction on the same three holes in 2011.

While Spieth was playing the 12th, Willett and Westwood were on the 15th, where the older Englishman thrust himself into the thick of things with a chip-in for an eagle to get to three-under, while Willett—suddenly the leader—parred to stay four-under.

Seeing the red "1" go up on the leaderboard to show Spieth's fall from grace, Willett consolidated his position with an eight-iron to seven feet and a successful birdie putt on the 16th. Westwood dropped to three behind with a three-putt from 45 feet, his old nemesis of short putts coming back to haunt him as he missed a four-footer.

One more player was in the mix. Johnson birdied the 15th with a two-putt from 20 feet after a daring second shot through a small gap in the trees. It got him to three-under for the round and tournament on a day of brilliant ball-striking where he couldn't convert any of three eagle putts from between 12 and 20 feet. He had double bogeyed the second hole with a four-putt and ended his quest with a double bogey from the bunker on 17 to finish T4. The 32-year-old would finally break through and win his first major two months later at the U.S. Open.

Spieth, honestly and accurately, said to his caddie after the 12th, "Buddy, it looks like we're collapsing." To his credit, he rallied with birdies on 13 and 15 to pull within two. An approach into the bunker on 17 and missed 10-foot putt gave him a bogey that extinguished his hopes as a closing 73 and back-nine 41 left him in a second-place tie with Westwood (69) at 286.

"Big picture, this one will hurt," Spieth admitted after joining the long list of players who blew a Masters lead on the back nine.

Willett had reached the clubhouse at 283 with a 67, preserving his bogey-free round with an outstanding chip from behind the 17th green. He also saved par with putts of eight feet on the seventh and ninth holes in a round featuring mostly solid ball-striking. In a week of harsh conditions, steady play won out. Willett had just nine bogeys in the tournament, compared to 10 bogeys, three double bogeys, and a quadruple bogey for the distraught Spieth.

An Ill Wind

The wind was a challenge for everybody the first three days, but what it did to Billy Horschel in the third round was downright cruel. He replaced his ball on the green for a 15-foot birdie putt on No. 15, walked to the other side of the hole to look it over, and watched in dismay as a gust of wind nudged the ball and started it rolling downhill all the way into water in front of the green. Under the rules, he had to take a one-stroke penalty and go back to the spot of his previous stroke, a chip from behind the green. To his credit, he got up and down from there for a bogey.

2017

In February, Sergio Garcia claimed the European Tour's Dubai Desert Classic for only his second victory since 2014. It was the same tournament that Danny Willett won before capturing the previous year's Masters. That was perhaps a good omen; on the other hand, the 37-year-old Garcia had gone winless in his first 73 major championship starts.

As the Masters approached, the focus was on Dustin Johnson, playing the best golf of his career and threatening to become a dominant force in the absence of Tiger Woods, whose bad back continued to keep him out of action. Johnson won his last three starts before the Masters, two of them World Golf Championships events, and took over the No. 1 spot in the World Ranking.

Unfortunately, Johnson's Masters ended before it started. He slipped and fell down a wooden staircase in his rental home on Wednesday afternoon, injuring his back. He showed up at Augusta National on Thursday, painfully hit a few balls on the practice range, and walked to the first tee before deciding he wouldn't be able to play.

Masters veterans called Thursday, when winds gusted into the 30s, one of the toughest days they'd ever seen in Augusta, but you wouldn't know it from Charley Hoffman. The 40-year-old four-time PGA Tour winner made birdies on five of six holes starting at the 12th for a 65 that was four strokes better than anybody else.

Garcia and Justin Rose, among others, were tied for fourth at 71. Sergio navigated the course without a bogey, with a lone birdie at the eighth hole. Rose had five birdies and four bogeys, missing several short putts while making three from 10 feet or longer.

Jordan Spieth was unable to put the nightmares of the back nine behind him. He made it past the 12th hole with a par, but for the second consecutive Masters round had a quadruple bogey, this one on the 15th hole. He hit his third shot in the water, took a penalty, knocked his next one over the green, chipped on, and three-putted. Headed for a pretty good round, he instead finished with a 75.

The second-round conditions were similar, and Hoffman felt their effect this time as he shot a 75. He didn't lose the lead, but had to share it at 140 with Garcia, Rickie Fowler, and Thomas Pieters. Fowler holed out from a bunker for an eagle on the second hole to spark the day's best round, a 67. Belgium's Pieters had been five-under through 10 holes of the first round before fading to a 72. He held it together all the way for a 68 on Friday.

Garcia birdied the first three holes on the way to a 33 on the front nine. His drive went so far to the left on the 10th that he hit a provisional ball in case the first one was lost. The original ball actually hit a tree and kicked into the fairway, from where Garcia made a bogey. (The walking scorer, thinking Garcia had played out with the provisional, marked him for a triple bogey, and that's what the leaderboards showed him with for a few holes.) A near hole-out from a plugged lie in the front bunker on the 12th—"hands down the best bunker shot I've ever hit"—was the highlight of a 36 on the back nine.

Garcia had been coming to Augusta since he was a 19-year-old sensation in 1999, and this was his 19th appearance. He had only a fourth (2004) and a couple of eighths to show for it on a course that often seemed to bring out his petulant side. Recently engaged, and also older and wiser, the Spaniard was working on his attitude. "I think I'm a little bit calmer now. I think I'm working on trying to accept things," he said.

The third round had been particularly troublesome for Garcia in past Masters, his scoring average a ghastly 74.9. So, it was a sign that this might indeed be a new Sergio when he shot a 70 for a 210 total to share the lead with Rose. Garcia hit 15 greens in regulation and took advantage of a break when he birdied the 13th after his second shot held up on the bank of the hazard instead of rolling down into the water. Rose caught fire with birdies on Nos. 12, 13, 15, 17, and 18 for a 31 on the back nine and Saturday's best round of 67.

Spieth continued his comeback from his first-round middle-of-the-pack status, following a 69 on Friday with a 68 in the third round to pull within two of the lead. He birdied the 13th with a bold four-iron second shot from the trees on the right, a television microphone picking up his comment to his caddie while discussing the shot, "What would Arnie do?" (four-time Masters champion Palmer had died the previous fall). The 23-year-old would be in the final-round mix for the fourth straight Masters, playing on Sunday in the next-to-last twosome with Fowler (71 for 211).

Hoffman led by two strokes before a bogey at 14 and double bogey at 16 left him with a 72, tied with Spieth and Ryan Moore at 212, followed by 2013 champion Adam Scott at 213.

While virtually half the field broke par in relatively calm weather in the final round, the five players who started within three shots of Garcia and Rose all shot over par, including a 75 by Spieth and a 76 by Fowler. Charl Schwartzel, the 2011 champion, claimed third place by completing a 68-68 weekend, but the final round was strictly a battle between the Spaniard and Englishman in the final twosome. What a back-and-forth battle it was, with Garcia gaining the upper hand early, Rose staging a reversal, Garcia making a comeback, and finally ending in a playoff.

Garcia got off to a great ball-striking start, with a birdie from six feet at the first, a missed birdie putt from five feet at the second, a birdie from eight feet at the third, and two-putt pars on the fourth and fifth. Rose started with four pars and a three-putt bogey from long range on the fifth to fall three behind.

Three holes later, they were tied again thanks to Rose birdies from 12 feet at the sixth, four feet at the seventh, and 15 feet at the eighth. Garcia saved par from a bunker with a seven-foot putt at No. 7 (he was five-for-six in bunker saves for the week), but wasted an opportunity when he missed a five-foot birdie putt at the eighth. Both parred the ninth for 34s on the front.

2017		
1	Sergio Garcia	71–69–70–69—279*
2	Justin Rose	71–72–67–69—279
3	Charl Schwartzel	74–72–68–68—282
T4	Matt Kuchar	72–73–71–67—283
T4	Thomas Pieters	72–68–75–68—283
6	Paul Casey	72–75–69–68—284
T7	Kevin Chapell	71–76–70–68—285
T7	Rory McIlroy	72–73–71–69—285
T9	Ryan Moore	74–69–69–74—286
T9	Adam Scott	75–69–69–73—286
*Garcia won on first playoff hole		

The pendulum continued to swing toward Rose when Garcia bogeyed the 10th and 11th to fall two behind, set up by a weak three-wood tee shot on the 10th and a hooked drive at 11.

Garcia seemed headed for yet another major championship disappointment when his tee shot hit a tree at the corner of the dogleg on the 13th and caromed to the left, finishing under a bush and forcing him to take a one-stroke penalty for an unplayable ball.

Garcia hacked his way off the pine needles into the fairway and watched Rose hit his second shot just over the green with a good chance to chip close for a birdie. There was a real possibility the deficit could double from two to four with five holes to play. Instead, Garcia hit a wedge to eight feet and made the putt for a par and Rose missed a five-foot putt and only managed a par himself.

Garcia's improved attitude paid off at what could have been a desperate time. "I was like, if that's what's supposed to happen, let it happen," said the Spaniard of his thoughts in the woods to the left of the 13th fairway. "Let's try to make a five here and see if we can put a hell of a finish to have a chance."

Garcia followed up his all-world par with two brilliant iron shots. An approach to five feet on the 14th set up a birdie to pull within one. Then after a huge drive on the 15th, his eight-iron second shot landed inches in front of the hole and glanced off the flagstick, settling 14 feet to the left of the cup. He rolled in the putt for a stirring eagle, netting a tie for the lead as Rose two-putted from the fringe for a birdie.

Rose went back ahead by one with an eight-foot birdie putt at 16, while Garcia missed from six feet after another laser-precision iron shot. Justin gave it right back with a bogey on 17, bunkering his approach and missing a seven-foot putt, sending them to the 18th all square.

Both faded their drives perfectly into the fairway. Rose got a break when his second shot barely missed the right bunker, caught a friendly slope, and rolled within eight feet of the hole. Garcia dialed in yet another on-target iron shot, a wedge to five feet behind the hole. Rose misread his putt, which slid by the lip on the high side, giving Garcia a putt for the victory. Sergio played too much break on his putt, too, for a par that could have felt like a dagger to the side of a player who seemed fated to major heartbreak.

Instead, the new Sergio felt "a lot of belief" heading to the playoff because of his solid ball-striking down the stretch of regulation. The duo headed back to the 18th tee after final-round 69s for 279 totals. The pure shots continued for Garcia on the first extra hole, a tee shot to the fairway and an approach to 12 feet. It was Rose who faltered with a tee shot into trouble behind a magnolia tree, from where he could only punch out. A good third shot left a 15-footer for a par, which he missed. Needing only to two-putt, Garcia provided theater by holing for a birdie and letting out a scream that released years of frustration, then blew kisses to a crowd that was chanting, "Ser-gee-oh!"

The third Masters victory by a Spaniard occurred on what would have been the 60th birthday of the first, Seve Ballesteros, who died at age 54 in 2011. It was also inspired by the second, Jose Maria Olazabal, who sent Garcia a note earlier in the week saying that he wasn't yet sharing his locker with anyone in the Champions Locker Room and would like to share it with Sergio. Done.

2018

In the last two years, Tiger Woods had come to Augusta only for the champions' dinner on Tuesday, unable to compete because of a painful back condition. Eleven days after the 2017 Masters, Woods underwent a fourth surgery, a spinal fusion, which finally restored his ability to play golf following a long recovery period. After playing in just one tournament in 2016-17, Woods returned to the PGA Tour for five events before the Masters in 2018 and finished second and fifth in his last two, making a run at a fifth green jacket not an unrealistic possibility.

He would be facing a formidable field of top players in good form. World No. 1 Dustin Johnson had a victory on the season, No. 2 Justin Thomas had two, Bubba Watson had won twice, 47-year-old Phil Mickelson ended a five-year victory drought, and Rory McIlroy won three weeks before the Masters.

The first-round leader turned out to be a familiar name who *wasn't* playing particularly well in 2018, though he did finish third in Houston the previous week. Jordan Spieth fired a 66 to sit atop the Masters field at the end of the day for the ninth time in his career at age 24. An eagle at the eighth put him two-under and five straight birdies starting at the 13th brought him to seven-under, before a pulled drive into the trees forming the narrow chute on the 18th got him into so much trouble that he ended up having to make a great up-and-down to save a bogey.

Spieth was two strokes ahead of Matt Kuchar, who had a 31 on the back nine, and Tony Finau, who dislocated an ankle while celebrating an ace in the Par-3 Contest on Wednesday and underwent an MRI on Thursday morning to determine there was no structural damage. The Masters rookie played with his ankle taped and was undeterred by a slight limp.

McIlroy was in a group at 69 thanks to par saves at the last three holes. Also at that number was Patrick Reed, his first Masters round in the 60s. In fact, the

27-year-old had been over par in nine of his 12 Masters rounds, while missing two cuts in four starts and a best finish of T22. Reed actually started his Masters career with more Augusta National experience than most. As a star golfer at Augusta State, where he led the team to two NCAA Championships, he got to play once a year at the site of the Masters, though it didn't seem to do him much good when he made it there as a pro.

For all the fanfare surrounding Woods' Augusta return, Tiger shot a 73 and wouldn't be a factor, going on to finish T32. Defending champion Sergio Garcia fared even worse, going from the sublime to the ridiculous in the course of a year. He hit five balls into the water on the 15th hole in the first round to make a one-putt 13, matching the highest score on any hole ever in the Masters, and badly missed the cut with 81-78.

Reed moved to the forefront on Friday with a round that included three streaks of three straight birdies—Nos. 1, 2, 3 and 7, 8, 9 for a 31 on the front and Nos. 13, 14, and 15. Three bogeys on the day, including a late one at the 16th, left him with a 66 and a 135 total, ahead of Marc Leishman by two strokes and Henrik Stenson by four.

Spieth continued his Jekyll-and-Hyde act of recent years, posting his 10th straight round that was either in the 60s (four of those) or over par (six of those). His 74 put him five strokes back, but it could have been worse. He double bogeyed the first hole and shot a 40 on the front nine before steadying himself for a 34 on the back. McIlroy joined him at 140 with a 37-34—71.

McIlroy shot into a tie for the lead by playing the first eight holes in five-under on Saturday, capped by holing out from 32 yards for an eagle at the eighth. He was the recipient of a couple of breaks on the back nine, playing out of an azalea bush to par the 13th and having his tee shot come off a tree into the fairway on the 18th where he made a birdie for a 65. Could this finally be his year?

Reed answered with some fireworks of his own on a day of intermittent showers that softened the greens. He had yet another three-birdie run on 8, 9, and 10 and a pair of eagles on the back nine with a 14-foot putt on the 13th and 27-yard pitch-in on the 15th. Despite another bogey at 16, he shot a 67 for a 202 total and a three-stroke lead on McIlroy.

Rickie Fowler and Jon Rahm took advantage of the conditions to shoot 65s and move into third and fourth place, respectively, at 207 and 208. Fowler would be in the next-to-last twosome on Sunday for the second straight year, hoping to do much better than the 76 he shot in 2017 when he started just one off the lead. The 24-year-old Rahm, already with two wins each on the PGA and European tours and ranked No. 3 in the world, had made up ground from an opening 75 and was looking to make it two winners in a row from Spain.

Most of the anticipation, however, centered on the Sunday showdown between Reed and McIlroy, who had staged a stirring singles duel in the 2016 Ryder Cup, Reed coming away with a one-up victory. McIlroy was continuing his annual Grand Slam quest at Augusta, while Reed was looking to add to his total of five PGA Tour victories. While he hadn't won since 2016, he came into the Masters off three straight top-10 finishes.

Sunday turned into the lowest scoring round ever at the Masters with a field average of 70.49. Fortunately for Reed, McIlroy didn't join the red-number party, as his long game and short putting were both off in a round of 74. With everybody else starting at least five strokes behind, Reed had some leeway to deal with challenges from far behind.

Before we get to those challenges, some scoring feats from those who didn't have a chance to win deserve mention. Finau, who dropped back in the second and third rounds, birdied six straight holes starting at the 12th, one short of the consecutive birdie record, for a 66 to finish T10. Paul Casey was nine-under through 16 holes (five-under for a four-hole stretch from 11 to 14) with a chance to tie or break the course record of 63 until he bogeyed the last two holes for a 65. It was the Englishman's fourth straight Masters final round of 68 or better; the other three netted him top-six finishes, this one a T15.

Australia's Cameron Smith shot a back-nine 30 and missed a five-foot birdie putt on the 18th that would have tied the record of 29. With a 66, he tied for fifth with McIlroy (his fifth straight Masters top 10), Stenson (his first top-10 in 13 tries), and Watson (his third top-10, the other two were wins).

At the top of the leaderboard, Reed bounced back and forth between his 14-under starting position and 13-under on the front nine. He bogeyed the first after driving behind a tree on the left, birdied the third with a 20-foot putt from the fringe, bogeyed the sixth where he came up short, and birdied the seventh with an approach to tap-in range. When he parred the eighth hole, while McIlroy was bogeying, Reed had a four-stroke lead.

He would, however, need to persevere through a wave of heat on the back nine, especially that applied by Spieth. The 2015 champion had fallen nine strokes behind with a frustrating 71 in the third round, lipping out five putts. Spieth shot himself into a tie for second with a 31 on the front nine on Sunday, none of his five birdies from longer than 12 feet. Spieth kept on charging by conquering his Waterloo hole, the 12th, with a 27-foot birdie putt from the back fringe and adding a two-putt birdie at the 13th after a brilliant hybrid second shot to 12 feet.

When Reed bogeyed the 11th after a drive into the right trees forced a punch-out, Spieth was suddenly within one. Reed showed his moxie by following a bogey with a birdie on the next hole for the second time in the round, holing a 22-foot putt on the 12th. Spieth quickly answered with a two-putt from long range at the 15th, making a six-footer for birdie.

Spieth continued to look like a man on a mission when he drained a 33-foot putt for a birdie on 16. From nine strokes back, he was now tied for the lead—and nine-under for the round. Reed didn't birdie the 13th. In fact, he was lucky not to make a bogey when his second shot landed inside the hazard line but stayed playable on the bank. Reed did produce the birdie he desperately needed at the 14th hole, with an approach to eight feet and a dead-in putt to finally get to 15-under.

Spieth narrowly missed an 18-foot birdie try at 17 and moved to the finishing hole one behind, needing a par to tie the course record but perhaps a birdie to have a chance to win and set the record for the largest final-round comeback. Instead, his tee shot caught a limb of a tree at the end of the chute on the left, dropping straight down and leaving him no chance to get closer than 90 yards from the green in two. He hit a nice third shot to eight feet but missed the putt to finish with a 64. He had given it his all, but was now helpless in the clubhouse two behind at 13-under.

Reed also received pressure from Fowler and Rahm in the twosome ahead of him. Rahm got within two when he birdied 14 only to see his bid come to an end when his second shot found the water on 15 for a bogey. He shot a 69 for fourth place at 11-under.

2018		
1	Patrick Reed	69–66–67–71—273
2	Rickie Fowler	70–72–65–67—274
3	Jordan Spieth	66–74–71–64—275
4	Jon Rahm	75–68–65–69—277
T5	Rory McIlroy	69–71–65–74—279
T5	Cameron Smith	71–72–70–66—279
T5	Henrik Stenson	69–70–70–70—279
T5	Bubba Watson	73–69–68–69—279
9	Marc Leishman	70–67–73–70—280
T10	Tony Finau	68–74–73–66—281
T10	Dustin Johnson	73–68–71–69—281

Fowler was one-over through seven holes, and it could have been worse if not for unlikely par saves on Nos. 6 and 7. He then reeled off birdies on 8, 9, 12, 13, and 15, all from 10 feet or less, to reach 13-under. The 29-year-old with seven top-five finishes in majors, but no victories, made a bid to change his major fortunes, hitting his approach to seven feet on 18 and making it for a birdie. That gave Fowler a 67 for a 14-under 274 total, forcing Reed to par the 18th to win outright.

Reed had already made a nervy five-foot putt for a par on 17 after a drive in the rough and second shot to the fringe some 75 feet from the hole. It was one of many par putts he made from between three and six feet in the final round. He would need one more on the 18th, where his delicate downhill birdie putt from 24 feet rolled a little more than three feet past. Reed rolled that into the heart of the cup for his first major title with a 71 and a 15-under 273 total.

On a day of brilliance from Spieth and Fowler, it was easy to forget just how impressive Reed had been over the course of the first three rounds to set the stage for his victory. On Sunday, he was just good enough.

Score One for the Old Folks

Two-time champion Tom Watson played his last Masters in 2016, but at the age of 68 he won Wednesday's Par 3 Contest with a score of six-under 21, matching the third-best score ever shot in the event on the club's nine-hole Par 3 course. He was playing with 78-year-old Jack Nicklaus, who shot four-under, and 82-year-old Gary Player, two-under.

2019

At the age of 43, Tiger Woods was looking to make the most of the new lease on his golf career. His 2018 comeback featured Sunday contention at the last two majors

(T6 at the British Open, second at the PGA Championship) and was capped by a victory at the season-ending Tour Championship. Next on the to-do list: attending to the unfinished business of tacking on to his total of 14 major championships, a number he'd been stuck on since 2008. Of immediate concern was trying to add to his total of four victories at Augusta National, where his last triumph was in 2005.

Woods had entered five tournaments in 2019 with finishes ranging from T5 to T30. There was a troubling sign in March when he didn't make his scheduled start at the Arnold Palmer Invitational due to neck pain. He returned the next week for the Players Championship, where he said that the neck problem was related to his back issues but that his withdrawal was a precautionary measure and he was fine. He declared that his Masters preparation was "right on track. I'm able to shape the ball both ways, which I'm going to need there."

Woods got off to an OK start on Thursday with a 70 that was good for a tie for 11th. A bogey on the 17th hole cost him a chance to open the Masters with a round in the 60s, something he'd now done only once in 22 starts. It was his sixth first round of 70; he'd gone on to win three of the first five times.

Driving was a concern, as both of Woods' bogeys were set up by poor tee shots, into a bunker at the fifth and trees at the 17th. He also found the trees to the left of No. 14, but was able to loft his shot over the tall timber to 25 feet and made that putt for a birdie. He birdied two of the par fives, Nos. 2 and 13, and added a five-foot birdie putt on the ninth.

It appeared the lead would be four-under until late starters Brooks Koepka and Bryson DeChambeau went on birdie binges down the stretch to both shoot 66, Koepka with four straight birdies starting at the 12th and DeChambeau with birdies on the last four holes. The 28-year-old Koepka was especially formidable, having won two U.S. Opens and a PGA in 2017-18, establishing himself as a player who elevated his game for the majors. While it was uncertain whether Woods still retained any intimidation factor at this point in his career, it certainly wouldn't apply to Koepka, who held off a charge by Tiger at the 2018 PGA.

Friday brought a logjam at the top with a record five players tied for first at 137 and four more just one stroke behind. Koepka had a double bogey at the par-five second in a 71 and he was joined in the lead by Jason Day (67), Francesco Molinari (67), Adam Scott (68), and Louis Oosthuizen (66). Xander Schauffele had the best round, a 65, to sit at 138 along with top guns Dustin Johnson (68-70) and Woods (70-68).

Tiger was even par through eight holes with birdies on the two front-nine par threes and bogeys on two holes where he drove into fairway bunkers—the fifth and the par-five eighth, which he three-putted. A 37-foot birdie putt on the ninth got him going in the right direction, and he hit all nine greens in shooting a 33 on the back nine. He birdied the tough 11th from 13 feet and for the second straight day made a spectacular birdie from the left trees on 14. This time he threaded his second shot through a gap instead of up-and-over, but the result was virtually the same, finishing 28 feet from the hole and he again drilled the putt. The second shot was followed by a dangerous moment when a security guard trying to hold back a moving throng slipped and blindsided Woods in the right ankle. Tiger hopped around for a few seconds on his left leg, wincing in pain, but fortunately wasn't seriously hurt.

Woods had to lay up from the trees on the 15th, but still walked away with a birdie after a wedge third shot and 30-foot putt. He missed birdie tries from eight and 14 feet on the last two holes, though he couldn't complain after the long putts he'd made.

The course was softened by rain on Monday and Tuesday, and the greens never really firmed up as it remained humid throughout the week with not much wind until Sunday. With approach shots sticking predictably close to where they landed, the second-round field average of 71.98 was the second lowest second round ever. Saturday's average of 70.77 was the second lowest of any round behind 2018's final round. And the cumulative scoring average of 71.87 for the tournament was a record, bettering the 1992 mark of 71.91.

Molinari took over the top spot with a 66 in the third round for a 203 total. The 36-year-old Italian was playing the best golf of his life in a 10-month stretch that included the British Open among three victories in the summer of 2018 and a victory at the Arnold Palmer Invitational a month before the Masters with a final-round 64. Like Koepka, he had bested Woods in a 2018 major, and had done it eye-to-eye in the same twosome at Carnoustie in Scotland. His third round was highlighted by a tee shot to four inches on the 12th hole, igniting a stretch of four straight birdies, all from within seven feet.

For the second straight day, Woods hit 16 greens and all nine on the back nine. He finished with a 67 and a tie for second at 205. The only scorecard blemish was on the fifth hole, where he drove into a fairway bunker for the third straight day. That was a particularly costly mistake this year, as the fifth hole had been lengthened by 40 yards to 495. The fairway bunkers had correspondingly been moved to a similar distance from the tee as before, making the second shot from there so long that it was impossible to reach the green.

The rest of the round was nearly impeccable, except for some errant drives from which Woods recovered. He birdied the sixth from 18 feet, the seventh with an approach to a foot, and the eighth with a two-putt from 11 feet, finishing the front nine with a 34 after saving par with a pitch and putt to three feet after a drive into trees on the ninth.

Woods pushed his drive so far to the right on the 11th that he found an alley and had a clear shot to the green. Then he got a break on 13 when his drive was headed left of the creek before it clipped a tree and came back into the fairway. He had to lay up but wedged to six feet and made a birdie. He added an up-and-down birdie from behind the 15th green and a seven-foot birdie on 16.

Tony Finau fired a 64 to earn a tie for second with Woods. Trying to follow up on a T10 in his Masters debut in 2018 with something even better, Finau hit a second shot to eight inches to eagle the eighth to go six-under for the round. He then lipped out a birdie putt on the ninth that would have given him the front-nine record, settling for a 30.

Koepka was next, three strokes back at 206, after a 69 that featured an eagle on the 15th to go five-under on the par fives for the round. Webb Simpson gained ground with a 64, playing the last 12 holes in eight-under, and was tied with Ian Poulter at 207. Schauffele was at 208, having hit into the water to bogey 15 and also making a bogey on 18, losing shots that would be precious come Sunday (the same for Day, who double bogeyed 15 and bogeyed 18 for 73—210).

Johnson, ranked No. 2 in the world, was going along rather quietly at 208 after a 70 where all four of his birdies were on par fives (No. 1 Justin Rose missed the cut).

Never before had there been more than one 64 (or better) in the same round; on this day there were three. The third was by Patrick Cantlay, who birdied only one of the par fives yet got into the scoring parade with an eight-birdie round to move up in the field after opening with a pair of 73s.

Anticipation was keen for what promised to be a thriller of a final round. The anticipation wouldn't linger through Sunday morning as it usually does. A forecast of severe thunderstorms in mid-afternoon caused a decision to start the final round early. With a larger than usual contingent of 65 making the cut due to the 10-shot rule, the field was put into threesomes and sent off both tees—the first tee time at 7:30 and the last at 9:20. That put Woods in the final threesome. If it had been the usual twosomes, Molinari and Finau would have been the last pair, with Finau getting the nod over Woods because he finished his round first on Saturday. It also gave Woods an early wakeup call of 4 a.m. to give him time to go to the gym and loosen up his back.

Molinari had once caddied in the Masters for his brother Edoardo, who made the field in 2006 as the U.S. Amateur champion. Francesco was already a second-year European Tour pro when he carried his brother's bag at Augusta National in the same threesome as Woods, who was the defending champion. Now Molinari was trying to beat Woods for the Masters title.

Francesco had only one bogey in the first three rounds and had gone his last 43 holes without one. He clearly wasn't as sharp as the final round got underway. Molinari scrambled to make putts for par of 12 feet on the first hole, eight feet on the fifth, and six feet on the sixth. He couldn't escape on the seventh, however, missing a 12-foot par putt after getting in bad position with a tee shot to the left. The Italian rebounded with a birdie from 14 feet on the eighth and parred the next three.

Woods went back and forth between a one- and three-stroke deficit during an inconsistent first 11 holes. He had to scramble on No. 2 after a tee shot into the trees on the left, ultimately making a six-foot putt for a par five. Tiger birdied the third from eight feet, then immediately retreated with back-to-back bogeys. He came up short with his tee shot on the fourth and missed a 10-footer for par. After driving into a bunker for the first three days on the fifth, he took a three-wood this time and found the fairway—and still made his fourth bogey on the hole when he three-putted, missing an 11-foot second putt.

A par on the sixth was followed by back-to-back birdies on Nos. 7 (approach to two feet) and 8 (second shot over the green, pitch to seven feet). The ninth was a two-putt par that felt like a save. Facing a severely breaking downhill putt from the back of the green, 70 feet from the hole, Woods displayed uncanny touch as his ball rolled slowly down the putting surface and stopped less than a foot from the cup.

Unfortunately, he gave one stroke back with his third bogey of the day on the 10th hole, driving into jail behind a tree on the right, forced to punch out and leave a full third shot to the green. He got away with another drive far to the right on the 11th, able to find an opening to hit a nice draw onto the green and make a par.

Through 11 holes, Woods and Molinari were even par and Finau one-over. In the threesome ahead of them, Koepka and Poulter had just hit into the water on the 12th and double bogeyed. On the tee, Molinari decided to hit an easy eight-iron instead of a hard nine, but mishit it and came up short, the ball rolling down the bank into the water. Finau found the water too and both made double bogey as the 12th hole took perhaps its greatest toll ever. Woods smartly aimed left of the flag and pulled his tee shot, leaving him a tough two-putt from 51 feet which he managed to negotiate.

The complexion of the tournament had drastically changed due to Molinari's mishap, which dropped him to 11-under. Not only was Woods now tied for the lead, a host of players were in the process of making their moves on the back nine and were now in the mix, many of whom started well behind.

Schauffele made his fourth birdie in six holes at the 13th to get to 11-under in a three-way tie for first, with four players at 10-under, all of whom began the final round either seven or eight strokes behind. Bubba Watson had just gone birdie-birdie-eagle on 13-15, Day birdied the 15th and Jon Rahm the 16th, while Cantlay was rolling along at four-under for the day.

Cantlay began the round inconspicuously at seven back and remained so until Molinari's retreat. Now he holed a 17-foot eagle putt at 15 to seize the solo lead at 12-under. Not for long, as Schauffele added yet another birdie at 14 to get to 12-under. The action was fast and furious, Koepka recovering from his double bogey at 12 with an eagle at the 13th to get back to 11-under.

It was getting tough to keep track. Cantlay disappeared as suddenly as he appeared, with bogeys on 16 and 17. The same for Watson with bogeys on the last two. Their places as contenders would soon be taken by Johnson, Simpson, and Rickie Fowler.

"There were so many different scenarios that could have transpired on that back nine. There were so many guys with a chance to win," said Woods after the round.

Tiger grabbed that chance the most firmly with birdies on three of four holes starting at the 13th. For the second straight day, his tee shot on 13 clipped a tree on the left side and was deflected to the fairway. This one was caused by his foot slipping on wet turf during his swing; the fortunate result was an unintentional big hook around the corner that left him with only an eight-iron second shot. He hit that to 30 feet and two-putted to get to 12-under along with Molinari, who also birdied. After a solid par on the 14th, Woods hit a good drive on 15 and, as he walked down the fairway, was in a five-way tie for the lead with Molinari, Schauffele, and two players who had just joined them at 12-under. Koepka got there with a two-putt birdie at 15 and Johnson, under the radar for most of the round, made a third straight birdie

2019

1	Tiger Woods	70–68–67–70—275
T2	Dustin Johnson	68–70–70–68—276
T2	Brooks Koepka	66–71–69–70—276
T2	Xander Schauffele	73–65–70–68—276
T5	Jason Day	70–67–73–67—277
T5	Tony Finau	71–70–64–72—277
T5	Francesco Molinari	70–67–66–74—277
T5	Webb Simpson	72–71–64–70—277
T9	Patrick Cantlay	73–73–64–68—278
T9	Rickie Fowler	70–71–68–69—278
T9	Jon Rahm	69–70–71–68—278

at 17. Just to add another player to the top section of the ever-changing leaderboard, Fowler birdied 13, 14, and 15, lipped out a six-foot birdie putt at 16, and birdied 17 to reach 11-under, one behind.

Woods broke the tie, jumping to 13-under with a five-iron second shot to 44 feet and two-putt birdie at 15. Molinari's bid ended on that hole. He drove to the right, laid up in the left rough, and watched his third shot catch an overhanging tree limb and plunge into the pond in front of the green for a second water ball, and second double bogey, on the back nine.

Finally, out of all the chaos, Woods struck the decisive blow on the 16th hole, where his eight-iron tee shot had the perfect distance and made its way down the slope from the right side, stopping three feet below the hole. The resulting birdie put him at 14-under with a two-stroke lead. Down the stretch, with a host of players looking to make this Masters their own, Woods dug deep to summon the inner resolve he possessed in his prime—and just enough of what remained of his game.

Schauffele remained stuck at 12-under down the stretch, Johnson ran out of holes, Fowler bogeyed 18, Day had finished earlier with a birdie at 18 for an 11-under total that couldn't stand up to the onslaught behind him, and Finau had fallen too far behind for his birdies on 13, 15, and 16 to make him a factor. It was left to Koepka to challenge Woods at the end. The U.S. Open and PGA champion showed his clutch shot-making with an approach to 10 feet at the 72nd hole, but he couldn't get the putt to fall and finished at 12-under.

Woods was trouble free on 17, where he missed a nine-footer for birdie, and strolled to 18 with a two-stroke lead over Koepka, Johnson, and Schauffele in the clubhouse. With trees in his line on a second shot from the right edge of the fairway, Woods "overcut" his second shot because he didn't want to go left, and landed well short and right of the green. A pitch, a 14-foot putt, and a tap-in produced a finishing bogey and garnered his 15th major championship. The 14 years between Masters victories was the longest ever, a year longer than Gary Player (1961-74).

Woods became the second oldest Masters winner to Jack Nicklaus' 46 in 1986—Tiger was an older 43 than Ben Crenshaw in 1995—while his fifth green jacket moved him past Palmer and within one of Nicklaus. It was all the more remarkable considering his two-year absence from competition and his physical condition before his last surgery. "I could barely walk. I couldn't sit. Couldn't lay down. I really couldn't do much of anything," Woods said.

It was a spectacle most assumed would never again be witnessed—Tiger Woods, the greatest golfer of his generation and some may argue the greatest ever, celebrating a major championship on the green of the 72nd hole. The fans knew they were witnessing a historic moment—no less so than Woods' first Masters title as a 21-year-old in 1997. The crowd roar reached a crescendo as Tiger shouted with joy, showing as much emotion as he ever has. It somehow seemed appropriate that Woods had not only returned to major championship winning form, he had also done so on golf's premier stage: the Masters at Augusta National.

2020

Dustin Johnson entered the 2020 Masters with three victories and two runner-up finishes in his last six starts. Two of the wins were in PGA Tour playoff events, one with a 30-under total and the other in the Tour Championship to wrap up FedExCup and Player-of-the-Year honors for the 2019-20 season. One of the second-place finishes was in a major, the PGA Championship, and the other was in Houston the week before the Masters. He was No. 1 in the World Ranking. For a human interest angle, Johnson had tested positive for the COVID-19 illness a month before the Masters and spent 11 days isolated in a hotel room.

Despite all of that, Johnson received scarce attention in the days leading up to the tournament. That was soaked up by Bryson DeChambeau, the talk of the golf world with a power game that helped him capture the U.S. Open two months earlier. While the PGA Tour took a three-month break from mid-March to mid-June due to the coronavirus pandemic, DeChambeau bulked up and worked on his swing to make the step up from long hitter to ultra-long basher. It paid off with a victory in July and his first major title at Winged Foot in September.

The 27-year-old only teed it up in one event in the nearly two months before the Masters. But with driving distance being such an important factor at Augusta National, DeChambeau stoked the fire. He shared with the press that he was experimenting with a 48-inch driver. He asserted that, for him at least, Augusta could be looked at as a par-67 course (he was planning on shooting for the green off the tee on the par-four third in addition to reaching the par fives in two with mostly short irons). The buzz was about Bryson.

The other main topic was that the tournament was being played in November, and without spectators due to the pandemic. Every previous Masters had been played in the spring, always in April except for March in 1934 and March/April in 1936. The absence of gallery roars—typically such an important part of the Masters—promised to be eerie. In terms of course conditions, the fairways, overseeded with ryegrass, were much softer, and the normally light rough of the "second cut" was thicker than usual.

While the course was playing longer and the rough a bit tougher, the tournament produced the lowest scoring ever, with a cumulative average of 71.75 and 43 players finishing under par for 72 holes. Greens that were already relatively soft became saturated by rain on Thursday morning. They were like dartboards during the first round, with approach shots staying almost exactly where they landed, and firmed up only very slightly as the week progressed.

A rain delay of nearly three hours after only a few players had teed off on Thursday made it impossible to complete the round, given the early sunset in November. (Due to the shorter daylight hours, the field went off both the first and tenth tees all four days). Paul Casey, with a 65, led among the half of the field that finished. The 43-year-old Englishman was ultimately unable to add to his total of four top-six Masters finishes, sliding to T38 by the end of the week.

DeChambeau needed to rally for a 70 after making a double bogey on the 13th hole (his fourth), where his second shot finished in a flowerless azalea bush left of the green. The second round would be worse. It was marred by a triple bogey on the third hole, where DeChambeau took a lost-ball penalty after his hooked tee shot plunged into the wet turf in the left rough and wasn't found during the allowed three-minute search period. Despite making seven birdies, he shot a 74 that relegated him to sidebar status on the weekend, when he finished T34.

Johnson asserted himself when the first round concluded on Friday. Having completed the front nine in three-under 33 with an eagle on the second and birdie on the eighth before Thursday's suspension, he added a 32 on the back nine with birdies on both par threes (11 feet on 12 and two feet on 16), and Nos. 15 and 18. The 65 tied him for first with Casey and South Africa's Dylan Frittelli, another Friday finisher.

Starting on the back nine in the second round, Johnson threatened to pull away with birdies on 11 (10 feet), 12 (11 feet), and 13 (four feet). He quickly gave two of those strokes back, though, with bogeys on 14 (three-putt from a tough position above the hole) and 15 (three-iron second shot into the water). The up-and-down beginning was followed by 12 straight pars and then a birdie from six feet on his finishing hole, the ninth. The 70 in good scoring conditions was nothing special, but it was a solid round in which Johnson hit 16 greens.

At the end of the day, with the second round suspended, Johnson was tied for first at nine-under 135 with Justin Thomas (66-69), Australia's Cameron Smith (67-68), and Mexico's Abraham Ancer (68-67). When the second round concluded on Saturday morning, they were joined by Jon Rahm (69-66), marking the second consecutive year five players were tied for the 36-hole lead. Johnson, Rahm, and Thomas were ranked 1-2-3 in the world, while 27-year-old Smith and 29-year-old Ancer had combined for just two PGA Tour victories (both by Smith).

Five players were just one stroke behind the leading fivesome, foreshadowing a probable crowded group of contenders as the tournament headed toward the stretch. Instead, Johnson launched a successful breakaway from the peloton early in the third round.

Dustin unleashed a 363-yard drive on the downhill second hole and fired a five-iron second shot directly at the back left pin, a shot that could be pulled off only to a soft green. It finished a foot from the hole for an eagle. He followed with a 56-yard approach to the short par-four third to eight feet for a birdie. His longest drained putt of the week was a 38-footer for a birdie at the fourth to go four-under through four holes. A wedge approach to two feet on the seventh gave him another birdie and a 31 on the front nine.

Two-putt birdies on both par fives and pars on the other holes gave Johnson a 34 on the back nine and his second bogey-less 65 in the first three rounds. It was a stunning exhibition of ball-striking, especially the combination of distance and accuracy off the tee. The South Carolinian hit all 14 fairways, with seven of his drives traveling at least 310 yards. He hit 16 greens in regulation or better (reaching three par fives in two) and had a routine 25-footer from

2020		
1	Dustin Johnson	65–70–65–68—268
T2	Sungjae Im	66–70–68–69—273
T2	Cameron Smith	67–68–69–69—273
4	Justin Thomas	66–69–71–70—276
T5	Dylan Frittelli	65–73–67–72—277
T5	Rory McIlroy	75–66–67–69—277
T7	Brooks Koepka	70–69–69–70—278
T7	C.T. Pan	70–66–74–68—278
T7	Jon Rahm	69–66–72–71—278
T10	Corey Conners	74–65–71–69—279
T10	Patrick Reed	68–68–71–72—279
T10	Webb Simpson	67–73–71–68—279

the fringe on one of the greens he missed. He also used his putter from well right of the green on 18 to within four feet of the hole for his only true save.

Johnson's 54-hole total of 200 tied Jordan Spieth's record of 2015 and left him four strokes ahead of a trio of players—Smith and Ancer with 69s and South Korea's Sungjae Im a 68.

Thomas and Rahm were disappointments at 71 and 72, respectively. Thomas hit several loose shots, as he bogeyed three of the last five holes. Rahm had appeared to be having a charmed week, with an ace on the fourth hole in one practice round and an unconventional—and incredible—ace on the 16th in another practice round. It has become a practice tradition on that hole for players to move to the front of the teeing ground and skip a shot across the pond and onto the green. When Rahm tried his trick shot on Tuesday, his ball skipped onto the putting surface and rolled like a putt with perfect speed as it curled into the hole at the back of the green. On Saturday, though, he hit an ugly, nearly topped, second shot into the woods on the eighth, hit a tree with an attempted escape, had to take a penalty for an unplayable ball, and made a double bogey that essentially knocked him out of it.

Meanwhile, Johnson displayed the same form that made him the Player of the Year, maybe even playing better than he had in his late summer-early fall streak. Still, he was anything but a lock, even with a four-stroke lead. After all, the 36-year-old had an 0-4 record with the 54-hole lead in major championships and owned only one major title (the 2016 U.S. Open) among his 23 PGA Tour victories. He had finished second in all four of the majors, five runner-up finishes in all, coming in all manner of frustrations.

Sure enough, he got off to an unsteady start on Sunday. Johnson's tee shot on the first hole found a fairway bunker; he recovered for a par. On No. 2, he chunked a pitch shot into a greenside bunker, escaping to two feet for another par. He appeared to right himself with a birdie from 12 feet on the third hole, then went the wrong direction with bogeys on the fourth (weak putt from the front fringe) and fifth (drive in a fairway bunker from which he couldn't reach the green). Suddenly, his lead was down to one stroke over Im, who birdied Nos. 2 and 3. Was another major slipping from Dustin's grasp?

Unshaken, Johnson hit his tee shot on the par-three sixth to seven feet, sank the birdie putt, and went back ahead by three after Im bogeyed. That was followed by another scramble on the seventh, where Johnson drove into the right trees, hit his next into a front bunker, and blasted out to two feet.

That was the end of Dustin's troubles. From that point on, his game clicked on and he was virtually mistake-free. Starting at No. 8, he hit every fairway the rest of the way and missed only one green, the 11th, where he pitched to four feet and made a par.

Johnson two-putted for a birdie on the eighth, but made the turn under pressure from Smith, who birdied the seventh and ninth with a pair of spectacular shots from the trees and shot a 33 on the front nine to pull within two strokes.

The margin widened to three when Smith bogeyed 11. Johnson took full possession of the tournament with birdies on 13, 14, and 15. He laid up on both par fives, discretion being the better part of valor with mud on his ball on 13 and trees in his way on 15. Johnson rewarded himself for the smart strategy with wedge shots to 13 feet on 13 and seven feet on 15, sinking both putts. He also made a six-footer after a wedge approach to the 14th.

Im, playing in his first Masters at age 22, and Smith performed admirably, each shooting 69s to share second place at 15-under 273, with Smith becoming the first player ever to record four rounds in the 60s in the Masters. But with Johnson reaching 20-under to lead by five through 15, the only remaining suspense was what score he would post for 72 holes. Two-putt pars on the last three holes brought Johnson home in 268, two strokes better than the old record shared by Tiger Woods and Jordan Spieth.

Johnson's final round was impressive, and not just because of the way he responded to the pressure. With the wind kicking up for the only time all week, the 68 matched the best score of the day. Johnson not only held or shared the lead after every round, he also owned the best score of the round three times (shared twice and outright once). For a player who had made a career of making winning major championships look so hard, he made this one look easy.

....

Double Digits, Then a Bounceback

Tiger Woods' title defense fizzled when he followed an opening 68 with rounds of 71 and 72 to fall 11 strokes behind. Then he had his worst score on a hole as a pro when he made a seven-over 10 on No. 12 in the final round, hitting three shots into Rae's Creek—the third coming from the back bunker after he'd finally cleared the water on his third try. The disaster put him at nine-over in the final round. Obviously feeling that was no way to finish the Masters, Woods proceeded to birdie five of the last six holes, including the last four, for a 76.

....

Acknowledgments

The top source for accounts of the Masters through the years was the comprehensive coverage in the pages of the event's hometown newspaper, the *Augusta Chronicle*. The secondary newspaper source was the *Atlanta Constitution*, particularly for some years when the *Chronicle* archives were unavailable.

Other vital sources were the substantial tournament reports in *Golf World*, *Sports Illustrated*, and the annual books by Mark H. McCormack, *The World of Professional Golf*. The CBS-TV Masters telecasts are available on YouTube starting from 1967 and transcripts of all press interviews from ASAP Sports starting from 2001; I also used my own notes of press interviews from the 1980s and 1990s. Information on statistics and results were found in the PGA Tour database and the Masters Media Guide.

Several books have been written about particular years of the Masters. Chronologically, that starts with my own book, *Making the Masters*, about the 1934 and 1935 events. Also there are *The Lost Masters*, by Curt Sampson, on 1968; *The Masters—The Winning of a Golf Classic*, by Dick Schaap, on 1970; *The Magnificent Masters*, by Gil Capps, on 1975; *One For the Ages*, by Tom Clavin, *The Greatest Masters*, by Stephen Goodwin, and *The 1986 Masters*, by John Boyette, all on 1986; *The 1997 Masters: My Story*, by Tiger Woods, with Lorne Rubenstein, on 1997; and *One Magical Sunday*, by Phil Mickelson with Donald T. Phillips, on 2004. *The Second Life of Tiger Woods*, by Michael Bamberger, has the 2019 Masters as its focus.

Portions of biographies and autobiographies that cover Masters experiences for particular players include *Golf Is My Game*, by Bobby Jones; *The Game I Love*, by Sam Snead with Fran Pirozzolo; *Ben Hogan: An American Life*, by James Dodson; *Hogan*, by Curt Sampson; *A Golfer's Life*, by Arnold Palmer with James Dodson; *Jack Nicklaus: My Story*, by Jack Nicklaus with Ken Bowden; *Seve*, by Seve Ballesteros; and *A Feel for the Game*, by Ben Crenshaw with Melanie Hauser. Past histories of Augusta National that have focused more on the club and longtime chairman

Clifford Roberts are *The Making of the Masters,* by David Owen, and *The Masters: Golf, Money, and Power in Augusta, Georgia,* by Curt Sampson.

Other newspaper sources were used as supplements, particularly in the early years when the *Chronicle* coverage was less extensive, and most were accessed through newspapers.com. They include: the *New York Times, Washington Post, Atlanta Journal, Chicago Tribune, Baltimore Sun, Philadelphia Inquirer, New York Herald-Tribune, The Tennessean, Miami News, Knoxville Journal, Knoxville News-Sentinel, Charlotte Observer, Tampa Tribune, Cincinnati Enquirer,* and *Greenville News*. Wire service reports included the Associated Press throughout the Masters history and, in earlier years, United Press, International News Service, and Grantland Rice's syndicated column. Periodicals with tournament reports in the 1930s include: *The American Golfer, PGA Magazine,* and *National Golf Review*. General golf publications as occasional sources were *Golf Digest, Golf Magazine, Senior Golfer,* and *Golfing*.

The extensive collection at the library of the USGA Golf Museum is appreciated, and especially the help from librarian Tara Valente, who kindly scanned material while the library was closed during the coronavirus pandemic in 2020.

In the process of bringing this book to print, thanks go to the watchful eye of proofreader/designer Isabella Piestrzynska and the cover design of Mimi Bark. Most of all, a very large thank you to Chris Sulavik, the publisher of Tatra Press, for believing in this project, giving it the green light, and his support and helpful editing along the way. In a sense, my career in golf writing has been pointing me toward this book, and, because of Chris, the idea has become reality.